Second Edition

UNDERSTANDING LIFESPAN DEVELOPMENT

Christopher Stanley
Florida Gulf Coast University

Cover images © Shutterstock, Inc.

Kendall Hunt
publishing company
www.kendallhunt.com
Send all inquiries to:
4050 Westmark Drive
Dubuque, IA 52004-1840

ISBN 978-1-4652-7947-7

Printed in the United States of America

CONTENTS

CHAPTER 4: PRENATAL DEVELOPMENT 35

CHAPTER 5: PHYSICAL AND COGNITIVE DEVELOPMENT IN INFANCY 49

CHAPTER 6: SOCIOEMOTIONAL DEVELOPMENT IN INFANCY 63

CHAPTER 7: PHYSICAL DEVELOPMENT IN CHILDHOOD 77

CHAPTER 8: COGNITIVE DEVELOPMENT IN CHILDHOOD 91

CHAPTER 9: SOCIOEMOTIONAL DEVELOPMENT IN CHILDHOOD 101

CHAPTER 10: PHYSICAL DEVELOPMENT IN ADOLESCENCE 123

CHAPTER 11: COGNITIVE DEVELOPMENT IN ADOLESCENCE 135

CHAPTER 12: SOCIOEMOTIONAL DEVELOPMENT IN ADOLESCENCE 145

CHAPTER 13: EMERGING ADULTHOOD 159

CHAPTER 14: MIDDLE ADULTHOOD 179

CHAPTER 15: LATER LIFE 189

CHAPTER 16: DEATH AND DYING 203

GLOSSARY 217

ACKNOWLEDGMENTS

I would like to dedicate this book to my wife Lauren, daughter Savannah, and sons Cy and Declan. They are my teachers, and deserve all the credit for any personal understanding of human development. I look forward to many more chapters together.

CHAPTER 1

Introduction

This book is devoted to the field of **lifespan developmental psychology**, which is the scientific study of human growth and adaptation across the life span. This field was sprung from two "book ends" in **child psychology** (the scientific study of behavior and mental processes of children) and **gerontology** (the scientific study of behavior and mental processes in aging populations). Lifespan developmental psychology includes some significant life stages that are not necessarily captured in child psychology and gerontology, such as adolescence, emerging adulthood, and middle age. Accordingly, throughout this book, there will be a discussion of the history, people, theory, research methods, and classic and contemporary scientific findings that relate to *all* stages of human development: prenatal development, infancy, childhood, adolescence, emerging adulthood, adulthood, later adulthood, and end-of-life.

In addition, certain findings will be elaborated upon. For example, in childhood, play is a crucial context to consider in relation to its relative role for development. Thus, some greater attention will be given to it during the relevant chapter. Other life stages will incur corresponding factors that warrant inclusion. Together, the reader will be given an opportunity to appreciate how each stage of the life span is distinct or unique.

Context and Cohort

As you consider the numerous issues discussed in this textbook, consider the **context** in which the variable is occurring. In a grammatical or mechanical sense, context is given by the words and phrases leading up to and following a key word or phrase in a statement. It is not uncommon for words to be taken "out of context"

simply by removing the words before and after. In a psychological sense, the context refers to the circumstances surrounding a particular experience or event. Once again, these circumstances may be leading up to or following the experience. Moreover, these circumstances may include a milieu of historical, social, and/or psychological factors.

For instance, a school teacher may take into account the relative levels of social skills his or her students maintain. The teacher observes this through multiple interaction students have with each other. Certainly, there would be variable levels of social skills in the classroom—some appearing quite popular while others may display anxious or shy behaviors. However, when taken in context, the teacher may also consider other contextual factors as they relate to social skills. One student who appears particularly shy may be an only child that is new to the community. A child that appears very popular with others may have a parent who works at the school and he or she feels particularly comfortable in the environment, putting them at ease to interact with others. To offer some other examples: the rates at which children grow physically may be understood in the context of how much food and nutrition is available to them in childhood, parents' willingness to corporally punish their children may be understood in the context of their religious beliefs, an elderly individual's happiness may be clarified by his or her mobility and familial presence. The contextual factors in these simple examples further clarify developmental pathways and variables by giving additional relevant information. When attempting to view human development in its appropriate context, you may be doing so through a "wider lens," enabling yourself to see more precisely why development is occurring in a certain way or at a certain rate. In the next chapter, a useful ecological theory will be offered that does well to capture context.

Another term that warrants mention is **cohort**, which refers to the group of individuals with whom you were born into the world concurrently, and pass through time with. You do not necessarily know all the members of your cohort. While friends and classmates in a community would certainly illustrate members of the same cohort, two individuals born—regardless of geographic location—at approximately the same time in the course of history would also be members of the same cohort. In a sense, they would be members of the same generation; in the same way members of the Baby Boomer generation are comprised of all individuals born shortly after World War II. A cohort has relevance for development because it is part of a broader historical context. The Baby Boomer cohort may have a variety of different values, attitudes, and experiences than does a cohort from before or after them.

Capturing Context and Cohort: Life Expectancy

One manner in which the collective impact of context and cohort upon development may be viewed simply in **life expectancy,** which is the number of years a newborn can expect to live, *assuming conditions in a particular region remain unchanged.* In 2010, Japan maintained the greatest life expectancy in the world; where males born that year could expect to live 79 years, while females could expect to live 86 years. In the United States in 2010, life expectancy for men was 76, and 81 years for women (People living longer, but sicker, 2012).

There are numerous contextual and historical factors (i.e., cohort) that impact life expectancy. For instance, one of the correlates of increased longevity may be income. Regions with higher income per person tend to have higher life expectancies. This does not imply income levels necessarily cause enhanced life span. Rather, subsumed within more stable economic regions may be higher education rates, and access to health care and health care programs. Indeed, a primary factor that drives life expectancy down is when child mortality rates are high at any one historical time. For instance, in Sweden in the early 1770s, there were several consecutive years of poor agricultural conditions, causing about 100,000 deaths, many of which were children. Two centuries later, in 1994, Rwanda was engulfed in civil strife, and genocide took the lives of several hundreds of thousands of individuals; again many children. In either of these cases, when life expectancy was calculated in one of those years, it would have been relatively low—even less than 20 years of age. However, as agricultural and political situations improved, the life expectancy increased accordingly. A low life expectancy does not imply all individuals living there will die younger when compared to other countries. Thus, where and when you are born may impact how long you can expect to live. The current life span in the United States (i.e., 76 years for males; 81 years for females) affords many the adolescent and emerging adulthood years as a time to more gradually mature into adulthood. During these years, one may crystallize their identity, consider and reconsider their career, and their attitude toward marriage and family. In different places and times, there was not such a "luxury," and late childhood appeared to pass quickly into young adulthood. In this way, life expectancy impacts human development, too.

Principles of Development

As you progress through the textbook, consider the following ideas regarding human development:

- Human development occurs continuously across the life span.
- Everyone experiences typical and unique development.
- Human development is probabilistic.
- Human development depends on many factors.

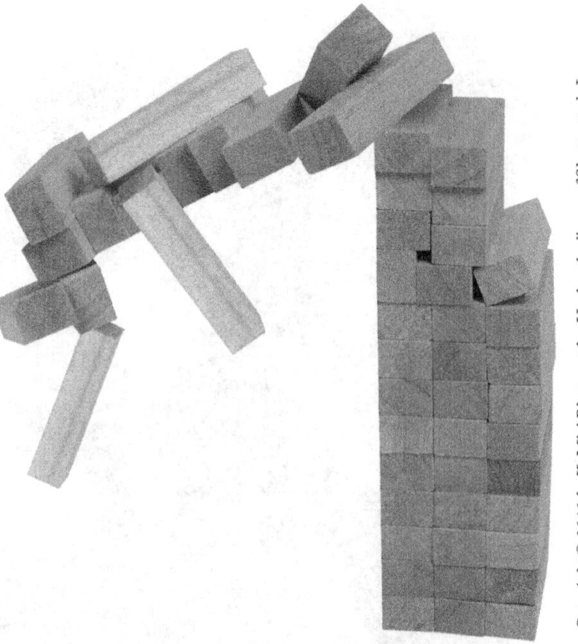

First, human development should not be understood merely as discrete or disconnected life stages; one after another. Rather, there is some level of continuity across life stages, and at any one point in time an individual may be a byproduct of their past experiences. While it may generally be argued there are indeed "critical periods" for certain aspects of development (e.g., ideal language learning, attachment), there are unique aspects to all points along the developmental trajectory.

Second, everyone experiences some degree of typical (or expected) and atypical (or unique) development. For the most part, you will move through life along with your cohort meeting certain physical, social, and cognitive milestones at approximately the same time. However, there may be variation with how some milestones are met (i.e., early or late) and there will most assuredly be variation in terms of how those milestones are met.

Third, human development is probabilistic. As noted above, there are typical milestones that are met at typical ages. However, there are no guarantees with human development. Slight variations in developmental contexts may produce different outcomes for different individuals. Moreover, there are influences such as **risk factors** that increase the likelihood of an undesirable outcome and **protective factors** that protect against the undesirable outcomes or increase the likelihood of a positive outcome. To illustrate, parental divorce may be a risk factor for children; associated with increased risk of academic decline, and deviant behavior. However, even in the context of a divorce, the continued presence of an adult with whom the child maintains a supporting, loving relationship is protective—it may guard against the otherwise negative academic and social consequences. Typically, one risk factor is not enough to warrant severe negative developmental consequences. Rather, an accumulation of risk factors in one's life may more accurately predict the outcome. As an analogy, consider the block game of Jenga, and that the toppling of the blocks as akin to a negative developmental outcome. In the course of play, it may be unfair to state the last person to attempt to move a block before it toppled was the one "at fault." Rather, there were numerous moves (or factors) leading up to the final move that were equally influential in terms of the outcome. Each removed block decreased the stability of the structure and increased the likelihood of it toppling. To build further on this analogy, protective factors would be akin to putting blocks into the structure, reaffirming its stability.

Fourth, human development depends on many factors. Similar to the notions of context, it is impossible to understand human development without considering numerous components. There are a variety of factors, including biological, familial, racial, cultural, social, academic, political, and/or historical issues which may act independently (or interact) to explain how an individual has developed, clarify how they are currently developing, or determine how an individual may develop in the future. While the inclusion of a seemingly endless array of factors into the human development picture may appear to make it more complex, they may be important to more accurately capture the complexities of human development.

Key Terms

- **Lifespan Developmental Psychology** – the term refers to the scientific study of human growth and adaptation across the life span. This field was sprung from two "bookends" in child psychology and gerontology.
- **Child Psychology** – the scientific study of behavior and mental processes of children
- **Gerontology** – the scientific study of behavior and mental processes in aging populations
- **Context** – the circumstances surrounding a particular experience or event
- **Cohort** – the group of individuals with whom you were born into the world concurrently, and pass through time with
- **Life Expectancy** – an average (or mean) based upon whether conditions in a particular region remain unchanged
- **Risk Factors** – variables that increase the likelihood of an undesirable developmental outcome
- **Protective Factors** – variables that protect against the undesirable outcomes or increase the likelihood of a positive outcome

Reference

People living longer, but sicker (2012, December). *Associated Press.* Retrieved from http://www.usatoday.com/story/news/world/2012/12/13/people-global-diseases/1766831/

CHAPTER 2

Developmental Psychology as a Science and Practice

Developmental Psychology

Human development is a broad term that captures not only life stages from conception through death, but also numerous variables and issues within each life stage. At the broadest level, most human behavior, thought, and emotional patterns can be conceptualized as having developed in some way. In other ways, a developmental perspective may be taken with most psychological variables. This latter point addresses why and how human development may also be found in psychological science.

While psychology traditionally is defined as the study of human behavior and thought processes, **developmental psychology** is the study of the changes and adaptations (over time) to human behavior and thought processes. The field of developmental psychology is comprised of both **scientists**, who examine what changes occur, why they may happen, and when; and **practitioners**, who are those that aim to intervene and modify human developmental trajectories. The practitioner most likely aims to modify human development in positive and fruitful ways, as with a social worker who strives to teach children with emotional problems healthy ways of coping with childhood stress.

The field of developmental psychology traditionally was limited to certain "developmental stages." Most notably, infancy, childhood, and adolescence typically were viewed as life stages that were truly "developmental" in nature. That is, a vast majority of physical, cognitive, emotional, and behavioral growth occurred during these stages, and thus considerable attention was placed upon them. More recently, developmental psychology (the field and in college courses) may take more of a life-span approach, where attention is distributed more equally among life stages from birth through death. Sometimes, this approach may be termed a "cradle to grave" perspective.

It is important to consider that while life stages can typically be "split up" according to age (in years), human development does not necessarily occur so neatly. For instance, infancy encompasses the first two years of life; that is, birth through the entire second year of life, an individual can reliably be described as an infant. This is true for other life stages (e.g., childhood, adolescence, etc.) as well. However, that does not imply that all infants or children are experiencing physical, social, or cognitive development similarly. A child may be significantly more mature physically, intellectually, or socially than his or her peers. Conversely, a child may lag behind his or her peers in various ways. Similarly, an older adult may appear to act much younger than he or she really is in terms of their professional or recreational lives, while others may demonstrate qualities more typically seen in individuals their own age. Drawing on these examples and the idea that human development may occur in various rates for different individuals, one may consider development as occurring in four main ways:

- chronological development,
- biological development,
- social development, and
- psychological development.

The first type is **chronological development** (or chronological age), which may be the simplest form and may be calculated with a simple mathematical problem. Your **chronological age** (i.e., the number of years and months since birth) may signify an approximate stage of development (e.g., childhood, adolescence, adulthood). However, considering the other types of development may give a clearer picture. **Biological development** is related to one's physical self. Genetically and biologically, all individuals are quite different and predisposed to various physical talents and bodily structures. However, one's biological state is also determined by behavioral factors such as diet and physical activity. Some individuals are biologically sound in relation to their peers, while others may be suffering from biological and medical issues that tend to have an onset in later years. Along those same lines, **social development** is related to one's social self, or the ways in which one interacts with others. Spending time in certain recreational or leisure activities, romantic attitudes and behaviors, and even technological or virtual social presence (e.g., Facebook) may be considered social variables. Once again, someone's "social age" may be ahead of, concurrent with, or behind, their peers. Finally, **psychological development** may subsume numerous mental activities that change over time. For instance, logical reasoning and decision making skills develop over time. Together, chronological age is just one—and rather crude—way of assessing development. Individuals are free to vary biologically, socially, and psychologically throughout the life span.

Developmental Psychology as a Science

The behavioral sciences (e.g., psychology, sociology, gerontology) employ what is typically referred to as "the scientific method" to attempt to answer important questions. At a very fundamental level, **the scientific method** includes steps related to: a) observing a phenomena or behavior; b) inventing (or finding) a theory consistent with the phenomena; c) formulating hypotheses; d) testing hypotheses through experiments; and e) evaluating the results.

It is likely that you encountered these very steps—or something very close—in a high school biology or physics course. Whether it is in such a high school classroom or a state-of-the-art laboratory, the scientific method culminates in one of two distinct outcomes. It is possible that: a) the original hypotheses were supported (in which case the researcher guessed correctly); or b) the original hypotheses were not supported (in which case it may be necessary to reformulate and re-test).

In any case, the scientific method is aimed at answering important questions by testing, and thereby strengthening a theory. In addition, the scientific method (which also may be called the *empirical process*) may establish cause and effect relations between variables (the term variable will be covered in the next unit). It is increasingly important to verify *causal* (not *casual*) information. **Causal information** lets someone know—with reasonable accuracy—that one antecedent (phenomena A) tends to have a certain consequence (phenomena B). For example, physicians want to know whether a certain drug improves health.

Parents and teachers want to know if a certain teaching strategy facilitates academic development. Coaches want to know whether a certain training routine improves athletic performance. Dieters want to know whether a certain nutritional regiment results in weight loss. Of course, this is not an exhaustive list of the causal information the research process lends itself to.

The scientific method (which can use several different methods) aims to capture cause and effect relations between variables. A **variable** is anything that is likely (or at the very least, able) to change. In the context of development, variables are a broad set of biological, behavioral, psychological, social, and emotional phenomena that may fluctuate between individuals, or between time points for the same individual. Simply speaking, sex would be one variable that may fluctuate between two or more individuals (i.e., male or female). One may also conceive an emotion (e.g., anger) as being a variable. The level of anger for one individual is not necessarily the same as it is for another individual. Moreover, the level of anger someone may be feeling at the present moment is not necessarily the same as how angry this same person may be at a later point in time. Above and beyond this general definition of variables, it's important to be able to classify variables in distinct ways.

Variables may be either independent or dependent variables. **Independent variables** are predictor variables, while **dependent variables** are the outcome variables in any one particular study. For example, a researcher may be interested to know whether enrollment in Head Start is related to subsequent educational achievement. In this particular scenario, the enrollment in Head Start is being viewed as a potential predictor (i.e., independent variable) of some type of outcome (i.e., dependent variable)—in this case, educational achievement. Another researcher may examine the effects of substance use on anxiety symptoms. In this scenario, the independent variable of substance use is thought to be a potential predictor of the dependent variable of anxiety symptoms. A simple rule may allow you to remember which variable is dependent and which variable is independent in any scenario. The dependent variable always *depends upon* the independent variable. From the aforementioned examples: a) educational attainment may depend upon enrollment in Head Start, and b) anxiety symptoms may depend upon substance use.

It is important to note that variables are categorized as independent or dependent variables in the context of each particular research question. In the example above, educational attainment was conceived as a dependent variable. However, that does not imply educational attainment will always be a dependent variable. A researcher could easily conceive a study in which someone's educational attainment is thought to predict some outcome variable, such as quality of life. In this case, educational attainment would be the independent variable. Thus, each specific research question has its own independent and dependent variables. From this point forward in the textbook, most topics can be viewed as a variable.

The research process implies that experiments be undertaken. Thus, there is some type of "design" that must be implemented. However, it should be noted that all research designs are *not* created equal in terms of establishing cause and effect relations. To illustrate, one type of design that is used in the behavioral sciences is a **single-subject design** (i.e., case study). In a single-subject design, researchers examine one (possibly more) individual(s) very closely. The "experiment" is the in-depth look at the individual(s). Thus, case studies tend to be very thick in descriptions and qualitative data. To illustrate, Stanley and Robbins (2001) examined a case study of a bi-racial athlete. The researchers looked more specifically at the developmental and athletic contexts which promoted or inhibited racial identity formation. In doing so, the individual participated in in-depth interviews. An apparent strength of the case study approach is that researchers may get a more intimate look at psychosocial processes than you may if you are otherwise studying large groups, where each individual is only a fraction of the whole group under study. An apparent weakness of the case study approach is also grounded in the idea that researchers examine select individual(s). You lose most, if not all ability to generalize to many individuals what you find to be the case in just one individual. Think about some of the aforementioned examples. Would you conclude a drug worked after testing it one individual? Would you conclude you have found the perfect diet after it results in weight loss in one client? Of course, the answer to these questions is "no." Thus, case studies offer little or no causal information. Nonetheless, they are quite useful in the early stages of research.

Another type of research design is an **associational design.** This may be also referred to as a **correlational design.** In fact, a later unit covers correlations. When a researcher engages in associational or correlational designs, they are still investigating relations between at least two variables. However, they are merely "taking the data as they are." More specifically, associational designs are aimed at capturing the direction and strength of the relations between two variables. Think again of the drug example given above. Not only is it important to know *if* the drug works, but it's also good to know how consistently and in what direction it may work. The "consistency" is related to strength. That is, does a certain dose of the drug appear to have an incremental effect? Does a certain dose generate a predictable consequence? The direction is related to whether the drug produces the same effect for most individuals. That is, does it appear that for many individuals the drug produces a change in the desired outcome or does it have a desirable effect for some, but an undesirable effect for others? One of the strengths of the correlational design is that you can assess many individuals (not just a few) and establish patterns of relations between variables. However, there are some important steps that have not been undertaken which allow you to make causal inferences with correlational data. Thus, correlational designs are still significantly impaired when it comes to establishing causal relations. There is an old saying that "correlation does not imply causation."

The aforementioned steps that are not undertaken in correlational (or case study) designs are absolutely essential for establishing cause and effect between two variables. The two types of designs that do take these necessary steps are: *experimental* and *quasi-experimental designs.* First we will consider the **experimental design.** Once you understand this design, understanding the quasi-experimental design is rather simple. The features that an experimental design has that make it appropriate for capturing casual information includes: a) the presence of a control group, and b) random assignment of participants to groups. The presence of a **control group** (or **placebo**) group is important because it lets the researcher know *what would have otherwise happened had there been no intervention.* This control group is an "otherwise" condition. Drug studies are laden with placebo groups (e.g., sugar pills) in which the participants are not given the active biological agent that the experimental group receives. What if, upon analyzing the results, the placebo group members were just as well off as the experimental group members? Intuitively, the drug was not useful because individuals did just as well without intervention. As you can see, when you employ an experimental design there has to be at least two groups: a control group that does not receive the intervention and the experimental group that does.

The second step or feature of an experimental design is related to **random assignment** of participants. The participants that make up a sample must be randomly assigned to the groups in order for a true experiment. They each must have an equal chance of being selected into the experimental and/or control group. What this does hypothetically is "wash away" pre-existing differences. These pre-existing differences can be almost anything that you can (or cannot) imagine may impact the outcome (e.g., gender, age, education, marital status, level of physical activity, personality, etc.). A researcher may want groups to have the same general "complexion" with all of these pre-existing differences to ensure that the primary way the groups differ is only whether they receive the intervention or not. When a researcher puts the two features of the experimental design together (control group and random assignment), they are enabling themselves to more clearly see precisely what effect (if any) the intervention has upon a certain outcome when all other plausible pre-existing differences (that may impact the results) are no longer as apparent. Together, these form a very strong method for assessing cause-effect between two variables.

The difference between an experimental and quasi-experimental design is quite simple. In a quasi-experimental design, there is still a control group. However, random assignment is not always possible, and in this case you would be left with a **quasi-experimental design**. When you hear the word "quasi" think of "almost." A quasi-experimental is almost—but not quite—an experimental design. A simple example may illustrate a quasi-experimental design. For instance, perhaps a researcher is interested in the effect of injuries due to exercise on some psychological outcome. The researcher cannot randomly assign participants to an "injury group" and a "non-injury" control group. How do they know who will be injured? It may be more useful to recruit many people who exercise, monitor them over time, and as individuals get injured, they become your experimental group members. Thus, you still have a control group—which is very important—but your ability to randomly assign participants is impaired. Taken together, listed in descending order (most to least) are the designs covered thus far, from which causal information may be gleaned:

1. Experimental design,
2. Quasi-experimental design,
3. Associational/correlational design, and
4. Single-subject design (case study).

As mentioned, the first two are very nice designs in establishing causal information, while the latter two are not. In addition, all research questions and designs are not equal in terms of assessing developmental variables (i.e., variables that change over time).

Another research design that warrants mention in this unit is a **longitudinal design**. Intuitively, if one is interested in how behavioral, physical, emotional, or cognitive processes change or adapt over time, it may make sense to observe individuals over time. A longitudinal design does just that, allowing researchers to observe and collect data over time to verify changes that take place. Some longitudinal designs are rather simple in design and application, but others are more far-reaching and complex.

To illustrate the latter, in 2009, scientists began recruiting mothers-to-be from New York and North Carolina—eventually hoping to track 100,000 individuals from conception to 21 years of age. Participants gave blood, urine, and hair samples and permitted researchers go into homes to test water and dust. Regular health interviews were performed during pregnancy, with exams and checkups thereafter. This longitudinal design was necessary to answer some important

questions. Primarily, the investigators were interested in "how various environmental and behavioral factors (e.g., diet, exposure to certain chemicals) may interact with genetic factors to affect health and development." Moreover, if health issues (e.g., autism, asthma, birth defects) are genetically driven, do certain environmental factors make them more likely?

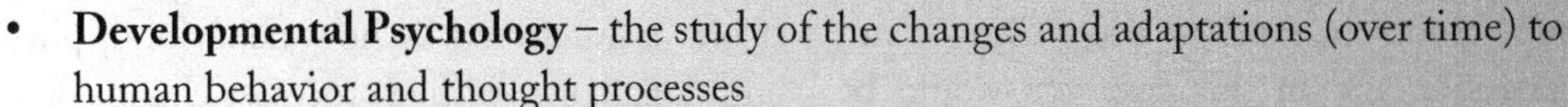

Key Terms

- **Developmental Psychology** – the study of the changes and adaptations (over time) to human behavior and thought processes
- **Scientist** – professionals who examine what changes occur, why they may happen, and when
- **Practitioner** – professionals who aim to intervene and modify human developmental trajectories
- **Chronological Development (or Chronological Age)** – the number of years and months since birth. Chronological age is just one—and rather crude—way of assessing development.
- **Biological Development** – related to one's physical self, health, and adaptive capabilities, and may be impacted by genetic and environmental influences
- **Social Development** – the ways in which one interacts with others
- **Psychological Development** – subsumes numerous mental activities that may change over time (e.g., memory, self-esteem, cognitive processing, etc.)
- **The Scientific Method** – a process related to answering questions; involving steps related to observing and forming hypotheses akin to human phenomena, then orchestrating steps to test those hypotheses
- **Causal Information** – lets one know—with reasonable accuracy—that one antecedent (phenomena A) tends to have a certain consequence (phenomena B)
- **Variables** – anything that is likely (or at least, able) to change; a broad set of biological, behavioral, psychological, social, and emotional phenomena that may fluctuate between individuals, or between points in time for the same individual
  - **Independent Variables** – predictor variables
  - **Dependent Variables** – outcome variables
- **Single-Subject Design (Case Study)** – a close examination of select individual(s); case studies tend to be very thick in descriptions and qualitative data. This design provides little or no causal information.
- **Correlational Design (Associational Design)** – this design is aimed at capturing the direction and strength of the relation between two variables. Although quite useful, this design also does not imply causation.
- **Experimental Design** – considered the most useful design in capturing causal relations between variables, it incorporates random assignments and maintains the presence of a control group
- **Control (Placebo) Group** – this "otherwise" group lets the researcher(s) know what would have happened had there been no intervention

- **Random Assignment** – a process thought to equalize groups; helps ensure the groups have the same "complexion" in regard to a wide array of pre-existing differences. In doing so, random assignment helps to ensure that the primary way the groups differ is the intervention.
- **Quasi-Experimental Design** – Generally the same as an experimental design, but lacking random assignment, which may be impractical in a given setting. Causal information may be inferred from this design.
- **Longitudinal Design** – allows researchers to observe and collect data over time (i.e., weeks, month, years, decades, etc.) to verify physical, social, and/or psychological changes

Critical Thinking Questions

1. Define and discuss human development. In doing so, what different ways are there to conceptualize development above and beyond mere chronological development? Personally, where do you fall in terms of these various forms of development in relation to your peers? Whether you believe yourself to be more or less advanced than your peers (or about the same), support your points with examples.
2. What is the scientific method? Compare and contrast the five main research designs offered in this chapter in terms of the characteristics that define them, as well as the relative amounts (if any) of causal information they may provide.
3. Design your own study. This study should be related to human development, broadly speaking. What is your main independent and dependent variable(s) (terms covered in chapter 1)? For this hypothetical study, which study design would you deem most appropriate? Why? Finally, given your design, how much causal information would you eventually be able to infer from this study?

Reference

Stanley, C.T., & Robbins, J.E. (2011). Racial identity and sport: The case ofa biracial athlete. *International Journal of Sport and Exercise Psychology, 9*, 64-77.

CHAPTER 3

Theoretical Bases

Theory

As mentioned in earlier units, research processes are laden with theories. **Theories** may generally be understood as educated guesses, although they may have some complexities. That is, a theory may have numerous terms, postulates, and contingencies that work together to form the basis of the educated guess. Theories not only guide the formation of hypotheses, but conclusions drawn from research projects are further used to reformulate theory. Thus, researchers employ theory a great deal in their work. Practitioners also employ theory in their work, by using them to understand, clarify, and predict behavior and development. Theories relevant for human development aid researchers and practitioners alike in understanding why human development may be occurring and how it will continue to occur.

For example, a parent may bring their 18-month old child into a pediatrician's office, complaining that her child is not expressing interest in walking. Not seeing any physical reasons why the child should not be walking, the pediatrician begins to probe about the environment at home, and comes to find that there are numerous siblings in the home that—along with the parent—always carry the infant wherever they need to go. As the pediatrician comes across this bit of "evidence," they piece together a theory (based upon social and familial factors) that clarifies why this infant is not yet walking. Then, based upon this theory, the recommendations are simple: refrain from picking up the infant. Rather, encourage them to stand and walk on their own at home. In this example, the theory—based upon evidence—suggested a certain reason and offered a corresponding modification plan. Should the pediatrician have noted other reasons why the child may not be walking yet (e.g., biological), they certainly would have a different understanding and intervention plan. In summary, theories enable researchers (and really

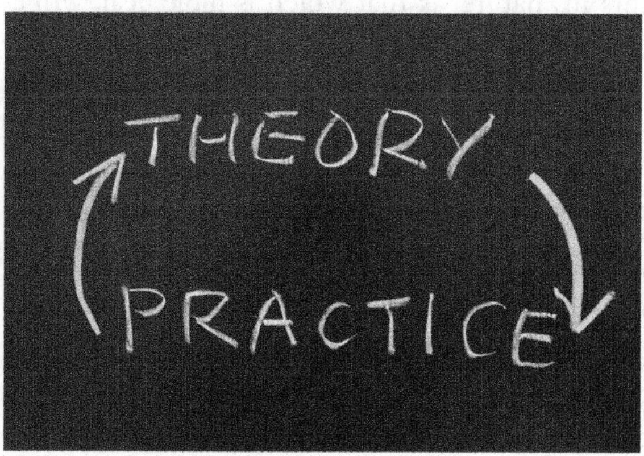

anyone for that matter) to better understand behavior and development, and predict future development and behavior.

There is an old adage from sociologist Kurt Lewin that "there is nothing as useful as a good theory." In terms of human development, certain theories are more applicable than others. You may well encounter other theories in other psychology courses or textbooks as they are more applicable to other areas. The theories that are covered in this unit are particularly relevant to understanding how humans develop over time. One such line of theory is learning theories. More specifically, humans may develop, change, and adapt due to environmental experiences that cause them to change in definite ways. In a sense, humans develop because they learn. Indeed, whether we are the teacher (e.g., potty-training a child) or the learner (e.g., trying to maintain a healthier diet), we have a great deal of familiarity in the *relatively permanent change(s) in behavior that occur due to experience.* This chapter is related to theoretical frameworks of learning. These theories try to clarify precisely how the relatively permanent changes take place.

Nature and Nurture

At a broad level, theories may emphasize two general areas: biological factors and environmental factors. This notion has been popularized as the "nature versus nurture" debate. What occurs in "nature" is that which is biological, while that which is linked with environmental factors is "nurtured." Theories that emphasize biological processes underscore biological and genetic contributions to human development. According to these theories, hereditary contributions from families or neurological maturation heavily influence human development. On the other hand, theories that emphasize environmental influence may contain postulates related to how social factors (e.g., peer groups, socioeconomic status) impact development. While many theories may emphasize one area over the other, in reality it is more likely that development depends on both. The theories described in the following paragraphs distinctly and uniquely clarify human development by nature, nurture, or some type of combination of the two.

Classical Conditioning

Conditioning theories are "nurture" theories. In terms of the following theories, conditioning is akin to learning. **Learning** is a relatively permanent change(s) in behavior that occur due to experience (Terry, 2009). Accordingly, **classical conditioning** theory posits that the learner's interactions with stimuli are the *experience* and the changes (if any) in the reaction to those particular stimuli represent the observable *behavioral changes* we see in a learning scenario (Olson & Hergenhahn, 2009).

Classical conditioning was a popular notion decades ago, as it enabled researchers to study observable forms of behavior, rather than relying upon philosophical or psychodynamic notions of the human mind. Pavlov (who was not a scientist but rather studied gastrointestinal processes in canines) once observed that dogs would start to salivate at the mere sight of his research assistants who typically brought the food into the laboratory. From there, Pavlov devised his hypotheses, and corresponding study with food, bell, and salivation paradigm. Thus, classical conditioning (and the most famous example illustrating the classical conditioning paradigm) was born. The main idea of this particular theory is behavior may be broken down into simple stimulus-response relations. Moreover, there is a consistent reformation of these links as—over time—unconditioned (or unlearned) stimulus and responses links may be paired with neutral stimuli, and subsequently become conditioned stimuli and/or responses. The reformation process represents conditioning, or learning (Olson & Hergenhahn, 2009; Terry, 2009).

Individuals bring instinctual reactions to certain stimuli in any given environment. During infancy and childhood, when so many experiences are new—that many stimuli have yet to be encountered—some of the reactions may be raw instinctual reactions resulting in changes in mood or physiological state. Given initial reactions are instinctual; they are unlearned or **unconditioned responses (UCR)** to **unconditioned stimuli (UCS)**. That is, you do not have to "teach" a canine to salivate to food; this is instinctual. You do not have to "condition" an infant to startle with loud noises; these are also instinctual reactions. Over time, the UCS may be paired with a secondary, or **conditioned stimulus (CS)**. This pairing may occur intentionally or unintentionally. The learner—in a passive sense—associates the old (UCS) and new stimuli (CS); thereafter, the CS may actually elicit the old response, too (UCR). In sum, the UCS used to elicit at UCR, then the CS was able to elicit the UCR, giving way to a new connection: a CS eliciting a **conditioned response (CR)**. The "conditioning" occurs as a result of repeated interaction or exposure with environmental stimuli and reacting to them (see Figure 3.1).

A typical illustration of classical conditioning is with **taste aversions**, which occur when an individual associates the taste of a certain food with some symptoms of sickness; in other words, a person will become disgusted by said food. Consider how the aforementioned classical conditioning terms (UCS, UCR, CS, CR) may help clarify how this occurs. In this case, the UCS and UCR are represented by the toxic or spoiled agent or a bacterium that produces some form of discomfort or sickness (e.g., nausea). Being "unconditioned," these reactions occur naturally—you do not need to teach someone to become nauseous from eating spoiled food! However, the original stimulus (UCS) was paired with the food (CS). This pairing was perhaps salient enough for the individual to experience similar discomfort with future encounters (even from the sight or smell) from the same type of food. Thus, the individual now maintains a CS (food) and a CR (nausea) pair which has been learned due to experience.

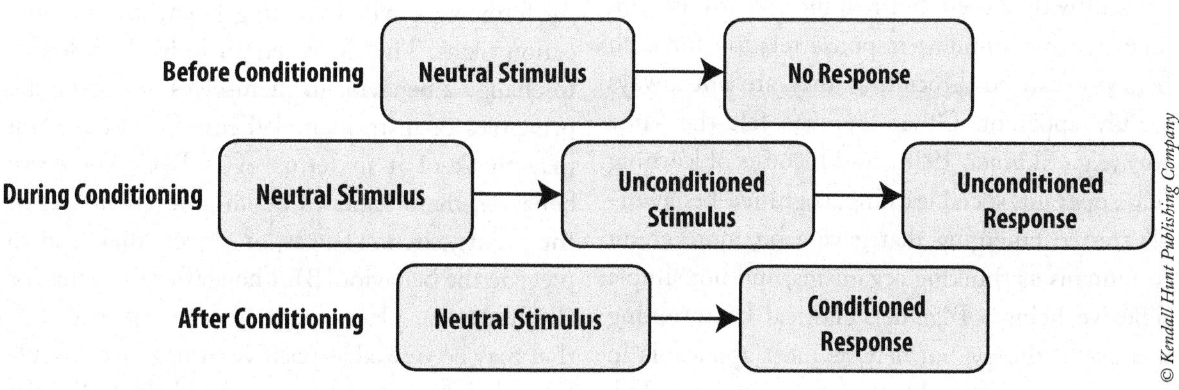

FIGURE 3.1 *Classical Conditioning*

This example related to taste aversion was used for pedagogical purposes—it's a nice way to illustrate classical conditioning principles. However, although many individuals can readily identify their own taste aversions, they may not have deep implications for human development. For the most part, classical conditioning may clarify how some seemingly instinctual and reactive behaviors are learned. Depending upon the intensity or frequency of the pairings, some classical conditioning may have more meaningful long-term consequences. For example, consider the natural warmth and positive feelings (UCR) that arise when an infant's basic needs (e.g., food, warmth, or nurturance) are met (UCS). If one particular individual (e.g., mother or father) is always being paired with the UCS, then over time, that person alone (CS) may elicit warm and affectionate feelings (CR) from the infant, having implications for attachment—the earliest and most fundamental emotional connection for an infant.

From early on to present day, many researchers employing a classical conditioning paradigm do so with non-human samples (e.g., Harlow, 1958; Watanabe & Mizunami, 2007). This may be that these samples typically lack the higher order thinking that we now understand adult humans have. Classical conditioning is rather reflexive and involuntary in principle, and in learning contexts that are more complex, this theory may not clarify human behavior. However, the theory and some of its principles (e.g., extinction, generalization) are still widely used and helpful in learning. Yet, identifying a stimulus-response relation for each behavior can be difficult, as they are not always readily apparent. Other theorists felt the same way (e.g., Skinner, 1938), and theories of learning (e.g., operant, social learning, cognitive-behavioral) started emerging that gave a bit more credit to humans as thinking organisms, and not simple reflexive beings. Together, classical conditioning is a useful theory, but may be most applicable in some forms of animal behavior or simpler, reflexive forms of human behavior.

Operant Conditioning

A basic tenet of instrumental conditioning is positive consequences strengthen a response and negative consequences weaken a response. That is, when an individual engages in a certain behavior—or set of behaviors—and it yields a positive outcome (i.e., intrinsic or extrinsic), he or she is more likely to engage in that behavior again. The reverse is also true. Negative outcomes lessen the likelihood of engaging in the action(s) that lead to that particular outcome (Brown & Jenkins, 2009). This tenet pre-dates the theory of formal instrumental conditioning theory, and may be recognized in Thorndike's (1898) original **law of effect.**

Decades later, Skinner (1938) formalized the **operant conditioning theory** that drew from the law of effect in that the consequences of a behavior alter the probability (enhance or lessen) of the behavior's reoccurrence. Thorndike and Skinner argued that behavior could be carefully controlled, monitored, and modified according to this general principle. Animal studies dominated much of their work. Thorndike attempted to teach cats to unlatch a door to obtain a piece of fish, while Skinner created his famous "Skinner boxes" and trained rats to obtain pellets (Hernstein, 2009). Much of the readings in this unit are related to the principles of reinforcement (i.e., types, schedules) which may help clarify how and why individuals learn (or don't learn) various tasks (Terry, 2009).

Instrumental (i.e., operant) conditioning is a useful framework when creating behavioral modification plans. That is, when an individual desires to change a behavior in themselves or others, the principles of instrumental theory are useful. You may think of it in terms of A-B-C. For every behavior, there tends to be an antecedent (A) or the events, circumstances, or objects that tend to precede the behavior (B). Then, after the behavior (B) has taken place, there are consequences (C) that may be viewed as positive or negative, but ultimately increase or decrease the likelihood of the behavior occurring again. If you want to change behavior(s), it may be useful to examine the antecedents and/or consequences that surround it. Change and/or manipulate those, and you may be able to alter behavior, too (Beck, 1995).

In the preceding descriptions of classical and operant conditioning theories, it may appear as though there are some similarities between the theories. In both, some type of "association" is a key principle. In addition, both theories assume the learner is engaged in the learning process and directly experiencing the conditioning processes. However, there are some key differences as well. Specifically, with classical conditioning, the "association" is between stimulus and response; whereas with operant conditioning principles, the "association" is between behavioral response and consequence. While classical conditioning implies reflexive and involuntary behaviors, operant conditioning suggests behavior is more complicated and voluntary. Generally, the basic premise of classical conditioning is the stimuli (conditioned or unconditioned) that make the responses happen. With operant conditioning, behaviors are a result of more complex reinforcement systems.

Social Learning

In the aforementioned classical and operant conditioning theories, one critical assumption is that the learner needs to be directly interacting with the stimuli and environment to actually learn. However, it is possible that learners may watch and imitate others as well. In doing so, they are not directly engaged with stimuli, but rather indirectly observing others who are. Such a scenario may be observed when a young child observes his or her older siblings, watching which behaviors were desirable and which were undesirable. Subsequently, the young child may select which behaviors it may be useful to adopt and which to discard. The "observations" referred to may be known as modeling, and an intricate part of **social learning theory**. With the inclusion of modeling in this theory, humans are given a bit more credit as being thinking, dynamic organisms than the classical and operant models permit.

The individuals that are observed or modeled are not restricted to family members of friends, but may also include most anyone that enters the

learner's visual field. In addition, observations are not necessarily only made face-to-face. It is possible modeling may occur via electronic (e.g., television, videos, video games, social networking sites) means as well. This latter point may illustrate the role of media in behavior and development. According to social learning theory, what the learner sees (regardless of form) may be internalized and/or imitated. Indeed, a classic study in observational learning included video observations.

More specifically, Albert Bandura—who is credited with the formation of social learning theory—performed a hallmark study known more popularly as the "bobo doll" study. In this particular experiment, children were divided into two groups: the experimental group watched a video in which other children were interacting rather aggressively with a bobo doll (an inflatable clown doll). In the video, the children could be observed hitting, punching, and throwing objects at the bobo doll. In the second group (the control condition) children watched a video in which other children interacted non-violently with the doll. Afterwards, all children entered a room with the same bobo doll originally viewed in the video. Perhaps not surprisingly, the children who had watched the aggressive behavior in the video appeared to mimic these behaviors, and they punched, kicked, and otherwise were aggressive toward the doll. The children in the control condition did not display the same intensity or frequency of aggressive behaviors. Based upon such findings, Bandura began to piece together a more formal social learning theory. All the conditioning and learning theories emphasize learning through action.

Biological Theory

Contrary to a strict learning approach, biological theories and perspectives underscore a mind and behaviors that are "already adapted" to some degree. **Biological theories** underscore the role that physical systems have upon human development, including behavioral, emotional, and cognitive adaptations. In terms of psychology, neurological systems may hold particular importance.

A classic case study in psychology, which directly supports a biological theory, is that of Phineas Gage. Phineas was 25 years old, and working on the railroad in 1848 when a terrible accident occurred. A large explosion sent a 4-foot iron bar careening through the air and through Phineas' head. The accident did not kill Phineas, and he eventually regained consciousness, even to the point of being able to walk home. There was no obvious negative impact to his memory, intelligence, or decision-making abilities. In this regard, he seemed unchanged. However, there were some noticeable differences in terms of behavior and personality. For instance, after the accident, Phineas was described as being disagreeable, stubborn, and emotionally reactive, which was in stark contrast to his demeanor before the accident. Thus, it was hypothesized that the iron bar damaged a specific part of the brain reserved for emotion regulation. This message is at the core of biological theory: Human behavior may always be explained by the biological systems that govern them. Behavioral, emotional, and cognitive development (i.e. overt processes) that occurs is a manifestation of the underlying neurological changes (i.e. covert processes). Underlying it all is something called a **neuron.** An image of a neuron may be viewed in Figure 3.2.

Neurons are actual cells that exist with human organisms. They are derived from **neural stem cells**, and are microscopic in nature, but they do exist, along with other biological components which will be covered shortly. Originally, some stem cells were reserved for the formation of the nervous systems (e.g. central and nervous systems). These particular cells became neurons, which represent the most basic unit of the nervous systems. Some of the neurons make up the peripheral nervous system (PNS), which consists of various nerve tissues. Other neurons make up the central nervous system (CNS), which consists primarily of the brain and spinal cord. As the brain is part of the CNS, this system may have particular relevance to understanding how biological theory operates. Prior to coverage of some of the other neurological components and principles, suffice it to say that all behavioral, emotional, and cognitive activity flows through the brain.

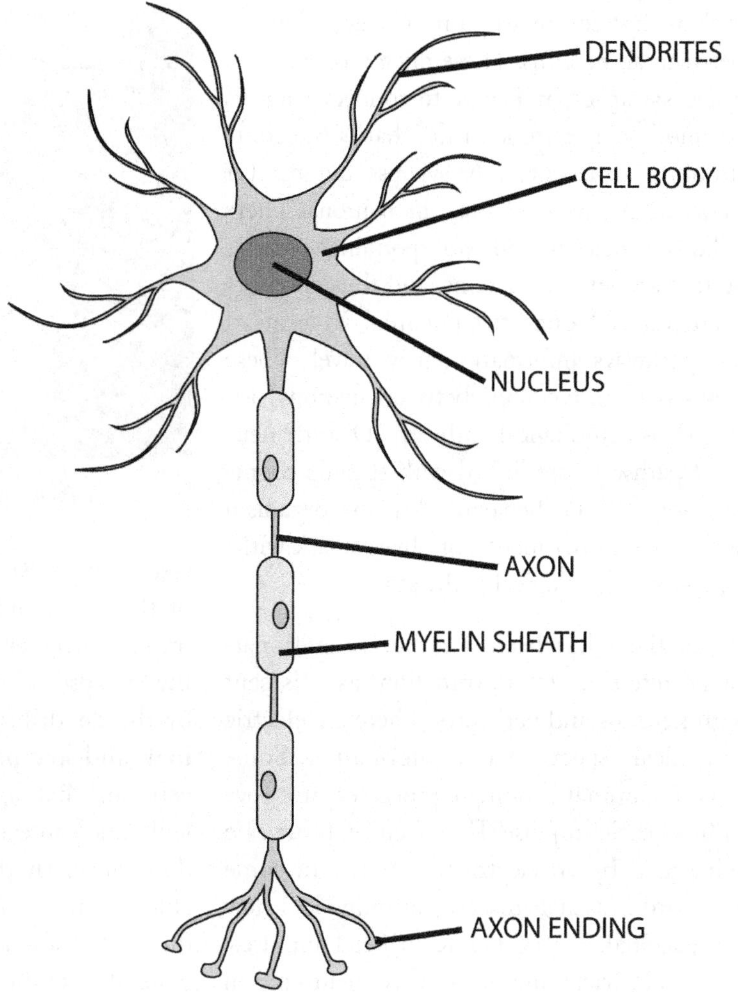

FIGURE 3.2 *Neuron*

Being microscopic in nature, billions of neurons exist within the CNS and PNS. Independently, each individual neuron may not hold importance. Rather, meaningful connections between neurons are made. Subsequently, **neurological pathways** are formed. In the following paragraph, the components and principles may help clarify how information is sent along these pathways. The "information" referred to is responsible for all behavioral, emotional, and cognitive activity. The neuron may be further broken down into constituent parts. First, each neuron has a **cell body** that contains the **nucleus** and the cell's DNA. The cell body is the main processing area for the neuron, and the other parts of the neuron emanate from the cell body. More specifically, information is received and delivered from the cell body. The reception of information occurs via the **dendrite**. There may be multiple dendrites per neuron, but they all maintain the same function. Dendrites resemble the branches of a tree, and are largely responsible for receiving information and guiding it toward the cell body. On the other end, the **axon** delivers messages away from the cell body. There is one axon responsible for dissemination of information through the neuron, as opposed to numerous dendrites. The axon is a "living cable" of varying lengths—in the brain axons may be microscopic in length as many neurons and axons are bunched together, while others may span up to 6 feet, running from the brain to the legs. Regardless of length, electrical impulses are sent practically instantaneously, and up to 200 miles per hour (Doidge, 2007)! In sum, information is received by the dendrites, passed along to the cell body (including the nucleus), and then sent along through the axon. This sequence is standard, and is termed the **law of forward conduction**. Neurological pathways do not travel in the opposite direction.

The descriptions of the component parts of the neuron were necessary for a basic understanding of this important type of cell. However, neurons do not function independently, but rather rely upon billions of other neurons. When information is passed through the axon, it does not cease to travel there, but continues on into "space" that exists between all neurons. These microscopic spaces are called **synapses,** and serve to connect neurons to one another. The information that is transmitted (from the axon) enters the synapse and may (or may not) be received by adjacent neurons. There are billions of neurons and corresponding synapses in the human nervous systems, and thus an enormous amount of "connective potential" in terms of various pathways information may travel. These pathways (i.e., connections between neurons) are referred to as neurological pathways. Distinct neurological pathways are linked with specific cognitions, emotions, and behavior. A living organism cannot engage in any mental or physical task without activating neurological pathways.

Thus far, there has been a rather (intentionally) vague reference to "information" as it is sent through neurons and pathways. There are electric and chemical aspects of this information. Some important automatic human processes are governed by electric impulse. For instance, heart rate is maintained by an electrical impulse. In some cases of cardiovascular disease, an individual may need a "pacemaker" to generate artificial impulses. Similarly, electrical impulses drive neurological activity. An extensive discussion of the physiological mechanisms underlying neurological activity is beyond the scope of this book. Briefly, however, when any of the senses (i.e., visual, auditory, tactile, olfactory, gustatory) are stimulated, there are biochemical changes in adjacent neurons which alters ionic content, which in turn creates an electrical impulse that is sent along to various destinations. Thus, there needs to be an initial "spark" which is part of the informational message traveling through neurons. It is important to note that these impulses travel through a neuron completely, or not at all. This is referred to as the **all-or-none principle.** There is no partial activation of neurons. However, the spark triggering the impulse would be relatively meaningless if not accompanied by some important chemicals.

The chemicals also necessary for information transfer are **neurotransmitters.** These chemicals

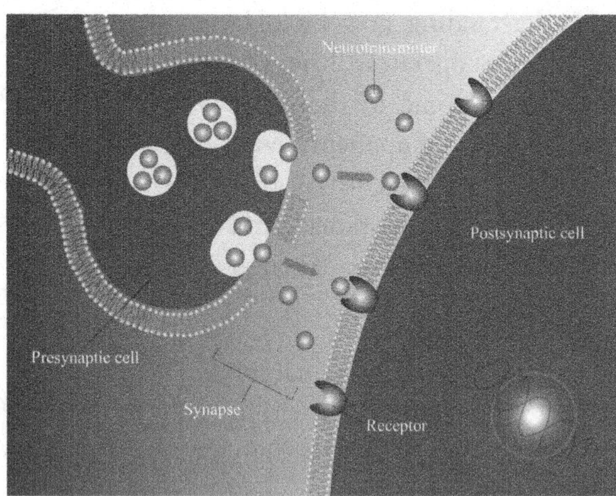

FIGURE 3.3 *Neurotransmitter*

(see Figure 3.3) are stored in small sacs at the end of the axon, and within the synapse. The nerve impulses trigger the release of the chemicals into the synapse, where they are potentially absorbed by the dendrites of adjacent neurons. There is a **lock-and-key principle** to neurotransmitter reception. That is, when a key properly fits a door-lock, one can easily lock or unlock that particular door. Similarly, distinct neurotransmitters are only able to "fit into" certain receptor sites on dendrites. If they do fit, they will cause one of two general reactions: a) they may excite the next neuron, or b) relax the next neuron. These are called **excitatory** and **inhibitory** responses, respectively. Again remembering the all-or-none principle, an inhibitory response would suggest a certain pathway will not activate. Together, nerve impulses stimulate neurotransmitter release into synaptic areas which—contingent upon whether they excite the adjacent neuron(s)—further stimulate neurons along the larger pathway. In this general way, the brain (CNS) is able to receive information from the environment (from the PNS), and subsequently send reaction messages via an identical process in the opposite direction.

Within the CNS, the brain—and the processes that occur within it—is critically important in determining the manner in which environmental stimuli are reacted. While an understanding of neurons may clarify how information is transmitted via the nervous systems, there are additional parts of the brain that also warrant attention, as they will bear mention in subsequent units. A significant amount of the cells in the brain are neurons, and function as described above. There are other cells that make up brain matter, and may be recognized without a microscope, given that one is able to view the brain, perhaps through advanced imaging techniques. The brain may be organized into three main pieces: the hindbrain, midbrain, and forebrain. The **hindbrain** is located toward the rear and typically responsible for automatic processes including breathing, blood circulation, and digestion. Above the hindbrain, the **midbrain** is responsible for processing some auditory and visual information. Perhaps most important, the **forebrain** is located at the front of the brain and responsible for most higher-order thinking (cognition) and feeling (emotion).

A structure called the **thalamus**, which means "inner room," is located in the forebrain. The thalamus initially receives the neural messages sent to the brain, and subsequently transmits them to appropriate areas of the brain for processing. Thus, many forms of human activity will stimulate neural activity in the thalamus, as it is a sort of "entry gate" to many other brain regions. Directly below the thalamus lies the **hypothalamus**, which maintains control over the **pituitary gland,** and subsequently the **endocrine system**. The pituitary gland has been called the "body's drug store" for its role in disseminating chemicals (Greenberg, 1998). More specifically, this gland is capable of releasing hormones into the bloodstream, eventually arriving at bodily organs for health and maintenance. In this way, the hypothalamus controls internal bodily processes (e.g., hunger, fatigue, sexual drive, body temperature, etc.). An image of the human brain is shown in Figure 3.4.

Above and beyond the thalamus and hypothalamus, which are considered "sub-cortical" areas due to their deep placement within the brain, there

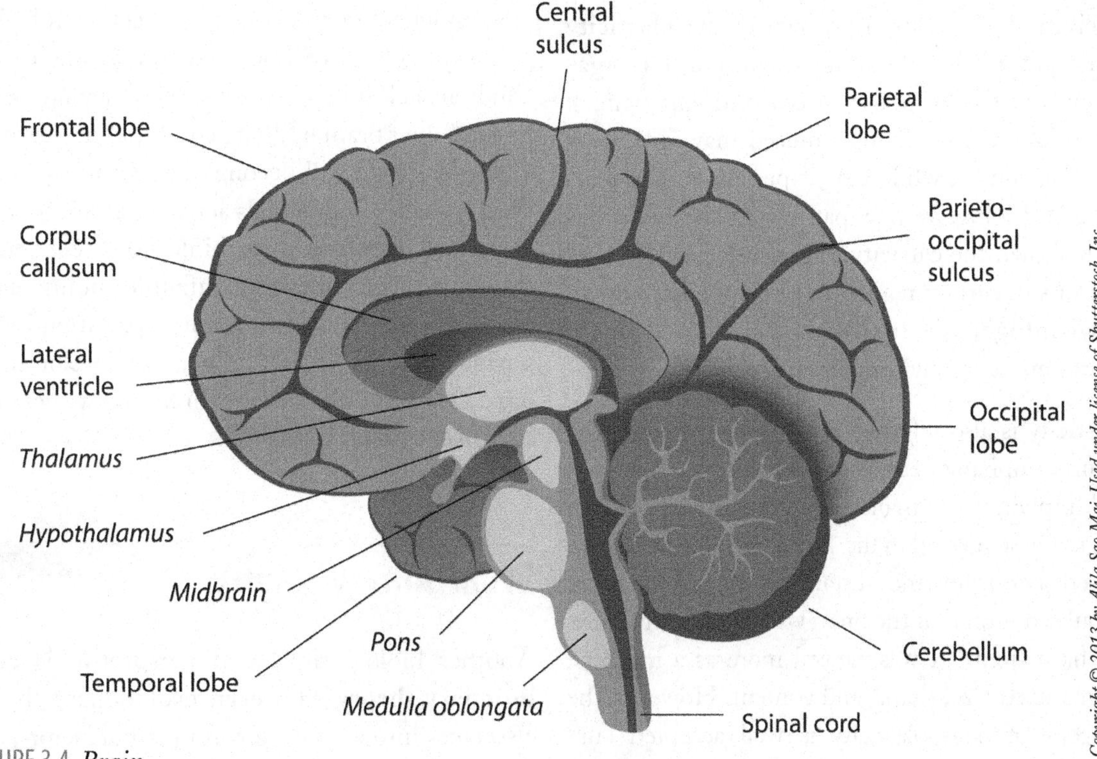

FIGURE 3.4 *Brain*

are other outward regions responsible for distinct functions. The concept of **brain localization** posits specific regions of the brain are adapted for specific functions. For instance, one region may activate when auditory information is being processed while another may be activated when visual information is being processed. One area may be involved with a negative emotion such as depression, while another may be linked with elation. Perhaps one of the most important brain areas to consider is the **cerebral cortex**. The cerebral cortex, which consists of the entire upper portion of the brain, is responsible for most thinking, feeling, or activity. The "folded" appearance of the cortex is due to it being compressed, or "wrinkled" to fit into a relatively small space. Within these folds, there is significant neural activity.

Plasticity Principle

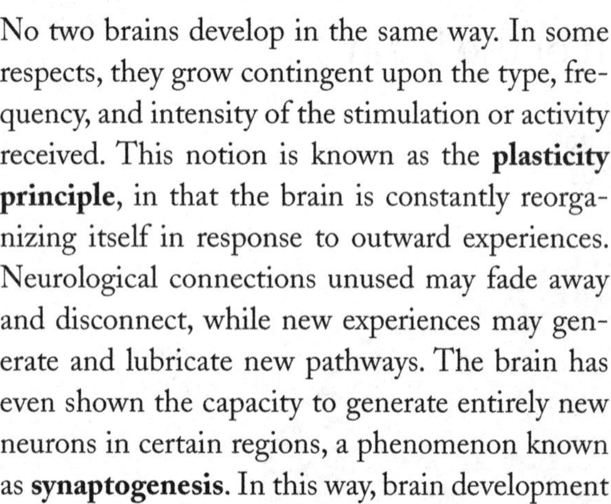

No two brains develop in the same way. In some respects, they grow contingent upon the type, frequency, and intensity of the stimulation or activity received. This notion is known as the **plasticity principle**, in that the brain is constantly reorganizing itself in response to outward experiences. Neurological connections unused may fade away and disconnect, while new experiences may generate and lubricate new pathways. The brain has even shown the capacity to generate entirely new neurons in certain regions, a phenomenon known as **synaptogenesis**. In this way, brain development is responsive to environmental conditions.

Plasticity is also referred to as *neuroplasticity* – the "neuro" implying neurons are involved and "plasticity" implying it is malleable or modifiable. When originally suggested in the 1960s and '70s, it was received skeptically, and in stark contrast to the more popular notion that the brain was fixed in structure, or "hardwired." It was viewed more as a machine with a fixed size, shape, and content. However, the concept of neuroplasticity is well accepted currently, and it is evident the brain may change its very structure for each activity performed, and importantly, if certain brain areas "fail," other brain regions may take over. Neuroplasticity principles have some important implications: children are not necessarily "stuck" with the mental abilities they are born with; damaged brains can reorganize and repair themselves, dead brain cells may be replaced, and most neurological networks and circuits are not hardwired (Doidge, 2007).

Neuroplasticity is a process, and requires experience to alter brain structure. With each experience, a series of old neurons active and connect. Importantly, when new experiences are being had, or when old networks don't fire, new neurological connections and networks may emerge. There is an old saying (although only as old as the concept of neuroplasticity) that the "neurons that fire together, wire together" (Doidge, 2007). During infancy and early childhood, the brain is rather undifferentiated in that experiences and stimuli may activate large portions of the brain, consisting of many networks. Many neurons fire together and wire together. Over time, the brain becomes more selective in that certain experiences or stimuli activate smaller brain regions and select neurological pathways. Think of how effortlessly infants and children pick up a new language (they are using most of their brain in doing so). Later on, learning a new language will become a much more calculated process—individuals activate far fewer pathways, and therefore must think more deliberately about linguistic rules. An infantile undifferentiated brain may allow the infant to pay attention to a wide range of stimuli; only as we develop more organized and differentiated brains do we begin to selectively attend to stimuli.

Evolutionary Theory

Another biologically based perspective is **evolutionary theory.** However, evolutionary theory also takes into account environmental factors, but does so across generations. Modern evolutionary

Charles Darwin.

theory—as it relates to behavior, emotion, and cognition—has roots in the original theory formed by Darwin, which primarily addressed how species may evolve physically over time. Many do not know, however, that Darwin also examined what would be considered "psychological" phenomena (the field of psychology was not recognized until after Darwin's death and hallmark publications). For instance, original observations appeared to show some degree of consistency in emotional expression across species and cultural groups in animals and human infants and adults. More specifically, under conditions that may cause stress or anger, humans continue to bear their teeth, which was viewed as a genetically inherited emotional characteristic. This singular example may not have profound relevance on its own, but may help illustrate how an emotional response or behavior is "passed" down. Humans develop over the course of their own lifetime, but may also be part of a larger ancestral chain, where adaptations—ultimately aimed at survival—are genetically transmitted. Thus, each individual is born with a certain set of cognitive, emotional, and behavioral predispositions. Together, evolutionary theory may offer principles linked with genetic transmission and adaptation to clarify human development.

However, evolutionary theory is not one of **genetic determinism**, which refers to the notion that individuals are completely biologically pre-programmed for a certain developmental sequence irrespective of environmental conditions. If genetic determinism were legitimate, the impact from social and environmental factors (e.g., parenting style, friendships) would be negligible in relation to developmental outcomes (e.g., physical maturation, intellectual capacity, emotional regulation, etc.). It is unlikely many theorists take such a strict approach to development. Rather, evolutionary theory suggests modifications are based upon environmental conditions (i.e. adaptations) that may in turn be genetically transmitted. Thus, evolutionary theory is interactional in nature and observed cross-generationally.

Ecological Theory

In the biological sciences, "ecology" refers to an interrelationship between a plant or animal and its environment. While decades ago (and perhaps according to learning theories), the environment above and beyond their most immediate surroundings was not viewed as exerting a substantial impact on development. The term *ecology* was adopted and transferred to the behavioral sciences to describe how broader environments and settings may impact development. Thus, ecological theory was born.

A contemporary version of **ecological theory** was offered by Urie Brofenbrenner (1977). At a broad level, this theory suggests that interaction with others and the environment is what is paramount to development. According to this theory, there are four primary systems that exert influence on development. The first system is the **microsystem**, which includes the individual's most immediate environmental circles. The microsystems for a typical child may include face-to-face contact and relationships

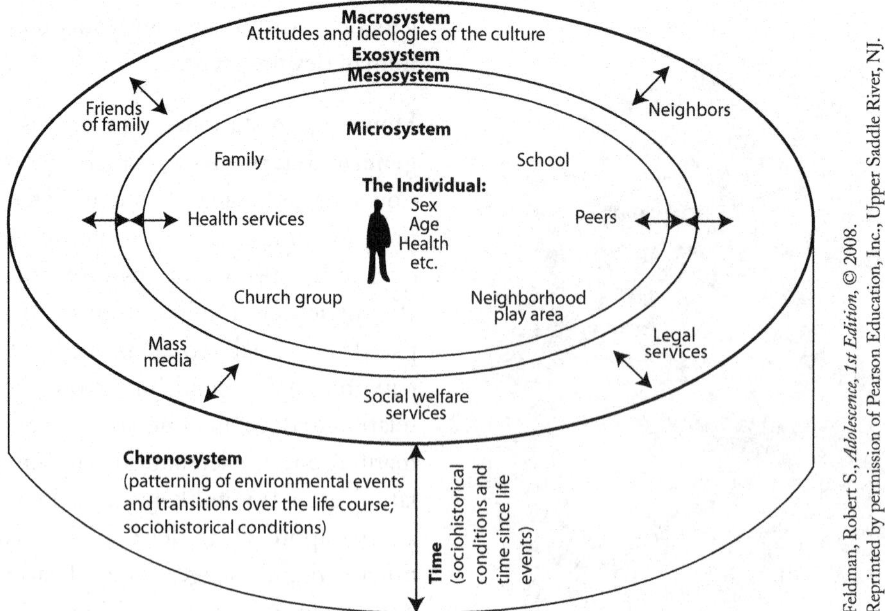

FIGURE 3.5 *Bioecological Approach to Development*

that occur within the home, school, or in peer groups. When interrelations are apparent between two or more microsystems, then the **mesosystem** may be apparent. For example, parenting style at home (microsystem A) may well impact how the child behaves at school (microsystem B), or vice versa. In addition, involvement in a church (microsystem C) may further impact all other settings and contexts. Together, this interaction illustrates a mesosystem. Beyond the mesosystem level, the **exosystem(s)** are related to settings that are not necessarily immediate settings for the child as with home and school, but may still impact the microsystems. For example, a child's microsystem is not necessarily their parents' workplace, but their parents' work may well impact their microsystems nonetheless. A parent working long hours may mean the child stays in an after-school program and/or spends time at home alone. Lastly, the **macrosystem** is the most remote course of influence, and involves historical and cultural phenomena. The macrosystem encompasses attitudes, practices, expectations, ideologies, and economic conditions of larger societal groups (see Figure 3.5). The macrosystem would describe how a cohort impacts development. Different generations may maintain different attitudes, practices, expectations, ideologies, and economic conditions, etc.

Some additional points worth noting with ecological theory: 1) the environment is dynamic in that certain events at any level (i.e. micro-, meso-, exo-, macrosystem) may alter the previously existing relations and create new conditions, and 2) systems are perceptual to the individual. To illustrate the first point that environments are dynamic, the birth of a sibling or the passing to the next grade may alter a microsystem. A parent and teacher who no longer are able to communicate amicably may impact a mesosystem. Should a parent change jobs and hours, then an exosystem has been impacted. Lastly, a macrosystem may change during an economic recession. Changes that occur at the macrosystem level, as it is the widest reaching level, may impact changes at all other levels. When considering how environments are perceptual, consider how one child may relish the structure and organization they receive from an experienced teacher, while another may prefer environments with less regulation. The idea that the impact of any or all of the aforementioned systems can change over time is referred to as the **chronosystem.** Together, ecological theory may clarify how there is such a wide array of developmental trajectories.

In the above description of ecological theory and the constituent systems, you may appreciate that ecological theory is very much related to context, as was described earlier. Ecological theory describes and clarifies in more detail the circumstances that define a particular context. When employing ecological theory, one is ascertaining how development "depends" on many different factors. This is a useful way to approach human development. The relative strength of ecological theory rests in that it incorporates elements of biological *and* environmental factors and also postulates the importance of contextual factors. In the coming chapters, certain contexts (or systems according to ecological theory) will be elaborated upon.

Research Paradigms

An interesting way to study the relative influence of biological and environmental factors is through study designs that capture conditions under which biological and genetically similar family members (e.g., siblings, offspring) have different environmental experiences. This is done in a variety of ways, but perhaps most classically through:

- twin studies,
- adoption studies, and
- twin/adoption studies.

A variety of researchers—each interested in tearing apart the relative influence of biological and environmental factors upon a certain developmental variable—have employed one of these designs, or a variant of one of these designs. Note how in each design, the paradigm uniquely "holds biological factors constant" while comparing two groups (or individuals) on some measure. First, **twin studies** are those that compare identical and fraternal twins on certain abilities. Identical twins—also known as monozygotic (MZ) twins—are those sets of twins that developed prenatally after one egg was fertilized (i.e., zygote) and later split into two developing embryos. Thus, MZ twins share 100% of their genetic material. On the other hand, fraternal twins—also known as dizygotic (DZ) twins—are those that came from two distinct, yet concurrently fertilized eggs. In the case of DZ twins, they share about 50% of genetic material; about the same as non-twin siblings do. However, DZ twins still have the same age, may have the same sex, and typically shared the same environment (e.g., parents, siblings, schools, peers, etc.). Therefore, in twin studies, two groups emerge: a MZ group that shares all genetic material and a DZ group that shares less genetic material with one another. By comparing these two groups on any measure or variables, it may give insight into whether or not that measure appears to be genetically or environmentally driven. To illustrate, suppose a researcher is investigating a personality measure such as extraversion (i.e., the degree to which someone is outgoing). The researcher desires to know whether extraversion is genetically or environmentally based. The research recruits sets of MZ and DZ twins and administers an extraversion scale. Now, suppose the MZ twins demonstrate identical extraversion scores, while the DZ twins demonstrate much more variability. This may give insight into extraversion being genetically driven—when you hold genetics constant (as with MZ twins) then extraversion is constant also. Conversely, if DZ twins

were quite similar in terms of extraversion as MZ twins, then **shared environmental influences** (i.e., those factors shared by their respective environments) may be inferred—genetics does not exert primary influence. Furthermore, if MZ and DZ twins did not look similar on a trait or behavior, then **non-shared environmental influences** (i.e., those factors that are exclusive to their respective environments) may be at play. Some rather intriguing cases have emerged from twin studies. One of the largest efforts was the Minnesota Study of Twins Reared Apart. The most striking case may have been that of the "Jim twins"—identical twins separated at birth and reunited at age 39. At that time, both had first wives named Linda and second wives named Betty. Both chain-smoked, drove a Chevrolet, and served as sheriff's deputies. They even each had similar jobs (one installed fire suppression systems; the other burglar alarms). Notwithstanding the high (perhaps improbable) degree of coincides, the researchers argue that something about the genetic make-up of these twins drove them towards similar experiences. In a sense, they each made their own independent, albeit similar environments, which heightened the likelihood of such similarities (Winerman, 2015).

Second, **adoption studies** compare children with their biological and adoptive parents. Children share genetic material with their biological parents and none with their adoptive parents (assuming a relative did not adopt them). If a researcher is able to gather data on all parties (i.e., children, biological and adoptive parents) then some interesting conclusions may be drawn, again in relation to the general influence of biological and environmental factors on any one variable. Consider this example: a researcher is interested in the heritability (i.e., genetic basis) of depression. Upon entering adolescence, an individual begins to demonstrate depressive symptoms, far more intense than expected in adolescence. On depression scales and measure, the individual does in fact score higher, indicating high levels of depression. There is also depression apparent in at least one biological parent, but there is no indication of depression in either of the adoptive parents. With results such as this, the research may infer depression is partly genetically driven. Consider the alternative scenario: the adolescent is demonstrating depression in adolescence. However, an adoptive parent, and not either of the biological parents also demonstrates this mood disorder. In this case, it appears more closely that some environmental factor(s) may be contributing to the onset of depression.

Third, **twin/adoption studies** are those that compare identical twins who have been raised apart, or otherwise maintain some type of difference in their development or environment. Admittedly, this may be quite rare for psychologists to observe, but it does occur nonetheless, offering a unique glimpse into what factors may be biologically linked and what environmentally linked.

The aforementioned "family-based studies" is not an exhaustive list. Consider the following study, in which researchers aimed to investigate the impact of fathers upon the age at which daughters experience menarche. More specifically, Tither and Ellis (2008) wanted to examine why girls growing up without the biological fathers tend to go through puberty earlier than their peers. To investigate this phenomenon, the researchers employed a **differential sibling exposure design**. This design again captures the genetic similarity that exists between siblings, although not in identical twins. Rather, to be included in this study, it was necessary for there to be at least two female sisters of different ages sharing the same two biological parents, and there was some type of familial disruption (e.g., separation, divorce) that resulted in the father leaving the home. Seemingly, the younger of the two sisters would have more prolonged exposure (leading up to puberty) to such a disruptive event and would therefore be more susceptible to it causing her to experience menarche earlier than the older sister. Therefore, while the sisters share a relatively large amount of genetic material, and much of their environmental material is shared, one key difference is the amount of exposure (in months and years) to the father being absent. Using these sister pairs who had experienced family disruption (i.e., father leaving) as an experimental group, and comparing them to sister pairs from intact families (i.e., father still present) as a control group, findings revealed that the stress presumably associated with an absent father does appear to earlier reported incidences of when a female experiences menarche (Tither & Ellis, 2008).

Erikson's Stage Theory

Erikson studied at Freud's institute for psychoanalytic training. He accepted much of Freud's theory, and the concept of internal conflict remains key. However, Erikson (1980) added his "psychosocial" stages as well:

- If significant others offer basic physical and emotional needs, an infant develops a sense of **trust.** If needs are not met, an attitude of **mistrust** develops, especially toward interpersonal relationships.
- A time for developing **autonomy.** Basic struggle is between a sense of self-reliance and sense of **self-doubt.** A child needs to explore and experiment, to make mistakes and test limits. If parents promote dependency, a child's autonomy is inhibited and capacity to deal with the world may be inhibited.
- Basic task is to achieve competence and **initiative.** If children are given freedom to select personally meaningful activities, they tend to develop a positive view of self and follow through with projects. If they are not allowed to make their own selection, they tend to develop **guilt** over taking initiative. They may then refrain from taking an active role and allow others to choose for them.
- Child needs to expand understanding of the world, continue to develop appropriate sex role identity, and learn basic skills required for school success. Basic task of **industry** relates to setting and attaining personal goals. Failure to do so results in a sense of **inadequacy.**
- A time of transition between childhood and adulthood. A time for testing limits, for breaking ties, and for establishing a new identity. Major conflicts center on clarification of **identity,** life goals, and life meaning. Failure to achieve identity results in **confusion.**
- Developmental task is to form **intimate** relationships. Failure to do so may lead to alienation and **isolation.**
- Generativity refers to the ability to care for another person(s). The most important event is parenting. Does the adult have the ability to care and guide the next generation? **Generativity** has a broader meaning than just having children. Each adult must satisfy and support the next generation, or risk a sense of **"stagnation."**
- The most important event here is coming to accept one's whole life and reflecting upon it in a positive manner. Achieving **integrity** means fully accepting oneself and coming to terms with one's own mortality. Accepting responsibility and achieving satisfaction is essential. The inability to do so results in **despair.**

Summary

When reading the theories of learning, keep in mind that you do not have to adopt and adhere to one particular theory. There are differences between the theories, but the learning situation and the individual may guide which particular theory seems to clarify the scenario in the most appropriate way. Many students may rack their brain trying to break down certain behaviors into stimulus-response relations. Indeed, that is the hallmark of classical conditioning and you may think you should be able to find this relation with all behaviors. However, this can be difficult, and you may appreciate that where classical conditioning does not clarify behavior, operant conditioning may. Where operant conditioning does not clarify behavior, social learning theory may, and so on. It is important to note learning does not just occur in any one context. There are numerous physical, social, and emotional mechanisms that are learned in any situation. Some learned mechanisms are "adaptive" in that they promote more desirable consequences. That is, the individual has learned something constructive. On the other hand, learned mechanisms may also be "maladaptive" (i.e., destructive). In sum, individuals can learn good and bad behaviors.

Key Terms

- **Theory** – somewhat like a complex "educated guess," theories relevant for developmental psychology are created to aid researchers and practitioners in clarifying and predicting behavioral phenomena
- **Nature and Nurture** – these two terms relate to biological and genetic (nature) or social and environmental (nurture) factors and their relative influence of any aspect of human behavior or development
- **Learning** – a relatively permanent change(s) in behavior that occurs due to experience. This term is akin to conditioning.
- **Classical Conditioning** – behavior may be broken down into simple stimulus-response relations, consisting of (un)conditioned stimuli and (un)conditioned responses
- **Unconditioned Response (UCR)** – an unlearned reaction; instinctual reaction
- **Unconditioned Stimuli (UCS)** – a naturally occurring stimuli in the environment to which someone has an UCR
- **Conditioned Stimulus (CS)** – the CS becomes paired with the UCS and the learner—in a passive sense—associates the old (UCS) and new stimuli (CS)
- **Conditioned Response (CR)** – the learned reaction to the CS
- **Taste Aversions** – may occur when an individual associates the taste of a certain food with some symptoms of sickness; people may become disgusted by said foods
- **Law of Effect** – the notion that when an individual engages in a certain behavior and it yields a positive or rewarding outcome, he or she is more likely to engage in that behavior again
- **Operant Conditioning** – this theory, developed by B. F. Skinner, elaborated upon the law of effect; that the consequences of a behavior alter the probability (enhance or lessen) of the behavior's reoccurrence
- **Social Learning Theory** – this theory gives humans a bit more credit as being thinking, dynamic organisms than the classical and operant models permit. A central tenet of this theory is "modeling," that suggests an important part of human learning occurs through observing others.
- **Biological Theory** – underscores the role that physical systems have upon human development, including behavioral, emotional, and cognitive adaptations
- **Neuron** – the most basic cellular unit in the nervous system
- **Neural Stem Cells** – the stem cells that were reserved for the formation of the nervous systems (e.g. central and nervous systems)
- **Neurological Pathways** – meaningful connections between neurons that permit the transmission of neural messages from the nervous systems to the brain and vice versa
- **Cell Body** – the main processing area for the neuron
- **Nucleus** – located in the cell body, all information must pass through the nucleus
- **Axon** – this feature delivers messages away from the cell body. There is one axon responsible for dissemination of information through the neuron.

- **Dendrites** – these features resemble the branches of a tree, and are largely responsible for receiving information and guiding it toward the cell body. There are numerous dendrites in any one neuron.
- **Law of Forward Conduction** – the standard sequence by which information is received by the dendrites, passed along to the cell body (including the nucleus), and then sent along through the axon. Neurological signals do not travel in the opposite direction.
- **Synapses** – the microscopic spaces between neurons that serve to connect neurons to one another
- **All-or-None Principle** – electrical impulses travel through a neuron completely, or not at all. There is no partial activation of neurons.
- **Neurotransmitters** – these chemicals are stored in small sacs at the end of the axon, and within the synapse. The nerve impulses trigger the release of the chemicals into the synapse, where they are potentially absorbed by the dendrites of adjacent neurons.
- **Lock-and-Key Principle** – the idea that distinct neurotransmitters are only able to fit into certain receptor sites on dendrites
- **Excitatory and Inhibitory Responses** – when a neurotransmitter enters a dendrite, it serves to excite or inhibit that particular neuron. While an excitatory response would facilitate continued passage of a neural signal, an inhibitory response would suggest a certain pathway will not activate.
- **Hindbrain** – located toward the rear and typically responsible for automatic processes including breathing, blood circulation, and digestion
- **Midbrain** –located above the hindbrain, responsible for processing some auditory and visual information
- **Forebrain** – located at the front of the brain and responsible for most higher-order thinking (cognition) and feeling (emotion)
- **Thalamus** – located in the forebrain, the thalamus initially receives the neural messages sent to the brain, and subsequently transmits them to appropriate areas of the brain for processing. Thus, many forms of human activity will stimulate neural activity in the thalamus as it is a sort of "entry gate" to many other brain regions.
- **Hypothalamus** – maintains control over the pituitary gland, and subsequently the endocrine system
- **Pituitary Gland** – capable of releasing hormones into the bloodstream, eventually arriving at bodily organs for health and maintenance. In this way, the hypothalamus controls internal bodily processes (e.g., hunger, fatigue, sexual drive, body temperature, etc.).
- **Endocrine System** – consists of the endocrine glands and functions to regulate body activities
- **Brain Localization** – the notion specific regions of the brain are adapted for specific functions
- **Cerebral Cortex** – this area of the brain consists of the entire upper portion of the brain, is responsible for most thinking, feeling, or activity. The "folded" appearance of the cortex is due to it being compressed, or "wrinkled" to fit into a relatively small space.
- **Plasticity Principle** – the idea the human brain is constantly reorganizing itself in response to outward experiences. Neurological connections unused may fade away and disconnect, while new experiences may generate and lubricate new pathways.
- **Synaptogenesis** – the capacity to generate entirely new neurons in certain regions

- **Evolutionary Theory** – a biological theory that posits humans develop over the course of their own lifetime, but may also be part of a larger ancestral chain, where adaptations—ultimately aimed at survival—are genetically transmitted
- **Genetic Determinism** – a rather strict and narrow evolutionary perspective that refers to the notion that individuals are completely biologically pre-programmed for a certain developmental sequence irrespective of environmental conditions
- **Ecological Theory** – a developmental theory that posits development depends upon the interaction of multiple sources (or systems) of influence
    - **Microsystems** – the individual's most immediate environmental circles
    - **Mesosystems** – interrelations are apparent between two or more microsystems
    - **Exosystems** – settings that are not necessarily immediate settings for the individual, but may impact the microsystems nonetheless
    - **Macrosystems** – the most remote course of influence, and involves historical and cultural phenomena, and encompasses attitudes, practices, expectations, ideologies and economic conditions of larger societal groups
    - **Chronosystems** – the impact of any or all of the aforementioned systems can change over time
- **Twin studies** – a family of studies that compare identical and fraternal twins on certain abilities
- **Shared Environmental Influences** – those factors shared by respective environments
- **Non-Shared Environmental Influences** – factors that are exclusive to respective environments
- **Adoption Studies** – compares children with their biological and adoptive parents
- **Twin/Adoption Studies** – compares identical twins who have been raised apart, or otherwise maintain some type of difference in their development or environment
- **Differential Sibling Exposure Design** – these studies employ a design that compares siblings and captures genetic similarity that exists between siblings
- **Erikson's Theory** – suggests humans develop according to eight psychosocial tasks that must be negotiated across the life span

Critical Thinking Questions

1. Apply classical, operant, and social learning to your own life. Take each theory and apply the corresponding principles to a behavior or aspect of development in your own life. For example, describe a behavior that appears to have been classically conditioned by describing the behavior in terms of (un)conditioned stimuli and responses. Describe another behavior that seems to follow operant conditioning principles (e.g., reinforcement and/or punishment). Lastly, apply social learning theory by describing a behavior that you modeled after observing others.
2. What is a theory and what makes a theory appropriate for human development? At a broad level, what makes a developmental theory "nature" or "nurture" in particular? Which theories covered in this chapter are nurture theories? Which are nature theories? Select a theory in particular and discuss why it may be a particularly good developmental theory in your opinion. If necessary, use examples to support your points.

3. What is "genetic determinism"? What broader theory is this related to? Is this too strict a view of human development? Why or why not?
4. What is the main idea of ecological theory? In answering this question, define and discuss the competing and interacting systems that are thought to impact development. Apply ecological systems theory to your own life by discussing the systems and how they may have positively or negatively impacted your development.

References

Beck, J. S. (1995). *Cognitive therapy: Basics and beyond.* New York: Guilford Press.

Brofenbrenner, U. (1977). Toward an experimental ecology of human development. *American Psychologist, 32*, 513-531.

Brown, P. L., & Jenkins, H. M. (2009). On the law of effect. In D. Shanks (Ed.), *Psychology of learning.* Thousand Oaks, CA: Sage.

Cairns, R. B., & Cairns, B. D. (2006). The making of developmental psychology. In William Damon & Richard M. Lerner (Eds.), *Handbook of child psychology: Theoretical models of human development* (pp. 89-165). Hoboken, NJ: Wiley.

Doidge, N. (2007). *The brain that changes itself.* New York: Penguin.

Erikson, E. H. (1980) *Identity and the life cycle.* New York: Norton.

Greenberg, N. (1998). "The evolutionary physiology of creativity." Human Behavior and Evolution Society, Tenth Annual Meeting, University of California - Davis, July 12-13, 1998.

Harlow, H. F. (1958). The nature of love. *American Psychologist, 13*, 673-685.

Hernstein, R. J. (2009). Selection by consequence. In D. Shanks (Ed.), *Psychology of learning.* Thousand Oaks, CA: Sage.

Money, J. & Tucker, P. (1975). *Sexual Signatures on Being a Man or a Woman.* Little Brown & Company: United Kingdom.

Olson, M. & Hergenhahn, B. R. (2009). *Introduction to theories of learning* (8th ed.). Upper Saddle River, NJ: Prentice-Hall.

Skinner, B. F. (1938). *The behavior of organisms: An experimental analysis.* New York: Appleton-Century-Crofts.

Terry, W. S. (2009). *Learning & memory: Basic principles, processes, and procedures.* (4th ed.) Boston: Pearson Higher Education.

Thorndike, E. L. (1898). *Animal intelligence: An experimental study of the associative processes in animals* (Psychological Review, monograph supplements, no. 8). New York: MacMillan.

Tither, J. M. & Ellis, B. J. (2008). Impact of fathers on daughters' age at menarche: A genetically and environmentally controlled sibling study. *Developmental Psychology, 5*, 1409-1442.

Watanabe, H. & Mizunami, M. (2007). Pavlov's cockroach: Classical conditioning of salivation in an insect. *PloS One, 6,* e529.

Winerman, L. (2015). A double life. *Monitor on Psychology, 46,* 30-33.

CHAPTER 4

Prenatal Development

Biological Bases of Prenatal Development

Prenatal development refers to the stage of development prior to the birth event. That is, a pregnant female is carrying an embryo or fetus of an individual in their prenatal phase of life. Thus, unlike other life stages that also have social and emotional areas of development, the prenatal stage is reserved only to biological or physical development.

The prenatal stage may be viewed as the **gestational phase**, which in humans is approximately 40 weeks long. To put the gestational length of humans in perspective, consider that rabbits have a gestational period of about 4 weeks, whereas the rhinoceros has a gestational period of almost 70 weeks. The Indian elephant has the longest gestational period of any mammal: almost 90 weeks! It may be hard to imagine carrying a fetus for almost 2 years. Generally, the larger the mammal, the longer the gestational period and the longer the expected life span.

For the purposes of this text, suffice it to say the human organism begins its journey at the point of **fertilization**, when the sperm of a male and egg of a female combine to form one cell. Of the hundreds of sperm that reach the egg (or ovum), one will penetrate the innermost part. At this point,

Copyright © 2013 by bikeriderlondon. Used under license of Shutterstock, Inc.

the walls of the egg actually shut out the other sperm, and the nuclei of the male and female cells fuse, completing the fertilization event. Thereafter, there are many rapid and important changes that occur.

After fertilization, chromosomes become integral to development. **Chromosomes** are threadlike strands of DNA located in the nuclei of cells that carry genetic material. The chromosome and genetic material inside are protected by **telomeres,** which are nucleotide sequences at the tail ends of the chromosome that protect it from deterioration and fusion with other neighboring cells (see Figure 4.1). Telomeres are somewhat like the casings that protect the end of shoelaces. When they are intact, they maintain the strength and integrity of the entire shoelace; when they deteriorate, the shoelace falls apart and is relatively useless. It is vital to protect this genetic material, as without it no other bodily organs (including those that differentiate sex) or processes (e.g. heart beat) that permit life would develop.

All cells in the human body have 46 chromosomes, except for sperm and ova. It may make instinctive sense that these have 23, and upon fertilization, combine in pairs to account for the 46 chromosomes of all other cells. The 23 pairs of chromosomes (46 total) in the newly combined cell align in matched pairs, with the exception of the pair that determines sex (i.e., X and Y chromosomes). While the ovum only contains an X chromosome, the sperm may contain an X (female) or Y (male) chromosome. If the sperm that ultimately reaches the nucleus of the ovum contains an X chromosome (forming an XX pair), a female will begin to develop. However, if the sperm that ultimately reaches the nucleus of the ovum contains a Y chromosome (forming an XY pair), a male will begin to develop. Thus, in a manner of speaking, the male contribution (i.e., sperm) determines the sex of the individual. Interestingly, it takes several weeks for the genetic commands differentiating sex to take place, and in a sense, all individuals start out as females.

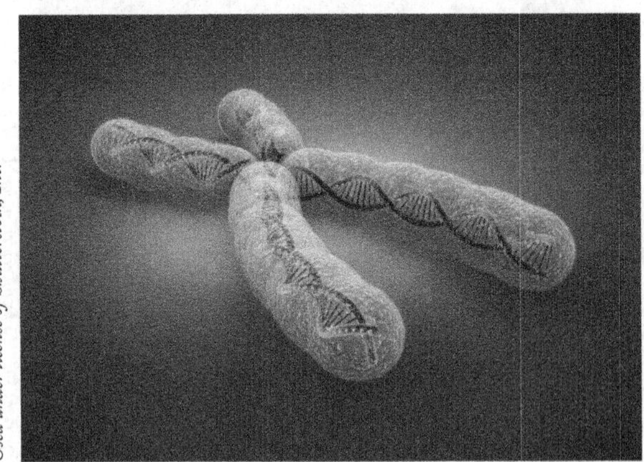

FIGURE 4.1 *Chromosome*

After about 36 hours, the combined sex cells, or **zygote**, begins an important process of cell division. The DNA found in the chromosomes of the zygote is a "blueprint of sorts" for the creation of proteins and material that will promote growth. The zygote is still relatively mobile, not attached to anything in particular. However, over time, the cell descends into the uterus and attaches to the uterine wall. This process is called **implantation.** An event after implantation is the formation of the **placenta**, which will serve as the "lifeline" between the fetus and the mother.

Interestingly, the growing organism (i.e., embryo and placenta) are not recognized and treated, and ultimately rejected, as foreign agents by the female immune system. At the earliest stage of gestation, when the embryo is implanting (or adhering) to the wall of the uterus, a pathway is "turned off" that ultimately does not permit immune cells to function normally in that particular area. Thus, the placenta, embryo, and subsequent fetus are recognized as "normal" body parts and permitted to grow (Nancy, Tagliani, Tay, Asp, Lev, & Erlebacher, 2012).

Gestation may be further broken down into **trimesters**. More specifically, there are three trimesters approximately three months long each, and referred to more simply as the first, second, and third trimester. Although all three trimesters are part of a broader gestational process, they are distinct in terms of what they signify about the biological development of the prenatal organism.

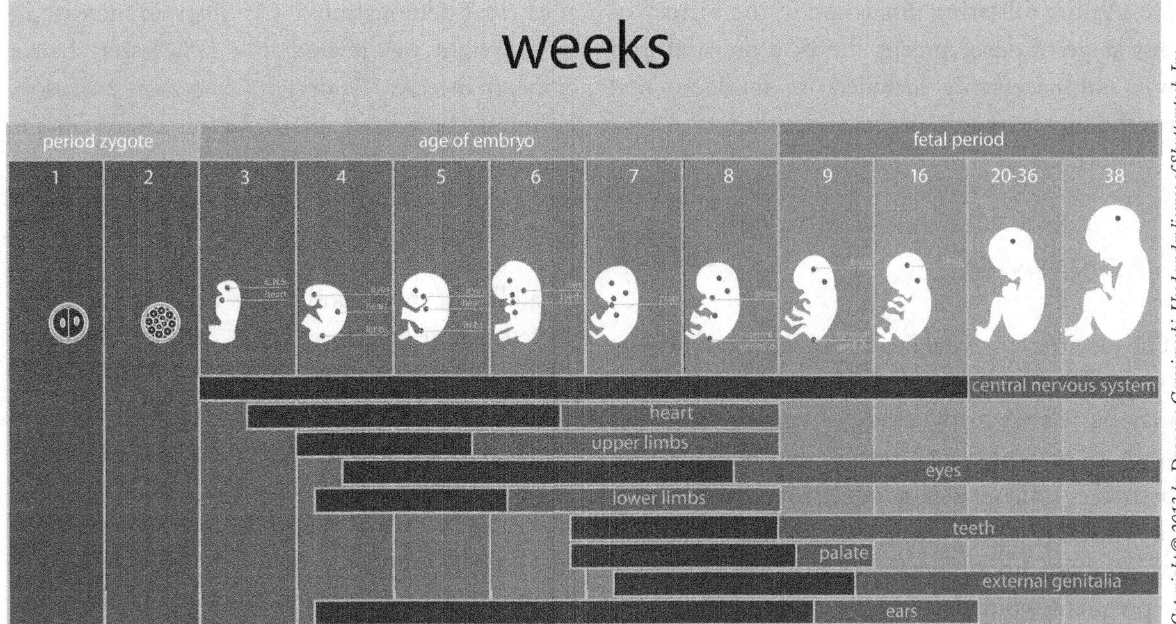

FIGURE 4.2 *Prenatal Development*

For instance, the first trimester roughly corresponds to the **embryonic stage** of development. During these first months, the prenatal organism has not yet developed human-like features (e.g., facial features, limbs, genitalia). Rather, the organism begins as a rather small, grayish, and cloudy embryo during the first weeks after conception. Thereafter, the brain and spinal cord begin to emerge. In the coming sections in this unit, you may further appreciate how vital prenatal care is considering the brain and spinal cord (which constitutes the central nervous system) is apparent for most of the gestational process. The fundamental pieces of the brain and spinal cord may resemble a tadpole to some degree, and may more appropriately be referred to as a **neural tube**. As the neural tube continues to grow and as it approaches the second trimester, limbs, facial features, and genitalia begin to form. Thus, when parent(s) want to verify the sex of a baby, they must do so at a time when it is reasonable to assume it can be verified.

All of the structures that form during gestation originate as **stem cells**. The fluid surrounding the developing organism(s), called **amniotic fluid**, is rich in stem cells. Stem cells are undifferentiated cells capable of increasing in number and forming various structures. The most primitive types of stem cells are totipotent or pluripotent stem cells, which can ultimately create an entire human organism, including the CNS and PNS. Some of these primitive cells are the same being proposed for clinical applications. It may also be possible some stem cells are reserved for the formation of specific structures. For instance, **neural stem cells** are capable of generating neural tissues (Gage, 2000). Without stem cells, fetal development would not be possible.

The second and third trimester are marked by further body development and refinement, and may generally be referred to as a stage of **fetal development**. Together, embryonic and fetal stages bring the fetus to a stage of "biological preparedness" for the birth event and thereafter (see Figure 4.2). The human gestational period (40 weeks) is typically necessary for neurological, cardiovascular, immune, and all nervous systems to have developed to a point of such "readiness." An infant of low birth weight—which may occur from slow prenatal growth or early birth—may warrant more attention from doctors and nurses to be sure they are equipped to meet the demands of infant life. As the following discussion of the history of this stage of development shows, a prenatal unit was not necessarily included in developmental psychology textbooks in recent decades.

A Brief History

The idea that prenatal health impacts later life has received increasing attention over the years, and may be related to the study of **epigenetics**—the study of environmental factors that may produce permanent changes in gene activity. Suffice it to say in decades past there was not the same level of emphasis upon prenatal care. Many years ago, a pregnant woman may have received biological treatments for her own non-pregnancy related health issues with the doctor having relatively little knowledge about how the treatment may (or may not) impact the fetus.

One particular scientist (David Barker) had a lot to do with necessary attention given to prenatal issues. Dr. Barker was a medical researcher investigating cardiovascular disease. In one landmark study, Dr. Barker noted the areas in England with the highest rates of cardiovascular disease (his dependent variable) were the same areas that had the highest rates of low birth weight (his independent variable) 50 years earlier (Hall, 2007). These initial findings sparked what has since been referred to as the "Barker hypothesis." This particular hypothesis was that prenatal growth and development (broadly speaking) was somehow linked with cardiovascular health even decades after birth. The researcher continued to test his hypothesis, and it was rather consistently and robustly supported (Hall, 2007). At the time Dr. Barker first reported his findings and advocated his hypothesis, there likely was not widespread support. Recall this was a time before the presence of thick volumes of pregnancy-related books.

Over time, other researchers found support for this hypothesis as well. These supporting studies came from other countries, as in a large-scale Finnish study that demonstrated a 1 kilogram increase in birth weight was related to a 17% lesser chance of heart disease (Andersen, Ängquist, Eriksson, Forsen, & Gamborg, 2010). In this same vein, researchers revealed a diagnosis of type 2 diabetes was more common for a twin who had low birth weight (Poulson & Vaag, 2001).

In addition, the hypothesis was tested and supported in non-human samples. Although one may argue that non-human samples may not generalize well to humans, there may be a basic strength to employing animal studies in a case such as this. In some animal studies, experimental designs may be employed, which from last unit you may recall are the best designs in terms of capturing causal information between two variables. In this case, researchers examined whether the nutrition (independent variables) of pregnant rats impacted the health (dependent variable) of the baby rats. To do so, the researchers divided the rats into two groups: a control group that received the typical amount of protein in their diet, and an experimental group that received a low protein diet. At this point, perhaps you may appreciate why such experimental designs cannot be performed with humans, in that you would be denying beneficial variables. One of the primary findings was that the rats born to those in the experimental group (i.e., low protein diet) had significantly less stem cells than those in the control group. Such findings strengthened Barker's hypothesis, and the medical community at large began to pay closer attention to prenatal health. In particular, it became more apparent that maternal environments mattered in terms of the baby's eventual health and development. Accordingly, Barker once stated, "you live in two worlds—the world in which your mother creates for you, and the world into which you are born."

The mother may be responsible for "creating" some environmental factors, but others may be more difficult to combat. For instance, in April 1956, two sisters entered a hospital in southern Japan. Previously bright and attentive, they could not walk or speak coherently. Many children from the same neighborhood began to emerge with the same complaints. As it turned out, tons of mercury was being dumped into Minamata Bay—the bay from which the community derived much subsistence. Infants were being born with intellectual difficulties and chromosomal issues (e.g., cerebral palsy). By 1993, over 2,000 individuals had what was termed "Minimata disease." In reality, it was a case study in the dangers of teratogenic exposure during gestation (Hall, 2007).

Teratogens

Generally speaking, **teratogens** are substances that may cross the placenta and harm the embryo or fetus during gestation. These may include, but are not limited to: drugs (i.e., prescription and nonprescription), environmental pollutants, infectious diseases, and nutritional deficiencies. Conceivably, any agent or substance that may enter the maternal blood stream may enter into the embryonic or fetal organism as well, via the placenta. Moreover, the embryo or fetus does not maintain the same level of immune functioning or maturity to handle such substances or agents in the same way as a child or adult may. Through this general process, teratogens may negatively impact embryonic and fetal development. There are some general principles that may clarify teratogenic exposure.

- Teratogens are more likely to cause structural damage during the embryonic stage and functional damage during the fetal stage.
- Teratogens can cause damage to the brain throughout gestation.
- Teratogens tend to operate in dose-response manner.
- However, teratogens can be unpredictable (Belsky, 2010).

According to these general principles, whether or not damage occurs to the fetus may be linked with other factors. For instance, the first principle cited above is a timing issue. If there is some degree of teratogenic exposure in the first trimester—during an embryonic stage—damage may be structural in nature. That is, as the exposure is occurring before bodily structures have formed, it is possible the damage may occur as body deformities (e.g., limbs, facial features). On the other hand, if the damaging exposure occurs after limbs and structures have formed (i.e., fetal stage), then the damage is not structural, but rather functional in nature. Functional damage refers to difficulties and abnormalities in the functionality (i.e., how something works) of the body. An example of functional damage may be hearing or vision loss. While the eyes and ears appear to have formed normally to the casual observer, they may not work ideally.

According to the second principle, teratogens may cause brain damage throughout gestation. For instance, a recent study demonstrated that prenatal exposure to household chemicals (i.e., DnBP and DiBP) typically found in a variety of household (e.g., vinyl materials) and personal care products (e.g., lipstick, hairspray, nail polish) was linked with lower intelligence scores in childhood. It should be noted that these associations were observable only for the mothers and offspring with the highest rate of exposure to DnBP and DiBP (Factor-Litvak, Insel, Calafat, Liu, Perera, Rauh, & Wyatt, 2014). Another study demonstrated that a variety of endocrine disrupting chemicals - such as those found in paints and adhesives - may interfere with normal maternal thyroid functions, and subsequently impact prenatal brain development (Wadzinksi, Geromini, McKinley Brewer, Bansal, Abdelouahab, Langlois, Takser, & Zoeller, 2014). Recall that the neural tube is evident in the earliest stages of gestation. The neural tube—which is the basis for the brain and spinal cord—constitutes the central nervous system, and must be in place for the organism to survive even as an embryo. Thus, teratogenic exposure at any point in time may negatively impact the brain, whether structurally or functionally. This principle is rather "loaded" in that the brain will have primary importance throughout the life span in terms of development. The third principle is related to the "dosage" of the teratogen. This principle may suggest little or moderate levels of exposure will be unlikely to cause embryonic or fetal damage. However, the principle suggests that large amounts of exposure may have negative impact. This principle may include numerous teratogens, ones that even may be considered rather harmless in most cases (e.g., caffeine). Lastly, the fourth principle suggests that different doses of different teratogens at different times have different effects. The usage of the term "different" in the preceding sentence may capture the notion that individuals' differences exist when it comes to gestation, teratogenic exposure, and embryonic and fetal damage. One individual may have relatively high levels of exposure to a teratogen, yet the infant displays no apparent negative effects. On the other hand, it is possible that a small amount of exposure leads to some form of abnormal embryonic or fetal development. Together, many substances may hold teratogenic potential depending upon timing and dosage. For the pregnant female, thorough and regular communication regarding the relative risk of teratogens with a doctor may be warranted. It should be noted that although teratogens represent a certain level of risk—they may heighten the likelihood of negative biological, psychological, and/or social development—most babies are born on time and normal weight (Dunkell-Schetter & Glynn, 2011).

Prenatal Care and Diagnostic Tests

Recall from the introduction of ecological development that human development may be contingent upon the interaction of numerous social systems, extending from one's immediate surroundings to also include a milieu of social and cultural factors. Intuitively, and in line with what researchers and practitioners now know of the importance of prenatal development, the systems in which the biological carrier resides also hold importance for fetal development. Accordingly, the general course of prenatal development may be dependent upon maternal environment and behavior, including prenatal health care.

Compared to developing countries, the United States and other developed nations have relatively well established modes of health care, including the knowledge and practices devoted to prenatal health. The fields of obstetrics, gynecology, and pediatrics broadly encompass research and practice devoted to the health and well-being of pregnant females, unborn children, and newborns. Prenatal care knowledge and practices evident in developed countries include routine physical examinations for the pregnant female. Such examinations are laden with recommendations relating to physical activity (e.g., reduction or cessation of exercise) and diet (e.g., nutrition and vitamins). For instance, a pregnant female may be advised to limit physical activity to walking as she nears her anticipated delivery date, or take vita-

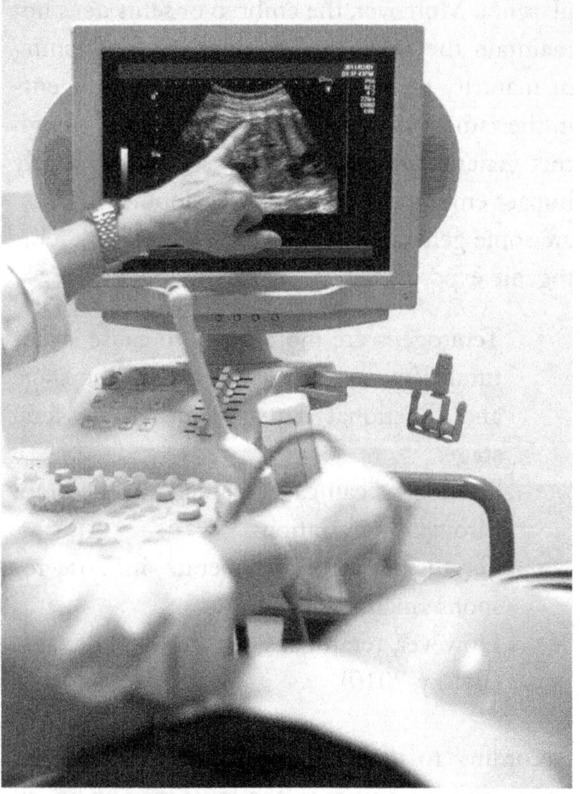

FIGURE 4.3 *Ultrasound*

mins including folic acid, which may be linked with neural tube development. Lastly, there are a variety of prenatal diagnostic tests available that permit careful monitoring of prenatal health and development.

Prenatal diagnostic tests offer insight into the embryonic and fetal health and progression. During the earlier stages of gestation, **blood tests** may be performed. Simple blood tests may demonstrate the relative presence or absence of various chemicals necessary for fetal growth. Moreover, blood tests are able to show when some chromosomal abnormalities are present (e.g., Down syndrome). Another widely used prenatal test is **ultrasound.** Ultrasounds (as shown in Figure 4.3) offer nurses and parents an actual image of the fetus, and are typically given sparingly in the course of gestation. However, under conditions of closer monitoring, a pregnant female may receive numerous ultrasound images of her baby. Ultrasound images allow doctors and nurses to track prenatal growth, and also observe structural development. Concerning the latter, structural development is of interest when attempting to note structural abnormalities or merely verifying the sex of the baby. The aforementioned tests (i.e., blood tests, ultrasound) are relatively non-invasive.

Some other more invasive (but useful nonetheless) prenatal tests include **chorionic villus sampling (CVS)** and **amniocentesis**. The CVS method is performed by inserting a catheter into the mother (abdominally or vaginally) and extracting a piece of the placenta. The piece of placenta then may be further examined to verify numerous chromosomal or genetic disorders. CVS may be necessary to confirm what a blood test and/or ultrasound suggested, and carries a higher risk of miscarriage than do other types of prenatal tests. Thus, CVS is used only under strict conditions. Another type of prenatal test is an amniocentesis. As you may appreciate from the name, this test involves an analysis of the amniotic fluid. The amniotic fluid contains stem cells that may reveal the presence or absence of disorders.

The Birth Event

Prenatal monitoring typically increases as the birth event approaches. For instance, doctors and parents are often able to observe the head of the fetus moving down toward the lower portion of the uterus. In the final days and weeks, the uterus begins to contract and the **cervix**, which is the narrower portion of the lower uterus that the baby must pass through, begins to thin and soften. Such events are clear signals the birth event is approaching, although it is unclear precisely what may trigger the birth itself, assuming it is not medically induced. Thereafter, some important stages characterize the birth event:

- dilation,
- birth, and
- placental expulsion.

In the first stage, dilation (or widening) of the cervix occurs. **Dilation** is responsible for the widening and opening of the cervix, which will ultimately allow the baby to progress from the uterus to the outer world. An important mechanism that facilitates dilation is **contractions**, which are muscular fluctuations at the base of the uterus that occur with increasing frequency as the birth event approaches. In the second stage, aptly termed the **birth stage**, the baby descends from the uterus—through the opening the cervix has vacated—and into the birth canal. The baby's head typically emerges first (i.e., **crowning**) followed by the torso and legs. The umbilical cord is severed, and the newborn is given some immediate medical at-

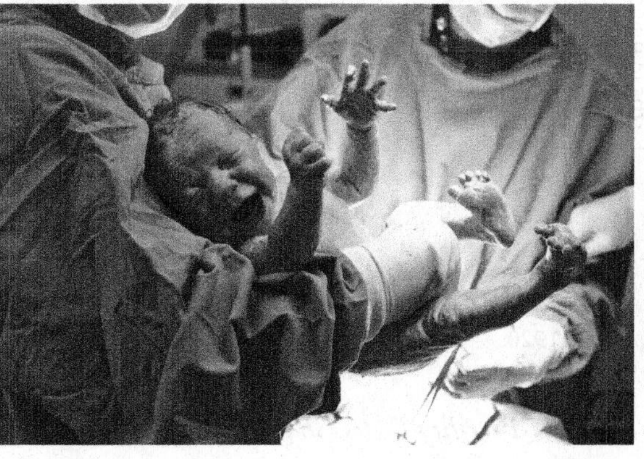

tention. The third stage is referred to as **placental expulsion**, and involves removing from the mother's body what is commonly called the "afterbirth." The afterbirth consists of the placenta and other materials that were necessary for prenatal development, but unnecessary post-birth.

The aforementioned stages are characteristic of the childbirths that occur through the birth canal. Contemporarily, it is fairly common for these to occur in hospitals, although some may wish to experience a natural childbirth. A **natural childbirth** may generally lack many of the traditional factors of a hospital birth, including the staff, room, and even anesthetics. For instance, a natural childbirth may occur at a birthing center or even one's own home. Rather than a doctor, a midwife may perform the delivery. Moreover, women choosing natural childbirth may opt out of the epidural or other anesthetics hospitals offer for pain relief associated with delivery. In 2010, 98.8% of all U.S. births occurred in hospitals. Among the 1.2% of out-of-hospital births, 67% were in a home or residence and 28% were in a birthing center. Medical doctors attended the most (86.3%) hospital births, followed by certified nurse midwives (7.6%) (Martin, Hamilton, Ventura, Osterman, Wilson, Mathews, 2010).

There is a delivery method that does not necessarily involve the birth canal. From time to time, a **cesarean section** (i.e., c-section) may be performed, that requires the doctor to enter the womb by making incisions in the abdominal wall to remove the newborn. While many c-sections are pre-arranged, some c-sections are ordered after traditional birth has already begun, perhaps due to some unforeseen complications. In 2010, c-sections accounted for 32.8% of all births; a slight decrease from 2009. While this was the first decrease since 1996, overall there are 60% more c-sections than in 1996 (Martin et al., 2010). There are a variety of reasons why a c-section may be performed, but all generally related to health concerns for the mother or baby. Some individuals may interpret such a drastic increase in the rates of c-section as being evidence c-sections are overused in developed countries, perhaps performed for reasons other than medical necessity or emergency. Notwithstanding this argument, a c-section remains a vital and life-saving birthing alternative. Figure 4.4 demonstrates the number of live births in the United States from 1920 to 2010.

Shortly after birth, it is common that a baby be given their first assessment. Namely, an **APGAR test** is given initially at 1 and 5 minutes after birth,

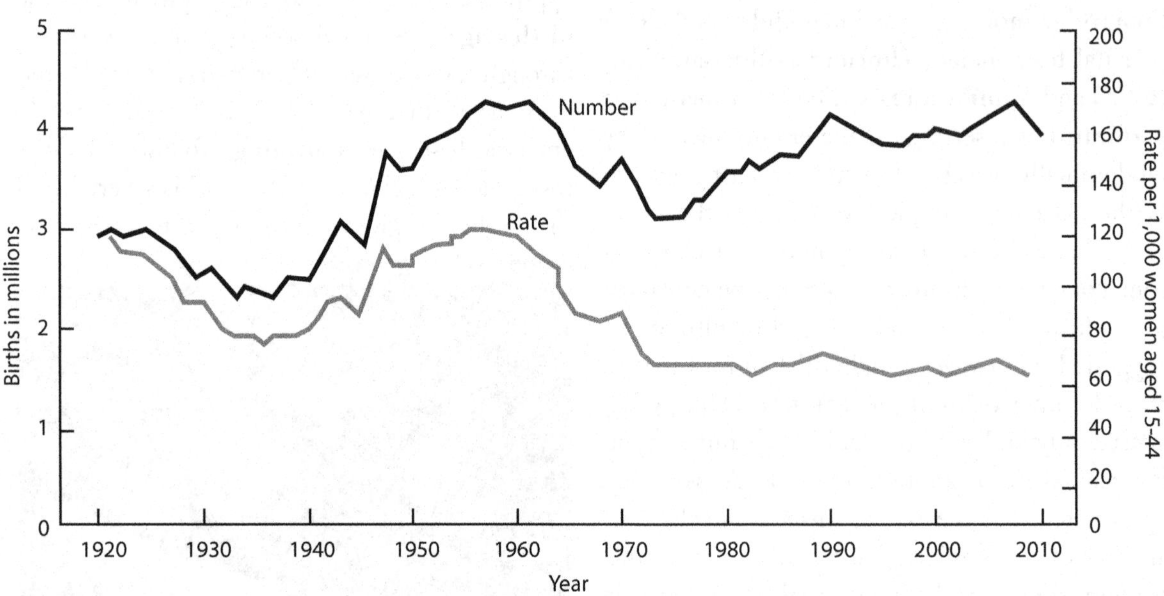

FIGURE 4.4 *Fertility Rates Chart*

Courtesy of CDC/NCHS, National Vital Statistics System

and multiple times thereafter. The acronym APGAR is derived from the dimensions it measures. Namely, it assesses relative levels of activity, pulse, grimace, appearance, and respiration (Belsky, 2010). In other words, this particular test evaluates heart rate, body color, muscle tone, respiratory effort, and reflex irritability. This test is intended to be employed rather quickly and conveniently. On the five dimensions mentioned above, a baby may be assigned a score of 0, 1, or 2. A score of 0 in each case would reflect a relative absence of that particular dimension. Conversely, a score of 2 in each case would indicate normal, and presumably healthy, functioning. A score of 1 in any dimension would indicate an infant may have lacked the qualities necessary for the assignment of a score of 2, but also did not display a total lack of activity, pulse, grimace, appearance, or respiration. For instance, a newborn having considerable difficulty breathing, or not at all, may be assigned a 0. An infant who breathes clearly or cries upon having his or her breathing pathways cleared may be assigned a score of 2. An infant assigned a score of 1 may have demonstrated some labored breathing in the first minutes. It should be noted that the APGAR is given more than once during a newborn's first minutes. Thus, scores may fluctuate, and doctors and nurses are using the scores to inform them of the type and intensity of assistance needed, if any. Generally, a newborn scoring a 7 or above on the test at 1 minute after birth is considered in good health (Belsky, 2010). However, a lower score doesn't necessarily mean that a baby is unhealthy or abnormal, but rather may indicate area(s) that warrant close attention (Dunkell-Schetter & Glynn, 2011). Infants that are of low birth weight may score low in some areas as their cardiovascular and respiratory systems may be underdeveloped. Generally speaking, and in accordance with Barker's hypothesis, adequate prenatal growth (which may be expressed in birthweight) may be ideal. Along those lines, a recent study showed that heavier weight at birth may be advantageous in terms of future academic achievement. According to researchers, the greater birthweight may indicate enhanced brain development in utero (Figlio, Guryan, Karbownik, & Roth, 2014). However, other researchers have

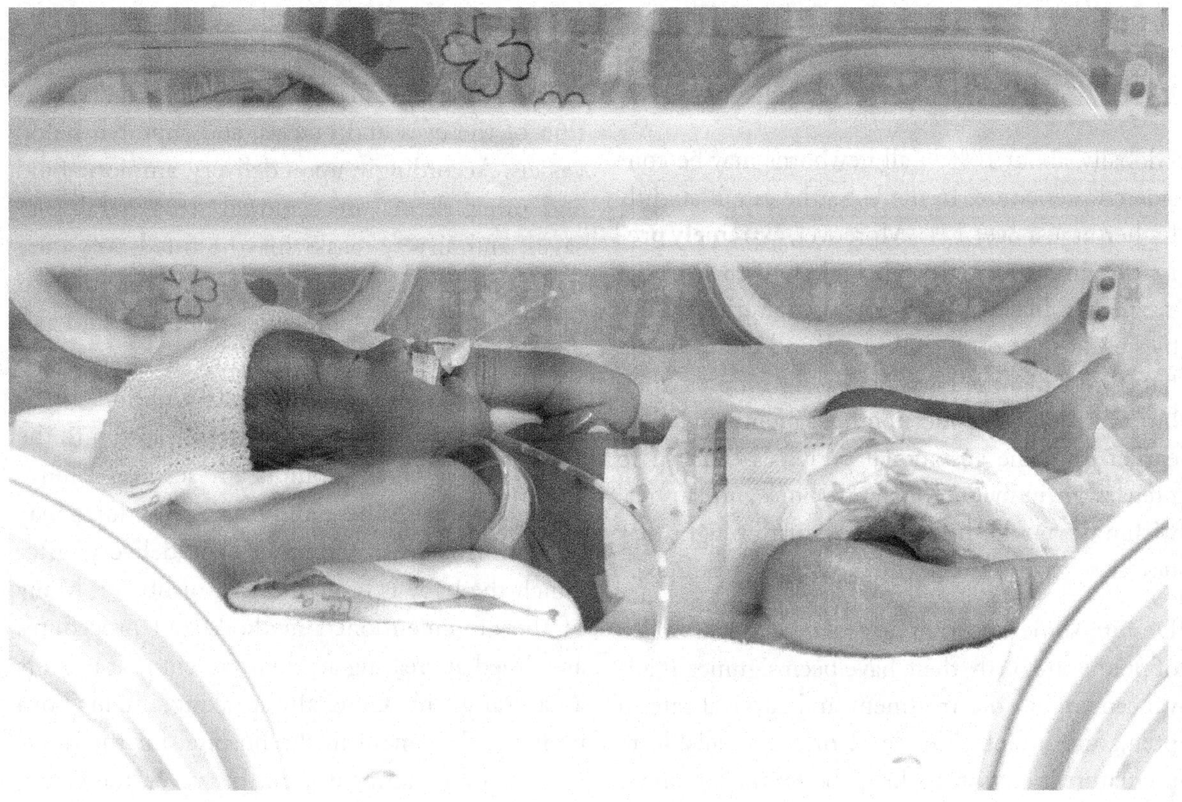

argued that birthweight charts may be tailored to specific ethnic groups to better predict adverse outcomes (Urquia, Berger, & Ray, 2014).

Low Birth Weight

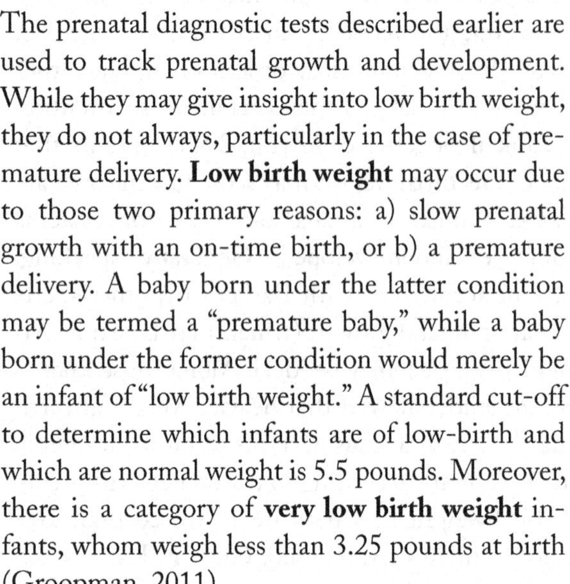

The prenatal diagnostic tests described earlier are used to track prenatal growth and development. While they may give insight into low birth weight, they do not always, particularly in the case of premature delivery. **Low birth weight** may occur due to those two primary reasons: a) slow prenatal growth with an on-time birth, or b) a premature delivery. A baby born under the latter condition may be termed a "premature baby," while a baby born under the former condition would merely be an infant of "low birth weight." A standard cut-off to determine which infants are of low-birth and which are normal weight is 5.5 pounds. Moreover, there is a category of **very low birth weight** infants, whom weigh less than 3.25 pounds at birth (Groopman, 2011).

Premature Delivery and Care

Globally, about 10% of all newborns may be considered premature. In the U.S., the rate is slightly higher, at just over 12%. Moreover, **extremely premature infants** are those born before 28 weeks of pregnancy. In cases of extreme prematurity, the babies eyelids are often still fused, and their ears are flat (Groopman, 2011). The reasons for premature birth are not well understood. As mentioned in an earlier unit, the gestational period is thought to prepare an individual for entry into and survival within the world. Infants of low birth weight may not have attained an adequate stage of readiness.

Despite some uncertainties related to the causes of premature birth, there have been significant advancements in the treatment and survival rate of premature infants. The level of care available to premature infants is markedly better than in previous decades, when doctors were not able to readily recognize and address the problems that typically arise for premature infants. Currently, parents of premature infants may be relatively confident of a good outcome, and subsequent development. Survival for infants born after 32 weeks, but not full-term, is almost 100%. Decades ago, this was not the case, as in the example of John F. Kennedy and his wife, who lost the five and half week premature infant son born to them in 1963.

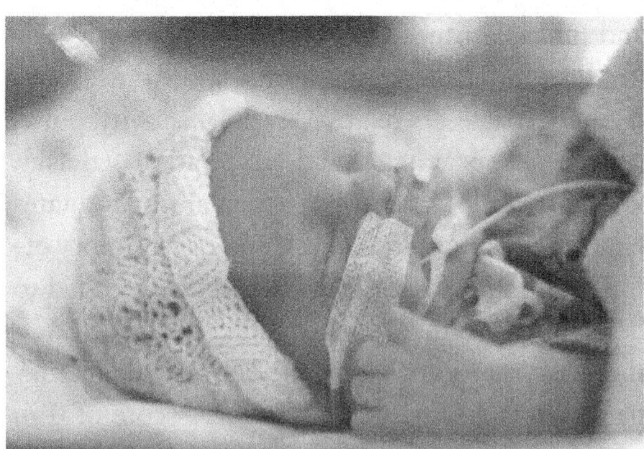

Neonatal intensive care units (NICU) house numerous professionals and instruments equipped to handle many of the physical problems that may accompany low birth weight. Premature infants may be at increased risk for collapsed lungs, body temperature regulation and fluid loss, inflammation of the eyes and bowels, and ruptured blood vessels. Accordingly, upon delivery, amniotic fluid and other debris are removed from nasal passages, and airway masks may be fitted over their mouth and nose. A thin catheter may be inserted into the umbilical vein, which pumps in fluid and medication. Catheters may be inserted to monitor blood circulation and pressure. In addition, a material called surfactant may be introduced into the baby's lungs, which prompts air sacs in the lungs to remain open. These and other procedures may be performed within minutes of delivery, after which the baby is brought to an incubator. Many of the aforementioned methods and procedures are aimed at creating an environment that mirrors a natural womb. Generally speaking, infants born prematurely remain in the hospital for the duration of the gestational term. However, the extent of the premature delivery, or the presence or absence of difficulties, may dictate how long an infant will actually remain under hospitalized care.

Infant Mortality

Despite the advances in prenatal and neonatal care, there are still cases of **infant mortality**, apparent when an infant dies within the first year of life. At a broad level, developed parts of the world, including the U.S., have relatively low infant mortality rates when compared to developing regions. The relative availability and quality of health care before, during, and immediately after the birth event is much higher in developed regions. Figure 4.5 demonstrates the rates of infant mortality for the United States from 1998 to 2008. When these factors are lacking, the risk of infant mortality increases. However, even within the U.S., there appears to be disparity when it comes to availability and quality of health care. Lower socioeconomic populations demonstrate a rather high infant mortality rate due to a lack of health care. This trend drives up the overall infant mortality rate in the U.S. Thus, in recent estimates, for every 1,000 infants, only about 7 die within the first year. Although this is a relatively low rate, it still ranks behind 40 other developed countries.

Regions of the world with the lowest infant mortality rates also have the highest **life expectancies**, as only a small number of infant mortality cases are being entered into this "average" age of life expectancy. Conversely, in regions where in-

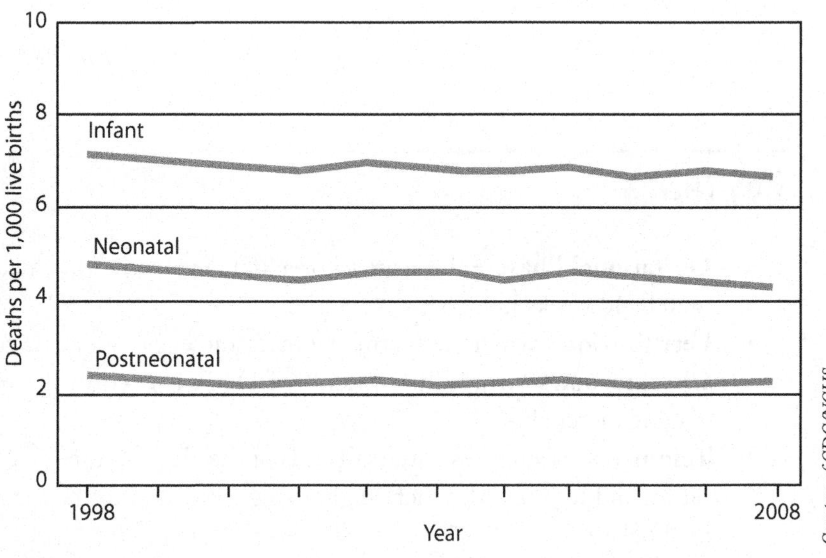

FIGURE 4.5 *Infant Mortality Chart*

Courtesy of CDC/NCHS

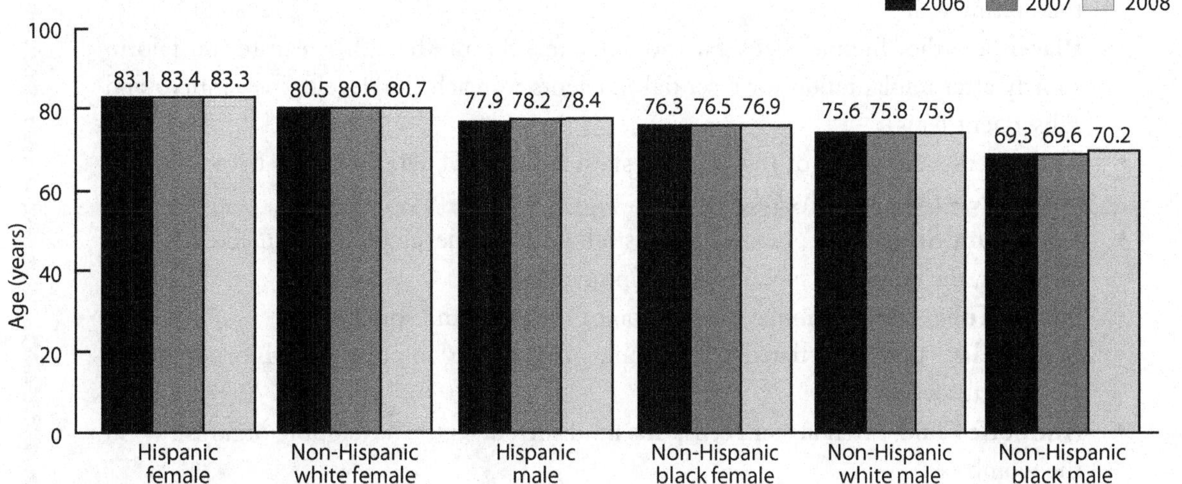

FIGURE 4.6 *Life Expectancy Chart...2006–08*

Courtesy of CDC/NCHS, National Vital Statistics System and Centers for Medicare & Medicaid Services

fant mortality is high, life expectancy is driven down. Together, there is a negative correlation between these two variables. Overall it is important to note that many of the undesirable issues discussed in this unit (i.e., damage due to teratogenic exposure, low birth weight, infant mortality, chromosomal and genetic disorders), while not necessarily uncommon, are still not viewed as normal parts of development. A healthy pregnancy and baby are the rules, rather than the exceptions. Figures 4.6 and 4.7 demonstrate life expectancies in the United States according to race and sex.

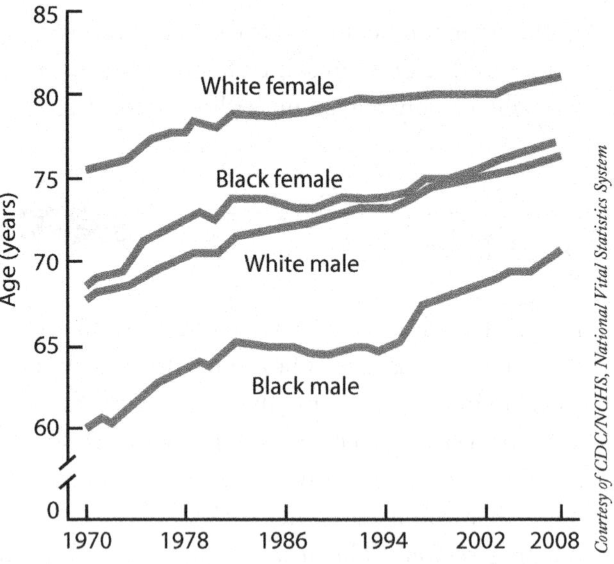

FIGURE4.7 *Life Expectancy Chart…1970–2008*

Key Terms

- **Gestational Phase** – the stage of prenatal development, which in humans is approximately 40 weeks long
- **Fertilization** – when the sperm of a male and egg of a female combine to form one cell
- **Chromosomes** – threadlike strands of DNA located in the nuclei of cells that carry genetic material
- **Telomeres** – sequences at the tail ends of the chromosome that protect it from deterioration and fusion with other neighboring cells, akin to the casings that protect the end of shoelaces
- **Zygote** – combined sex cells
- **Implantation** – the process of the zygote descending into the uterus and attaching to the uterine wall
- **Placenta** – the "lifeline" between the fetus and the mother; this feature must form shortly after implantation for essential nutrients to reach the developing embryo and subsequent fetus
- **Trimesters** – segments of the larger gestational stage. There are three trimesters approximately three months long each.
- **Embryonic Stage** – the prenatal organism has not yet developed human-like features. However, the brain and spinal cord begin to emerge.
- **Neural Tube** – the preliminary formation of the brain and spinal cord
- **Stem Cells** – undifferentiated cells capable of increasing in number and forming various structures
- **Amniotic Fluid** – rich in stem cells, this fluid surrounds the developing organism(s) in the womb
- **Neural Stem Cells** – stem cells capable of generating neural tissues

- **Fetal Development (or Stage)** – the second and third trimester are marked by further body development and refinement; human features are apparent
- **Epigenetics** – the study of environmental factors that may produce permanent changes in gene activity
- **Teratogens** – any substances that may cross the placenta and harm the embryo or fetus during gestation
- **Prenatal Diagnostic Tests** – any of a variety of tests that offer insight into the embryonic and fetal health and progression
- **Blood Test** – a relatively common prenatal test; may demonstrate the relative presence or absence of various chemicals necessary for fetal growth. Moreover, blood tests are able to reveal whether some chromosomal abnormalities are present (e.g. Down syndrome).
- **Ultrasound** – offers nurses and parents an actual image of the fetus. Ultrasound images allow doctors and nurses to track prenatal growth, and observe structural development.
- **Chorionic Villus Sampling (CVS)** – performed by inserting a catheter into the mother (abdominally or vaginally) and extracting a piece of the placenta. The piece of placenta then may be further examined to verify numerous chromosomal or genetic disorders.
- **Amniocentesis** – an analysis of the amniotic fluid. The amniotic fluid contains stem cells that may reveal the presence or absence of disorders.
- **Dilation** – responsible for the widening and opening of the cervix
- **Contractions** – muscular fluctuations at the base of the uterus, that occur with increasing frequency as the birth event approaches
- **Birth Stage** – baby descends from the uterus—through the opening the cervix has vacated—and into the birth canal
- **Crowning** – the emergence of the head from the birth canal
- **Placental Expulsion** – removal of the placenta and other materials that were necessary for prenatal development, but unnecessary post-birth
- **Natural Childbirth** – birth may occur in the home or a birthing center, and may generally lack many of the traditional factors of a hospital birth, including the staff, room, and even anesthetics
- **Cesarean Section (or c-section)** – a procedure in which the doctor enters the womb by making incisions in the abdominal wall to remove the newborn
- **APGAR Test** – given initially at 1 and 5 minutes after birth, the APGAR assesses relative levels of activity, pulse, grimace, appearance, and respiration in a newborn
- **Low Birth Weight** – this may occur due to slow prenatal growth with an on-time birth, or premature delivery. A standard cut-off to determine which infants are of low-birth and which are normal weight is 5.5 pounds.
- **Very Low Birth Weight** – a term reserved for infants weighing less than 3.25 pounds at birth
- **Infant Mortality** – infant death that occurs within the first year of life
- **Life Expectancy** – the average number of years one can expect to live, given various conditions (i.e., physical, social, economic) remain the same

Critical Thinking Questions

1. Discuss gestation. In doing so, discuss the important physical processes and features that characterize this phenomena. In addition, be sure to discuss the features and processes that facilitate growth of the embryo and fetus.
2. What are teratogens? In defining this term, be sure to also discuss the four principles that may be applied to clarify if and when teratogenic exposure may cause damage to the embryo or fetus.

References

Andersen, L. G., Ängquist, L., Eriksson, J. G., Forsen, T., & Gamborg, M. (2010). Birth weight, childhood body mass index and risk of coronary heart disease in adults: Combined historical cohort studies. *PLoS ONE, 5*, e14126.

Belsky, J. (2010). *Experiencing the lifespan.* New York: Worth.

Dunkel-Schetter, C., Glynn, L. (2011). Stress in pregnancy: Empirical evidence and theoretical issues to guide interdisciplinary researchers. In R. Contrada & A. Baum (Eds). *Handbook of Stress* (pp. 321-343). New York: Springer Publishing Company.

Factor-Ltvak, P., Insel, B., Calafat, A.M., Liu, X., Perera, F., Rauh, V.A., & Whyatt, R.M. (2014). Persistent associations between maternal prenatal exposure to phthalates on child IQ at age 7 years. *PLoS ONE, 9*: e114003 DOI: 10.1371/journal.pone.0114003.

Figlio, D., Guryan, J., Karbownik, K., & Roth, J. (2014). The effects of poor prenatal health on chidlren's cognitive development. *American Economic Review.* Retrieved from: www.sciencedaily.com/releases/2014/12/141202082533.htm

Gage, F. H. (2000). Mammalian neural stem cells. *Science magazine, 280*, 1433-1438.

Groopman, J. (2011, October 24). A child in time: New frontiers in treating premature babies. *New Yorker*, 26-35.

Hall, S. S. (2007, November 19). Small and thin: The controversies over the fetal origins of adult health. *New Yorker,* 52-57.

Martin, J. A., Hamilton, B. E., Ventura, S. J., Osterman, M. J., Wilson, E. C., Mathews, T. J. (2010). Births: Final data for 2010. *National Vital Statistics Reports, 61*, 1-72.

Nancy, P., Tagliani, E., Tay, C. S., Asp, P., Levy, D. E., Erlebacher, A. (2012) Chemokine gene silencing in decidual stromal cells limits T-cell access to the maternal-fetal interface. *Science, 336*(6068), 1317-1321.

Poulson, P., & Vaag, A. (2001). Glucose and insulin metabolism in twins: influence of zygosity and birth weight. *Twin Research, 4*, 350-355.

Wadzinksi, T.L., Geromini,K., McKinley Brewer, J., Bansal, R., Abdelouahab, N., Langlois, M.F., Takser, & Zoeller, R.T. (2014). Endocrine disurption in human placenta: Expression of the dioxin-inducible enzyme, Cyp1a1, is correlation with that of the thyroid hormone-regulated genes. *The Journal of Clinical Endocrinology and Metabolism.* DOI: 10.1210/jc.2014-2629.

CHAPTER 5

Physical and Cognitive Development in Infancy

Infancy

Infancy may be rather easily understood as ranging from birth to 2 years of age. These chronological markers leave little doubt as to when a baby may be called an "infant" and when they move on to toddlerhood. Thus, the following units will focus on select physical (i.e., neurological, motor), cognitive (i.e., language, memory), and socioemotional (i.e., attachment) variables in infancy. The range and degree of milestones that typically occur during infancy are impressive. For instance, infants will likely take their first steps, begin to communicate linguistically, and display clear preferences for certain caretakers. Along these lines, the subsequent paragraphs will describe developmental features of infancy. As you consider these features, also bear in mind that some of the "largest developmental leaps" are made during infancy. Thus, while infants may appear to maintain relatively simple lifestyles comprised of eating, sleeping, fussing, and playing, there is significant growth occurring in many areas.

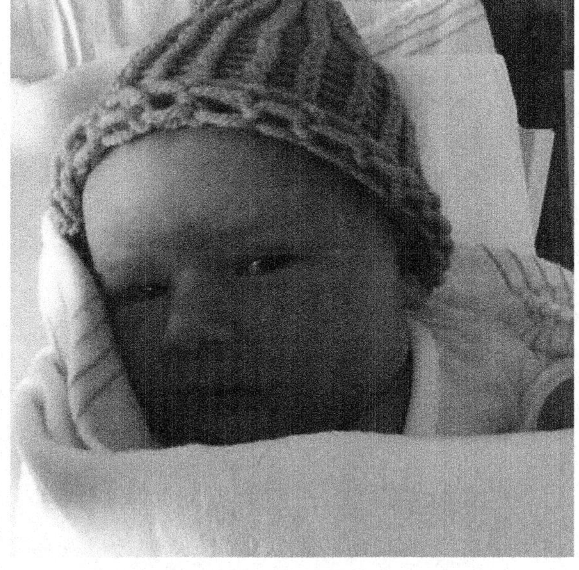

Courtesy of the author

Neurological Development

When considering neurological development in infancy, some of the terms and principles originally introduced in previous units on theory will be revisited. More specifically, biological theory was laden with relevant terms such as the neuron, synapse, and neurotransmitter. Moreover, the plasticity principle and the process of synaptogenesis will be revisited. However, some new terms will be introduced as well.

For instance, the rate of brain growth during infancy, although not directly and casually observable, is impressive. During the first two years, the overall gray matter in the brain will grow from one quarter of its adult size to three quarters of its adult size. Thus, the brain nearly triples in size in just two years. Put simply, if our brains continued this rapid growth, the adult brain—and skull covering—would be enormous. One particular brain region, the **cerebral cortex**, is part of this growth. Recall the cerebral cortex, which consists of the entire upper portion of the brain, is responsible for most thinking, feeling, or activity. Thus, during infancy, the brain regions available for higher order thinking increase dramatically. However, brain size alone does not account for enhanced brain capabilities in infancy. Neurological processes occurring within the cortex and other brain regions occur concomitantly.

Synaptogenesis and Myelination

First, **synaptogenesis** occurs at a rapid rate. Recall synaptogenesis is the formation of linkages between neurons, ultimately forming neurological pathways and permitting the transmission of messages along nervous system channels. Generally speaking, environmental stimuli (i.e., objects and forces detected by the senses) prompt the activation of these neurological pathways. When applied to infancy, the people and objects the infants encounter are the stimuli, and cause many neurological pathways to fire for the first time. A movement as simple as grasping a mother's finger may be sensed visually and tactilely, and prompt a message sent to the brain for processing.

Second, **myelination** occurs intensely during infancy. Myelination is a process that strengthens the protective covering surrounding the axon of the neuron (see Figure 5.1). This covering is the **myelin sheath**, and when strengthened, is linked to faster and more efficient information processing. Thus, neural impulses may travel more safely and effectively through the neuron to stimulate

neurotransmitter release at the terminal sites. Myelination may be underlying enhanced balance and motor coordination in infancy. Conversely, some degenerative diseases in later life are due in part to a breakdown of the myelin sheath. Together, it is evident the synaptogenesis and myelination processes that occur during infancy are critical for growth.

Physical and Motor Development

The average weight for a newborn is approximately 6 pounds, with an average length of about 19 inches. Another important measurement is

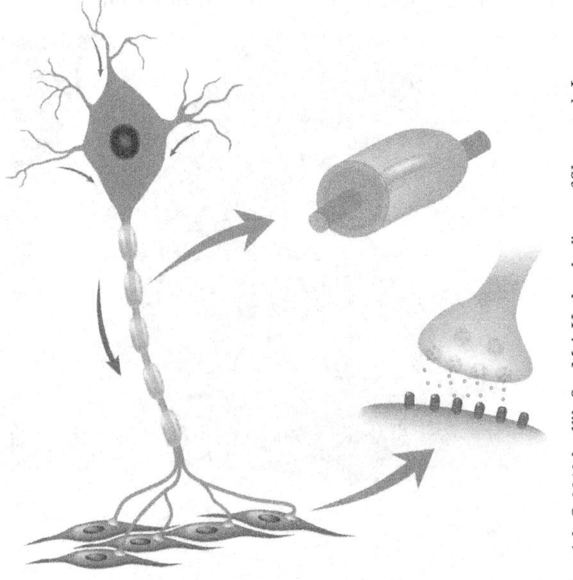

FIGURE 5.1 *Motor neuron w/details of myelin*

head circumference. Throughout infancy, length, weight, and head circumference will be monitored consistently, assuming the infant is regularly seeing his or her pediatrician. There are expected rates of infantile growth in terms of length and weight, and any lack of such growth in an infant may be an indication of malnutrition, digestive problems, or other problems. This may be particularly important as individuals must be at least 2 years old to be covered by U.S. dietary guidelines. For infants, no formal guidelines exist other than those created by organizations emphasizing breastfeeding for at least the first 6 months. Recently, researchers investigated dietary patterns of infants and found that much depends upon sociodemographic variables. Results revealed that infant diets high in sugar, fat and protein were associated with lower maternal education level and socioeconomic status. Such research is important given that it appears infants develop a taste and preference for what they are fed (Wen, Kong, Eiden, Sharma & Xie, 2014). In addition, head circumference should increase at a certain rate in relation to body shape and size, and a failure to do so may indicate certain physical problems. For example, infants accumulating fluid may demonstrate enhanced rates of head growth.

With the aforementioned physical assessments, parents and caregivers may become familiar with **percentile scores**, as these scores typically accompany the raw measurements for length, weight, and head circumference. A percentile score indicates the percentage of scores that fall at or below an infant's personal measurement(s). For instance, an infant at the 85th percentile for weight is as heavy or heavier than 85% of all other infants within a particular group. Doctors are able to generate percentiles for infants in relation to "all other infants" because they have the luxury of knowing the population parameters for infantile length, weight, and head circumference. That is, due to the frequency of such assessments being taken globally, and the sharing of this data, researchers and practitioners have a solid idea of what an average score is, and thus where one particular score ranks in relation to that average. In addition to these dimensions of physical growth, infants also display motor development.

Even newborns engage in motor movement, although their movements may lack some physical and cognitive properties apparent in older children. The most fundamental movement is in the form of basic reflexes. These reflexes, unlike more advanced motor movements, are not necessarily volitional. They are processes in sub-cortical and instinctual areas of the infantile brain, and do not rely upon cortical processing as do more advanced motor movements. Nevertheless, infants may respond motorically to certain stimuli in predictable ways.

For instance, a **sucking reflex** causes young infants to suck rather frequently and indiscriminately. It is not uncommon to see an infant picking up an object such as a block, bring it to their mouth, and instinctively suck on it. Infants also may show a **rooting reflex,** in that they turn toward touches on their cheeks. From on evolutionary perspective, these two reflexes may have an important purpose in that they promote feeding. Another basic reflex worth mentioning is a **grasping reflex**. Infants tend to wrap their fingers around objects (e.g., adult fingers) placed in their palm. The grasping reflex, similar to the sucking and rooting reflex, are automatic and instinctual movements. However, they are also basic motor movements reactive to environmental stimuli. Thus, they represent fundamental forms of motor activity. During the first two years of life, infants will move from these automatic non-volitional movements, to more advanced deliberate, volitional motor activity.

Numerous motor milestones characterize infancy. Similar to the developmental leaps that occur neurologically during infancy, there is also significant physical and motor advancement. However, unlike the covert neurological development, motor and physical development is directly observable. Although there is much variability in terms of when infants meet certain milestones, there are broad expectations for when some should occur. For instance, most parents become aware that infants tend to begin to walk around one year of age. While some may walk earlier, even as young as 9 months, some infants may continue to crawl well into their second year. Thus, while one year may be an average age of infants' first steps, there is variability. However, other motor milestones precede walking.

While infants are often held (and sleep) belly-up, some pediatricians and parents encourage "tummy-time." When laid on their stomachs, infants will begin to push themselves up, and at about 12 weeks may be capable of extending their arms so as to lift up their heads. Infants may be able to sit up, but require some support, such as an infant chair or pillow. In the coming weeks and months, infants can typically sit with little or no support without consistently falling over.

At about 4 or 5 months, infants may become more mobile, turning over on their own. Parents may no longer be able to put their baby on a surface and rely upon them remaining there. Rolling over and scooting may be an infant's first means of movement. At about 9 months, many infants begin to crawl, as they have advanced to being able to

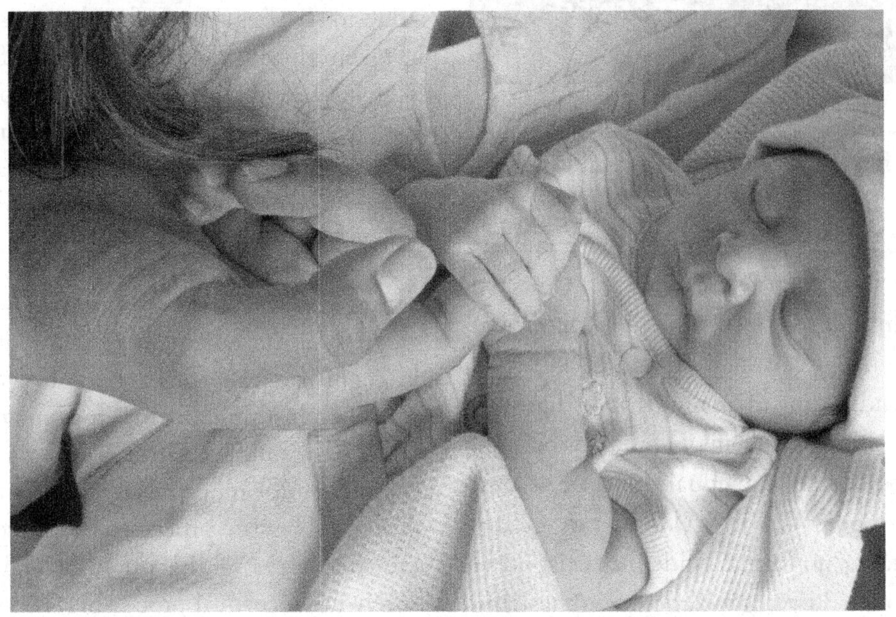

elevate their lower half as well, and propel themselves forward. Crawling may demonstrate volitional activity, as the infant crawls toward people and objects that are desirable or interesting. Interestingly, some infants may skip the crawling stage completely, and proceed directly from scooting to walking.

Walking fluidly and uniformly does not appear immediately. Rather, the infant tends to first support themselves standing with an object such as a chair or footstool. From that position, infants may take a few steps into the arms of a parent or to the safety of another nearby supportive object. During these initial steps, it is typical for an infant to fall frequently, often falling forward after just a few steps. Over time, though, the infant is capable of walking longer distances without misstep. Eventually, walking becomes relatively routine.

Language

A discussion of language in infancy may be neatly placed between discussions of motor and cognitive development, respectively. There are motor components to language: The vocal and facial movements are necessary to produce sounds that ultimately form words. However, there is a cognitive component to language as well, involving the use of memory, symbols, and images. Infants appear to be born with a natural inclination to communicate. Fundamental crying, fussing, and smiling may all be viewed as forms of communication. Thereafter, **cooing** may become apparent. Infant cooing broadly captures the noises they may make. Coos are not necessarily made to indicate a need for food, attention, or sleep, but are sounds nonetheless. At about 7 or 8 months, **babbling** may emerge. Babbling is distinct from cooing in that recognizable syllables are being uttered, but not in a sequence necessary for word formation. For instance, an infant may consistently babble "deeter." In this utterance, there are syllables (i.e., dee-, ter) that are useful in the English language in words such as "deer" or "meter." However, babbling is marked by a lack of proper expression of words. It is not uncommon for a parent to report his or her infant spoke at a remarkably early age, only to find they did not repeat the word consistently. What may have occurred is the infant was merely babbling and happened to place syllables in such an order to resemble a given word. Infantile cooing and babbling may serve another useful purpose -- allowing infants to hear themselves make noise. That is, hearing may be a critical form of motivation for producing early sounds. In one study, Fagan (2014) observed that infants with profound hearing loss had produced significantly less vocalizations that infants with normal hearing capabilities. However, when the infants with hearing loss received cochlear implants, there was no longer an apparent difference between groups. Thus, is was apparent infants wanted to hear themselves and explore their own sound production (Fagan, 2014).

The infant's true "first word" typically appears at about one year of age, although there is much variability in terms of when parents report the first word. When the first word does appear, it is indicative of a stage of **holographic speech**, in

which syllables are deliberately and—over time—consistently used to form words and communicate specific desires. To some degree, holographic speech may be recognized in words used solely between the infant and caretaker(s). For instance, an infant and mother may exchange the word "binkie" often, referring to a blanket or pacifier. Although the word *binkie* may have little or no long-term linguistic value, its deliberate and consistent production demonstrates language development. However, holographic speech is perhaps most exciting when words are used in a proper context. Of course, the classic example is an infant uttering "momma" or "dadda" for the first time, identifying their parents. Communication is further enhanced when infants, typically well into their second year, demonstrate **telegraphic speech**. This particular stage is marked by words being connected to one another to form more complete ideas or desires. For instance, an infant with telegraphic speech capabilities may be able to ask for specific objects such as a "blue toy" or "big ball." Even these two-word utterances are significantly more informative than if the infant merely was able to ask for a "toy" or "ball." The descriptions (i.e., blue, big) further allow the infant to specify what he or she wants. Together, infants typically move from crying to one or two (or more) word utterances aimed largely at communication. When holographic and telegraphic speech is apparent, it may seem as though the infant is "getting it." It is about two years of age that language really begins to develop quickly.

The word spurt, or **vocabulary spurt**, refers to a rapid increase in the words infants appear to repeat and grasp. Analogous to a growth spurt, significant development is seen in a relatively short amount of time. Research has shown that 18-month olds learn two to five new words per day. In addition, researchers have demonstrated that a limit may exist in terms of how many new words may be retained: In one experiment, a day after learning 6 new words, toddlers best remembered only the first 3 words they had been taught (Brady & Goodman, 2014). Such findings may cohere well with other researchers and practitioners whom emphasize the importance of the quality of language development over quantity. As one researcher stated ""...it's not about shoving words in. It's about having fluid conversations around shared rituals and objects...that is the stuff from which language is made." (Quenqua, 2014). As infants approach the end of their second year, they may have 300 words or more in their lexicon. They appear to absorb words like sponges, and parents and caregivers may report needing to "watch their language" at this stage. Moreover, children learn words differently as they age, perhaps becoming more adept at using linguistic context and social cues to determine the meaning of new words (Brady & Goodman, 2014). Language development occurs concurrently with general cognitive development. Therefore, a basic understanding of cognitive development is helpful.

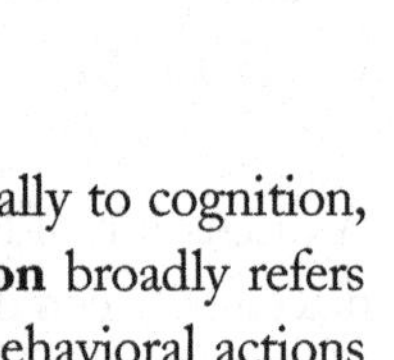

Cognitive Development: Piaget

Being the first unit related specifically to cognition, a definition is warranted. **Cognition** broadly refers to mental activity. All observable behavioral actions and reactions correspond to mental action(s). That is, humans rely upon mental processes and mechanisms to interpret and act upon stimuli and situations they may encounter. These cognitive processes may include relevant processes such as attention, concentration, decision-making, and memory, to name a few.

Originally, in 1762, Jean-Jacque Rousseau called a newborn baby a "perfect idiot." More than a century later, William James portrayed an infant's mental life as being "one great blooming, buzzing confusion" (Bloom, 2010). There are perhaps some developmentalists who still hold such a view; that infants are largely "ignorant." However, there is widespread and compelling research in recent decades suggesting the opposite; infants are quite cognitively active, and this infantile cognition may be critically important for subsequent cognition in childhood, adolescence, and adulthood. Consider some of the following theories and studies.

Bill Anderson/Photo Researchers, Inc.

Jean Piaget proposed a theory of cognitive development that may help clarify to some degree how cognition changes over time. More specifically, Piaget's stage theory suggests there are four general stages that individuals must pass through to attain mature thinking capabilities, beginning in infancy. The first stage is the **sensorimotor stage**. This stage encompasses infancy, and Piagetian theory suggests infants are literally stumbling into experiences. By name, the stage implies the infant moves around and interacts with people and objects. Together, they must sense their environment, and interact motorically with the objects within it. However, this movement and sensation alone are not the critical part to cognitive development. Rather, there is supposed cognitive activity that occurs concurrently with the physical activity. Most pertinent to infancy, schema (plural for scheme) develops.

Schema are organized structures that make sense of experience. The "experience" in this case is motor movement. The "structures" are akin to thinking patterns related to the experience. Theoretically, schemas develop naturally, as infants are naturally inclined to play with objects, which in turn prompt schema development. Indeed, it is not uncommon to observe infants engaging in the same action over and over again. For instance, an infant may grasp an object and release it; the object falling to the floor. The infant may engage in this same general sequence of activity with the same (or different) object, consistently producing the same result. Along with these behaviors, a "dropping" schema may develop. The infant now has the benefit of an "organized rule" related to how a certain action produces a predictable result. Moreover, some older infants request the same movie again and again. When it finishes, they want to watch it again. It appears as though infants are attracted to events they are able to predict in some way.

Piaget believed schema were clearly being created and used during what he called **circular reactions**, which are repetitive action-oriented movements, that the infant or child repeats again and again. Many can appreciate that infants and young children often do the same thing over and over and over again, seemingly with continued fervor and interest. The most fundamental form of circular reactions is **primary circular reactions**, perhaps evident in the first half year of life. Very little of the "outside world" appears to exist at this stage of life, and subsequently, primary circular reactions are those in relation to one's own body. An infant

may stare as they rotate their wrist for an extended period of time, or they may continually grab their feet. Thereafter, **secondary circular reactions** are those actions and reactions occurring in the outside world with tangible objects, such as toys or other people. In a sense, infants are capturing cause and effect relations; they press a button, and a light goes on; they kick a ball and it rolls; they squeeze a toy and it squeaks. **Tertiary circular reactions** are the final type of reaction, and are comprised of organized and flexible schemas. An infant or young child may readily adapt or experiment with new environments and new objects, always engaging in new actions, observing the consequences, and repeating. Infants in this stage are sometimes referred to as "little scientists." Throughout these reactions, it is apparent that infants and young children appear to get a kick out of being able to predict "what comes next." It is quite common that infants and young children can watch the same movie over and over again; perhaps attracted to scenes where they know what's coming next.

Over time, schematic development occurs and is guided by two main principles: **assimilation** and **accommodation**. According to Piaget, assimilation is apparent when existing schema work well to explain the world and the objects, events, and experiences therein. On the other hand, accommodation - which more genuinely fuels schematic and cognitive development - is apparent with existing schema need to be modified in order to match up with new events, experiences, or outcomes. Both of these processes may be demonstrated in a simple example consisting of a "dumping" schema. Consider an infant that has mastered the art of dumping items out of containers. In the playroom, they pick up boxes and dump out the toys; in the sandbox they pick up a bucket and pour out the sand; in the bath they pick up a cup and pour out the water; at the dinner table they pour milk onto the floor. In all instances, the actions and ideas inherent in a general dumping scheme work perfectly, and assimilation is evident. However, consider what may happen when the same infant picks up an open jar of peanut butter, lifts it up and turns it over to spill out the contents. At first dismayed, the infant cannot dump the contents. It is possible the infant needs to accommodate the dumping schema to account for different (in this case sticky) contents. In these cases, accommodation requires that existing schema become more elaborate, consisting of more complex rules and contingencies.

Habituation and Object Permanence

Researchers have been creative in the efforts to examine infantile cognition. Some hallmark studies in developmental psychology have been undertaken to investigate infant cognition. One of the limitations of working with infants is they cannot be asked to self-report on thought processes, and they cannot neatly and observably work out discrete problems as children and adults can, for the researcher to infer cognitive skills. In addition, human infants are quite limited motorically; they cannot press levers or find their way through mazes as even some non-human infants may do. Therefore, researchers have been drawn to one skill that infants do appear to maintain command over: their eye movement. The infant eye movement (e.g., direction, intensity, duration) may reflect some fundamental cognitive processes. For instance, eye gaze may intensify when something is new, interesting, or unexpected. Accordingly, in the following section, habituation, object permanence, and depth perception will be discussed.

One way in which infantile cognitive activity may be recognized is in **habituation**, which is the gradual decrease in the strength of a response after repeated exposure to a particular stimulus. The reverse relation, or **dishabituation**, is an increase in the strength of a response after a change in stimuli. The typical infantile responses are gazing and sucking. In other words, according to the habituation paradigm, infants may gaze or stare at a new or novel object or toy rather intently. However, over time, they would lose interest, and this would be

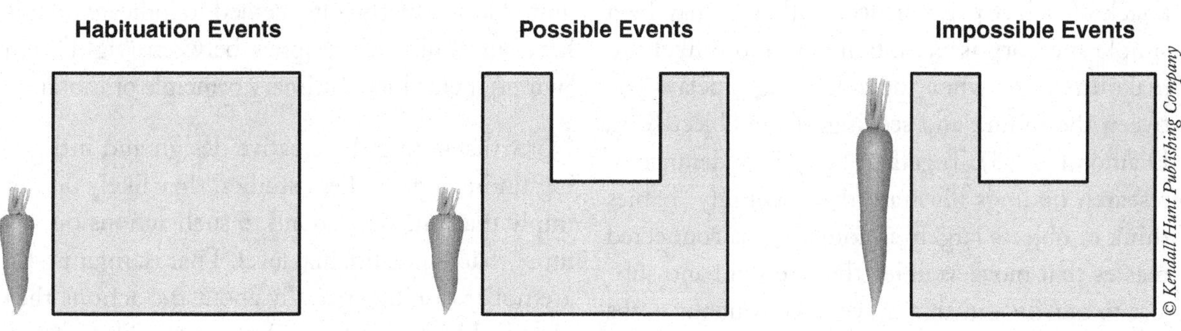

FIGURE 5.2 *Carrot 'impossible event' image*

observable in a gazing response that lessens until it is perhaps nonexistent. The infant has "habituated" to the object. However, if a new object is brought to the attention of the infant, the gaze response returns, demonstrating a dishabituation response. To illustrate, when caregivers are going on a plane trip for the first time with infants, a common piece of advice may be to bring a couple of new toys along, with the hope the infant dishabituates, and immerses him or herself with the toy. The habituation paradigm has been employed in research settings to investigate whether infants see something new (which may be an indication of memory) or see something they did not expect (which may be an indication of expectations).

A classic study demonstrated that infants have expectations (Baillargeon, 1987). In this study, often referred to as the "carrot study" or the "impossible event study," infants were shown several images (see Figure 5.2). In the first "habituation" phases of the study, infants were shown short and tall carrots pass behind a wall with an open window. Expectedly, they could not see the short carrot as it passed behind the wall. However, they could view the tall carrot as it passed behind the wall, as it was tall enough to eclipse the window opening. The infants were shown these events over and over until they were habituated to it (i.e., they were no longer interested). The next phase of the study something unexpected occurred. The infants were once again shown the same events, however, this time as the tall carrot passed behind the wall; it did not become visible through the window. For this particular event, the infants dishabituated, and their gaze response returned. These findings may infer infants do in fact maintain certain expectations about the environment, and are thereby cognitively active in this way.

The aforementioned study may also offer evidence of **object permanence**, which is a basic understanding that objects continue to exist even when unseen, unheard, or unfelt. In other words, objects do not cease to exist when they are taken away. Accordingly, infant gazing is thought to indicate when an infant is "searching" for something they expect to be there. In the carrot study, the infants may understand the tall carrot still exists and therefore should have appeared in the window opening. The same responses were evident in other studies (e.g., Baillargeon & Devos, 1991; Kotovksy & Baillargeon, 1994).

Interestingly, Piaget originally proposed infants did not clearly maintain object permanence. For instance, he proposed they were susceptible to something termed the **A-not-B error**. This error may be demonstrated simply by taking an object and hiding it, first in location A (e.g., behind a pillow) and second in location B (e.g., under a blanket). If the object is initially hidden in location A, the infants may correctly find it there. However, when hidden at location B, even when the infant is able to see it being hidden, they continue to search at location A first. Piaget thought this may demonstrate a general inability to appreciate the permanence of the object. Generally, this idea has not received much support, and infants may be more capable than Piaget gave them credit for. The A-not-B error may not be due to a lack of object permanence. Rather, it may be a simple memory issue; infants are more likely to make the error when there are longer delays between the hiding and seeking of the object (e.g., Diamond, 1985). Together, the preponderance of research findings illustrate the possibility "babies think of objects largely as adults do, as connected masses that move as units, that are solid and subject to gravity and that move in continuous paths over time" (Bloom, 2010, p. 3).

Some contemporary work has offered some more compelling results. Researchers including Karen Wynn, Kylie Hamlin, and Paul Bloom, at the Infant Cognition center at Yale University, have conducted an intriguing series of studies aimed at investigating infantile morality. To that end, the researchers were initially interested in babies' reactions to two main forms of observed actions: helping and hindering. In the first set of experiments, 9- and 12-month-old infants were shown a video of a red ball going up a hill. At various time points, a yellow square got behind the red ball and "helped" it up the hill; at other times, a green triangle got in front of the red ball, pushing it down, and "hindering" its progress. Thereafter, researchers showed videos of the red ball approaching the yellow square (i.e., the helper) or a video of the red ball approaching the green triangle (i.e., the hinderer). The infants gazed much longer when the ball approached the triangle. This may have been an indication of surprise; the infants expected the ball to approach the helper, not the hinderer (Bloom, 2010).

A follow-up study was quite similar, but was performed with actual three-dimensional objects (i.e., balls, squares, triangles). The same helping and hindering scenarios as before were carried out. Thereafter, instead of looking at babies' gazes, the researchers placed the helping and hindering objects on a tray and allowed the infants to select one. Almost all of the babies selected the helper (i.e., yellow square). A separate series of studies—which showed one-act morality "plays" to infants—seemed to corroborate these findings, with infants overwhelmingly preferring the helper, or the "good guy." These experiments seemed to indicate infants have an ability to decipher between "right" and "wrong" behaviors, a primary principle of morality.

Notwithstanding the creative design and intriguing findings from these studies, they likely do not imply that infants respond to such actions on any more than an instinctual level. That is, infants still are not reasoning critically about the actions they observed in these (or similar) events. The infants' preferences may be laden with as much (or more) emotion as it is cognition. However, these seemingly innate preferences will be subject to developmental and cultural interventions over time, giving higher order moral capabilities to the individual. Some theories that may clarify higher order moral reasoning will be discussed in a later unit.

Memory

Memory may be understood as the storage of images and ideas for later retrieval. Memory may be broken down into **working memory**, a form of short-term memory used for day-to-day tasks, and **long-term memory**, which may be stored for many years or decades, consistently available for retrieval. Working memory permits an individual to remember where their room is located upon reentry into a hotel. This type of memory does not typically remain beyond the time period that it is required. Long-term memories are evident when an individual is relaying a story from years prior. Infants don't necessarily maintain the same capacity to store memory that children, adolescents, and adults do. Some interesting new research has demonstrated that infants as young as 5 months old are more likely to remember an event from the previous day if there was some type of positive affect associated with it, including smiling and laughing (Flom, Janis, Garcia, & Kirwan, 2014).

As mentioned in earlier, habituation and object permanence may certainly suggest infants are capable of remembering items. However, this form of memory may be akin to working memory, enabling infants to store information for relatively short periods of time. The more enduring aspect of memory (i.e., long-term memory) appears to be absent in infants. More specifically, there appears to be a general inability to remember specific events prior to about three years of age. This phenomenon has been termed **infantile amnesia**. It is more typical for individuals to report their very first memories at three and a half years, or sometime thereafter. There are several competing hypotheses as to why infantile amnesia exists. However, two notions in particular may be helpful.

First, infantile amnesia may be apparent due to neurological immaturity, while infancy is a period of significant neurological growth, there is still relative underdevelopment when compared to children or adolescents. The frontal lobe in particular is immature, and perhaps impairs the infant from efficiently processing and storing information related to events. After two years, myelination and synaptogenesis slow down somewhat, indicating the infant may be approaching a more advanced neurological state. Second, infantile amnesia may occur due to unfamiliarity with a native language. The infant has yet to learn language, and many memories may be stored in forms only interpretable after linguistic capabilities have developed. At about 3 years, telegraphic speech is evident, and accompanied by the vocabulary spurt. Thus, according to this hypothesis, it is intuitive memories that would begin to appear shortly thereafter.

Concurrent Developmental Processes

In infancy, some motor milestones may promote growth in other areas as well. For instance, some researchers have placed considerable importance on the motor milestone of crawling in terms of what other forms of development it may promote (Bertenthal, Campos, Kermonian, 2009). Crawling may represent the first significant advancement in "self-produced locomotion." In other words, the infant is now capable of voluntary and independent movement, which may have implications for overall development. One of the underlying sources of evidence for the importance of crawling is that a variety of other cognitive, social, and emotional capabilities appear to emerge concurrently with this motor milestone. For instance, the emotion of "fear" may be precipitated by the crawling activity.

A classic study in the field of developmental psychology is the visual cliff study. This study requires a thick pane of glass be suspended about four feet above the floor. Beneath the glass, there are two sections: one shallow end that is directly beneath the glass and one deep end that is on the floor. There is a checkerboard pattern over the entire surface beneath the glass. The infants are placed on the shallow end of the glass, which to them appears merely as they are on the surface of a sturdy checkerboard table (see image below). Thereafter, the infants are encouraged by a caretaker to come to the deep end. As they approach the deep end, an apparent drop off occurs. Truthfully, they are protected from the drop off by the thick glass surface. However, as they approach, their avoidance and wariness (or lack thereof) to enter the deep end indicates their ability to perceive depth or possibly experience fear. Interestingly, while infants that just learned to crawl appear to cross into the deep end rather indiscriminately, infants

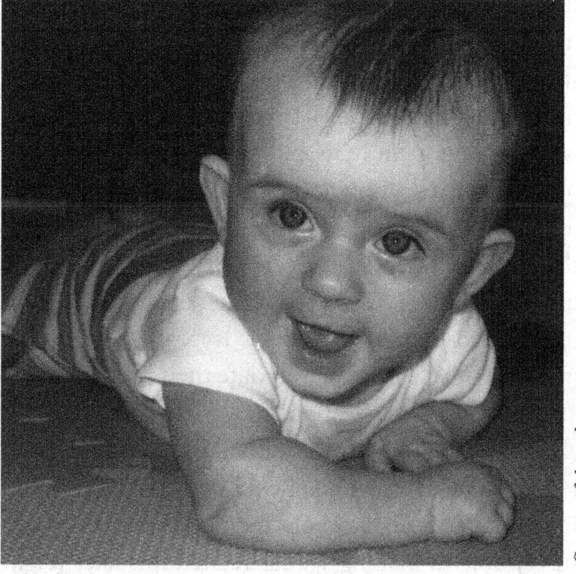

Courtesy of the author

who had been crawling for about six weeks demonstrated consistent avoidance of the deep end. Thus, the experience of crawling may give rise to new perceptual and emotional ranges.

In addition, spatial intelligence may be impacted by crawling, as evidenced by the A-not-B error covered earlier in the chapter. Infants are less susceptible to making the A-not-B error as they enter their ninth month. That is, infants about 9 months old are less likely to look for an object in an incorrect location (where it was hidden before) after being shown it is hidden in a new location. Researchers hypothesize that while newborns and younger infants are immobile (i.e., before they can crawl), they may understand their environment by how objects are placed in relation to their own fixed position. However, when infants achieve mobility by crawling, they are no longer fixed in one position, and must now rely upon other ways of understanding and organizing their environment. More specifically, infants may use landmarks (i.e., objects in their environment) to understand their environment. If an infant is moving, they must continually update their placement in an environment in relation to a variety of landmarks (Bertenthal, Campos, Kermonian, 2009). The need for a continual updating of environmental cues ultimately arose from crawling, and may make them less susceptible to making spatial-related mistakes (e.g., A-not-B error). Related research has suggested that regularly playing with puzzles and blocks may also contribute to spatial skill development. Such activities require the deliberate manipulation of objects in space (Jirout & Newcombe, 2014).

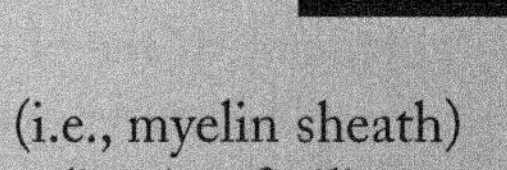

Key Terms

- **Myelination** – a process that strengthens the protective covering (i.e., myelin sheath) surrounding the axon of the neuron. Along with synaptogenesis, myelination facilitates neurological maturation.
- **Percentile Score (or Rank)** – indicates the percentage of scores that fall at or below an infant's personal measurement(s). In infancy, these are often given in terms of length, weight, and head circumference.
- **Sucking Reflex** – an automatic and instinctual movement in which infants suck rather frequently and indiscriminately on objects that touch their lips
- **Rooting Reflex** – another instinctual movement in which infants turn toward touches on their cheeks
- **Grasping Reflex** – infants tend to wrap their fingers around objects placed in their palm
- **Cooing** – after crying, cooing is the first observable stage of communication (language); infant cooing broadly captures the noises they may make
- **Babbling** – this type of infantile communication is distinct from cooing in that recognizable syllables are being uttered, but not in a sequence necessary for word formation
- **Holographic Speech** – syllables are deliberately and consistently used to form words and communicate specific desires
- **Telegraphic Speech** – this particular stage is marked by words being connected to one another to form more complete ideas or desires
- **Vocabulary Spurt** – typically occurring toward the latter portion of infancy, this refers to a rapid increase in the words infants appear to repeat and apparently grasp
- **Cognition** – this term broadly refers to mental activity (e.g., attention, concentration, decision-making, and memory)
- **Sensorimotor Stage** – this is a Piagetian term referring to the first stage of cognitive development, encompassing infancy. During this time, infants are literally stumbling into experiences; the infant moves around and interacts with people and objects. In doing so, cognitive activity occurs concurrently with the physical activity.
- **Schema** – these "organized rules" are mental structures that make sense of experience. The "experience" in this case is motor movement. The "structures" are akin to thinking patterns related to the experience.
- **Circular Reactions** – behaviors engaged in consistently to produce a particular result. These circular reactions facilitate schema formation.
  - **Primary Circular Reactions** – evident in the first half year of life; primary circular reactions are those in relation to one's own body
  - **Secondary Circular Reactions** – actions and reactions occurring in the outside world with tangible objects, such as toys or other people
  - **Tertiary Circular Reactions** – comprised of organized and flexible schemas
- **Accommodation** – existing schema are modified to match up better with new events or experiences.
- **Assimilation** – existing schema work well to explain the world, including events, objects and experiences.
- **Habituation** – the gradual decrease in the strength of a response after repeated exposure to a particular stimulus
- **Dishabituation** – an increase in the strength of a response after a change in stimuli
- **Object Permanence** – a basic understanding that objects continue to exist even when unseen, unheard, or unfelt
- **A-not-B error** – this error may be demonstrated simply by taking an object and hiding it, first in location A (e.g., behind a pillow) and second in location B (e.g., under a

blanket). If the object is initially hidden in location A, the infants may correctly find it there. However, when hidden at location B, even when the infant is able to see it being hidden, they continue to search at location A first.

- **Memory** – the storage of images and ideas for later retrieval
- **Working Memory** – this type of memory is more short-term in nature, and necessary for day-to-day tasks. This type of memory does not typically remain beyond the time period that it is required.
- **Long-Term Memory** – these types of memory may be stored for many years or decades, consistently available for retrieval
- **Infantile Amnesia** – refers to a general inability to remember specific events prior to about three years of age, perhaps due to neurological immaturity or a lack of linguistic sophistication

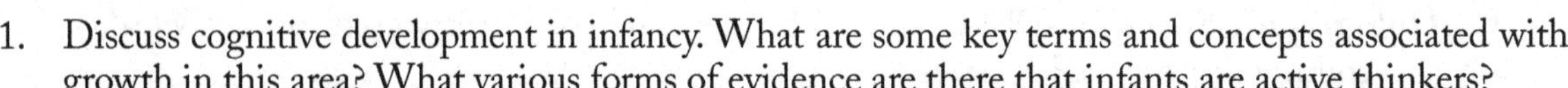

Critical Thinking Questions

1. Discuss cognitive development in infancy. What are some key terms and concepts associated with growth in this area? What various forms of evidence are there that infants are active thinkers?
2. What is your earliest memory? Do you think you have memory of events that occurred in infancy? What are some explanations for why individuals are generally unable to recall events (i.e., long-term memories) that occur during infancy?

References

Baillargeon, R. & Graber, M. (1987). Where's the rabbit? 5.5-month-old infants' representation of the height of a hidden object. *Cognitive Development, 2,* 375-392.

Baillargeon, R. & Devos, J. (1991). Object permanence in young infants: Further evidence. *Child Development, 62,* 1227-1246.

Belsky, J. (2010). *Experiencing the lifespan.* New York: Worth.

Bertenthal, B. I., Campos, J. J., & Kermonian, R. (2009). An epigenetic perspective on the development of self-produced locomotion and its consequences. In L. Liben (Ed.), *Current directions in developmental psychology* (pp. 45-53). Boston, MA: Pearson.

Bloom, P. (2010, May 5). The moral life of babies. *The New York Times.* Retrieved from http://nytimes.com/2010/05/09/magazine/09babies-t.html

Brady, K.W., & Goodman, J.C. (2014). The type, but not the amount of information available influences toddlers fast mapping and retention of new words. *American Journal of Speech-Language Pathology, 23.* doi: 10.1044/2013_AJSLP-10-0013.

Diamond, A. (1985). Development of the ability to use recall to guide action, as indicated by infants' performance on AB. *Child Development, 56,* 868-883.

Fagan, M.K. (2014). Frequency of vocalization before and after cochlear implantation: Dynamic effect of auditory feedback on infant behavior. Journal of Experimental Child Psychology, 126. doi: 10.1016/j.jecp.2014.05.005.

Flom, R., Janis, R.B., Garcia, D.J., & Kirwan, C.B. (2014). The effects of exposure to dynamic expression of affect on 5-month-olds memory. Infant Behavior and Development, 37. doi: 10.1016/j.infbeh.2014.09.006

Jirout, J.J., & Newcombe, N.S. (2014). Building blocks for developing spatial skills: Evidence from a large representative U.S. sample. Psychological Science. doi: 10.1177/0956797614563338 Kotovksy, L. & Baillargeon, R. (1994). Calibration based reasoning about collision events in 11-month-old infants. *Cognition, 51,* 107-129.

Piaget, J. (1950). *The psychology of intelligence.* Oxford, England: Harcourt.

Quenqua, D. (October 16, 2014). Quality of words, not quantity, is crucial for language skills. New York Times. Retrieved from: http://www.nytimes.com/2014/10/17/us/quality-of-words-not-quantity.

Wen, X., Kong, K.L., Eiden, R.D., Sharma, N.N., & Xie, C. (2014). Sociodemographic differences and infant dietary patterns. *Pediatrics,* DOI: 10.1542/peds.2014-2015.

CHAPTER 6

Socioemotional Development in Infancy

Temperament

The social and emotional life of infants is comparatively simple when in relation to children, adolescents, and adults. However, the social and emotional life of infants is dynamic, with its own unique brand of complexities. In the following unit, relevant social and emotional issues observed in infancy will be covered, including temperament, attachment, and daycare.

Although a newborn may be somewhat limited to fussing and crying when they are upset, or otherwise sleeping, over time the infant begins to interact with caretakers in meaningful and perhaps predictable ways. Infants may quickly begin to show features of what appears to be a "personality." By definition, personality consists of enduring qualities, and a true personality may take years to develop and mature. Over time, a constellation of traits and behavioral tendencies—unique to an individual—are demonstrated. During infancy, however, **temperament** may emerge. Temperament may be viewed as behavioral and reactionary aspects of oneself that are thought to be innate. The "innate" quality of temperament makes it a relevant construct to examine in infancy.

The modern exploration of temperament began with the *New York Longitudinal Study*, which took place over many years in the 1950s and '60s (Thomas, Chess, and Birch, 1968). The primary aim of this study was to investigate whether certain characteristics present at birth impacted infant and child development in significant ways. The characteristics present at birth were largely observable via infantile activity. For instance, persistence was viewed when an infant would continue a behavior without interruption. Similarly, distractibility was observed according to how

easily an infant was distracted by light, noise, or other stimuli. Another characteristic was initial reaction, which was assessed according to how the infant reacted to new or novel objects, people, and situations. More specifically, did they seek out the new item(s) or withdraw from them? A regularity characteristic was indicated by the extent to which certain diurnal patterns (e.g., sleeping, eating, and elimination) varied. While some infants were very predictable with feeding and sleeping, others were not. The researcher isolated nine such characteristics, and noted how they may impact relationships and interactions with others.

While the researchers acknowledged that all infants show each characteristic at one time or another, it appeared as though most infants fell into one of three categories, each carried a cluster of the aforementioned innate characteristics. These clusters are currently viewed as types of temperament. Generally, there are three types of temperament: Easy, slow-to-warm-up, and difficult.

The term **"easy"** in relation to temperament is relative. Many would argue there is no such thing as a truly easy infant or easy parenting; however, some infants may maintain qualities that may make them *easier* to manage. For instance, infants with an easy temperament are flexible above all. They adapt to new objects and situations relatively easily and calmly, and demonstrate a positive mood (as indicated by smiling and babbling) often. These infants have very regular sleeping, eating, and bowel movement cycles, perhaps taking some guesswork out of what they may need at one particular time. For parents and caretakers of easy children, it may be easier to act spontaneously. For instance, travel with the infant will go relatively smoothly as they are typically open to new places and situations. Caretakers may be able to leave infants of easy temperament in the care of a babysitter, as they tend to respond positively to new people. Together, this temperamental style is quite attractive for caretakers.

Conversely, a **difficult** temperament may almost be viewed in stark contrast to the easy variety. An infant with a difficult temperament does not react well to novel situations or new people, resorting first to fussing, crying, or tantrums. To illustrate, when a difficult infant is brought to a daycare for the first time, they will likely protest actively and loudly immediately, and take a longer time to adjust to the new situation than other infants may. Socialization patterns are integral to the lives of difficult children, and they protest when they sense disruptions. Moreover, these infants tend to have irregular schedules with sleeping, feeding, and bowel movements. These infants would not react as well to travel or babysitters. Together, caretakers may feel they have less flexibility and spontaneity.

Somewhere between easy and difficult children lies the **slow-to-warm-up** (or **wary**) infants. As the term implies, these infants generally may respond negatively (e.g., fussing, crying) to new situations, but they tend to accept them more quickly than their difficult counterparts. However, when pushed to become immediately involved in something new, these infants and children would exhibit withdrawal or clingy behavior. For instance, if a caretaker was dropping off their child for the first day at daycare, and had to leave shortly thereafter, the child may cling tightly to the parent and choose to not socialize with others for the time-being. Accordingly, these children are sometimes described as "shy" although the shy behavior(s) do disappear after repeated exposure to a particular stimulus or environment. In addition, their schedules are relatively consistent.

Of course, not all infants are categorically easy, difficult, or slow-to-warm-up. As the researchers originally noted, all infants in their sample displayed all of the characteristics to some extent (Thomas, Chess, & Birch, 1968). Together, as temperament appears to impact the nature of interactions the infant has with objects and people in the environment, temperament is broadly considered a social factor in infancy. However, one may also consider the nature of the relationship the infant forms with a caretaker.

Ethological Evidence of Bonding and Attachment

Contemporary theories and concepts related to infantile needs and social relationships are grounded in ethological studies. **Ethology** is the study of behavior in animals (including humans) in natural settings. The following paragraphs will include descriptions of some classic ethological research studies focused on the factors associated with the relationships that form between an infant (generally of any species) and a caretaker. In the coming paragraphs, it may be useful to note support related to what an infant needs, and the connections that may form between them and those that provide for those needs.

Konrad Lorenz (1935) was one such ethological scientist. He studied goslings (i.e., baby geese) and their natural inclination to follow certain stimuli in their environments (see image below). More specifically, Lorenz reported that during certain stages in infancy, babies tend to follow and even prefer a certain stimulus. The process of "following and preferring" may be known as **imprinting**. Lorenz even noted that if the biological mother was not present, the goslings would imprint on other moving stimuli, even Lorenz himself. It appeared as though the goslings were attracted to characteristics their biological mother would have. Some of the visual images of Lorenz depict the researcher in "goose-like" behaviors such as walking, swimming, and quacking. Indeed, to the casual observer, it would not appear a well-known ethological scientist was engaged in research that would make major contributions to developmental psychology. To the contrary, it would have appeared to be rather eccentric behavior.

Nonetheless, two of the key contributions from Lorenz's work include the notion that *infants may be inclined to seek out stimuli in their immediate environment*, and also that there *appear to be specific developmental periods where imprinting needs to occur*. This latter notion is akin to a **critical period**, which refers to a chronological window of time that is ideal for acquiring a new behavior or establishing a connection. The "critical" nature of this period is that if it is missed, it cannot necessarily be revisited at a later time point.

In addition to Lorenz's work with goslings, Harlow (1958) initially was interested in the origins of love, thinking the capacity to feel this emotion originated in infancy, and from there moved on to study emotional attachments in rhesus monkeys. Rhesus monkeys were chosen because they tend to mature more quickly than human infants and they appeared to demonstrate a range of emotions. Together, the developmental processes of this species could be observed more efficiently. Specifically, Harlow was interested in the emotion of love, and hypothesized that love originally sprung from a feeding bond between the infant and the mother (or caretaker) and thereafter may be applied to other individuals. To test this hypothesis, Harlow staged an experimental design of sorts. Given a sample of infant rhesus monkeys and their biological mothers, some infant-mother pairs were separated by placing the infant in a separate environment. This new environment contained two "artificial mothers." One artificial mother was made from wire while the other was made from cloth. Moreover, the wire model was fitted with a bottle containing food. Harlow and colleagues (1966) observed the infant monkeys strongly favored the cloth model, preferring to cling to it, particularly when frightened (see image below). The infants would move to the wire model to feed, but return to the cloth model thereafter. Thus, even with a primary necessity such as food available elsewhere, the infants sought the warmth and comfort of the cloth model. When the bottle was placed on the cloth model, the infants did not stray from the cloth model.

In sum, although the aforementioned ethological studies did not involve human emotional bonds, they have offered useful evidence of the emotional needs and processes relevant for infancy. A discussion of such needs and processes in human infants is warranted. More specifically, the following sections will include a discussion of the attachment bond.

Attachment

From birth, a bonding process begins to form between a human infant and the primary caretaker(s). Such a bond may be viewed as an emotional connection that is created between the infant and an immediate and nurturing adult. This bond is more typically called the **attachment bond**, and is thought to be a strong connection, relatively robust to other factors that may otherwise threaten relationships. In fact, infants may maintain several characteristics or behaviors that promote attachment. For instance, over time infants begin to smile, coo, and babble, which adults may find endearing. Moreover, infants may show preference for humans over other stimuli, and imitate gestures. Lastly, infants maintain infantile features and body composition that many adults find "cute," thereby increasing the likelihood they will want to bond with the infant.

John Bowlby's (1980) seminal work outlined three main phases the attachment process follows. Through these phases, Bowlby describes how infants become increasingly more selective and attuned to their primary caretaker(s), or attachment figure(s). A simple and contemporary view of the attachment process may include phases of pre-attachment, attachment-in-the-making, and clear-cut attachment.

In the **pre-attachment** phase, which may be recognized from birth to about 3 months, infants are relatively indiscriminant when it comes to adults. At this time, they are not necessarily showing preference, and may more easily be held and cared for by numerous adults without protest. Over time, and as the infant enters an **attachment-in-the-making** phase, they may become more selective and begin to show preference for particular caretaker(s). Not surprisingly, when preferences begin to emerge, so do protests when the infant is separated from their primary attachment figures. During this middle phase, these preferential and protest behaviors are not necessarily consistent, though. Lastly, a **clear-cut attachment** is defined by an undeniable preference for one or more attachment figures. Not only is the preference clearly indicated, but the reaction to separation events is more predictable. For instance, an infant who has established an attachment will more regularly fuss and protest when they sense they are being separated. This may be due to **separation anxiety**. Together, the attachment bond emerges over time.

The attachment bonds that exist between an infant and a caretaker are not all the same. There are some consistent and qualitative differences in terms of these bonds. There are numerous forms of attachment bonds. At the broadest level, attachments may be viewed as secure or insecure. Furthermore,

there is more than one form of an insecure bond; namely, insecure resistant and insecure avoidant. Before considering the subtle differences that exist between these attachment types, it is useful to consider the research paradigms that originally were employed to investigate them.

Strange Situation Paradigm

The **strange situation paradigm** is a research method—originally created by Mary Ainsworth (1973)—that intends to manipulate and capture the reactions and behaviors that occur when an infant is separated from (and reunited with) their attachment figure. First, the caretaker and infant enter a laboratory room. The room itself does not appear to be a laboratory per se, but rather may have some chairs, a rug, and some toys. The caretaker and infant are initially alone, and the infant is free to explore the room and its contents as they please. After some time, a stranger enters the room, and immediately converses with the parent. Thereafter, the parent leaves the room inconspicuously. This represents a "separation episode" and researchers observe the infant's reaction to noticing the caretaker has left coupled with a stranger being in their presence. After some time, there is a "reunion episode" in which the caretaker returns and greets the infant. Together, the infant's behavior, particularly upon the reunion episode, was used to categorize the infant into one of the three aforementioned attachment types.

First, **securely attached** infants would explore freely while their caretaker was there, and also get noticeably upset when they realized they had been separated. Upon reunion, the securely attached infants greet and seek contact with their caretaker, and while in the presence of the caretaker, interacted with the stranger positively. It may be tempting to view secure attachment as being void of any negative emotions, such as those observed when the infant noticed they had been separated from their caretaker. However, consider another example to clarify this. Suppose you are taking a genuine friend to the airport so they can catch a flight for a trip they are taking. If you have a genuine and healthy affection for this person, you

are understandably upset to see them leave, but likely trust they will be back, at which time you will resume your relationship. Thus, healthy and secure attachments may in fact predict some degree of negative emotions upon separation.

Second, some infants demonstrated insecure attachment. For instance, **insecure resistant** infants showed a general reluctance to explore the new environment, even when in the presence of only their caretaker. When the stranger does enter the room, the infant is wary and avoids interaction. Rather, these infants prefer to stay close to the caretaker, and may be described as "clingy." These infants were extremely upset when they noticed the caretaker had left. The negative emotions displayed by insecure resistant infants, when compared to secure infants, was greater in intensity and duration. Often, they continued to be upset even upon reunion with the caretaker and surprisingly do not seek contact with them. Together, this attachment style may be marked by anxious and clingy behaviors, with less apparent emotional regulation. While it is natural for caretakers to desire for their infants and children to show them affection to some degree, the clinginess described above may be problematic in some situations where the infant or child and caretaker are separating (e.g., daycare, school, babysitter, etc.).

Lastly, **insecure avoidant** infants display behavioral and emotional patterns that are unique. The insecure avoidant infant shows little or no interest in exploring the new environment or interacting with the stranger in any way. In addition, they appear to avoid contact with the caretaker when they return. Together, they appear to "avoid" contact and exploration, and lack the emotional and behavioral reaction to separation and reunion that are present in other attachment styles.

Thus far, temperament and attachment style have been discussed in relation to how they may be viewed in infants and children. It should be noted that while characteristics of certain temperament and attachment styles appear similar, they are two different constructs. Temperament is thought to be an innate level of activity and reactivity, while attachment style is an emotional bond between the infant and caretaker(s) and observed via separation and reunion behaviors. While an infant may appear to have an easy temperament overall, over time an insecure attachment may form. Conversely, an infant with a seemingly difficult temperament may establish a secure attachment over time. These possibilities raise an interesting question: What variables facilitate attachment development?

Attachment Development

Attachment does not have the same innate quality that temperament does. However, temperament and caretaker responsiveness are thought to interact to facilitate attachment development. Thinking back to what characterizes the different temperament styles, it may be intuitive that easy children may be easier for parents and caretakers to "read." If an easy infant begins to fuss, a caretaker may rely upon the regular schedule the infant maintains to inform them of what the infant needs (i.e., sleep, food, etc.). In addition, an easy infant is more flexible in many environmental and social situations. Thus, an infant in this particular case may have his or her needs more easily met. Conversely, one may consider a difficult infant, who may be very particular about his or her surroundings, and caretakers may not be able to satisfy their needs as quickly. The infant may also maintain a more irregular schedule, giving the parents more guesswork in terms of what they need.

From these simple illustrations, it appears as though it may be simpler to meet the needs of easy infants. On the other hand, it may be increasingly challenging to appease a difficult infant consistently, but not impossible. Thus, the resources and responsiveness of the caretaker(s) become an important variable. That is, for the most part, are the caretakers capable of meeting the infant's needs? Loving and diligent parents and caretakers will strive to meet the needs of their infants, even those with a difficult temperament. However, in some cases infant needs may not be met regularly. In some cases of difficult temperaments, the caretakers may find the infant too demanding. In other cases, even with an otherwise easy infant, caretakers may be unresponsive or neglectful. Regardless of the scenario, an important question to ask is: Are the infant's needs being met? If the answer is "yes," there may be a higher likelihood of a secure attachment developing. This may be a result of an underlying sense that develops with the infant that when they need something—day or night—certain individual(s) tend to provide it. If the infant's needs are not being met with some degree of regularity, then the chances of an insecure attachment may increase. Together, an interaction between temperament and responsiveness may facilitate attachment development.

Globally, it appears as though about 65% of attachment bonds are of the secure variety (Belsky, 2010). Thus, a secure attachment is the rule, rather than the exception. This is good news for parents and caretakers, as it may reflect the notion that responsiveness does not have to be perfect. Rather, there is a level of effort and responsiveness that is likely adequate to promote a healthy and secure attachment. While a secure attachment may be desirable, any type of apparent insecure attachment that exists does not imply the infant or child is being neglected or cared for improperly, nor does it imply the infant or child is destined for a lifetime of insecure relationship patterns. Rather, it may merely be an observation of some anxious, clingy, or avoidant behaviors.

Ecological Considerations of Daycare

The ways in which daycare may impact development may neatly be organized according to an ecological framework. Recall an ecological perspective emphasizes the concurrent presence and interaction of numerous systems, targeting immediate (i.e., microsystem) and more distal (e.g., exosystem, mesosystem) environments. Moreover, these systems and their interactions are subject to change over time (chronosystem). Together, development depends on many different factors. In terms of daycare, multiple factors must be considered to understand the ways in which daycare may impact development.

To illustrate how a **macrosystem** may impact daycare and development, consider the U.S. government's Family Medical Leave Act (FMLA), which is intended to protect the employment status of expectant mothers in the weeks leading up to and following delivery. However, the FMLA typically does not cover more than six to eight weeks, meaning the majority of mothers return to work well within the first year of an infant's life. To put the U.S. policy in perspective, Sweden offers up to a year off with a substantial portion of pay (Belsky, 2010). Some simple data describing trends in daycare usage may further show how an **exosystem** indirectly influences daycare experience. Driven by maternal employment rates, infants and children may require more time in daycare, as evidenced by the rate of over 60% of mothers with children under the age of 6 working in 2000, compared to 34% in 1975. Together, daycare has become a staple in U.S. culture as social and economic policies and practices have influenced the rates are which many infants and children experience non-maternal childcare.

For infants and children, family and daycare represent **microsystems,** or environments in which they spend face-to-face time. Moreover, parents may dictate the type and amount of daycare the infant or child experiences. Such an example of one microsystem (i.e., family) impacting another (i.e., daycare) would illustrate a **mesosystem.** Lastly, a **chronosystem** is apparent in changes that occur within any of the systems. For example, a mother may have multiple children and elect to stay at home with her children or a promotion may result

in more work hours. Nevertheless, it is possible the impact of daycare depends upon some important aspects at the microsystem level, including the type, quantity, and quality of daycare.

First, one may consider various forms of daycare. There are still many parents that care for their infants and children, primarily staying at home to tend to them during their early years. In addition, relatives may care for infants. In one of these two scenarios, the cost of childcare may be nonexistent. However, the caregiver may not be able to earn as much as they would otherwise, which is an important factor in determining when other forms of daycare are sought.

A majority of infants and children experience some form of full- or part-time non-maternal childcare. For instance, in 2000, more than 50% of all preschool age children in the U.S. attended a **daycare center** (Shonkoff & Phillips, 2000). A daycare center is an institution whose administration and staff maintain a primary focus upon caring for infants and children. These institutions are readily visible in many communities, inhabiting large buildings. Daycare centers may differ in terms of size, the age ranges they can handle, and cost. Many may enroll infants as young as 6 weeks, and have part-time or after school programs for older children. Typically, some basic curriculum and developmental teaching (e.g., potty-training) are interwoven into the daycare center program, and are regulated by state guidelines. A **family day care** is also an option, which refers to an individual who cares for a relatively small group of children in their home. In such a case, the home may be customized to handle childcare (e.g., cots, toys, play areas, monitors, etc.). Like daycare centers, family daycares also require state regulation. The family daycare and daycare centers that are regulated by state guidelines often have a rating system applied that is based upon a variety of factors (e.g., staff education, cleanliness, etc.). For instance, a star-system is used in North Carolina, with five-stars purportedly indicating a high quality daycare. In sum, the type of daycare may have a direct bearing on development.

Second, the *quantity* of daycare may be considered in relation to development. Belsky (1986) stirred much early debate regarding the maladaptive effects of too much childcare, in what he phrased a "slow steady trickle of disconcerting evidence" related to the negative impact of non-maternal care. The negative impacts he cited included infant dysregulation and irritability. Some of the negative outcomes associated with children included non-compliance, less peer likeability, aggression, and other behavioral problems (NICHD Early

Child Care Research Network, 2001). The early empirical examination of daycare, however, has been plagued by criticisms—the most notable of which was that daycare was often conceptualized merely in terms of quantity. That is, as more non-maternal daycare is experienced during infancy and early childhood, the more negative outcomes are realized. Some may characterize this as a dose-response relationship. In emphasizing quantity, researchers may leave out important considerations such as quality of daycare or parental responsiveness in conceptualizing what matters in terms of developmental outcomes.

To that end, the National Institute of Child Health and Human Development (NICHD) have been instrumental in broadening the scope of knowledge of the impact of daycare effects. In a landmark Study of Early Child Care, NICHD researchers reported that quality of care—rather than quantity—appears to have the most significant impact on the aforementioned outcomes. In fact, the *quality* of daycare is likely the most important factor in predicting socioemotional development. In this case, quality refers to the degree to which caregivers are affectionate, attentive, responsive, and stimulating (Belsky, 2001). Thus, while relative quantity of daycare appears to maintain a negative relationship with some outcomes, quality of care should be given primary consideration. Moreover, if quality of program is the crucial variable, then it becomes essential to set standards of quality for daycare and early elementary school programs.

The issue of quality is important in understanding the ways in which the daycare microsystem may impact development. While quality may be defined in different ways, a high-quality daycare may be one that supports learning and development in positive ways. Marshall (2009) suggested quality of daycare may be understood according to structures and processes. Structural features are those that are directly controlled, regulated, and observed. For instance, child-to-staff ratios, overall size and setting, and training and certification standards may all be structural indicators of quality. There are also features related to processes that indicate quality. These are not necessarily or explicitly regulated or observable, but include staff and infant interactions, personal attention and affection, and so on.

The research performed by the NICHD has allowed for some practical recommendations to be made. The NICHD and Belsky (2001) state that U.S. policy (i.e., mesosystem feature) does not currently adhere to policies and procedure that would allow for mothers to stay at home in the first year of infancy, thereby drastically reducing non-maternal daycare quantity. Although subsidization programs alleviate daycare costs, the cost of quality daycare still remains high and out-of-reach for many. Thus, reducing quantity and increasing quality of daycare is difficult.

The NICHD researchers suggested four essential features characterize overall daycare quality: features and practices that encourage attachment to school and peer group, constructivist learning, promoting intrinsic motivation, and a coherent focus that includes social development. Briefly, fostering a secure attachment to school may be beneficial, not unlike the adjustment of a securely attached infant. Constructivist classroom methods encourage interaction, autonomy, and competence, which in turn may foster attachment. The goal of teachers should be to encourage behavior that stems from internal sources, rather than external rewards and punishments. The latter may serve to create a competitive undertone, and de-emphasize personal commitment and achievement. Lastly, social development may be promoted by implementing the aforementioned guidelines.

Erikson

Recall Erik Erikson (1980) proposed a stage model of human development, spanning from infancy through later adulthood. Integral to each stage is a primary psychosocial task. For instance, according to Erikson, the first stage is **trust versus**

mistrust (roughly encompassing the first year of life). The psychosocial aspect of this stage is related to whether or not significant others offer basic physical and emotional needs, in which case the infant develops a sense of trust. A nurturing caregiver that is particularly attentive to their infant's needs may foster such trust. However, if needs are not met with enough consistency, an attitude of mistrust develops, especially toward interpersonal relationships. This particular stage may be juxtaposed to attachment theory to some degree. That is, a sense of trust may be integral to the attachment bond that forms between an infant and caregiver.

Still within infancy, and encompassing the second year of life, is a supposed **autonomy versus shame and doubt** stage. During this time, Erikson thought it was particularly important for the infant to begin developing autonomy, or a sense of self-sufficiency. The most basic struggle is between a sense of self-reliance and sense of self-doubt. The infant needs to explore and experiment, to make mistakes and test limits. It is typical to see infants in their second year exploring the environment and wanting to acquire new behaviors. It is also not uncommon for infants to want to be very involved and try things for themselves. If parents promote dependency, an infant's sense of autonomy and subsequent capacity to deal with the world may be inhibited to some degree. With this stage, the infant will ideally embark on a path toward developing a general sense of independence and competence that will be useful throughout life.

Recent research has supported the notion that autonomy in toddlerhood may be linked with higher cognitive skills and childhood. In one study, mothers were encouraged to help toddlers solve challenging problems, and were rated in terms of autonomy supportive behaviors, including encouragement, positive feedback, tone of voice, keeping the child on task, following the child's pace, perspective taking ability, and offering the opportunity for choices. Years later, the children were measured in terms of executive functioning (broad term related to cognitive functioning including memory, decision-making, reasoning and adaptability), with the highest scores being reported for those children whose mothers appeared to be the most supportive in terms of autonomy (Matte-Gagne, Bernier, & Lalonde, 2014). Together, promoting autonomy may have lasting impact upon development.

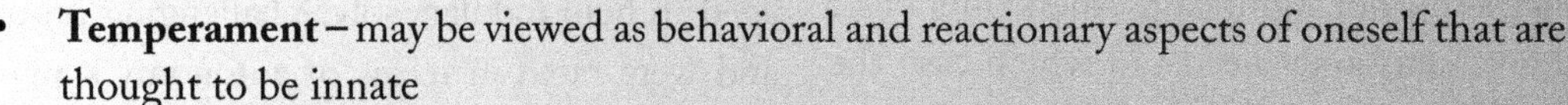

Key Terms

- **Temperament** – may be viewed as behavioral and reactionary aspects of oneself that are thought to be innate
    - **Easy** – infants with an easy temperament are flexible above all. They adapt to new objects and situations relatively easily and calmly, and demonstrate a positive mood (as indicated by smiling and babbling) often. These infants have very regular sleeping, eating, and elimination cycles.
    - **Difficult** – infants with difficult temperaments do not react well to novel situations or new people; they may protest when they sense disruptions. These infants tend to have irregular schedules with sleeping, feeding, and bowel movements.
    - **Slow-to-Warm-Up (Wary)** – these infants generally may respond negatively (e.g., fussing, crying) to new situations, but they tend to accept them more quickly than their difficult counterparts
- **Ethology** – the study of behavior in animals (including humans) in natural settings
- **Imprinting** – the idea that newborns tend to follow and prefer a certain stimulus
- **Critical Period** – a chronological window of time that is ideal for acquiring a new behavior or establishing a connection
- **Attachment** – an emotional connection that is created between the infant and an immediate and nurturing adult
- **Pre-Attachment Phase** – from birth to about 3 months, infants are relatively indiscriminant when it comes to adults. At this time, they are not necessarily showing preference.
- **Attachment-in-the-Making Phase** – infants begin to show preference for particular caretaker(s). Not surprisingly, when preferences begin to emerge, so do protests when the infant is separated from their primary attachment figures.
- **Clear-Cut Attachment** – an observable preference for one or more attachment figures
- **Separation Anxiety** – an infant who has established an attachment will more regularly fuss and protest when they sense they are being separated
- **Strange Situation Paradigm** – a research method that manipulates and captures the reactions and behaviors that occur when an infant is separated from (and reunited with) their attachment figure; used to assess attachment style
- **Secure Attachment** – demonstrated by infants who explore strange environments freely while their caretaker is there, and also noticeably (but controllably) upset when they realized they had been separated. Upon reunion, the securely attached infants greet and seek contact with their caretaker.
- **Insecure Resistant Attachment** – infants show a general reluctance to explore the new environment, even when in the presence of only their caretaker. When the stranger does enter the room, the infant is wary and avoids interaction, and is extremely upset (greater in intensity and duration) when they notice the caretaker has left. Often, they continued to be upset even upon reunion with the caretaker and surprisingly do not seek contact with them.
- **Insecure Avoidant Attachment** – infant shows little or no interest in exploring the new environment or interacting with the stranger in any way. In addition, they appear to avoid contact with the caretaker when they return. Together, they appear to "avoid" contact and exploration, and lack the emotional and behavioral reaction to separation and reunion that are present in other attachment styles.

- **Daycare Center** – a daycare center is an institution whose administration and staff maintain a primary focus upon caring for infants and children
- **Family Daycare** – an individual who cares for a relatively small group of children in their home
- **Trust versus Mistrust** – the first of the stages in Erikson's eight psychosocial task model, this stage is related to whether or not significant others offer basic physical and emotional needs, in which case the infant develops a sense of trust. However, if needs are not met with enough quality or consistency, an attitude of mistrust develops, especially toward interpersonal relationships.
- **Autonomy versus Shame and Doubt** – during this time, Erikson thought it was particularly important for the infant to begin developing autonomy, or a sense of self-sufficiency. The most basic struggle is between a sense of self-reliance and sense of self-doubt.

Critical Thinking Questions

1. Describe temperament. What are key differences between the three main types of temperament? Do you think infants and children can fit neatly into one of these three categories? Also, do you think temperament is something that lasts with an individual over time, or do new personality traits emerge as one approaches adolescence and adulthood?
2. How do temperament, parental responsiveness or attentiveness, and attachment style all interact? What parenting behaviors may increase the likelihood of a secure attachment? In your response, be sure to clearly describe the temperament or attachment types you include in your analysis.
3. For an infant, do you think being raised at home (by a stay-at-home parent) is clearly preferable to daycare, or vice versa? Why or why not? In terms of attachment, do high amounts of daycare negatively impact the attachment bond between infant and primary caretaker(s)? What are some key considerations here? Include examples as necessary to support your points.

References

Ainsworth, M. D. S. (1973). The development of infant-mother attachment. In B. M. Caldwell & H. N. Ricciutti (Eds.), *Review of child development research* (Vol. 3, pp. 1-94). Chicago: University of Chicago Press.

Belsky, J. (1986). Infant day care: A cause for concern? *Zero to Three, 6*, 1-7.

Belsky, J. (2001). Emanuel Miller Lecture: Developmental risks (still) associated with early child care. *Journal of Child Psychology and Psychiatry, 42*, 845-859.

Bowlby, J. (1980). *Attachment and loss: Vol. 3 Loss: Sadness and depression.* New York: Basic Books.

Erikson, E. H. (1980) *Identity and the life cycle.* New York: Norton.

Harlow, H. F. (1958). The nature of love. *American Psychologist, 13*, 73-685.

Harlow, H. F., Harlow, M. K., Dodsworth, R. O., & Arling, G. L. (1966). Maternal behavior of rhesus monkeys deprived of mothering and peer association in infancy. *Proceedings of the American Philosophical Society, 110*, 58-66.

Lorenz, K. (1935). Der Kumpan in der Umwelt des Vogels. Der Artenosse als auslosendes Moment sozialer Verhaltungweishen. [The companion in the bird's world. The follow-member of the species as releasing factor of social behavior.] *Journal fur Ornithologie. Beiblatt (Leipzig), 83*, 137-231.

Marshall, N. (2009). The quality of early child care and children's development. In L. Liben (Ed.), *Current directions in developmental psychology* (pp. 144-150). New York: Pearson.

Matte-Gagne, C., Bernier, A., & Lalonde, G. (2014). Stability in maternal autonomy support and child executive functioning. *Journal of Child and Family Studies.* doi: 101007/s10826-014-0063-9

NICHD Early Child Care Research Network (2001). Child care and family predictors of preschool attachment and stability from infancy. *Developmental Psychology, 37*, 847-862.

Shonkoff, J. P., & Phillips, D. A. (2000). Growing up in childcare. In J. P. Shonkoff and D. A. Phillips (Eds.), *From neuron to neighborhoods: The science of early childhood development* (pp. 297-327). Washington, DC: National Academy Press.

Thomas, A., Chess, S., & Birch, H. G. (1968). *Temperament and behavior disorders in childhood.* Oxford, England: New York University Press.

CHAPTER 7

Physical Development in Childhood

Defining Childhood

Prior to discussing factors relevant for development in childhood, it may be useful to define the parameters of this life stage. Thus far, issues related to physical development during the prenatal stage, and the physical, cognitive, and socioemotional development during infancy have been covered. These stages have consistent and discrete beginnings and endings. For instance, a prenatal stage is defined as beginning at conception and continuing up to the birth event. Infancy begins upon birth, and persists through the first two years.

Childhood may have a similarly consistent and discrete beginning. More specifically, when infancy ends at two years of age, childhood begins. This next stage may commonly be known as toddlerhood, but it is broadly subsumed under childhood. The conclusion of childhood may be more variable. For the purposes of the upcoming units, childhood may be viewed as ending with the onset of puberty. Thus, while there is a chronological beginning to childhood, there is a biological conclusion. Of course, there is some degree of variability with the age at which individuals experience puberty. Some experience it particularly early, beginning even at age 8 or 9, while others do not experience pubertal changes until much later than average. In an attempt to capture more uniformity with this definition of childhood, it may be useful to remember the idea of a cohort. Within any given cohort, when a majority of its members have begun to experience puberty, it may be evident that everyone in that particular

cohort has grown out of childhood and entered adolescence. With the consideration of this cohort effect, it is possible that an individual may experience puberty significantly early, but may still be considered a child, along with the other members of their cohort. Conversely, if an individual experiences puberty significantly late, they have already entered adolescence, as have most of their peers. It is important to note that humans - in comparison most other animals - have a particularly long childhood. Other species reach biological maturity much more quickly relative to their overall lifespan. Neuroimaging and metabolic research has demonstrated this is in large part due to the human brain. Being more complex, it requires more "fuel" in early years, which may actually divert energy and resources from other organs and features. That is, the brain dominates early metabolic processes as it burns through about two-thirds of the calories the entire body uses while at rest. In that vein, one researcher labeled the 5-year old brain an "energy monster." For some children, it may even be difficult to guess their age by size alone, and it becomes necessary to listen to speech and watch their behaviors to gain a more accurate picture of their age. This may be due to the notion that body growth "grinds to a halt" during periods of rapid brain growth (Kuzawa, Chuganin, Grossman, Lipovich, Muzik, Hof, & Wildman, 2014).

It is important to note that puberty (which shall be covered in a later unit) represents a critical physical transition in human development. The hormonal and physical changes associated with puberty prepare the human body for reproductive capabilities, and may be indicative that the individual is no longer in an immature state (at least physically) when compared to childhood. The following sections will cover physical (e.g., neurological and motor development) and cognitive factors that are unique to childhood.

Neurological Development

It may be difficult to match the brain growth that occurs during infancy. The brain grows from 25% to 75% of its eventual adult size during infancy (Stiles & Jernigan, 2010). Thus, there is no room for equivalent growth at any other life stage. Additionally, processes underlying neurological growth

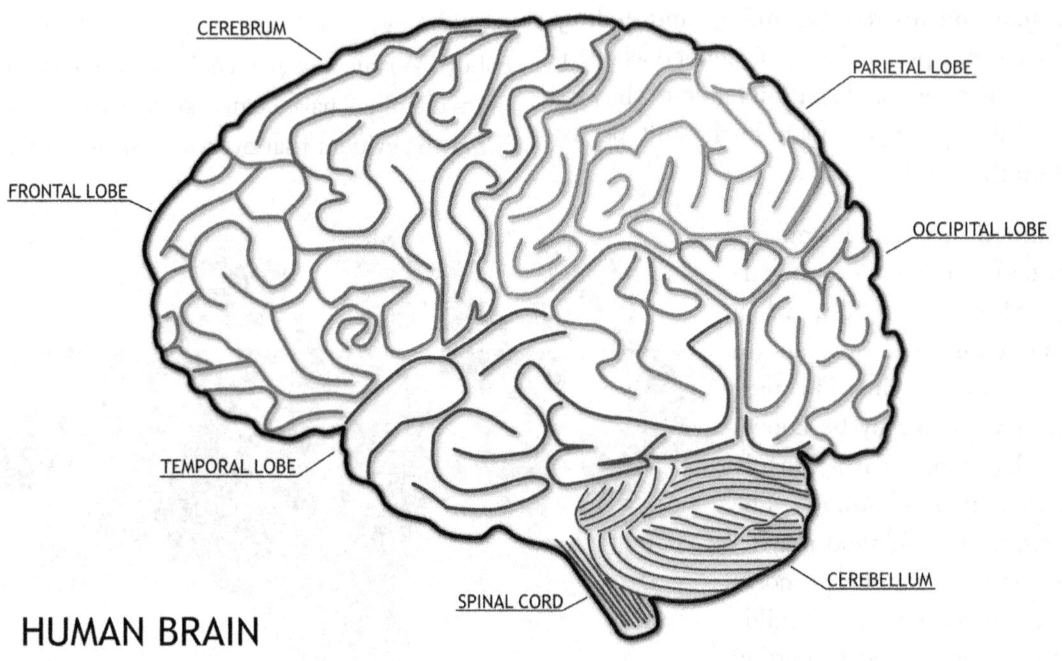

FIGURE 7.1 *Human Brain Structure*

demonstrate continued and significant growth during childhood. For instance, synaptogensis and myelination continue to exert their respective influences on the formation and strengthening of neurological pathways. With the amount of new experiences, behaviors, and emotions that are evident in childhood, there is extensive potential for neurological stimulation and growth.

In addition, the frontal lobe, which is associated with thinking, reasoning, and behaviors, demonstrates vital, albeit relatively slow, growth during childhood (see Figure 7.1). While the brain appears to grow naturally during childhood, there are factors that may inhibit normal and necessary neurological development. For instance, stress—broadly defined—in early years may delay brain development. One study illustrated that children who have been exposed to intense and chronic stressors score lower on working memory tasks compared to children who had not experienced this level of stress. In order to more closely examine the neurological bases of these findings, the same researchers took a Magnetic Resonance Imaging (MRI) scan—which offers a type of "snapshot" of the brain—reported that in children who had experienced intense stress, the prefrontal cortex took up much less space compared to the low-stress children (University of Wisconsin-Madison, 2012). The researchers were careful to note "stress does not necessarily permanently scar the brain." The plasticity principle suggests even when brain development is delayed due to stress in some children; they may catch up in later years. However, stress may be viewed as a risk factor in terms of neurological growth. However, there are protective factors as well.

For example, exercise and physical activity may promote neurological growth in childhood. Some of the research related to exercise and neurological benefit in children stems from observations that children with attention-deficit hyperactivity disorder (ADHD) *and* who participate in sport activities tend to respond better to behavioral interventions than do children with ADHD who do not participate in sport. This phenomenon may be an indication of a positive correlation between physical activity and neurological health. Researchers in neuro-imaging based studies suggest that as children are physically active at the same time their brain is experiencing rapid growth, neurological systems are strengthened supporting subsequent learning and memory (Hopkins, Davis, VanTieghem, Whalen, & Bucci, 2012).

More observable physical development in childhood may be in terms of bodily structure. Two general principles are evident in relation to childhood body structure. First, a **cephalacaudal principle** suggests that children tend to grow from the top down. Second, a **proximodistal principle** implies children tend to grow from the inside out. Children tend to grow most quickly in the head, shoulder, and torso, with relatively short limbs. Together, children (particularly young children) appear to have stout bodies and large heads. During adolescence, a **growth spurt** will incur lengthening of the limbs and overall body growth, reducing the ratio of head size to body size and giving an individual a more adult-like appearance.

A vast majority of children will grow according to these principles and with relative consistency across ages. However, in some extreme cases, such physical growth and motor development does not occur. More specifically, **stunting** refers to the cessation of physical growth, often due to having either too little caloric intake in infancy and childhood or too little nutritional variety during that time. When a child—during what is otherwise a critical growth period—does not receive enough calories, the body prioritizes vital organs maintenance over body growth. Therefore, while many children do survive, their growth (including the brain) is stunted. Brain scans of a healthy nourished 3-year-old brain to that of a malnourished 3-year-old are quite telling: the brain of the healthy child is almost twice as large—the "difference between a cantaloupe and a softball" (Rukmini, 2012). Given the link with caloric intake, stunting is more common in areas of the world where malnutrition rates are high.

Consider the community of Louri, located in central Africa. Several years ago, a devastating drought hit the region. Thereafter, equivalent droughts came every few years (a much higher frequency than is typical). Due to the consistent drought conditions, there was a general lack of food in terms of quality and quantity for all members of the community, including for all infants and children. A young girl named Achta was one such child, born during the original drought and subsequently malnourished through infancy and childhood. In 2012, Achta was 7 years old, but maintained a height and weight more consistent with a 3-year-old's body. Her brain has also developed accordingly, and is much smaller than would be expected. This is manifest in her inability to meet certain motor milestones, even rather simple ones such as drawing a circle on a piece of paper. Achta's growth and development illustrates a stunting effect, which is apparent in 40% of children in Louri (Rukmini, 2012)!

Motor Development

Motor development is related to adaptations in movement capabilities. During infancy, discussion of motor movement was limited to basic reflexes progressing into more voluntary movements, evident in many motor milestones (e.g., crawling, walking). Motor development continues through childhood, further allowing children to physically navigate their environment. At a broad level, motor skills may be gross or fine. **Gross (or mass) motor** movement are those that require the activation and use of large muscular systems. Any type

Courtesy of the author

Copyright © 2013 by s_oleg. Used under license of Shutterstock, Inc.

of activity that requires much of the lower (e.g., hopping on both feet) or upper (e.g., pouring out a large bucket of sand) body muscles would be considered a gross motor skill. Conversely, **fine (or precise) motor** skills are those that require the activation and use of smaller muscular units. A general principle evident in childhood is that *gross motor movement tends to precede fine motor movement.* Two useful ways to observe motor development is through play and drawing. Imagine a toddler who is given a crayon and a piece of paper. They may grasp the crayon in their palm, wrapping their fingers around it, and making large sweeping motions (that require movement of the shoulder, elbow, forearm, and wrist) to draw with it. However, an older child would be able to draw with the same material in a much more precise way, holding the crayon between select fingers, and perhaps only requiring wrist and finger movement to produce a drawing. Note the images above, which were generated by different children, but some years apart.

As evident in the monkey drawing, when 2.5 years old, the child was evidently unable to stay within the lines of the character; however, a much older child (perhaps 7 or so) demonstrated much better control in drawing an image of a car. It is interesting to note some research has demonstrated an association between drawing ability at age 4 and later intelligence. In the study, drawings (of the image of a person) by 4-year olds were rated for presence and correct quantity of features (i.e., head, eyes, nose, limbs, etc.). These ratings were positively correlated with intelligence scores at 4 and 10 years later (Arden et al, 2014). However, the lead author was cautious to warn that the correlation was moderate, so "parents should not worry if their child draws badly." Sex differences are also apparent. Young girls may develop fine motor skills at a faster rate than young boys, while boys may outperform females in many gross motor tasks (Geary, 1998).

Evidence of motor development in childhood may be gathered from other anecdotal experience. If one were to observe elementary school children during the course of a typical day, it would be apparent how the children display more advanced movement and coordination as their age increases.

The rule, rather than the exception, is that children are reared in an environment that permits and facilitates normal motor development. In some cases, there is an apparent delay in motor development. Although relatively rare, if certain criteria are met, a diagnosis of a **motor skill (or coordination) disorder** may be warranted. The fifth edition of the Diagnostic and Statistical Manual (DSM-V) of disorders includes the main criteria for developmental coordination disorder. First, there must be an apparent significant delay in motor skill attainment. Imagine a scenario in which a 5-year-old has the general gross and fine motor capabilities of a 3-year-old. This may impair his or her ability to navigate many social, recreational, and academic tasks. Such a motor delay may be observed early in failure to meet infantile milestones (e.g., walking) and later on in general clumsiness (e.g., dropping utensils frequently), particularly poor athletic capabilities in relation to peers, or inability to dress themselves or lace their shoes. Another important criterion for diagnosis of this particular disorder—and a hallmark for most disorders—is that the condition must cause some level of distress. Children do not express distress in the same ways an adolescent or adult may. While older individuals may explicitly express their distress, or indicate their relative level of distress on a survey; children may not have the communicative ability to do so. Rather, children may withdraw from activities where their motor delay may cause problems, even if they evidently found them enjoyable before. They may alter their socialization habits, breaking old friendships and forming new ones. In addition, their grades at school may suffer, indicating an inability to concentrate or regulate negative emotions.

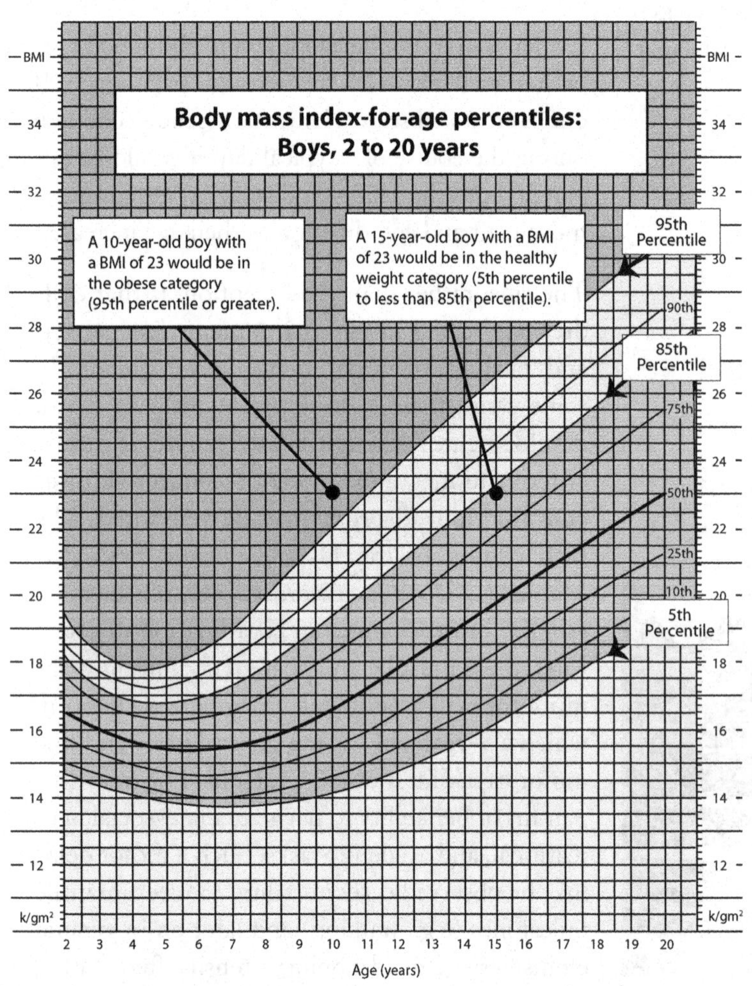

FIGURE 7.2 *BMI Chart for Boys*

Obesity

A discussion of the topic of obesity necessitates a discussion of body mass, which is related to an individual's body shape and size. In fact, the **body mass index (BMI)** is a specific ratio of one's weight to height. The precise ratio requires knowledge of one's height (in centimeters) and weight (in kilograms). In certain areas where inches and pounds are more common, a simple conversion may be necessary before calculating BMI. Even more simply, BMI calculators are available online, and quickly convert centimeters to inches and pounds to kilograms, ultimately generating a BMI score. It may be noted that calculation of BMI is relatively convenient, requiring at the very least a reliable scale and a tape measure. Its convenience may be one reason it is so widely used. There is a wide range of BMI scores, but these scores are typically between 20 and 30. This score may then be applied to a scale to indicate weight status, or whether a particular person is underweight, normal weight, overweight, or obese. However, for children and adolescents, the scale and corresponding ranges of BMI scores that capture the various weight statuses depend on two other factors; namely, age and gender.

Figure 7.2 depicts an age and sex (i.e., male) specific BMI chart. It is important to note the different colored areas of these charts as they define the ranges of BMI scores (for each age and gender) of the four primary weight statuses (i.e., underweight, normal weight, overweight, obese). The top portion on each chart defines the **obesity**, which by definition is the 95th percentile of BMI scores for any gender and age. Recall a percentile implies all the scores that lie at or below a particular score. Thus, the 95th percentile of BMI scores is greater than or equal to 95% of all other BMI scores for that age and gender. Together, someone at the 95th percentile (or greater) has a relatively large amount of weight for their height in comparison to others in their age group. The next weight status is **overweight**, and may be indicated by the scores that lie between the 85th and 95th percentile. **Normal weight** is defined by the 15th to the 85th percentiles. Thus, a large amount of the population is thought to exist in this range, and it is thought to represent relative healthy weights to maintain for height. Lastly, an **underweight** individual is at the 5th percentile or less for a BMI score, indicating relatively light weight for their height when compared to their peers. There is a general linear movement of the ranges in these charts (i.e., movement up and to the right as age increases) because they must account for natural growth. There is expected height and weight growth that would impact the normal expectations of weight in relation to height at different ages.

BMI scores are used for a variety of reasons but primarily as a convenient indicator of health. As BMI increases, and particularly as individuals fall into an obese category, there are a variety of negative medical correlates, including cardiovascular problems, hypertension, and type 2 diabetes onset (Dietz, 2004). Thus, reducing BMI may reduce the likelihood of the onset of such diseases or reduce their severity. Recent estimates of the prevalence of overweight and obese youth is impressive. In the United States alone, the prevalence of overweight and obese children has increased by over 180% from 1971 to the year 2000 (Joliffe, 2004). Globally, similar trends have been observed in Canada, Finland, and China (Kautiannen, Rimpela, Vikat, & Virtanen, 2002; Luo & Hu, 2002; Tremblay & Williams, 2001). In addition, it is important to consider the higher rates of children that are overweight and obese may carry over into their adulthood years, and nearly half of all severely obese adults were obese as children, and continued to amass pounds over many years (Associated Press, 2012). Experts at the Center of Disease Control believe they offer very reasonable estimates that over 40% of the population will be obese by the year 2030—a staggering proportion (Associated Press, 2012)! This is consistent with recent data observable in Figures 7.3 and 7.4, which visually display obesity trends.

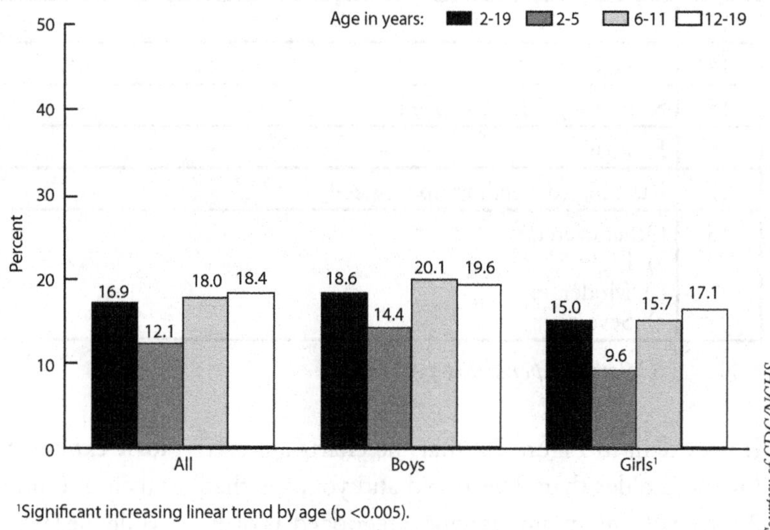

FIGURE 7.3 *2009-2010 Obesity Among Children*

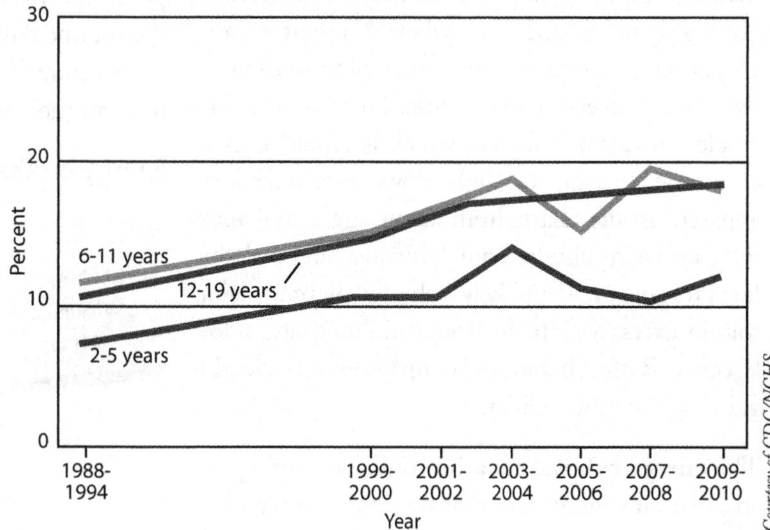

FIGURE 7.4 *1988-2010 Obesity Among Children*

	Activity	Calorie Expenditure
1	Laying still	1
2	Sitting, standing, reading, writing, eating, playing cards, hand-sewing, etc.	1.5
3	Driving car, tailoring	2
4	Washing floors, sweeping, and ironing	2.2
5	Playing golf	2.5
6	Walking 5 km/hr speed	3
7	Walking 7 km/hr speed	4.5
8	Walking 9 km/hr speed	9
9	Gardening, weeding, etc.	5
10	Cycling (depending upon speed)	3.5 to 8.0
11	Boxing, rowing	12
12	Dancing	5
13	Table tennis	5.5
14	Tennis	6
15	Swimming 3 km/hr speed	9
16	Football	8
17	Running (depending upon speed)	10 to 25
18	Other exercises: a) Light b) Moderate c) Severe	 2.5 4 8

TABLE 7.1 *Caloric Expenditure per Minute*

It is evident in Figure 7.2 that the charts are used for those older than 2 years old and younger than 20 years of age. Infants are not categorized as overweight or obese. Rather, they may be more informally described as "large" or "chunky." Even in rare, but highly publicized cases, when an infant weighs 15 pounds or more at birth you would not categorize them as overweight or obese. There is a considerable amount of baby fat, which is typically shed over time. In fact, the slight downward trajectory apparent in the charts from about age 2 to 4 may indicate when children are "growing out" of baby fat. However, it is unlikely baby fat plays a major role in excess weight in later childhood and adolescence. Rather, behavioral contributions to weight gain may be more salient.

The **energy balance equation** offers a simple perspective on weight gain that occurs for behavioral reasons. This ratio compares **caloric intake** to **caloric expenditure.** The former is linked with food taken in (and converted to calories for energy use) while the latter is related to the calories that are used or burned, either through resting metabolic rates or physical activity. Any type of physical activity, even the routine day-to-day movements, requires caloric expenditure. Table 7.1 illustrates some daily activities and the amount of calories they burn.

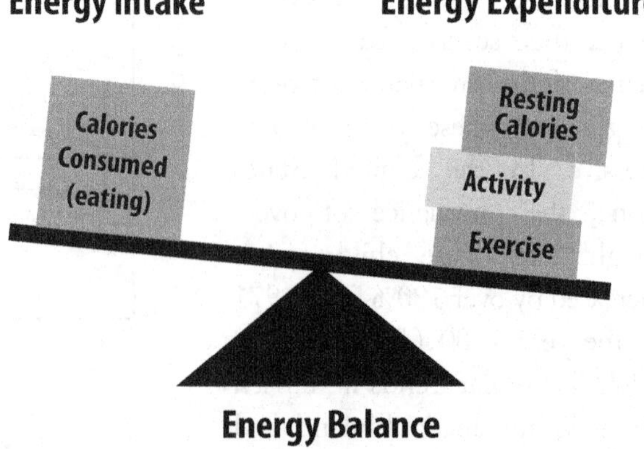

The energy balance equation simply posits that if an individual takes in more calories than they expend, weight gain will likely occur. On the other hand, if one expends more than they take in, weight loss will be more likely (see Table 7.1). Approximately 3,500 calories translate into one pound of weight gain or loss. Thus, the rate at which weight is gained or lost is related to how much the equation may be imbalanced. If one takes in large quantities of food with little metabolic or physical activity to compensate it, then weight gain may occur quickly. However, even slight imbalances may result in weight gain. Consider if an individual on average consumed 100 more calories per day than they expended. This may still translate into weight gain, but a rather slow and perhaps undetectable rate. This latter phenomenon has been termed **creeping obesity**.

There are numerous factors associated with weight gain in childhood, but they all seem to relate broadly to the energy balance equation. Some factors serve to increase calories taken in, while others reduce the amount of calories expended.

Dealing first with the former factor, there are variables that may impact caloric intake. First, it is not uncommon for children to exceed what is a recommended number of calories in a given day. A diet with plentiful snacks may contain much **energy dense food.** These foods are typically high in fat and have a large amount of calories in a relatively small package. When consumed frequently, the calories from such energy dense foods can accumulate quickly. Another way in which a recommended amount of calories may be surpassed is that typical serving sizes are rather easily exceeded. Often the nutritional content offered on the sides of food packages gives the amount of calories for one serving. Many individuals may be surprised that one bottled soft drink contains two or more servings. An individual bag of chips may contain multiple servings as well. Thus, the information offered on the side of a food package may actually be multiplied by the number of servings in that particular package if it is being treated as a single serving. Second, individuals that eat particularly quickly may be more susceptible to take in more calories. The pituitary gland controls the release of a hormone called leptin, which is released in response to the stomach being full. However, it may take several minutes for the brain to register a sense of "fullness." In the meantime, many calories may be taken in, particularly if they are the energy dense variety. The fast food industry has certainly capitalized on the distribution of energy dense food (which are desirable due to fat and sugar content) and the need to consume it relatively quickly. Research has also demonstrated that obese children's brains are more responsive to sugar. When compared to a control group consisting of children of healthy weight, a group of obese children produced brain images with heightened activity in response to sugar intake in the insular cortex and amygdala, which are regions associated with perception, emotion, taste, motivation , and reward (Boutelle, Wierenga, Bischoff-grethe, Grenekso-Stevens, Paulas, & Kaye, 2014).

Clinicians and nutritionists would have valuable feedback regarding what a healthy and balanced diet should be. They may have recommendations not only in terms of calories but also the types of food that should be consumed. In addition, they may have simple techniques aimed at slowing down the eating

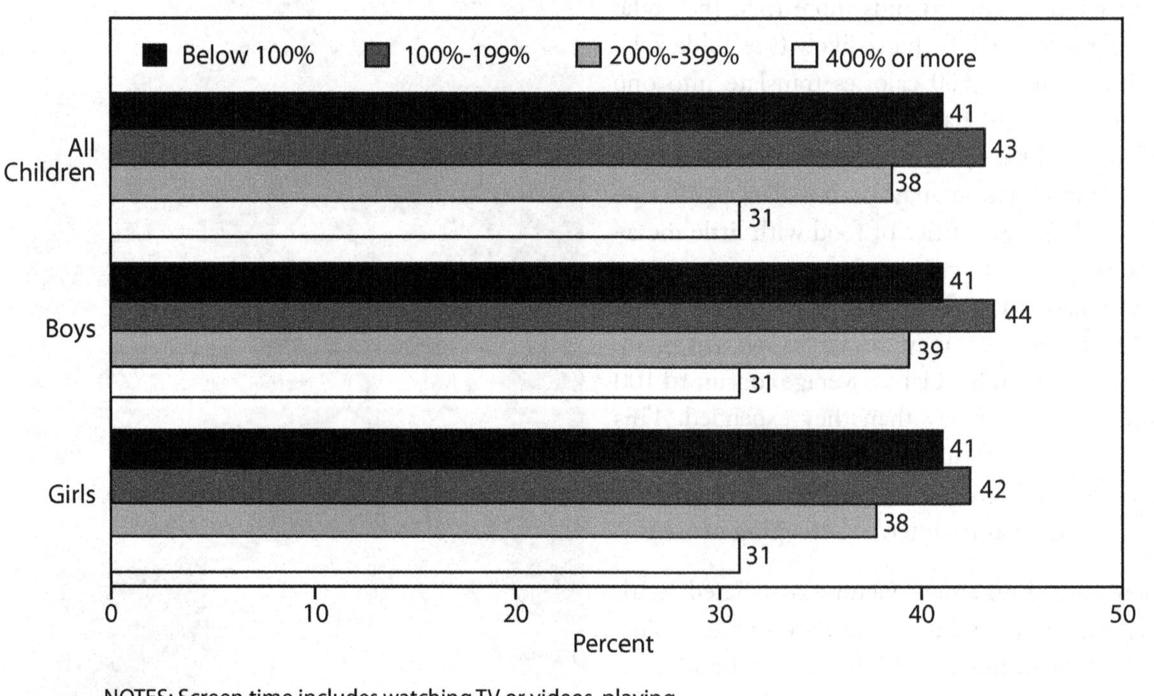

FIGURE 7.5 *Screen Time*

process. For instance, they may suggest eating dinner with your family. If there is some level of interaction while eating, this may slow down the eating process itself. Clinicians may also suggest that each bite of food be chewed deliberately a certain number of times or for a certain length of time, ensuring it is properly chewed to aid in digestion, but also to slow down the eating rate.

Regarding caloric expenditure, a sedentary lifestyle, or a lifestyle with a general lack of physical activity, certainly contributes to weight gain during childhood and adolescence. A relatively consistent and negative correlation emerges between physical activity (the primary source of caloric expenditure) and BMI. A large portion of sedentary time may be taken up by television, video games, and computer use. The technological advancements with these products has led to a dramatic increase in the time children spend being inactive. Together, it has been reported that general "screen time" is the most prominent factor related to a sedentary lifestyle (Biddle, 2007). Accordingly, a question may be raised: May active video games (i.e., those that require physical interaction) be employed to increase physical activity rates in children?

Foley and Maddison (2010) conducted a review of the literature related to use of active video games as a means to increase physical activity. **Active video games** require the player to physically move to interact with video images. Such active games are dependent upon movement detected through a camera, infrared sensors, pressure-sensitive mats, lasers, or ergometers. For example, an active bowling game would require the child make arm and wrist movements consistent with actual bowling form. An active dance game may require the child to move their feet to correspond to certain areas on a pad or mat on the floor. Regardless of the type, though, movement is required to play the video game, unlike traditional video games which require hand-held controllers with mere button pushing is used to play. Thus, there is some caloric expenditure. The purpose of the literature review was to assess the empirical evidence of video games as a means to increase physical activity rates in children.

One of the main types of studies considered in the review were "energy expenditure" studies, through which the researchers compared how much energy was used when playing various active video games, compared to a resting state or traditional physical activity. These studies demonstrated that active video games unquestionably require more energy output than a resting state, which is more evident in traditional video games with push-button controllers. Moreover, the more movement required was typically associated with more energy expenditure. Importantly, these active games did not induce physical activity intensity that surpassed what the American College of Sport Medicine (ACSM) has prescribed as a minimally acceptable amount and intensity of physical activity to appreciably impact body composition or cardiovascular health. Together, while active video game playing may be substituted for complete inactivity, it should not be viewed as fulfilling a necessary healthy amount of physical activity. The authors also noted that while participants in their studies typically adhered to the play requirements of the study, they do not necessarily adhere to them when playing at home. To illustrate, for the study, children may have been asked to play continually without break for 10 minutes or more so researchers could assess energy expenditure. However, at home when children are playing, there may be breaks, interruptions and rest periods which serve to lessen the amount of energy expended. Together, as active games require movement, there may be potential for them being suitable substitutes for standard exercise. However, there is little empirical support that active video games should currently be viewed as a proper exchange for the level of physical activity prescribed by the ACSM.

Key Terms

- **Childhood** – the life stage that begins when infancy ends and concludes with the onset of puberty
- **Cephalacaudal Principle** – the idea children tend to grow from the top down
- **Proximodistal Principle** – the idea children tend to grow from the inside out
- **Growth Spurt** – more typical in pre-adolescent (late childhood), this term refers to a lengthening of the limbs and overall body growth, reducing the ratio of head size to body size and giving an individual a more adult-like appearance
- **Stunting** – the cessation of physical growth, often due to having either too little caloric intake in infancy and childhood or too little nutritional variety during that time
- **Gross (or Mass) Motor** – movements that require the activation and use of large muscular systems
- **Fine (or Precise) Motor** – those movements that require the activation and use of smaller muscular units
- **Motor Skill (or Coordination) Disorder** – among other criteria, the primary feature for diagnose of this disorder is an apparent and significant delay in motor skill attainment, often observable in a failure to meet motor milestones
- **Body Mass Index (BMI)** – a specific ratio of one's weight to height
- **Obesity** – a term reserved for those who rank above the 95th percentile of BMI scores for any gender and age; indicating a relatively large amount of weight for their height in comparison to others in their age group
- **Overweight** – indicated by BMI scores that lie between the 85th and 95th percentile
- **Normal weight** – indicated by BMI scores from the 5th to the 85th percentiles
- **Underweight** – indicated by a BMI score at the 5th percentile or less; suggesting very light weight for their height when compared to their peers
- **Energy Balance Equation** – a ratio comparing caloric intake to caloric expenditure. The presumption is when intake exceeds expenditure, weight gain occurs; when expenditure exceeds intake, weight loss occurs
- **Caloric Intake** – linked with food taken in and converted to calories for energy use
- **Caloric Expenditure** – related to the calories that are used or burned, either through resting metabolic rates or physical activity
- **Creeping Obesity** – weight gain that occurs (and ultimately results in obesity) slowly over time, perhaps undetectable over the course of many years
- **Energy Dense Food** – foods typically high in fat and have a large amount of calories in a relatively "small package"
- **Active Video Games** – require the player to physically move to interact with video images. Game play and progression is predicated upon movement detected through a camera, infrared sensors, pressure-sensitive mats, lasers, or ergometers.

Critical Thinking Questions

1. Describe a typical physical growth pattern for children. In doing so, be sure to discuss the principles which govern growth in childhood, and ultimately, how children emerge to look a bit more "adult-like" as they approach adolescence.
2. Discuss obesity. What defines obesity and what are some of the current rates and prevalence of obesity in the U.S.? What factors are generally behind these trends? Support your points with examples.
3. Are active video games a plausible way to combat obesity? That is, can active video games—in terms of what they currently require of the user—replace traditional physical activity? Why or why not?

References

Arden, R. (2014). Genes influence young children's human figure drawing, and their association with intelligence a decade later. *Psychological Science.*

Associated Press (2012, May 8). Obesity study results mixed. *The Winston-Salem Journal,* p. A10.

Biddle, S. J. (2007). Sedentary behavior. *American Journal of Preventative Medicine, 33,* 502-504.

Boutelle, K., Wierenga, A., Bischoff-Grethe, A., Grenekso-Stevens,E., Paulas, M.P., & Kaye, W.H. (2014). Increased brain response to appetitive tastes in insula and amygdala in obese compared to healthy weight children when sated. *International Journal of Obesity.* doi: 10.1038/ijo.2014.206

Dietz, W. H. (2004). Overweight in childhood and adolescence. *New England Journal of Medicine, 350,* 855-857.

Foley, L., & Maddison, R. (2010). Use of active video games to increase physical activity in children: A (virtual) reality? *Pediatric Exercise Science, 22,* 7-20.

Geary, D. C. (1998). *Male, female: The evolution of human sex differences.* Washington, DC: American Psychological Association.

Hopkins, M. E., Davis, F. C., VanTieghem, M., Whalen, P. J., & Bucci, D. J. (2012). Differential effects of acute and regular physical exercise on cognition and affect. *Neuroscience, 215,* 59-68.

Jolliffe, D. (2004). Extent of overweight among U.S. children and adolescents from 1971–2000. *International Journal of Obesity, 2,* 4-9.

Kautiannen, S., Rimpela, A., Vikat, A., & Virtanen, S. M. (2002). Secular trends in overweight and obesity among Finnish adolescents in 1997-1999. *Internal Journal of Obesity Related Metabolic Disorders, 26,* 544-552.

Kuzawa, C.W., Chuganin, H.T., Grossman, L.I., Lipovich,L., Muzik, O., Hof,P.R., & Wildman,D.E. (2014). Metabolic costs and evolutionary implications of human brain development. *PNAS.* doi: 10.1073/pnas.1323099111

Loyola University Health System (2011, May 2). Kids who specialize in one sport may have higher injury risk. *ScienceDaily.* Retrieved May 7, 2012, from http://www.sciencedaily.com/releases/2011/05/110502121741.htm

Luo, J. & Hu, F. M. (2002). Time trends of obesity in pre-school age children in China from 1989 to 1997. *Internal Journal of Obesity Related Metabolic Disorders, 26,* 533-538.

Rukmini, K. (2012) Hunger stunts Chad children, cripples society. *U-T San Diego.* Retrieved from http://www.utsandiego.com/news/2012/dec/15/lack-of-food-stunts-chad-children-damages-minds

Stiles, J. & Jernigan, T. L. (2010). The basics of brain development. *Neuropsychology Review, 20*, 327-348.

Tremblay, M. S., & Williams, J. D. (2001). Secular trends in the body mass index of Canadian children. *Canadian Medical Association Journal, 163*, 1429-1433.

University of Wisconsin-Madison (2012, June 6). Stress may delay brain development in early years. *ScienceDaily.* Retrieved June 10, 2012, from http://sciencedaily.com/releases/2012/06/120606164936.htm#.T8_zWW59xk.mailto

CHAPTER 8

Cognitive Development in Childhood

As mentioned in an earlier unit, cognition is a broad term related to mental activity, or thinking, decision-making, and memory. Unlike various forms of physical development (e.g., neurological development), cognition cannot be directly observed. Rather, an observer may infer cognitive development in the ways in which children progress and adapt to solving problems, making decisions, and employing memory. There are very consistent ways in which young children may differ from older children in terms of cognitive capabilities. In addition, there are legitimate ways in which all children seem to differ from adolescents and adults in terms of cognitive processes and capabilities. The cognitive development theorists presented in this chapter (i.e., Piaget and Vygotsky) have offered useful terms and frameworks for clarifying how and why these adaptations occur. It may be important to note that each of these theorists have unique terms and principles associated with their views on cognitive development. However, each assumes some degree of activity and interaction with the world, including people and objects, to facilitate cognition and development. Indeed, it seems particularly beneficial that children appear to have a predisposition to be curious, and seek out activity and interaction. Research has demonstrated that children's curiosity motivates learning, and the more curious they are about a particular topic, the more they activate the hippocampus regions associated with memory, retention of information and reward (Gruber, Gelman, & Ranganath, 2014). Together, curiosity seems to naturally spark learning and cognition.

Piaget's Conservation Task

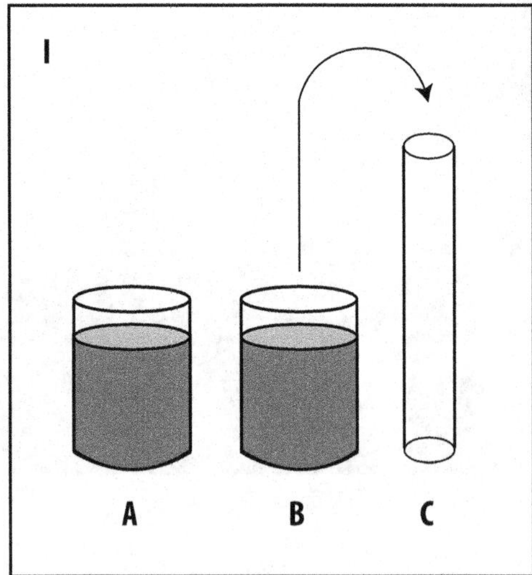

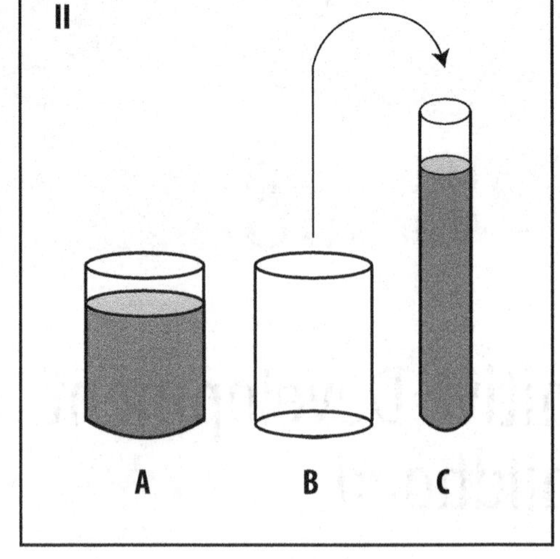

FIGURE 8.1 *Piaget's Conservation Task*

One of the primary ways to identify cognitive development is to observe how children of different ages approach and handle problems. The problems or dilemmas children encounter may be at home (with sibling), at school (with academic tasks), or with peers (with adopting and maintaining friendships or playing games). Theorists and researchers (such as Piaget and Vygotsky) may induce problems in laboratory settings as well to closely monitor how children solve problems. One of the class laboratory-induced problems is the "conservation" problem or task (see Figure 8.1).

In this particular task, a researcher comes into a room with three beakers, two of which are short and stout and full of equivalent amounts of liquid. The third beaker is taller and thinner, and does not contain any liquid. The researcher then takes one of the shorter beakers with liquid and pours all of the liquid contents into the tall thin beaker. Now, there is one short beaker and one tall beaker with liquid. The researcher asks the audience (or participants) which one of the beakers has the most liquid. The most telling piece to this particular task is that very young children are more inclined to state the taller beaker has more liquid in it. However, as children age and mature cognitively, they are less likely to claim the taller beaker does have more liquid. Indeed, by early adolescence, most would be surprised if there were still consistent errors made with this task. In other words, older children may be less susceptible to making decision-making errors as they have matured cognitively. It may be useful to ask yourself: At what age would children be significantly less likely to make this conservation error?

However, the mere observation of age-based differences in laboratory-induced problems does not clarify how and why such cognitive development occurs. That is where theory becomes useful.

Piaget

Piaget's (1950) theory was first covered in an infancy chapter, and related to the sensorimotor stage and the necessary formation of schema. During this stage, infants stumble into objects and experiences, and make sense of their physical reality. Their interactions require motor movement, and all movements promote the formation of schema, or an organized mental action. While schema is critically important in terms of cognitive development, they are not enough to permit advanced thinking. According to Piaget, other stages must be realized. More specifically, children must pass through preoperational and concrete operational stages. As the names of these stages imply, the term "operation" will be critically important to understanding this theory. An **operation** is an internalized *mental action* that is part of an organized structure. More simply put, an operation is mental action.

Following the sensorimotor stage, the **preoperational stage** may be evident from approximately ages 2 through 7. As the prefix "pre" implies, this stage is one that exists *before* proper operational thought exists. Piaget believed that the sensorimotor period led to internal images that children can label with words. Subsequently, this stage is marked by an explosion in language and use of **symbols**. Language, make believe play, and drawing are some important ways children demonstrate their advancement with the use of symbols. While language, play, and drawing are very salient activities, children are still very susceptible to errors in thought.

The preoperational stage is defined largely by what is missing (i.e., operational thought). In a sense, mental action cannot occur due to inherent limitations or cognitive obstructions. For instance, the inability to solve the conservation task may be understood via some limitations inhibiting mental action. One is that young children tend to be **centered**, implying they get "stuck" on striking features (e.g., tallness) of immediate objects. Imagine a child that holds firmly to the idea that a taller beaker must contain more liquid. In addition, children may not understand **reversibility,** in that what was done may be undone. In the conservation task, if a short beaker was poured into a taller beaker, then one could reverse the process and pour the contents of the taller beaker back into the shorter beaker, demonstrating that the contents of both were still equal. In the example above, centeredness and reversibility illustrate two obstructions that negatively impact a child's ability to "mentally act" or operate on problems to solve them logically. Indeed, operational thought may be used synonymously with **logical thought.** Piaget identified numerous limitations in the preoperational mind, including:

- **Identity Constancy**
  People maintain their personal integrity despite changes in external features (e.g., a scary mask turns a person into a monster).
- **Animism & Anthropomorphism**
  Giving life and human characteristics to inanimate objects.
- **Seriation**
  Related to ordering or grouping objects.
- **Artificialism**
  Humans make everything, including natural phenomenon.
- **Egocentrism**
  The inability to see another's point of view.

The latter limitation (egocentrism) is one of the most prevailing characteristics of cognition in childhood. One of the classic ways childhood egocentrism has been demonstrated is via the "three mountain problem." In this scenario, a child enters a room with a model consisting of three mountains, one larger mountain and two smaller mountains. The child is situated near the side with the two smaller mountains, and can clearly see some objects (e.g., houses) resting on the smaller mountains. Another person (or doll) is placed on the opposite side of the model adjacent to the taller mountain. From that angle, this person's (or doll's) vision of the smaller mountains is obstructed by the taller mountain. However, when you ask the preoperational child if the person or doll can see the objects on the smaller mountains, they invariably respond "yes." Such egocentrism may be evident in common settings as well. For instance, a child may ask another individual a question about what's on television as though they are in the same room, even though they are clearly not.

It is important to note that childhood forms of egocentrism are due to an inherent cognitive inability to see another point of view. The term *egocentrism* may be used to describe adolescents or adults, but is no longer linked with a cognitive inability. Rather, other factors fueling egocentric thought may be evident, as will be described in a unit on adolescence.

Together, while the preoperational stage is marked by advancements in symbolic and linguistic capa-bilities, there are numerous limitations. Most children in the preoperational phase would (by definition) not be able to solve the conservation task. However, children in the **concrete operational stage** may demonstrate higher order cognitive skills. Basically, whatever a child could not do before, they can during the concrete operational stage. To solve problems adequately, you have to "mentally act" upon them, rather than just reacting to immediate perceptions as in sensorimotor and preoperational stages. Older children are able to solve the classic conservation problem because they realize even though it appears different, it must logically be the same as long as no water is spilled. A key term is "concrete," implying what is tangible and observable. Children in this stage can mentally act upon concrete objects and situations (i.e., those they can see, feel, smell, hear, etc.). Thus, children in this stage can readily problem solve many day-to-day issues. Where they still encounter difficulty is generally thinking about that which is not concrete. Therefore, thinking that is hypothetical, abstract, retrospective, futuristic, or speculative is still difficult.

Vygotsky

Lev Semyonovich Vygotsky spent most of his academic and professional life in early twentieth century Moscow, investigating and analyzing literature, artistic creation, philosophy, and pedagogy. However, his greatest professional contribution was in the area of cognitive development. Prior to his death from tuberculosis at 38 years of age, Vygotsky had already developed what remains as one of the most influential theories in developmental psychology. Interestingly, the development of the theory may be understood in the context of Vygotsky's social and political environment (i.e., early twentieth century Russia). More specifically, Vygotsky was influenced in part by Marxist ideals. Briefly, Marxist ideology suggested that all societies were evolving toward a communistic society. To that end, Marx believed that the activities

in which people engage accounted for the "contents" of the mind (e.g., memory, attention). In other words, Marxist philosophy posited that social existence determines consciousness. There were apparent differences in the psychological make-up of different social classes. Moreover, Marx also believed that societies develop though "dialectic exchanges." These exchanges allow individuals within society to identify problems, formulate solutions, and act upon them. To illustrate, during Vygotsky's adult life in Russia, capitalism was viewed as the problem, and dialectic exchange eventually offered communism as a solution. According to Marxist ideology, these dialectic exchanges were essential for societal movement and development. Thus, the communistic movement was based upon the ideas that action influences cognition and dialogue encourages growth. Subsequently, Vygotsky applied these ideas to child cognitive development. He also advocated for the impact that play had upon cognitive development.

Play was viewed as a critical vehicle for cognitive development. Play-based activities offered children a world independent of the real world that was driven by authority figures such as parents, teachers, and caretakers. A primary benefit of play is that imaginary situations may be created that permit the child to act out in ways not possible in the real world. The fantastic nature of play allowed otherwise unrealistic goals and desires to be met. In this way, the child may behave in ways beyond his or her age. One may envision a child riding a big-wheel bicycle all the while pretending to be driving a car. A second benefit of play is that most play—whether solitary or group play—contain rules that must be followed. Even basic imaginative play scenes adhere to social rules. For example, a child that is pretending to be a professional dancer will adhere to the social rules often prescribed to that profession. The child must dress, speak, and act accordingly. According to Vygotksy, no form of play was without rules. Together, play was viewed as a means to nurture higher-order thinking in children. In more recent years, research has demonstrated that play may enhance memory, cognitive skills, social functioning, language abilities, and reasoning.

According to Vygotsky (1962), children construct the contents of their minds through social interaction. The content of a mind may consist of a variety of mental structures and images that underlie cognitive processes. Three core beliefs guided his theory of cognitive development:

- activity generates thinking,
- development requires the use of "dialectic exchanges, and
- development is a sociocultural process.

In general, environments with rich activities would promote cognitive development. Furthermore, Vygotsky gave emphasis to the importance of language and guidance by superiors (i.e., the zone of proximal development). Simply put, two children may have a similar biological make-up. However, the childhood activities of one are laden with opportunities for play, social interaction, problem solving, and rich cultural experiences. The other child may lead a less active lifestyle that is marked by little activity and social involvement. According to Vygotsky, the latter of these children may be less advanced cognitively and possess fewer psychological tools as a result of fewer opportunities to think in a social context. Most important, it appears as though many elements of the theory may be understood in the context of childhood play. The following sections will juxtapose childhood play to the three core beliefs of Vygotsky's theory, as well as highlight the relevance of language and the zone of proximal development.

At the center of Vygotsky's theory is the idea that activity generates thinking, which presumes that children must engage with stimuli in the environment in order to initiate thought. Activity in the broadest sense includes all familial, academic, physical, and social tasks that children typically encounter. Play represents a significant type of activity found in childhood, and would require very basic thinking processes. According to this idea, children are active agents in their own development. To illustrate, a child that desires to climb a tree will be forced to think to some degree about the intended action. For instance: Where will the climb begin? Does the tree appear sturdy enough? If not, how will the weak areas be traversed? Has anyone climbed the tree successfully before? How far can the climb continue up the tree? Is there adequate landing in the event of a fall? Although children—especially younger children—would not necessarily map out a complete tree-climbing plan, the task itself may require some degree of thinking. For example, a group of children that are playing a game of American football would have to employ several psychological mechanisms in order to play successfully, including: a) recall of game rules, b) game strategy, c) knowledge of their respective role and position on the team, d) who their teammates are, and e) the ongoing score. According to Vygotsky, such activity would enhance cognitive development by requiring children to utilize basic and necessary psychological skills.

As children engaged in activities, they may run into situations or problems that they couldn't readily solve. Subsequently, the child has to synthesize the conflict. More specifically, some forms of play will necessitate that the players identify and resolve problems via "dialectic exchanges." However, these dialectic exchanges do not necessarily need to be interpersonal verbal exchanges between children, but rather may be intrapersonal mental exchanges within the mind of each child. Problems that arise in play need to be identified and solved. Vygotsky employed some interesting research paradigms throughout his research career, many of which required children to play games that required problem solving. One such paradigm required children to play a "forbidden colors" game. Children were asked a series of questions, and the answer to several of these questions was a particular color. However, children were forbidden to use certain color terms (e.g., blue and yellow) in their game play. Children were also not allowed to use one color response more than once. Lastly, they were also informed that in order to win the game they must refrain from using these color terms. The researchers gave the children colored cards to use during game play in any way that they thought necessary. Vygotsky reported that younger children did not use the colored cards effectively—if at all—during game play. However, older children used the cards in several different ways. They used the cards to eliminate colors, remind themselves of previous answers, or to arrange potential correct responses. Vygotsky argued that older children used these cards as "tools" in their game play. These tangible tools are akin to cognitive tools (e.g., recall strategies, logical thought) that children may develop and use during other forms of play.

Perhaps Vygotsky's most well-known line of research involved the use of blocks. According to this paradigm, the researcher would place a collection of blocks of different sizes, shapes, and colors in front of a child. The researcher would then turn over one of the blocks to reveal a nonsensical word (e.g., "mur") written on the underside of the block. The child was then asked to select all of the other blocks that would likely have the same word written on it. Thus, the child was being asked to categorize the blocks in some systematic way. After each series of selections, the researcher would turn over a block that had not been selected, thereby informing the child to the "correctness" of their decision. Vygotsky was primarily interested in the ways in which children grouped the blocks together. The experiments revealed that younger children did not use any real type of systematic method to organize blocks, but rather clumped them into "unorganized heaps." Children that were somewhat older would "think in complexes" by using some form of objective criterion to classify blocks (e.g., color, size, or shape). The oldest children would demonstrate more adult-like capacities for thinking and were able to conceptualize correct block categories. Vygotsky argued that these research methods corroborated his notion that activity generates thinking and psychological tools are created and used to accomplish tasks.

Lastly, Vygotsky argued that cognitive development is also a sociocultural process. His theory presumes that thinking and learning shifts from the intrapersonal domains to interpersonal domains evident in cultural and ethnic groups. In this way, thinking becomes a social experience and most mental processes had social origins. Different cultural groups and regions maintain distinct patterns of thinking that tend to be transmitted inter-generationally. Along these lines, Vygotsky and his colleagues examined categorization schemes—similar to his block studies—in literate and non-literate populations. Vygotsky reasoned that non-literate individuals would have less advanced categorization capabilities than literate individuals. The literacy variable was thought to reflect one way in which cultures may differ cognitively. More recent research has demonstrated that cultural groups may also differ according to parental involvement, language usage, memory capacity, and so on. Similarly, the rules and expectations of play are well defined within each culture. Much like each game has its unique set of rules, strategies, expectations, and nuance, each particular culture has its own unique play-based activities. In sum, each culture may promote a unique set of psychological tools.

Vygotsky thought that cognitive development was influenced by certain "semiotic mechanisms." The semiotic nature of these mechanisms required the usage of symbols and mental image. These mechanisms were essential features that must be in place for development to occur. Most notably, language was thought to transform cognitive development. Words and the mental images that accompany them were considered an essential element for this cognitive growth to occur. This transformation may be viewed much the same way as mastery of a particular motor skill, such as walking transforms the nature of human physical activity. Once a child gains the strength, coordination, and confidence to walk, he or she is more readily able to move in fluid and adult-like ways. Furthermore, they are able to move faster and farther than crawling permitted. Similarly, once language is mastered, cognition will be redefined for a child. Vygotsky argued that the symbolic features of language enhanced cognitive capabilities greatly. To illustrate, when a young child is being introduced to American football, they are likely recognizing a ball and playing field and learning how to throw and catch a ball. When the child has an understanding of football vernacular, the learning of the game will augment greatly. In other words, when learning and playing a game of American football, children will likely need to communicate and use terms related to the game itself (e.g., touchdown, extra point, hand-off, receiver, offense, defense, kick-off, etc.). There is a symbolic component to each of these terms, and players should generate a mental image of each of them. After having attached a mental image to these relevant terms, they will be able to think about the game in more advanced ways. For instance, they may demonstrate the ability to think retrospectively, futuristically, and hypothetically about the game. Children will be able to reminisce about past games and describe in detail what occurred. They may describe play tactics and design other games. Children may envision how the activity may be altered to be more enjoyable. Therefore, after the basic mastery of language, children are capable of more adult-oriented, higher-order thought processes. Subsequently, the quality of their play has been enhanced.

Perhaps Vygotsky's most prominent idea focused on the differentiation between actual development and potential development. The **zone of proximal development (ZPD)** describes the distance between what a child can do alone versus what he or she can do with some assistance from an expert or a superior. A child's actual developmental level is recognized by the level of mental functioning that they currently maintain. A child's actual developmental level allows them to independently accomplish tasks. However, potential developmental level may be higher, and is related to the tasks that may be accomplished through guidance or collaboration with adults or peers. Thus, ZPD describes the gap between these two developmental levels. Moreover, ZPD captures mental tools, strategies, and processes that have not yet fully matured. The implications for childhood play are clear as games may have informal mentoring and imitative qualities to them. When observing a group of children at play, it is apparent that some are active participants in the games and some—frequently younger children—are observing and reproducing action. For example, a young child may not readily be able to play a game of tee-ball, but with assistance from an older sibling is able to make contact with the ball, run the bases in an appropriate way, and stay in the proper area while in the field. In this way, the child is able to engage in an activity and work with certain cognitive skills that otherwise would not be enabled. Together, a child's actual developmental level is not viewed completely by how a child can play independently, but rather also by how they are able to observe and imitate others.

In sum, Vygotsky's theory of cognitive development has proved very useful in clarifying how children learn. According to the theory, the interaction between the child and the environment is critical to the growth of mental processes. Most notably, the theory highlights the importance of: a) activity (including play), b) dialectic exchange (i.e., problem resolution), c) sociocultural context, d) language, and e) the zone of proximal development. Taken together, children develop psychological tools and strategies (e.g., language, counting, mnemonic devices, algebraic formulas, writing, art, schemes, diagrams, mapping, symbols, etc.) that enhance their cognitive capabilities and potential. In this way, children's learning begins long before they actually enter school. Vygotsky argued that long before studying specific topics in school (e.g., arithmetic), children have had experience with the content (e.g., operations of division, additions, subtraction, and determination of size). Thus, childhood play would appear to be a critical component to the eventual intellectual and academic achievement of children. Childhood play offers opportunities for children to temporarily depart the real world that is governed by adults and engage in thoughts and actions that are beyond his or her years. Childhood play offers children exposure to social rules and expectations outside of the familial setting. Furthermore, play will likely offer children the occasion to resolve conflicts, employ language and symbolic thought, and be mentored by older children. In such ways, cognition may be nurtured through play.

Key Terms

- **Operation** – central to Piaget's theory, this term refers to an internalized mental action that is part of an organized structure
- **Preoperational Stage** – following sensorimotor, this stage may be evident from approximately ages 2 through 7, and one that exists *before* proper operational thought exists
- **Symbols** – becoming more evident in the preoperational state, language, make believe play, and drawing are all examples of symbols and symbol use
- **Logical Thought** – perhaps akin to operational thought, the ability to think rationally and readily solve problems
- **Centered** – children may get "stuck" on striking features (e.g., tallness) of immediate objects
- **Reversibility** – what was done may be undone
- **Identity Constancy** – scary mask turns a person into a monster
- **Animism & Anthropomorphism** – giving life and human characteristics to inanimate objects
- **Seriation** – related to ordering or grouping objects
- **Artificialism** – the idea humans make everything, including natural phenomenon

- **Egocentrism** – the inability to see another's point of view
- **Concrete Operational Stage** – characterized by the ability to "mentally act" upon the concrete and tangible object and situations
- **Zone of Proximal Development (ZPD)** – perhaps Vygotsky's most famous notion, this term refers to the distance between what a child can do alone versus what he or she can do with some assistance from an expert or mentor

Critical Thinking Questions

1. Compare and contrast Piaget's and Vygotsky's theories. How are they similar? How are they different? In constructing a response, be sure to incorporate relevant terms and concepts for each theory.
2. Discuss the role that play has in cognitive development. That is, how might play (or lack thereof) promote (or inhibit) cognitive development? Use examples to support your points.

References

Berk, L. E., & Winsler, A. (2002). *Scaffolding children's learning: Vygotksy and early education.* Washington, DC: National Association for the Education of Young Children (NAEYC).

Berk, L. E. (1994). Research in review. Vygotsky's theory: The importance of make-believe play. *Young Children, 50*, 30-39.

Gruber, M.J., Gelman, B.D., & Ranganath, C. (2014). States of curiosity modulate hippocampus-dependent learning via the dopaminergic circuit. Neuron. doi: 10.106/.neuron.2014.08.060

Piaget, J. (1950). *The psychology of intelligence.* Oxford, England: Harcourt.

Rogers, C. S., & Sawyers, J. K. (1988). *Play in the lives of children.* Washington, DC: National Association for the Education of Young Children (NAEYC).

Vygotsky, L. S. (1962). *Thought and language.* (E. Haufman & G. Vakar, Eds. and Trans.). New York: MIT Press and Wily (Original work published 1934).

Werstch, J. V. (1985). *Vygotsky and the social formation of the mind.* Cambridge, MA: Harvard University Press.

CHAPTER 9

Socioemotional Development in Childhood

Erikson

Moving past stages more characteristic of infancy, during childhood Erikson proposed stages of initiative versus guilt and industry versus inferiority. The basic task during the **initiative versus guilt** stage, which largely comprises the preschool years, is to achieve competence and initiative. If children are given freedom to select personally meaningful activities, they tend to develop a positive view of self and follow through with projects. If they are not allowed to make their own selection, they tend to develop guilt over not taking initiative. Thereafter, they may refrain from taking an active role and allow others to choose for them. A critical element to this stage and the one that follows is the development of a sense of competence in day-to-day tasks.

Thereafter, during the elementary school years, and during a proposed **industry versus inferiority** stage, the child needs to expand his or her understanding of the world, and learn basic skills required for school success. Erikson (1997) asserted during this stage a child's "radius of significant relations" includes the school and neighborhood. The basic task of industry relates to setting and attaining personal goals, and failure to do so results in a sense of inadequacy. This stage is marked by an expanding worldview. The child begins to understand him- or herself in broader social contexts. Indeed, a sense of "inferiority" would not be possible without recognizing that others were perhaps more competent in certain areas.

Together, the psychosocial tasks linked with childhood are thought to drive children toward

pro-social behavior

developing competence and expanding their worldviews. More simply put, these stages imply children may move toward becoming more autonomous and independent individuals; confident in their attempts to try new things and solve problems. On the other hand, children may also develop a sense of dependence (upon parent, sibling, or teachers) or lack of competence in relation to their peers, which would result in a more negative sense of self. The theoretical stance that children grapple with their own sense of competence, and concurrently are expanding their knowledge of self in social contexts has relevance for many cognitive, social, and emotional variables, including self-esteem.

Self-Esteem

The construct of **self-esteem** is an affective sense of generally feeling good or bad about one's level of competence. Moreover, self-esteem is derived from evaluating oneself in relation to others. A child assesses his or her own level of competence in relation to their peers. That is, how would a child know if they are competent in a certain area unless they know what incompetence in that same area looks like? During childhood, self-esteem may become increasingly differentiated. Harter (1999) posited there are five general forms of self-esteem, including scholastic, behavioral conduct, athletic, physical appearance, and peer likeability. **Scholastic** (or academic) self-esteem arises when a student generates positive feelings about themselves in terms of academics. It is likely this sphere of self-esteem may be further differentiated into sub-domains. A student may have high self-esteem in mathematics or science, but not necessarily both. High self-esteem in **behavioral conduct** may be linked with a perceived level of competence in adopting and maintaining roles and behavioral expectations in social contexts. A child with low self-esteem in this area may avoid new social situations, fearing they will not act appropriately and be humiliated. **Athletic** self-esteem is related to athletic skills and sport. A child with high self-esteem is confident in his or her ability to learn and play games, and compete against others in athletic competitions. If in fact these individuals are skilled athletes, their self-esteem likely is reinforced from parents, coaches, physical education teachers, and being one of the first individuals picked for teams. While athletic self-esteem is more linked with motor skills and performance, **physical appearance** self-esteem is associated with how a child views their own outward appearances. This may include physical features such as body shape and size, but also modes of dress. Many children appear to have an acute sense of style, and base their self-esteem on how they present an outward appearance in relation to others. Lastly, **peer likeability** self-esteem is derived from a general sense of how well a child feels they are liked by their peers. A child with a high self-esteem in this area may be more likely to approach new children and befriend them, confident in their abilities to adopt and maintain friendships. A child with low self-esteem in this area may withdraw from others, doubting they will be liked.

Together, there may be numerous opportunities to build self-esteem. A child may have high self-esteem in one or two areas, but moderate or low self-esteem in others. As some of the examples above suggested, children with high self-esteem in a certain area may be more likely to approach novel tasks and situations or new people, as they are more confident in their abilities to successfully navigate the task or situation. On the other hand, children with low self-esteem may be less likely to put forth effort toward tasks where they predict failure. This scenario illustrates a **cycle of self-esteem.**

For instance, children who are low in scholastic self-esteem may expect to do poorly on a test. This expectation produces high anxiety and may lead them to reduce the amount of effort they apply to studying because they expect to do poorly anyway. Ultimately, the reduction in expectation and effort may indeed result in poor performance on the test. In this way, their poor self-esteem is maintained.

Contrarily, a student with high scholastic self-esteem is more inclined to study diligently and effectively. Subsequently, they do realize solid test performance, and their success reinforces their high self-esteem. Teachers and parents may need to customize tasks or outcome criteria so children that have low self-esteem can realize some degree of success.

In sum, self-esteem is an affective sense of feeling good or bad (i.e., competent or incompetent) in different areas. It is derived in part from self-evaluation and social comparison and represents an important form of socioemotional development.

Emotional Regulation

Socioemotional development in childhood is marked not only by the experience of various emotions, but also the ability to regulate them. **Emotional regulation** is the ability to manage ones' emotional state (Bridges, Denham, & Ganihan, 2004). It is important to note that all emotions may require some level of regulation. At a broad level, emotions may have a *positive* or *negative valence.* Emotions with a negative valence include anger, frustration, anxiety, depressive symptoms, or grief. On the other hand, emotions with a positive valence may include excitement, exhilaration, happiness, and joy. It may seem intuitive why negative emotions should be regulated. One may envision an upset child being able to calm himself down, or a particularly anxious child managing his or her nervousness in the classroom. However, positive emotions require regulation as well. Ideally, children will be able to temper their excitement if it's not befitting a certain context (e.g., the classroom, church, etc.).

Neurologically speaking, emotional regulation capabilities are associated with the frontal lobe, the area of the brain that demonstrates relatively slow, but vital growth in childhood. The frontal lobe gets "exercised" when a child attempts to regulate his or her emotions. In addition, emotional regulation may be temperamental in nature. A child with an easy temperament may be characterized by more managed emotions and less intense protest and reactivity when something occurs. For instance, a child with an easy temperament may be able to calm themselves down to fall asleep at night, or back to sleep should they wake up in the middle of the night. An infant or child with a difficult temperament may need assistance in calming down, by being talked to or rocked. Thus, some children may be more naturally prone to regulate their emotions. However, children may experience emotional regulation difficulties.

When emotions go unregulated, they tend to be externalized or internalized. **Externalizing** emotions is evident in those that act impulsively upon present emotional states. Emotions such as anger, anxiety, sadness, or joy may be expressed overtly, and displayed as acting out, aggression, disruptive behavior. An old adage that may be akin to externalizing behaviors is that these individuals "wear their emotions on their sleeve." What they are feeling is evident to others around them. When emotions are unregulated and externalized, they can interfere and disrupt familial and academic settings. On the other hand, **internalizing** emotions is not an overt process, but rather children deal with emotions by "tucking them away." Particularly with negative emotions, it may be important to share and process them with others in appropriate contexts. Children that internalize emotions do not, and the unregulated emotions may lead them to withdraw from others and exacerbate negative feelings of anxiety or depressive symptoms. Unlike children that externalize emotions, children that internalize them are not necessarily disruptive in familial and academic settings. In fact, they may be labeled as "quiet" or "shy." In any case, children with emotional regulation difficulties may require help in developing emotion regulation skills. Many schools or non-profit agencies may have programs devoted to helping children with emotional or behavioral problems that interfere with their natural social and academic development. These programs may include teachers, therapists, and social workers, who together work with the child to identify emotions, what stimuli may trigger the emotions, and offer practical solutions in regulating them.

Interestingly, children that have externalizing tendencies may maintain a higher than expected self-esteem. Subsequently, one of the difficulties with getting them to change behavior is they think they're okay and others may have the problem. Children with internalizing tendencies may have a lower than expected self-esteem. These children may be very self-critical, and think they're helpless to change.

Prosocial Behavior

As children move away from the egocentric confines of preoperational periods, they may adopt perspective-taking capabilities; meaning they can now understand those around them may have different views and emotions. Evidence of this may be in feelings of empathy and sympathy. **Empathy** is the ability to feel what another person is feeling, or being able to "put yourself in another person's shoes." Empathy may be related to positive and negative emotions. A child may empathize with the excitement a peer feels after receiving an award. A child may also empathize with the frustration a peer may feel with a difficult task. **Sympathy** is a bit narrower in definition, and restricted to more negative emotions. A child may sympathize—or feel sorry for—a peer who is experiencing difficulty at home or school. Sympathy does not imply one child can precisely relate to the same emotions their peer is experiencing, but rather feels bad they are going through it.

Perspective taking capabilities may drive children to engage in **pro-social behavior**, which is related to caring about others and acting upon that by helping where necessary. The most genuine form of pro-social behavior is **altruism**, which is complete selfless behavior aimed at helping someone in need (Eisenberg, 2003). A simple example may differentiate altruism from other pro-social

behaviors. A child may note his or her parents have been particularly busy and stressed of late, and take it upon themselves to help out with some chores around the house, knowing that it will alleviate some stress for the parents. Similarly, another child may help out with chores around the house, perhaps in part to help others, but with an underlying motivation to do so because there will be extra allowance money in it for them. The former example better illustrates the completely selfless nature that characterizes altruism. Some research has demonstrated that having a sibling - perhaps particularly for young males - may make them more self-less and pro-social behaviorally. While females generally appear to benefit more from social relationships (including peers and parents or caretakers), positive sibling interactions may equally benefit males, promoting altruism. The researchers state positive relationships with siblings are very important and may yield long-term effects. However, the researchers warn parents and caretakers it's not enough to just break up fights between siblings, they need to get through conflict and have positive interactions (Harper, Padilla-Walker, & Jensen, 2014).

Aggression

While positive and pro-social behaviors are evident in childhood, there are also antisocial behaviors that emerge. Most notably, aggression is viewed as a negative and problematic form of behavior in childhood. It is notable the amount of exposure children may have to such aggressive behaviors in school contexts. Indeed, in a recent study, it was reported that in the last year, 6% of U.S. children missed a day of school after having been a victim of aggressive or violent actions. Moreover, 14% had experienced some type of physical assault and 48% had been exposed to at least one form of victimization, most of which (about 30%) was bullying. The negative impact upon psychosocial state and academic performance (e.g., missed classes) is clear (Finklehor, Vanderminden, Turner, Shattuck, & Hamby, 2014). Undesirable aggressive behavior may also be driven by emotions. For instance, the **frustration-aggression hypothesis** posits that most aggressive acts are prompted by feelings of dissatisfaction, annoyance, and frustration.

Aggression may be clarified by the motives that underlie it. In a basic form, **instrumental aggression** is related to harmful actions that occur as a result of a pursuit of a goal. A child may hit another child to get a favorite toy in daycare. In this example, the goal was to obtain the toy, and a physically aggressive act was used as the means or "instrument" to achieve the goal. Instrumentally aggressive acts may not exist as isolated cases, however. Once a child is aggressed against, they may be in the position to retaliate. Reactive aggression is related to antagonistic acts that are done in response to an original aggressive act. From the earlier example, once the child was hit and the toy taken away, the child may react by hitting the first child back. These examples involve direct physical acts of aggression. However, aggressive acts may also be indirect, and non-physical in nature. **Relational aggression** is associated with acts designed to hurt a person's social relationships (Merrell, Buchanan, & Tran, 2006). Children that engage in relationship aggression may try to sabotage friendships another child has,

by spreading rumors or gossiping, or deliberately excluding an individual from social events such as birthday parties. While physical contact does not occur, there is still intent to harm another. For many years, it was widely assumed that if females were aggressive, they were aggressive via relational methods, whereas males were more likely to aggress in physical ways. However, this gender difference is less clear in recent years. Females appear to be equally likely to engage in physical aggression. This may be observed in the dramatic increases in rates of domestic violence involving females, and the number of young female athletes participating in traditionally "male" sports, such as American football, ice hockey, or wrestling (Garbarino, 2007).

Bullying and Popularity

An aggressive act that is repeated, and involves a "disparity of power between victim and perpetrator" is known as **bullying** (Wang, Iannotti, & Nansel, 2009). An important consideration in the definition of bullying is the notion of a "disparity of power." Social disparity may be viewed according to **popularity** statuses, which emerge during childhood. Popularity is related to peer-likeability and salience. That is, in determining popularity, two important questions must be answered: Are peers aware of a student *and* are they liked?

Popularity in social contexts has typically been done via **sociometric procedures**, that allow researchers to assess which children are actively liked, disliked, or neither. A sociometric procedure to assess popularity is relatively straightforward. In a classroom, all students could be issued a peer nomination form in which they name the one (or more) peers they like the most, and also the peer(s) they dislike the most. These forms may be collected from all children and the researcher can form a popularity map. Children that are consistently rated as being liked, and rarely (if ever) rated as being disliked are characteristically **popular** children. Moreover, **controversial** children are those that are frequently nominated as both liked and disliked. Controversial children appear to have a polarizing effect on their peers. Peers are well aware of their presence, in positive or negative ways. Popular and controversial are both well liked, however, and may both be considered a high popularity status. On the other hand, children that are consistently disliked are referred to as **rejected** children. For these children, peers are aware of them, but due to general dislike peers that do not appear on any nomination forms may be termed **neglected.** These children are not "on the radar" of their peers. Rejected and neglected children would be considered a low popularity status. Somewhere in between high and low popularity statuses lay **average** children. As the term implies, most children likely fall into this category. From a sociometric perspective, these children are nominated as liked several times, and even disliked on occasion. They are not as consistently salient or liked as high status children are, but also not as actively disliked or neglected as low popularity status suggests. In relation to bullying, children of low popularity status (i.e., rejected and neglected) tend to be the victims of bullies, perhaps because it is less likely these children will have peers

rush to their aid. Various forms of bullying will be revisited in the unit on socioemotional development in adolescence.

Bullying may take on many forms, consistent with the forms of aggression. Bullying may be physical, verbal, or relational (Wang et al., 2009). Physical and verbal forms are considered *direct* bullying behaviors, while relational bullying is considered *indirect*. In addition, a fourth form of bullying has emerged in recent years: **cyberbullying**. This type of bullying would also be indirect and can be defined as aggression through personal computers (e.g., email, instant messaging, social network sites) and cellular phones (e.g., text messaging). Its emergence in recent years is understandable when juxtaposed to the rise in popularity of online social networking (e.g., Facebook, Twitter, etc.) and personal cell phone use.

Bullying behaviors tend to peak in late childhood (i.e., middle school) and decrease thereafter into adolescence. Males are more likely than females to bully others, although when females do bully others they are more likely than males to engage in relational bullying, whereas males are more likely to engage in direct physical or verbal bullying (Wang et al., 2009). Wang et al. (2009) assessed the prevalence of various forms of bullying in middle and high school, reporting a high prevalence of bullying. In their sample, many students reported having bullied or having been bullied in the last two months, including 21% physically, 54% verbally, 51% relationally, and 14% electronically or cyberbullying.

Friendship plays a role in bullying behavior. First, individuals are more likely to bully others when they have friends. It may seem counterintuitive that a bully has friends; many may envision a bully as being a loner or outcast. However, bullies may derive some motivation to bully from the groups to which they belong. Bullies may feel some degree of peer pressure to continue bullying, if they perceive they are expected to do so. Bullies may even be described as popular, but seeing other classmates as being a threat to their friendship or popularity, may bully them to assert their social position. In addition, individuals are less likely to be bullied when they have friends. This seems a bit more intuitive; you are less likely to be bullied if you have friends that will come to your aid. Therefore, friends appear to not only support bullying behaviors, but also may protect against it on the other end. This friendship factor may be particularly true with direct forms of bullying (i.e., physical and verbal). However, the friendship factor does not appear to hold true as consistently in the case of cyberbullying. Specifically, people appear to bully (or be bullied) regardless of how popular they may be or how many friends they may noticeably have. Thus, while some researchers originally described cyberbullying as a "new bottle with old wine," this may not necessarily be the case (Li, 2007). Given the trends in computer and cell phone use with children, this form of bullying is likely to receive much more attention.

Play

Play is perhaps a more positive feature of childhood. Infants play in and around each other, and even with the same toys, but may not acknowledge one another nor engage in cooperative play, as may be viewed in the following image. In infancy, parents and other adults need to maintain a more active role in play experiences. However, in middle and late childhood, individuals are capable of their own play. In addition to the natural enjoyment that children seem to derive from play, it also facilitates vital growth in all areas of development. For instance, regular play would appear to facilitate gross and fine motor skill development, as well as balance and coordination. Play was interwoven into the unit on cognitive development in childhood, particularly how play may be an important factor in Vygotskian perspectives of cognitive development. In addition, play may be important because it facilitates the use of symbols (i.e., symbolic play) and helps develop peer relations.

Symbolic play may require mental representations in the form of symbols and images. Moreover, a

Courtesy of the author

child's symbolic play capabilities may be indicative of overall cognitive development (Piaget, 1962). Symbolic play involves pretending and requires imagination. Importantly, a child may engage in symbolic play by themselves or with others (e.g., peers, siblings, parents). Solitary symbolic play may be viewed as a child by themselves pretending to cook at a toy stove. On the other hand, cooperative symbolic play may be apparent when the child is not only pretending to cook at the stove, but also share with their playmates what they prepare. It is evident that a child's mother elicits particularly high levels of symbolic play (Bjorklund, 2000). In any case, the notion of symbolic play in social contexts has relevance for the process of **guided participation** (Rogoff, Mistry, Göncü, & Mosier, 1993). Guided participation may be viewed as an extension of Vygotsky's zone of proximal development, and is the "process and system of involvement of individuals with others, as they communicate and engage in shared activities" (Rogoff et al., 1993, p. 6). Guided participation may occur on an explicit level, as in messages that an adult gives to a child during their interactions. It may also occur on an implicit level, where the child may observe and process day-to-day behaviors and reactions of the adult(s) in their environments. Rogoff et al. (1993) viewed guided participation as an "apprenticeship of thinking" whereby children may vastly improve their cognitive and social skills and capabilities via interacting in meaningful ways with others. Together, cooperative symbolic and guided participation may serve to **socialize** children by making them aware of useful ways to think and act in society, but also gives them an opportunity to "act like adults" during imaginative play sessions.

In addition, play helps develop peer relations. A **peer** is someone who is about the same age and level of maturity. Thus, peers are encountered in a child's classroom and friendships as well. The trend in daycare has also increased the amount of peer exposure that young children receive. The ways in which children interact and play with their peers changes through the course of childhood.

Young children (e.g., toddlers) may demonstrate some level of difficulty in play with others. Relatively minor distractions (e.g., a loud noise) or a miscue (e.g., a toddler falls) can interrupt play between two young children. It has been consistently shown that toddlers are able to play more effectively with children with whom they are familiar (National Research Council, 2000). Together, parents and caretakers may need to go to some lengths to arrange a successful play session with two (or more) toddlers. The parents may have to introduce the toddlers to each other on multiples occasions, allowing them to become somewhat familiar with each other. Thereafter, the parents or caretakers may need to carefully monitor and structure the play sessions, attempting to avert the distractions and miscues that typically prevent extended play. Even when toddlers play, they are not necessarily engaged in **collaborative play** as older children may. They are still relatively egocentric in thought and actions, and while on the surface it may appear they are playing with another child, they may well be playing independently, but in proximity, to another child. Play in early childhood is marked by high amounts of conflict and even aggression (National Research Council, 2000).

As children mature, their capability to engage in prolonged and mutually agreeable play tends to increase. Play among older children involves enhanced use of symbols (as mentioned above) and pretense. Together, children are capable of pretending, and do not necessarily require toys, objects, or props to facilitate their play. Prolonged play in larger groups is more possible. Interestingly, **temperament** and **attachment** have been linked with friendships and play in childhood. More specifically, children demonstrating inhibition and anxiety, which may be evident in insecure forms of attachment and difficult temperaments, may have more difficulty adopting and maintaining peer relations. On the other hand, a secure attachment has been linked with relatively smooth transitions into harmonious and positive peer relationships (National Research Council, 2000). Thus, familial factors are linked with social and emotional development.

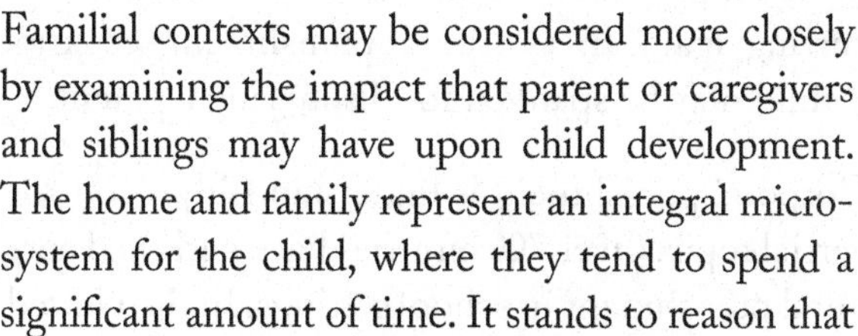

Family

Familial contexts may be considered more closely by examining the impact that parent or caregivers and siblings may have upon child development. The home and family represent an integral microsystem for the child, where they tend to spend a significant amount of time. It stands to reason that family members may exert considerable influence upon development. For instance, one may contemplate parenting style by considering the relative levels of some important variables. More specifically, a certain degree of **demandingness** may be evident in some parents. Such parents often have clear rules, boundaries, and expectations for their children, and when rules are broken or expectations are not met, there are well-defined and often immediate consequences (e.g., punishment). On the other hand, parents may also be marked by **responsiveness**. This style is linked with emotional warmth and a high degree of involvement in the child's life. Both of these variables (i.e., demandingness and responsiveness) exist on a continuum, and parents may exhibit varying levels of each of them. It should be noted that these two dimensions are both conceivably beneficial for children. Children may thrive on some degree of structure and consistency brought about by a demanding parent. Assuming the rules and enforcement strategies are not outlandish, such an environment prevents a chaotic atmosphere. In addition, parental responsiveness is viewed as a positive and protective factor in many areas of child development. For instance, as was reviewed in a previous unit, responsiveness may foster a secure attachment. By considering these dimensions together, four general parenting styles emerge (see Figure 9.1).

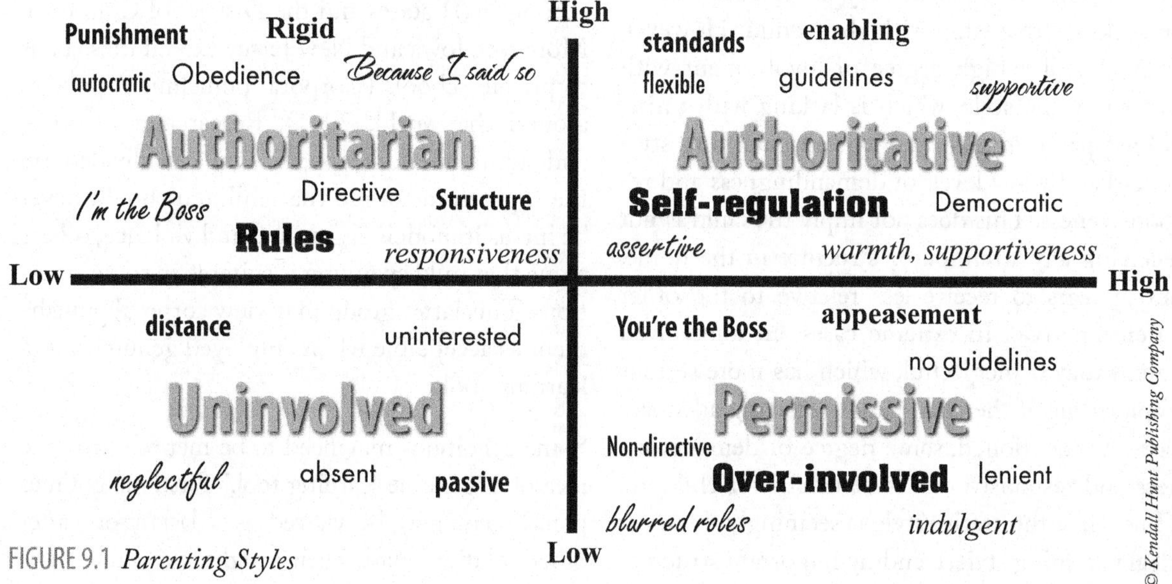

FIGURE 9.1 *Parenting Styles*

An **authoritarian** parenting style is discernible in high levels of demandingness in the form of structure, rules, and rule enforcement. However, there are relatively low levels of responsiveness in these parents. An authoritarian parent may have a "my way or the highway" attitude, and is more autocratic in nature. These parents are more likely to enforce rules and punish children, and less likely to follow up with any form of emotional warmth afterwards. If an authoritarian parent is more autocratic in nature, then an **authoritative** parent is more democratic in nature. Although the two parenting styles offered thus far, sound similar, there is an important difference. As may be viewed in Figure 9.1, an authoritative style combines high levels of demandingness and similarly high levels of responsiveness. Thus, authoritative parents are also likely to enforce rules with their children, but also exhibit emotional warmth at other times. With each of these parenting styles (i.e., authoritarian and authoritative) there are clear roles of parent and child in the house.

The remaining parenting styles lack the more demanding aspect of parenting. For instance, a **permissive** parent does not clearly create and enforce rules, but does display relatively high levels of emotional warmth. Sometimes referred to as "indulgent," there are less clear parental and child roles established with this parenting style. In fact, a permissive parent may at times appear to be seeking friendship with their child. However, there is still a high degree of involvement with this parenting style, which is lacking with **uninvolved** parenting. An uninvolved parenting style is marked by low levels of demandingness and responsiveness. This does not imply the child is not receiving any attention or structure in the home, but appears to receive less relative to the other parenting style. In extreme cases, an uninvolved parent may be neglectful, which has more serious implications if the child is not receiving adequate care. As mentioned, some degree of demandingness and responsiveness is beneficial for children. Thus, an authoritative style is seemingly the most ideal parenting style, blending important structural and socioemotional features. It should be noted that these styles may be employed to describe an individual parent, or a general climate that exists within a household. For example, a family may be comprised of an authoritarian father and a permissive mother, whose parenting styles converge to give the household an authoritative climate for the children.

Corporal Punishment

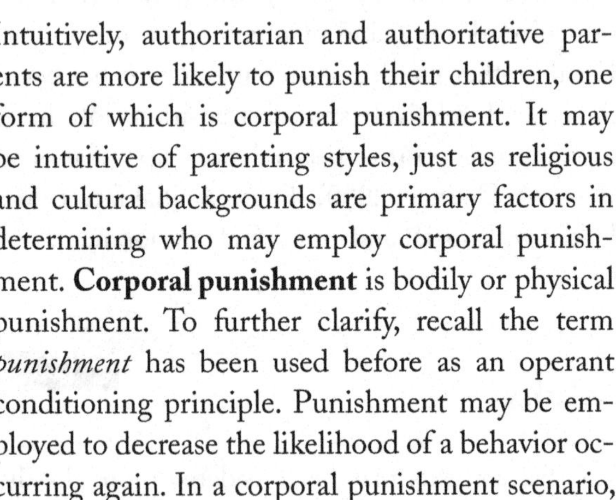

Intuitively, authoritarian and authoritative parents are more likely to punish their children, one form of which is corporal punishment. It may be intuitive of parenting styles, just as religious and cultural backgrounds are primary factors in determining who may employ corporal punishment. **Corporal punishment** is bodily or physical punishment. To further clarify, recall the term *punishment* has been used before as an operant conditioning principle. Punishment may be employed to decrease the likelihood of a behavior occurring again. In a corporal punishment scenario, a child may be spanked for disobeying a parent.

Corporal punishment is understandably a controversial topic. Over 70 countries have outlawed corporal punishment in school settings. In the United States, corporal punishment is prohibited in public schools in 31 states and the District of Columbia. Moreover, Iowa and New Jersey extend these bans to private schools (Corporal punishment policies around the world, 2011). Researchers, parents, and administrators appear similarly divided on the topic: some argue that children should never be hit, as it models aggression and violence; others argue that mild spanking is suitable in some situations. This latter group may view corporal punishment as acceptable when employed genuinely as a learning tool.

Some conditions may need to be met to satisfy the idea of a "genuine learning tool." First, many times punishment may be viewed as a last resort, after other solutions have been sought. Second, if it is to be employed, the punishment should clearly be linked—for the parent and child—with the negative or problematic behavior. The parent should not be making physical contact in an impulsive fashion, and there should not be long delays in behavior and punishment whereby the child may be confused about when he or she may have done wrong. Third, the punishment should not be excessive in terms of intensity, frequency, or duration. Researchers that do support corporal punishment typically use terms such as "mild spanking." Fourth, researchers do seem to agree that infants should not be corporally punished. Infants do not have the cognitive maturity to engage in such a learning process, or otherwise understand what they did wrong (Bugenthal, Martorell, & Barraza, 2003). When these conditions are met, one may perhaps view corporal punishment as being part of a broader learning principle. However, when these conditions are not met and when there is physical contact above and beyond what may be suggestive of a learning principle or process; other problematic behaviors may be evident. Some researchers may argue that corporal punishment puts the child being punished in a very aroused and defensive state, which impairs his or her ability to calmly process and understand the situation, make decisions, and solve problems.

At the heart of the controversial nature of corporal punishment is that some view it as being linked with maltreatment or abuse. More specifically, **child maltreatment** is evident when a child's physical or emotional integrity is threatened. Thus, by definition, corporal punishment and child maltreatment carry very different meanings.

There are three general forms of child maltreatment. First, **physical abuse** is evident when there is excessive physical contact that typically may result in bruises, scratches, and in more extreme cases sprains, and bone fractures. In most professional and school settings, there is protocol for reporting such observable physical marks on children. There is also **emotional abuse**, whereby children's emotional integrity is threatened. This may be evident in a parent that consistently berates or belittles their children, or employ tactics to emotionally manipulate them, attacking their self-esteem, or instilling anxiety or guilt. Lastly, **neglect** is a form of child maltreatment. This may be in cases of extremely uninvolved parents or families, when the child is not receiving adequate supervision, nutrition, or basic hygiene. Together, any form of maltreatment negatively impact a child physically, emotionally, or both.

Siblings

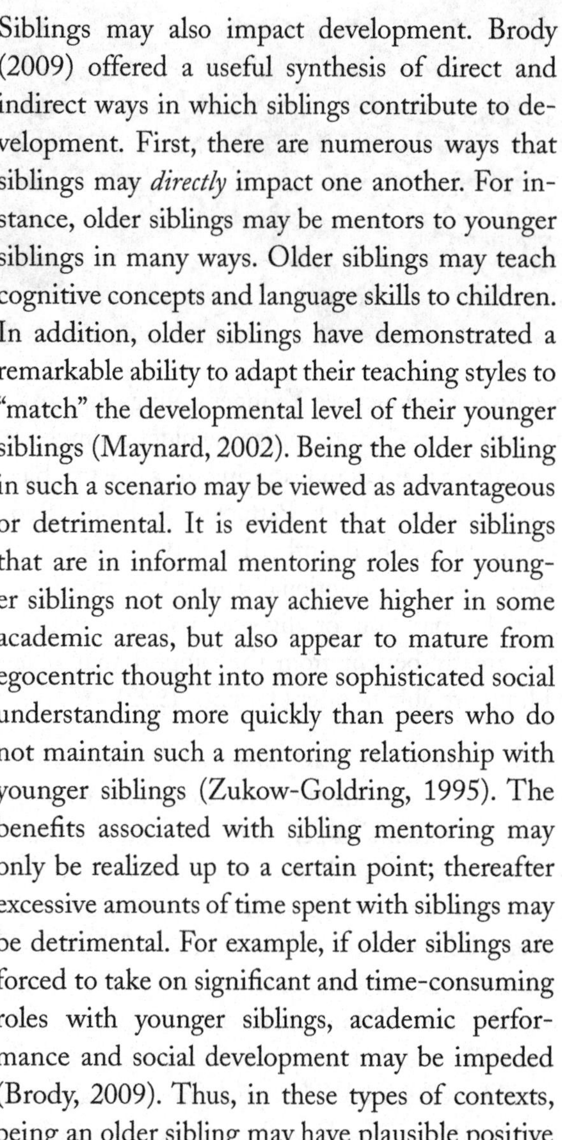

Siblings may also impact development. Brody (2009) offered a useful synthesis of direct and indirect ways in which siblings contribute to development. First, there are numerous ways that siblings may *directly* impact one another. For instance, older siblings may be mentors to younger siblings in many ways. Older siblings may teach cognitive concepts and language skills to children. In addition, older siblings have demonstrated a remarkable ability to adapt their teaching styles to "match" the developmental level of their younger siblings (Maynard, 2002). Being the older sibling in such a scenario may be viewed as advantageous or detrimental. It is evident that older siblings that are in informal mentoring roles for younger siblings not only may achieve higher in some academic areas, but also appear to mature from egocentric thought into more sophisticated social understanding more quickly than peers who do not maintain such a mentoring relationship with younger siblings (Zukow-Goldring, 1995). The benefits associated with sibling mentoring may only be realized up to a certain point; thereafter excessive amounts of time spent with siblings may be detrimental. For example, if older siblings are forced to take on significant and time-consuming roles with younger siblings, academic performance and social development may be impeded (Brody, 2009). Thus, in these types of contexts, being an older sibling may have plausible positive or negative benefits.

Similarly, being the younger sibling in a family appears to have potential for positive and

Courtesy of the author

negative consequences. Younger siblings that grow up with aggressive and antisocial older siblings are at greater risk for demonstrating the same troublesome behaviors (Bank, Patterson, & Reid, 1996; Brody, 2009). On the other hand, during times of intense social or emotional parental conflict (e.g., martial separation or divorce) younger siblings may greatly benefit from the support that older siblings are able to offer (Jenkins, 1992).

Second, there are ways in which siblings *indirectly* impact one another's development. Broadly speaking, parents' experiences with raising older siblings may impact how they approach, treat, and ultimately raise younger siblings. In the same vein, other adults that come into contact with a set of siblings (e.g., teachers, coaches, church members) may also treat siblings from the same family differentially based upon previous experiences with the older sibling(s). This phenomenon has been supported empirically, with parental expectations of their younger children being based upon their older children (Whiteman & Buchanon, 2002). In addition, Broffenbrenner (1977) originally reported that teachers form expectations regarding a child's academic capability and conduct based upon interactions with older sibling(s). Thus, parents, teachers, and other adults may form similar expectations of siblings, and treat them accordingly, even when unfounded.

However, differential treatment of siblings also occurs. A child's belief their parents are less affectionate or caring toward them, or that they receive more negative treatment, has been linked with negative social and emotional adjustment (Reiss, Neiderhauser, Hetherington, & Plomin, 2000). These negative effects of differential treatment may be particularly salient when the children feel the differential treatment is unwarranted (Kowal, Kramer, Krull, & Crick, 2002). However, parental attitude and attention toward older siblings is not always negative for a younger sibling. From time to time, parents may even engage in basking with their older children. **Basking** is apparent when a parent is deriving enhanced psychological enjoyment and fulfillment due to accomplishments and achievements of their children (Brody, 2009).

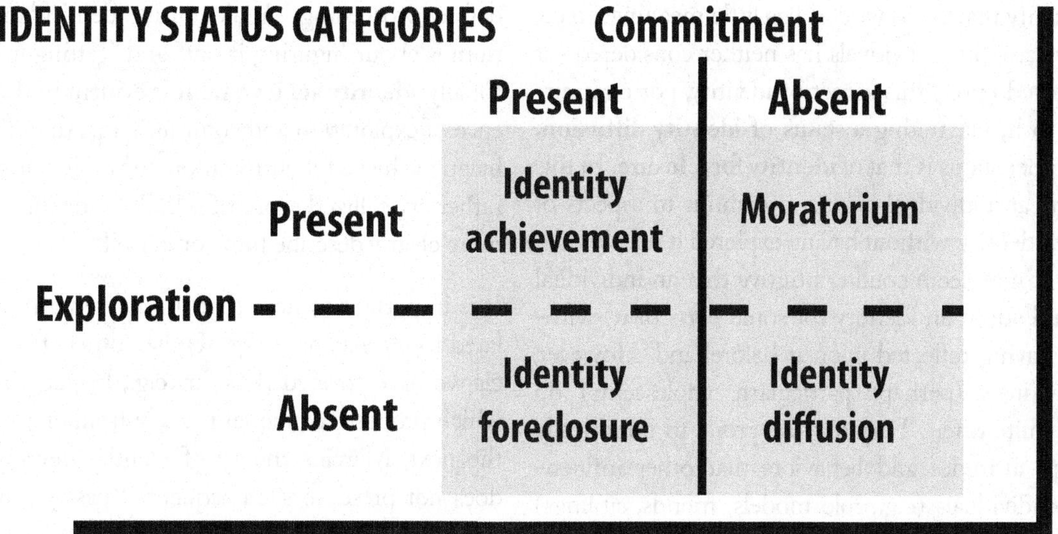

FIGURE 9.2 *ID Status*

When an older sibling excels in one or more areas (e.g., academically, athletically, socially) the parent may bask in this child's accolades, and this may have positive effects for younger children as the parents enhanced psychological state and functioning may promote better parenting (Brody, Kim, Murry, & Brown, 2003).

Identity

Identity has much relevance for adolescence. Piaget incorporated identity into his theory, positing that adolescence was primarily a time of transition between childhood and adulthood; a time for testing limits, for breaking ties, and for establishing a new identity. Major conflicts during this time period center on clarification of identity, life goals, and life meaning, and failure to achieve identity results in confusion.

Furthering this idea, James Marcia (1966, 1987) originally offered a framework that is useful in understanding identity development. According to Marcia's theory, there are two critical processes associated with identity formation: exploration and commitment. Exploration is akin to thinking and reflection. Presumably, when one genuinely understands themselves according to identity, it is after some degree of personal reflection. Commitment is an enduring characteristic of identity, and marked by personal confidence and assurance that the chosen aspects of identity are genuine, and will remain as such. The relative presence or absence of these processes at any one time in the broader identity formation progression may clarify the degree to which an individual has truly internalized one or more aspects of their identity. According to this model then, and as viewable in Figure 9.2, four statuses emerge:

- diffusion,
- foreclosure,
- moratorium, and
- achievement.

To further understand these stages, consider an example of an individual in terms of their sexual identity development. **Sexual identity** encompasses all the attitudes, knowledge, and behaviors related to one's sexual self. Typically, sexual identity development is more prevalent as adolescence approaches. Thus, during a core part of childhood, an individual may have yet to entertain any notions of this aspect of oneself. Even as this same individual enters adolescence and thinks about their sexual self a bit more, their personal knowledge of or attitudes toward sexuality may be so weak it has little meaning. In either case, the individuals has neither considered (or reflected upon) this aspect of identity, nor committed to it, illustrating a status of **identity diffusion.** Another status is that of **identity foreclosure.** In this stage, an individual begins to commit to aspects of their identity, without having explored it deeply (if at all). It may seem counterintuitive that an individual would adopt an identity (or some parts of it) without having reflected upon it beforehand. However, individuals (perhaps particularly adolescents) do this quite often. They may be prone to uncritically adopt attitudes and behaviors that other influential individuals (e.g., role models, friends, siblings) demonstrate. Recall during early adolescence, group membership is particularly important; adolescents may have a great desire to "fit in" and will seemingly modify their identity to do so. In the example of the individual developing sexual identity, they may begin to mimic others in terms of language and behaviors associated with sexuality. A lack of meaningful reflection, however, may imply that these behaviors and attitudes are not deeply ingrained elements of themselves. Thus, they may more easily be "shed," moving onto something else. This may help clarify why some adolescents go through "stages" where they seem to exhibit vastly different sets of behaviors. **Identity moratorium** is marked by exploration, but a lack of commitment. This is a very meaningful stage in terms of identity development because, in a sense, the individual is saying they are focused upon "getting it right." The uncritical adoption of aspects of identity apparent in foreclosure status is no longer apparent. In fact, there may appear to be little or no progress in terms of identity development on the surface; rather, the progress comes in the form of deeper introspection regarding oneself. In terms of sexual identity, an individual may more closely consider their own sexual self, independent of the influence of others. The term moratorium is sometimes applied in a legal context regarding the death penalty. In the history of the death penalty, some states put a moratorium on the death penalty; based upon the fact innocent individuals are apparently on death row. Thus, state legislators place the moratorium on the death penalty in order for the system to "get it right" before proceeding. Analogously, identity moratorium is about "figuring it out" and "getting it right." Finally, **identity achievement** is evident in the presence of exploration and commitment. An individual having achieved identity in one or more areas has a rather crystallized sense of self. An individual could more clearly describe him- or herself.

It is important to note that the above terms are related to *statuses*, not *stages*. Unlike other stage models we have covered thus far (e.g., Piaget, Erikson) which propose sequential passage from one stage to the next, Marcia's theory of identity development does not presume such sequential passage. Rather, individuals are relatively free to move in and out of these statuses. Moreover, there are various forms of identity (e.g., gender, sexuality, racial, ethnic, professional, athletic, etc.). An individual does not necessarily demonstrate the same identity status with all forms of identity. A simple example may be viewed in relation to sexual identity. Whereas gender identity comes along as young as age 2 or 3, sexual identity is more likely to develop thereafter. While there are multiple forms of identity, some of those that appear to receive the most attention are in terms of gender, sexuality, racial, and ethnic identities.

Gender Identity

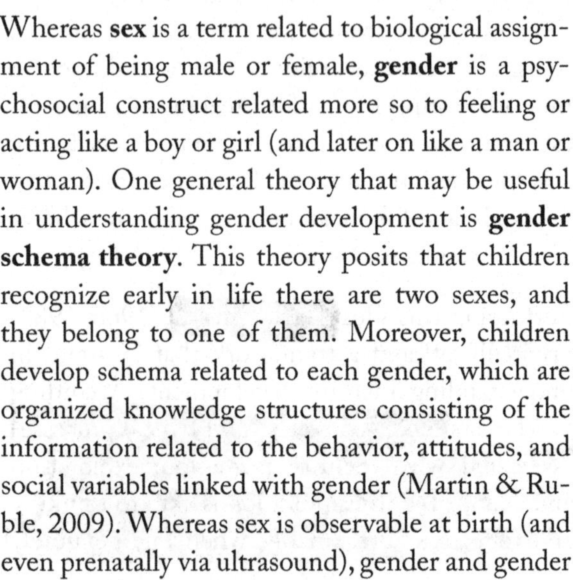

Whereas **sex** is a term related to biological assignment of being male or female, **gender** is a psychosocial construct related more so to feeling or acting like a boy or girl (and later on like a man or woman). One general theory that may be useful in understanding gender development is **gender schema theory**. This theory posits that children recognize early in life there are two sexes, and they belong to one of them. Moreover, children develop schema related to each gender, which are organized knowledge structures consisting of the information related to the behavior, attitudes, and social variables linked with gender (Martin & Ruble, 2009). Whereas sex is observable at birth (and even prenatally via ultrasound), gender and gender identity emerges over time. Not only do children begin to understand themselves as being a particular sex (i.e., male or female) but also adopt certain expectations for gender behavior they employ for themselves in terms of roles they may adopt, games they may play, or clothes they may wear. They may also apply these expectations for gender behavior toward others in that the child may come to expect other males or females to generally behave or dress in the same way.

Accordingly, **gender identity** is related to a sense of being masculine or feminine. It begins to develop in infancy, and is learned from expectations. Indeed, one of our first lessons in gender is that newborn baby girls receive pink clothing, blankets, toys, and nursery décor, while baby boys receive blue. Thereafter, but still during infancy, "gender appropriate" toys and games begin to infuse the household. These processes are complimented by **gender roles**, which are expectations of culture in terms of feminine and masculine behaviors and characteristics. While there is not necessarily a precise list of masculine and feminine behaviors, most can generally agree on many cultural factors that "belong" to one category or the other (see Figure 9.3). Gender role classification *does not* imply a particular sexual orientation. Gender roles may be identifiable to the observer, sexual orientation is not necessarily.

Researchers have investigated gender development in samples of infants as young as 6 months of age, reporting that these infants may well distinguish between male and female voices. Moreover, 9-month-old infants are able to distinguish between photos of men and women. Shortly thereafter, and around 12 months of age, infants are readily able to associate voices with men's and women's photographs. That is, they seem to sense which voice "goes with" a particular photo (Martin, Ruble, & Szkrybalo, 2002). Thus, from very early on there is evidence children are processing gender-related information.

There may be evaluative and motivational processes inherent in gender development. More specifically, when forming groups (e.g., gender) humans tend to *evaluate* their own groups more highly, emphasizing what they perceive as the most positive and salient characteristics of the group(s) they belong to. It has been demonstrated that children as young as 3 years of age appear to prefer their own sex and may assign more positive characteristics to their own sex group (Ruble & Martin, 1998). This may be observed when children so consistently appear to form homogeneous groups based upon sex. It is relatively rare for children to congregate and associate exclusively with the opposite sex (Maccoby, 1998).

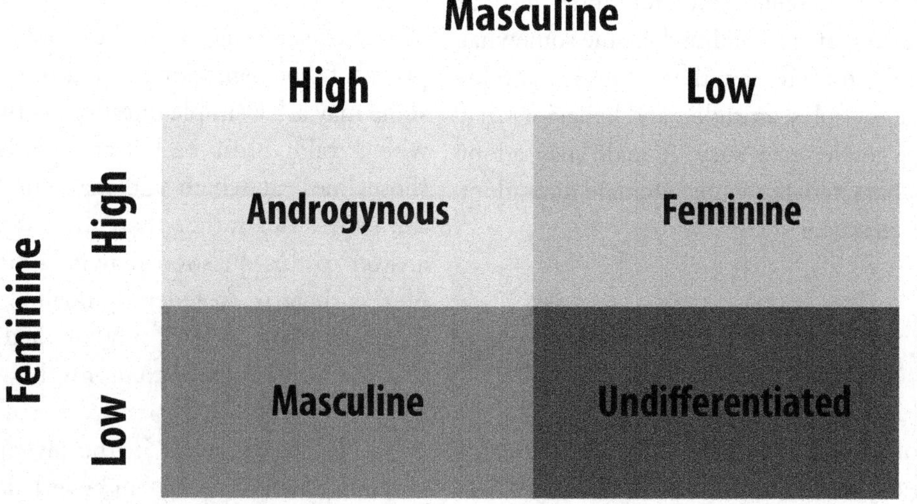

FIGURE 9.3 *Gender-role Classification*

In addition, children may be more *motivated* to be associated with, and learn about, their sex and gender groups. Together, children may be more driven to learn the features that characterize the group they associate with and also act those out. For instance, a young girl may have come to realize she is "more like her mom" in some ways. She can readily identify as a girl, as it is apparent in school and other social contexts she hangs out with other young girls. These girls may be taking in information from the environment in relation to games, toys, modes of dress, and behaviors that are pertinent to females (i.e., feminine). As their conceptions of their own sex and gender crystallizes, children are able to clearly differentiate between genders, and are even able to use one's sex to make judgments about that particular person (e.g., what the person is like, what the person likes to do, etc.) (Martin & Ruble, 2009). One may envision a young male electing not to befriend a young female because he makes assumptions the two will not cohere and share interests and activities.

Generally speaking, it appears as though gender development follows a three-stage pattern. First, during toddlerhood, children begin taking in gender-related information. Thereafter, during the next stage comprising ages 5 through 7, children develop a very categorical approach to sex and gender. During this stage, they view sex and gender as very fixed and consistent, with all males and females acting masculine and feminine, respectively. After this stage, children become somewhat more flexible in their view that while sex is relatively fixed, the roles, attitudes, and behaviors that encompass gender may vary. A male may adopt feminine characteristics while a female may adopt masculine characteristics.

Racial Identity

In addition, **racial identity** is thought to begin forming early in childhood. Racial identity refers to "a sense of group or collective identity based on one's perception that he or she shares a common heritage with a particular racial group" (Helms, 1993). Racial identity is often based upon stable biological features (e.g., skin color) and may cause individuals to categorize themselves into groups based upon those features.

Racial identity has been examined more generally in relation to racial socialization. **Racial socialization** has been conceptualized as the process by which Black individuals develop a healthy Black racial identity (Stevenson, 1995). Researchers have identified core areas in which this type of socialization is thought to occur (Stevenson, Cameron, & Herrero-Taylor, 1998). Recently, Stevenson et al. (1998) proposed that racial socialization is transmitted to individuals via messages that: a) promote cultural empowerment and pride, and b) promote an awareness of societal oppression. Together, these beliefs are thought to enhance racial identity and protect individuals against racially destructive environments. Furthermore, family is thought to be the primary socializing agent (Anglin & Wade, 2007) with some support that other contexts such as organized activities may also facilitate racial identity formation (Stanley, 2014).

When May Children Be Left Alone?

When considering all of the aforementioned aspects of socioemotional maturity in children, some may ask a simple question: Is there an age at which children can be left alone at home? Along those lines, at which age may children become the baby-sitter rather than the baby-sittee? The answer to this question may be a bit more complex as there is no federal guideline; states differ in terms of the laws (if any) applied here. Much of the following will exemplify how the answer to this is viewed in North Carolina, where there is no specific language in the juvenile code that specifies when children can be left alone at home. However, according to the N.C. Department of

Health and Human Services, state fire code says that children under the age of 8 should not be left alone without appropriate supervision:

> "If any person shall leave any child under the age of eight years locked or otherwise confined in any dwelling, building or enclosure, and go away from such dwelling, building or enclosure without leaving some person of the age of discretion in charge of the same, so as to expose the child to danger by fire, the person so offending shall be guilty of a Class 1 misdemeanor."

The statute above should not be taken to imply an adult in North Carolina may leave a child 8 or older unsupervised. What is particularly important is that the child(ren) can take care of themselves for the amount of time they are alone and under the conditions in which they are left.

The reliable discretion of parent or guardian to know how capable their child is is critical, as anyone who leaves a child alone can be charged with neglect or child abuse if the child is not capable of taking care of himself and is injured. An adult also can be charged if he or she leaves a young child with an older child who is not capable of taking care of the younger child. Below are some questions to ask before deciding to leave a child alone for a time:

- Does the child have a relative or neighbor nearby to call if help is needed?
- Can the child prepare a snack or meal without supervision?
- Does the child understand how to handle visits or phone calls from strangers?
- Is the child comfortable being left alone?
- Is the home environment safe?
- Does the child know first-aid procedures in case of minor injuries such as cuts?
- Does the child know how and when to call an emergency number?

Key Terms

- **Initiative versus Guilt** – the basic task is to achieve competence and initiative. If children are given freedom to select personally meaningful activities, they tend to develop a positive view of self and follow through with projects. If they are not allowed to make their own selection, they tend to develop guilt over not taking initiative.
- **Industry versus Inferiority** – the child needs to expand his or her understanding of the world, and learn basic skills required for school success. The basic task of industry relates to setting and attaining personal goals, and failure to do so results in a sense of inadequacy.
- **Self-Esteem** – an affective sense of generally feeling good or bad about one's level of competence; it is derived from evaluating oneself in relation to others. Evident in the following areas:
    - **Scholastic** – arises when a student generates positive feelings about themselves in terms of academics. It is likely this sphere of self-esteem may be further differentiated into sub-domains. A student may have high self-esteem in mathematics or science, but not necessarily both.
    - **Behavioral Conduct** – linked with a perceived level of competence in adopting and maintaining roles and behavioral expectations in social contexts.
    - **Athletic** – self-esteem is related to athletic skills and sport. A child with high self-esteem is confident in his or her ability to learn and play games, and compete against others in athletic competitions.
    - **Physical Appearance** – associated with how a child views their own outward appearances. This may include physical features such as body shape and size, but also modes of dress.
    - **Peer Likeability** – derived from a general sense of how well a child feels they are liked by their peers.
- **Cycle of Self-Esteem** – a phenomena observable when children with high self-esteem in a certain area appear more likely to approach novel tasks and situations or new people, as they are more confident in their abilities to successfully navigate the task or situation. On the other hand, children with low self-esteem may be less likely to put forth effort toward tasks where they predict failure.
- **Emotional Regulation** – the ability to manage, modify or regulate ones' emotional state
    - **Externalizing** – a difficulty in emotional regulation, it is characterized as acting somewhat impulsively upon present emotional states. Emotions such as anger, anxiety, sadness, or joy may be expressed overtly, and displayed as acting out, aggression, or disruptive behavior.
    - **Internalizing** – this is not an overt process, but evident when someone is unable to regulate and therefore tucking emotions away; those that internalize may often be characterized as "shy" or "quiet"
- **Empathy** – the ability to feel what another person is feeling, or being able to "put yourself in another person's shoes"
- **Sympathy** – to feel sorry for another who is experiencing difficulty at home or school
- **Pro-social behavior** – caring about others and acting upon that by helping where necessary. The most genuine form of pro-social behavior is altruism.

- **Altruism** – the most genuine form of pro-social behavior; complete selfless behavior aimed at helping someone in need
- **Frustration-Aggression Hypothesis** – the idea that most aggressive acts are prompted by feelings of dissatisfaction, annoyance, and frustration
- **Instrumental Aggression** – harmful actions (physical or non-physical) that occur as a result of a pursuit of a goal
- **Relational Aggression** – a non-physical form of aggression comprised of acts designed to hurt a person's social relationships
- **Bullying** – an aggressive act that is repeated, and involves a "disparity of power between victim and perpetrator"
- **Popularity** – related to peer-likeability and salience. That is, in determining popularity, two important questions must be answered: Are peers aware of a student *and* are they liked?
- **Sociometric Procedures** – a procedure to assess popularity is relatively straightforward. In a classroom, all students could be issued a peer nomination form which they name the one (or more) peers they like the most, and also the peer(s) they dislike the most.
    - **Popular** – a status associated with being consistently liked in a social context
    - **Controversial** – those that are frequently nominated as both liked and disliked
    - **Rejected** – a status for those whose peers are aware of them, but are generally disliked
    - **Neglected** – these children are not "on the radar" of their peers
    - **Average** – most children likely fall into this category; those who are liked and disliked to some degree
- **Cyberbullying** – an indirect form of bullying viewed as aggression through personal computers (e.g., email, instant messaging, social network sites) and cellular phones (e.g., text messaging)
- **Symbolic play** – involves pretending and requires imagination. Importantly, a child may engage in symbolic play by themselves or with others (e.g., peers, siblings, parents).
- **Guided participation** – perhaps an extension of Vygotsky's zone of proximal development; it is the process and system of involvement of individuals with others, as they communicate and engage in shared activities
- **Socialization** – a subtle sociocultural process whereby children may be made aware of useful ways to think and act in society, but also gives them an opportunity to "act like adults" during imaginative play sessions
- **Peer** – someone who is about the same age and level of maturity
- **Demandingness** – a variable related to parenting style; this is related to the relative presence within a household of clear rules, boundaries, and expectations for their children, and—when rules are broken or expectations are not met—the consequences
- **Responsiveness** – an element of parenting style linked with emotional warmth and a high degree of involvement
- **Authoritarian** – discernible in high levels of demandingness in the form of structure, rules, and rule enforcement; as well as relatively low levels of responsiveness in these parents
- **Authoritative** – more democratic in nature; an authoritative parenting style that combines high levels of demandingness and similarly high levels of responsiveness

Bully Prevention
1 - practice what you preach (don't engage)
2 - assess extent of problem

- **Permissive** – does not clearly create and enforce rules, but does display relatively high levels of emotional warmth; sometimes referred to as "indulgent" parenting
- **Uninvolved** – this parenting style is marked by low levels of demandingness and responsiveness; sometimes referred to as "neglectful"
- **Corporal punishment** – methods of bodily or physical punishment
- **Child maltreatment** – evident when a child's physical or emotional integrity is threatened
    - **Physical Abuse** – evident when there is excessive physical contact that typically may result in bruises, scratches, and in more extreme cases sprains, and bone fractures. In most professional and school settings, there is protocol for reporting such observable physical marks on children.
    - **Emotional abuse** – evident when a child's emotional integrity is threatened
    - **Neglect** – circumstances whereby the child is not receiving adequate supervision, nutrition, or basic hygiene
- **Basking** – apparent when a parent is deriving enhanced psychological enjoyment and fulfillment due to accomplishments and achievements of their children
- **Identity** – a term akin to a self-concept; it involves a "self-portrait"
- **Identity diffusion** – according to Marcia's identity status model, this status is marked by uncertainty, with neither reflection nor commitment to form of identity
- **Identity foreclosure** – in this stage, an individual begins to commit to aspects of their identity, without having explored it deeply (if at all)
- **Identity moratorium** – this stage is marked by exploration, but a lack of commitment
- **Identity achievement** – this is evident in the presence of exploration and commitment
- **Sex** – the biological assignment of being male or female
- **Sexual identity** – this term encompasses all the attitudes, knowledge, and behaviors related to one's sexual self
- **Gender** – a psychosocial construct related to "acting or feeling" male or female
- **Gender Schema Theory** – children may recognize early they belong to one of the two sexes. Thereafter, they develop schema, which are organized knowledge structures consisting of the information related to the behavior, attitudes, and social variables linked with gender.
- **Gender Identity** – the fundamental sense of being male or female, begins to form early in childhood
- **Racial Identity** – a sense of group or collective identity based on one's perception that he or she shares a common heritage with a particular racial group; often based upon skin color and may prompt individuals to categorize themselves into groups based upon that feature.
- **Racial Socialization** – the process by which individuals develop a racial identity

Critical Thinking Questions

1. Discuss pro-social behavior and aggression. In doing so, be sure to discuss the different forms of each, and provide examples of children engaging in these behaviors.
2. What's the difference between corporal punishment and child maltreatment? How can one detect the difference?

References

Anglin, D. M. & Wade, J. C. (2007). Racial socialization, racial identity, and Black students' adjustment to college. *Cultural Diversity and Ethnic Minority Psychology, 13*, 207-215.

Bank, L., Patterson, J. R., & Reid, J. B. (1996). Negative sibling interaction patterns as predictors of later adjustment problems in adolescent and young adult males. In G. H. Brody (Ed.), *Sibling relationships: Their causes and consequences* (pp. 197-229). Norwood, NJ: Ablex.

Bjorklund, D. F. (2000). *Children's thinking: Developmental function and individual differences.* Belmont, CA: Wadsworth.

Bridges, L. J., Denham, S. A., & Ganiban, J. M. (2004). Definitional issues in emotional regulation research. *Child Development, 75*, 340-345.

Brody, G. H. (2009). Siblings' direct and indirect contributions to child development. In L. S. Liben (Ed.), *Current directions in developmental psychology* (pp. 157-162). New York: Pearson.

Brody, G. H., Kim, S., Murry, V. M., & Brown, A. C. (2003). Longitudinal direct and indirect pathways linking older sibling competence to younger sibling competence. *Developmental Psychology, 39*, 618-328.

Broffenbrenner, U. (1977). Toward an experimental ecology of human development. *American Psychologist, 32*, 513-531.

Cillessen, A. H. N., Rose, A. J. (2009). Understanding popularity in the peer system. In L. S. Liben (Ed.), *Current directions in developmental psychology* (pp. 198-204). New York: Pearson.

Corporal punishment policies around the world (2011). CNN News. Retrieved from http://www.cnn.com/2011/WORLD/asiapcf/11/08/country.comparisons.corporal.punishment/index.html

Eisenberg, J. (2003). Pro-social behavior, empathy, and sympathy. In M. H. Bornstein, L. Davidson, C. L. M. Keyes, & K. A. Moore (Eds.), *Well-being: Positive development across the life course* (pp. 253-265). Mahwah, NJ: Erlbaum.

Erikson, E. H. (1997). *The life cycle completed.* New York: Norton.

Finklehor, D., Vanderminden, J., Turner, H., Shattuck, A., & Hamby, S. (2014). At-school victimization and violence exposure assessed in a national household survey of children and youth. *Journal of School Violence.* doi: 10.1080/15388220.2014952816

Garbarino, J. (2007). *See Jane hit: Why girls are growing more violent and what we can do about it.* New York: Penguin Books.

Harper, J.M., Padilla-Walker, L.M., & Jensen, A.C. (2014). Do siblings matter independent of both parents and friends? Sympathy as a mediator between sibling relationship quality and adolescent outcomes. *Journal of Research on Adolescence.* doi: 10.1111/jora.12174

Harter, S. (1999). *The construction of the self. A developmental perspective.* New York: Guilford Press.

Helms, J. E. (1993). Introduction: Review of racial and ethnic identity terminology. In J. E. Helms (Ed.). *Black and White racial identity: Theory, research, and practice.* Westport, CT: Praeger.

Jenkins, J. (1992). Sibling relationships in disharmonious homes: Potential difficulties and protective effects. In F. Boer & J. Dunn (Eds.), *Children's sibling relationships: Developmental and clinical issues* (pp. 127-138). Hillsdale, NJ: Erlbaum.

Kowal, A., Kramer, L., Krull, J. L., & Crick, N. R. (2002). Children's perceptions of the fairness of parental preferential treatment and their socioemotional well-being. *Journal of Family Psychology, 16*, 297-306.

Li, Q. (2007). New bottle but old wine: A research of cyberbullying in school. *Computers and Human Behavior, 23*, 1777-1991.

Maccoby, E. E. (1998). *The two sexes: Growing up apart, coming together.* Cambridge, MA: Belknap Press.

Marcia, J. E. (1966). Developmental and validation of ego-identity status. *Journal of Personality and Social Psychology, 3*, 551-558.

Marcia, J. E. (1987). The identity status approach to the study of ego identity development. In T. Honess & K. Yardley (Eds.), *Self and identity: Perspectives across the lifespan* (pp. 161-171). New York: Routledge.

Martin, C. L. & Ruble, D. N. (2009). Children's search for gender cues: Cognitive perspectives on gender development. In L. S. Liben (Ed.), *Current directions in developmental psychology* (pp. 165-172). New York: Pearson.

Martin, C. L., Ruble, D. N., & Szkrybalo, J. (2002). Cognitive theories of early gender development. *Psychological Bulletin, 128*, 903-933.

Maynard, A. E. (2002). Cultural teaching: The development of teaching skills in Maya sibling interactions. *Child Development, 73*, 969-982.

Merrell, K. W., Buchanan, R., & Tran, O. K., (2006). Relational aggression in children and adolescents: A review of implications for school settings. *Psychology in the Schools, 43*, 345-360.

National Research Council (2000). *From neurons to neighborhoods: the science of early childhood development.* Washington, DC: National Academy Press.

Piaget, J. (1962). *Play, dreams, and imitation in childhood.* New York: Norton.

Reiss, D., Neiderhauser, J. M., Hetherington, E. M., & Plomin, R. (2000). *The relationship code: Deciphering genetic and social influences on adolescent development.* Cambridge, MA: Harvard University Press.

Rogoff, B., Mistry, J., Göncü, & Mosier, C. (1993). Guided participation in cultural activity by toddlers and caregivers. *Monographs of the Society for Research in Child Development, 58* (Serial No. 236).

Ruble, D. N. & Martin, C. L. (1998). Gender development. In W. Damon (Ed.), *Handbook of child psychology: Vol. 3* (pp. 933-1016). New York: Wiley.

Stanley, C.T., (2014). The mediating role of racial socialization processes on the relations between organized activity involvement and Black racial identity. *Western Journal of Black Studies*, 38, 233-243.

Stevenson, H. C. (1995). Relationship of adolescent perceptions of racial socialization to racial identity. *Journal of Black Psychology, 21*, 49-60.

Stevenson, H. C., Cameron, R., & Herrero-Taylor, T. (2002). Development of the Teenager Experience of Racial Socialization Scale: Correlates of race-related socialization frequency from the perspective of Black youth. *Journal of Black Psychology, 28*, 84-106.

Trautner, H. M., Ruble, D. N., Cyphers. L., Kirsten. B., Behrendt, R., & Hartmann, P. (1998). *Rigidity and flexibility of gender stereotypes in childhood: Developmental or influential?* Manuscript submitted for publication.

Wang, J., Iannotti, R. J., Nansel, T. R. (2009). School bullying among adolescents in the United States: Physical, verbal, relational, and cyber. *Journal of Adolescent Health, 45*, 368-375.

Whiteman, S. D. & Buchanon, C. M. (2002). Mothers' and children's expectations for adolescence: The impact of perceptions of an older sibling's experience. *Journal of Family Psychology, 16*, 157-171.

Zukow-Goldring, P. G. (1995). Sibling caregiving. In M. H. Bornstein (Ed.), *Handbook of parenting: Status and social conditions of parenting* (pp. 177-208). Mahwah, NJ: Erlbaum.

CHAPTER 10

Physical Development in Adolescence

Adolescence is a time marked by a milieu of physical, social, emotional, and cognitive changes. In some ways, it is viewed as a transition period between childhood—marked by relative immaturity in most areas—and adulthood, which may require a certain degree of maturity in these same physical, social, emotional, and cognitive areas. However, it is important to be clear of what precisely signifies adolescence. While some life stages maintain chronological beginnings or endings, adolescence may be viewed as having a biological beginning. More specifically, when puberty begins, adolescence begins. In addition, when adolescents reach an age typically associated with the graduation from high school (approximately 17 or 18), adolescence is concluding. Thus, while there is a biological beginning, there is a chronological ending to adolescence. This conceptualization of adolescence may be useful for a couple of reasons. First, puberty involves hormonal and biological shifts that prepare the human body for reproduction. This definition of puberty given above is suggestive of the idea that the ability to reproduce is a significant shift from childhood to adolescence. Second, in most industrialized nations, adolescents spend a significant portion of time in high school, thereafter moving on to other, perhaps more adult-like roles and responsibilities. Together, the onset of puberty and the age associated with graduation from high school may be useful in determining who may be considered an adolescent.

With this definition, one may also consider a **cohort effect.** That is, when the majority of individuals in one cohort or generation have begun to experience puberty, then it may be said that particular cohort has entered adolescence. This is an

important perspective because if select individuals experience puberty significantly earlier than their peers, they have not necessarily entered adolescence yet. On the other hand, if select individuals experience puberty quite late, it does not imply they have been a child in the meantime, with all of their peers entering adolescence. In either case, when a majority of the cohort has experienced pubertal onset, adolescence has commenced. Seemingly, it would be easier to have a chronological beginning and ending to puberty. For instance, some have suggested that adolescence simply begins at age 10 and ends at age 20 (Feldman, 2008). However, such a definition may overlook the important biological feature of puberty.

Neurological Development

As noted previously, processes of synaptogenesis and myelination underlie significant neurological development during infancy and childhood. Such neurological development is related to enhanced behavior, cognitive and emotional capacities. When compared to their younger counterparts, older children appear quite capable in motoric (e.g., movement and athletics), cognitive (e.g., decision-making, language), and emotional (e.g., expression and regulation) ways. Thus, neurological growth may be indirectly inferred via observations of an individual's development. However, there are direct ways to monitor and study neurological growth. For instance, a type of **neuroimaging** called **magnetic resonance imaging (MRI)** provides scientists with direct information about the brain's structure, function, and connectivity. Ultimately, neuroimaging "involves unmasking the biological mechanisms that underlie behavioral development" (Amso & Casey, 2009, p. 86). To that end, MRI employs magnetic forces, radio waves, and intricate software to recognize signals from brain tissue; providing very accurate pictures of the human brain (see image below). Importantly, because MRI does not necessitate the use of radioactive material, it may be employed to scan one

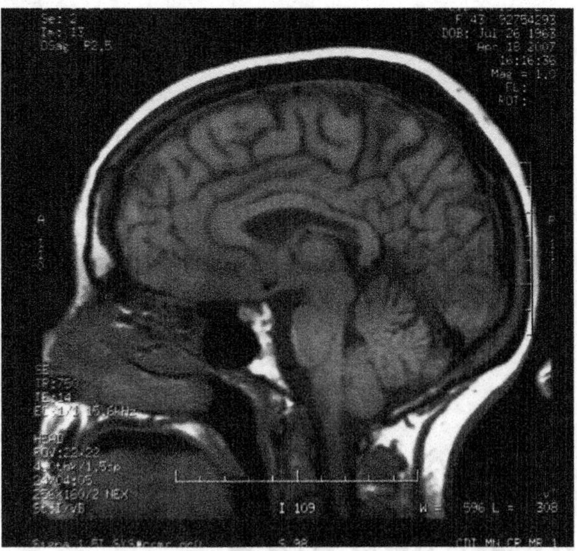

individual many times in a longitudinal design, noting anatomical changes in the brain during different life phases (Giedd, Stockman, Weddle, Liverpool, Wallace, Lee, Lalonde, Lenroot, 2012).

Researchers at the National Institute of Mental Health (NIMH) have been conducting a longitudinal study tracking participants from toddlerhood through early adulthood. For this study, MRI scans are taken every two years for approximately 2,000 individuals. Of this larger sample, many are from clinical samples (i.e., attention-deficit disorder, autism, etc.). In addition, there are numerous sets of identical and fraternal twins. Together, researchers may gain valuable images and insight into typically and atypically developing brains (Giedd et al., 2012). Imagine how a researcher may investigate the effect of childhood trauma on the brain. They may produce MRI images of children exposed to traumatic events and compare them to children who did not experience such trauma. Then, the researchers may make direct comparisons between the two groups, noting if particular areas of the brain (perhaps those linked with stress or emotional regulation) are in any way differentially developed.

For the NIMH study and others employing MRI methodology, two important variables are the relative growth and appearance of white and gray brain matter. **Gray matter** in the brain is associated with information processing areas, and consists mostly of cell bodies and some extracellular space. On the other hand, **white matter** derives its color and name from the presence of myelin, the fatty insulating material that covers axons. Thus, white matter in the brain has connective properties and capabilities. In fact, the relative presence of myelin in white matter allows neurological signals to travel approximately 100 times faster through these areas than others in the brain. The corpus callosum, the subcortical portion of the brain connecting the right and left hemispheres, is the most prominent white matter feature (Giedd et al., 2012). As one researcher put it "white matter is the long-distance wiring of the brain, while gray matter does the math" (University of Wisconsin-Madison, 2012).

Perhaps more useful still is a *functional* component of MRI, or ***f*MRI**. With *f*MRI, a scientist may determine brain activity through blood oxygenation levels. Thus, *f*MRI not only offers insight into the brain structure, but also the relative levels of activity within the brain. Lastly, **diffusion tensor imaging (DTI)** may be used to assess brain connectivity. Briefly, DTI offers scientists information related to interior changes in white matter in the brain. White matter is tissue containing nerve fibers and myelin. Water reacts differentially when placed in white matter containing strong, consistent nerve fibers (i.e., more connected) when compared to white matter with weaker and inconsistent nerve fibers (i.e., less connected). Thus, an image of brain connectivity may form, and may be monitored over time. Together, an individual's brain's structure, function, and connectivity may be viewed.

Consider a study undertaken by a team of researchers investigating the brain connectivity and emotional processing of children and adolescents at-risk for schizophrenia (Diwadka, Wadehr, Pruit, Keshavan, Rajan, Zajac-Benitez, Eickhoff, 2012). To conduct their study, the team recruited a sample of "at-risk" children and adolescents. Those children and adolescents deemed at-risk had parents who had been diagnosed with schizophrenia. Since there may be a genetic basis for disorders, these individuals were considered at-risk. The researchers also recruited a control sample of children and adolescents without family history of schizophrenia. Thereafter, all participants were shown multiple images of faces showing positive, negative, and neutral emotional expressions. These images were thought to activate parts of the brain (i.e., white and gray matter areas) responsible for emotional expression and processing. The researchers employed *f*MRI in order to examine how different areas of the brain activate and communicate with one another. Findings revealed that at-risk children and adolescents, when compared to the control group, demonstrated reduced network communication and disordered network responses to emotional faces. Moreover, the researchers stated these findings "suggest that brain developmental processes are going awry in children whose parents have schizophrenia" (Diwadka et al., 2012). Of course, these methods require costly equipment and laboratories. This equipment is not typically accessible to many developmental researchers. Nevertheless, some other very meaningful findings have emerged from studies involving MRI, *f*MRI, and DTI.

For instance, in the NIMH study, it appears as though the brain is already at 95% of its eventual adult size by age 6, and total cerebral volume (akin to brain size) peaks at about age 10.5 in females and 14.5 in males. In addition, studies have revealed that cortical brain regions related to sensory and motor movement, including the **cerebrum**, develop initially. Again in the NIMH sample, cerebrum size peaked at 11.3 years for females and 15.6 for males. This gender difference may mirror differences in puberty and a growth spurt discussed later in this unit. Thereafter, temporal and parietal areas linked with language and attention mature. Areas that integrate sensory, motor, language, and attention develop last (for full review see Amso and Casey, 2009).

Throughout the life span, gray matter in the human brain demonstrates an inverted-U shape of development, meaning that throughout childhood there are substantial increases in gray matter (i.e., the brain is growing). However, this relative growth rate of gray matter levels during later adolescence diminishes over time. That is, there are often "peak" growth rates in adolescence. However, white matter appears to continually develop linearly with age, and does not level off and diminish at one apparent time point. Brain size should be viewed as a limited capacity, but the ways in which inner structures and connections change is less limited. Together, the brain and its cortical and subcortical regions may grow primarily through adolescence (i.e., gray matter) but continues to connect (i.e., white matter) and develop in terms of processing speed and efficiency throughout the life span (Giedd et al., 2012). In the next chapter, this neurological development will be juxtaposed to cognitive development.

Puberty

The physical changes in adolescence are noteworthy, and puberty is responsible for much of the variability one may observe in adolescent physical development. **Puberty** is the "awakening of a complex neuro-endocrine machinery in which the primary mechanism is still unclear" (Parent et al., 2003). While this definition may appear complicated at first glance, it may cover several important aspects of puberty. First, an "awakening" refers to the initiation of an event; in this case a significant biological transformation. Second, the term *neuro-endocrine machinery* refers to the involvement of neurological and endocrine systems in this transformation. Neurological systems and components will need to work in conjunction with the endocrine system to release and regulate hormones essential for puberty. Lastly, the above definition includes the phrase "primary mechanism is still unclear." Although the primary mechanism that triggers puberty appears unclear, some researchers have reported deep sleep is particularly important with puberty. There is a neurological basis of puberty, and the portions of the brain that control puberty become active during sleep—and the deepest stages of sleep in particular. This conclusion is based upon research showing that a luteinizing hormone (LH) is secreted in greater quantities after deep sleep. This may be important because LH plays an active role in pubertal onset, and is vital for reproduction; LH triggers ovulation in females and testosterone production in males (Shaw, Butler, McKinney, Nelson, Ellenbogen, & Hall, 2012). Therefore, children and adolescents who do not receive enough quality deep sleep may be prone to a late or slowed puberty. Researchers also have shed light on the biological organs and processes that constitute puberty, and the average ages at which puberty tends to occur for males and females. In addition, researchers have isolated some factors that are linked with pubertal onset. The coming paragraphs will include descriptions of what research has informed us about puberty.

As mentioned above, neurological and endocrine systems are concerned with puberty. More specifically, a structure called the **thalamus**, meaning "inner room," is located in the forebrain. The thalamus initially receives the neural messages sent to the brain, and subsequently transmits them to appropriate areas of the brain for processing. Directly below the thalamus lies the **hypothalamus**, which maintains control over the **pituitary gland** and subsequently the **endocrine system** (see Figure 10.1). The pituitary gland has been called the "master gland" due to its control over the endocrine system (Feldman, 2008), or the "body's drug store" for its role in disseminating chemicals (Greenberg, 2004). Ultimately, this gland is capable of releasing **hormones (i.e., selective chemicals)** into the bloodstream, eventually arriving at bodily organs for health, maintenance, and growth.

Hormone levels are constantly monitored by the **gonadostat**. If the hormone level is too low, the gonadostat signals the pituitary to produce more hormones. If the levels go too high, the gonadostat restricts the pituitary's output. When puberty begins, the gonads begin producing more hormones, including **testosterone** (i.e., an androgen) and **estradiol** (i.e., an estrogen). This event may be referred to as **gonadarche**. More

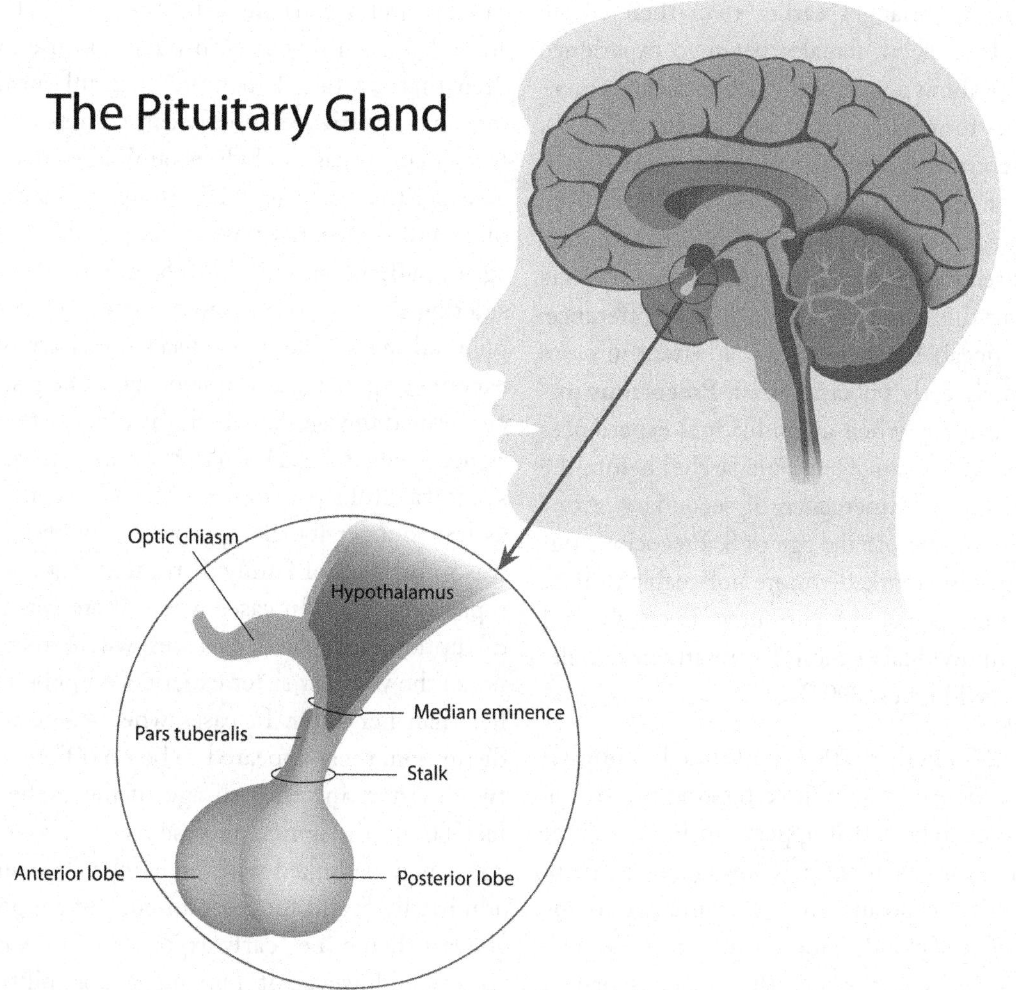

FIGURE 10.1 *Pituitary gland*

specifically, gonadarche may be recognized in females as **menarche** and males as **spermarche**.

At a broad level, puberty causes two types of changes or characteristics. First, **primary sexual characteristics** are physical changes directly involved in reproduction, such as menarche and spermarche. In addition, **secondary sexual characteristics** are physical changes not related to reproduction. Secondary characteristics may include breast development in females (i.e., thelarche), pubic hair growth, voice changes, or acne. A growth spurt may also be evident in adolescence, observed in a dramatic increase in weight and height. Typically, females experience this growth spurt before males. Together, as the original definition implied, puberty involves the interaction of the hypothalamus, pituitary gland, and gonads causing rapid physical changes involving hormones. Researchers also know factors that are associated with puberty; these factors should be viewed as associative and not causative.

Factors Associated with Pubertal Onset

Factors related to pubertal onset are also those that have been linked with early onset of puberty. That is, an individual exposed to certain factor(s) may be more likely to experience primary or secondary sexual changes earlier than their counterparts. In general, females begin to experience puberty at about age 11 years, while males generally begin around 12 years of age (Feldman, 2010). These descriptive statistics represent measures of central tendency, and there is expected variation. For instance, some females may report the emergence of secondary sexual changes around 10 years of age, but this may still be a negligible difference. More noticeable differences are apparent in cases of extremely early pubertal onset. **Precocious puberty** is evident when an individual experiences primary sexual change (e.g., menarche) before the age of 9, or the emergence of secondary sexual characteristics before the age of 8. Precocious puberty would be markedly more noticeable in relation to one's peers, and currently affects about 1 in 5,000 individuals—more frequently in females (Cesario & Hughes, 2007).

Cesario and Hughes (2007) performed a comprehensive review of studies investigating precocious puberty and reported it appears to be correlated with numerous factors, including genetics, pediatric obesity, exposure to environmental toxins, stress, and early and chronic exposure to sexualized society. First, the idea that genetics plays a role in pubertal onset is intuitive; an adolescent may reach puberty about the same time their biological parents and siblings did. Given the role of neurological and endocrine systems, it may make sense that there is a genetic basis for the age at which one experiences puberty. Second, excess weight—perhaps resulting in obesity—has been linked with early onset of puberty. A secular trend in menarche, juxtaposed to a secular trend in childhood overweight and obesity rates may confirm this. Consider that the average age of menarche has consistently dropped over many decades. Over these same decades, there has been an equally consistent rise in incidence of overweight and obese youth, demonstrating a negative correlation between these variables. Third, exposure to environmental toxins—broadly defined—may be linked with pubertal onset. Synthetic chemicals that enter the human bloodstream and organs can disrupt normal endocrine functioning. Fourth, stress has been linked with pubertal onset. Children that are raised in more stressful surroundings may experience puberty early. Stress can arise from many areas, including familial sources. Reconsider the study in which groups of sisters (one older and one younger) were compared in terms of age of pubertal onset (Tither & Ellis, 2008). Considering genetics is a primary factor determining pubertal onset, one may expect the sisters would experience puberty at the same age. The researchers verified the ages at which the older sister experienced menarche. During this time, the younger sister was still a pre-adolescent, and in some cases as the younger female approached puberty, there was some form of family disruption (e.g., divorce, separation, etc.). In cases where there was family disruption, compared to cases where there was none, the younger sister experienced puberty earlier than her sister. In cases where there was no disruption, there appeared to be no difference between sisters in terms of age of menarche. If in fact family disruption represents a stressor, then stress may be linked with menarche. The authors admittedly found the least amount of support for the last theme (i.e., early exposure to a sexualized society). However, it remains a possibility that sexual messages, attitudes, and behaviors may put some children on a "faster-track" to puberty.

Thus far, we have considered the factors (i.e., independent variables) that are linked with early puberty (i.e., dependent variable). However, experiencing puberty early may in turn be linked with psychosocial factors. Early puberty may be particularly problematic for females:

- depressive symptoms;
- externalizing behaviors;
- use of alcohol, drugs, and/or tobacco;
- earlier dating and sexual involvement with others; and
- disordered eating and eating disorders.

These trends and consequences may not be reserved exclusively for females. The aforementioned secular trend in puberty that has long been observed in females may be true for males as well. One of the reasons that this observations in males is less available is that some primary characteristics of puberty in females, such as breast development and menarche, are more observable and obvious signs. For males, the characteristics of puberty include enlarged testes and spermarche. Males may be less likely to report these features and researchers less willing to inquire about them (Wilson, 2007). However, Marcia Herman-Giddens performed such a study, and found that males are now experiencing puberty anywhere from 6 months to 24 months earlier than what many textbooks say is standard for males. For males, this means puberty may realistically begin at age 9 or 10. Thus, males and females may begin puberty much earlier than in previous generations, and perhaps earlier than many parents expect. Implications of this may mean parents and/or teachers need to talk to their children much sooner about the "birds and the bees" (Wilson, 2007).

Disordered Eating and Eating Disorders

Far more common and widespread than defined eating disorders is disordered eating. **Disordered eating** refers to troublesome eating behaviors (e.g., restrictive dieting, bingeing, or purging) which occur less frequently or are less severe than those required to meet the full criteria for the diagnosis of an eating disorder. Many adolescents, particularly females, may begin experimenting with such behaviors. It may be directly related to some of the weight gain that typically results from puberty. If weight gain is apparent in areas (e.g., hips, thighs) that an adolescent views as being incongruent with her ideal body shape or size, she may try to control the weight gain by changing eating behaviors. Regrettably, these changes in eating behaviors may not necessarily be part of a sound diet, nor guided and monitored by a nutritionist.

Eating problems and disorders are increasingly common in adolescence—most notably, anorexia nervosa and bulimia nervosa. More commonly referred to as merely anorexia or bulimia, the "nervosa" tag on reflects an emotional aspect of eating disorder. These eating disorders are complex issues, involving behavioral, cognitive, and emotional elements.

Anorexia nervosa is a disorder marked by voluntary starvation. Most anorexics are White adolescents, from middle- and upper-income families (Lawler & Nixon, 2011). According to the Diagnostic and Statistical Manual (DSM-IV), the four main criteria for anorexia nervosa are:

- Refusal to maintain body weight at or above a minimally normal weight for age and height (weight loss leading to maintenance of less than 85% of that expected).
- Intense fear of gaining weight or becoming fat, despite explicit contradictory evidence.
- Disturbance in the way in which the body is perceived or experienced (places too much importance on body image or denial of current situations).
- Amenorrhea (i.e., absence of three consecutive menstrual cycles).

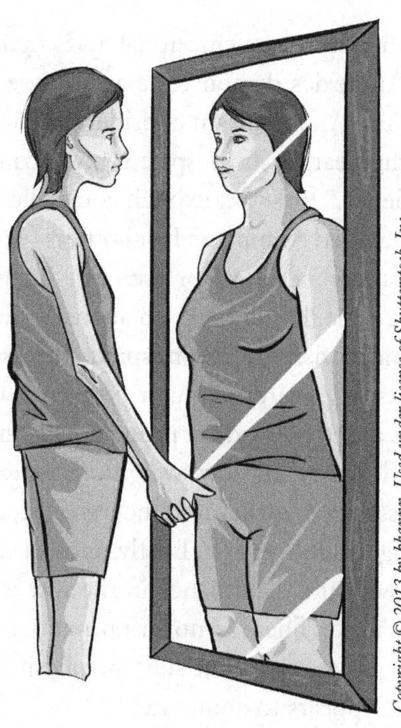

The criteria for anorexia include physical, emotional, and cognitive aspects. For instance, a clinician may observe an adolescent female that actively and adamantly refuses to maintain an expected or normal weight for her age and height. This is typically achieved through extreme calorie restriction, or **voluntary starvation**. The same BMI chart as was used when describing obesity may be applied here. For any age and sex (in this case primarily female) there is an expected range of BMI. It should be noted there are individuals that are naturally and genetically very tall and thin; yet anorexia is marked by a refusal to maintain 85% of a typical BMI. Also, a physical aspect of anorexia, amenorrhea is the apparent absence of three or more consecutive menstrual cycles and may be linked with a lack of nutrient intake (Thompson & Sherman, 2010). Amenorrhea may also be apparent in some adolescent athletes, particularly those that engage in sports or events that require high amounts of aerobic activity (e.g., cross country, distance swimming). However, amenorrhea in the absence of the other criteria does not define an eating disorder.

The other criteria are emotional and cognitive in nature. Anorexics demonstrate an intense fear of weight gain. An important consideration with this item is this fear exists "despite explicit contradictory evidence." Relevant explicit contradictory evidence included comments from others (e.g., close friends, family members) or even viewing the digits on the scale. In addition, an anorexic may have had to make visits to the hospital for associated symptoms (e.g., cardiovascular problems, fatigue) and been urged by medical professionals that they are at an unhealthy low weight. Despite these clear messages that they are underweight, the fear of gaining weight persists. Lastly, anorexia appears to carry with it a disturbance in the way the body is experienced. There is not a normal balance of various components of the self; the physical aspect of oneself appears to dominate.

There are some associated features of anorexia nervosa. For instance, anorexia may be linked with depressive symptoms, perhaps due to a general dissatisfaction with the body and low self-esteem. Anorexics may also demonstrate obsessive and compulsive behaviors. Obsessions are consistent thoughts that tend to generate anxiety or fear; while compulsions are the subsequent behaviors that the individual believes may mitigate the anxiety. In cases of anorexia, these obsessions and compulsions are associated with food and caloric intake. Together, anorexia involves a consistent drive to lose weight, and anorexic body shape and size is more consistent (i.e., extreme leanness). However, that is not necessarily the case with bulimia.

Bulimia nervosa is an eating disorder characterized by eating large amounts of food (i.e., bingeing) and consequently compensating for it in some way. Once again, the majority of cases are with females. According to the DSM-IV, the four main criteria for bulimia nervosa are:

- Recurrent episodes of binge eating (i.e., eating more than normal in a discrete period of time, and with a sense of lack of control).
- Recurrent compensatory behavior aimed at losing weight (e.g., purging behaviors,

fasting or excessive exercise).

- Behaviors last twice a week for three months.
- Self-esteem is too closely linked to body image.

Binge eating is a hallmark of this disorder, and typically involves food that are high in caloric content (i.e., sweets, fast food). The recurrent compensatory behaviors are aimed at ridding the body of the calories taken in during the binge episode. There is some variability with how bulimics compensate. At a broad level, there are purging and non-purging methods of compensating. **Purging** methods include self-induced vomiting, misuse of diuretics, laxatives, and enemas. Of these, self-induced vomiting is the most common. The primary **non-purging** methods include fasting and excessive exercise. In either case, an individual is attempting to account for those calories taken in during a previous binge episode. There is an apparent "secretive" component to bingeing and purging behavior; they are not done in public settings, but rather in privacy.

Bulimics are not necessarily as lean as anorexics may be. Recall the binge episodes suggest there are many calories being taken in. The type, timing, and "effectiveness" of the compensatory behaviors may determine how many calories were retained, and ultimately if weight will be gained or lost. It is not uncommon for an individual suffering with bulimia to be normal weight or even overweight according to BMI status.

Key Terms

- **Adolescence** – a life stage beginning with puberty and ending with the ages corresponding with high school graduation
- **Magnetic Resonance Imaging (MRI)** – MRI employs magnetic forces, radio waves, and intricate software to recognize signals from brain tissue, providing very accurate pictures of the human brain
- **Gray Matter** – brain matter associated with information processing areas, and consists mostly of cell bodies and some extracellular space
- **White Matter** – brain matter that derives its color and name from the presence of myelin, the fatty insulating material that covers axons; white matter in the brain has connective properties and capabilities
- ***functional* MRI, (*f*MRI)** – brain activity is assessed through blood oxygenation levels. Thus, *f*MRI not only offers insight into the brain structure, but also the relative levels of activity within the brain.
- **Diffusion Tensor Imaging (DTI)** – offers scientists information related to interior changes in white matter in the brain. Water reacts differentially when placed in white matter containing strong, consistent nerve fibers (i.e., more connected) when compared to white matter with weaker and inconsistent nerve fibers (i.e., less connected).
- **Cerebrum** – a cortical brain region related to sensory and motor movement
- **Puberty** – marking the beginning of adolescence, puberty is the "awakening of a complex neuro-endocrine machinery in which the primary mechanism is still unclear"
- **Precocious Puberty** – evident when an individual experiences primary sexual change (e.g., menarche) before the age of 9, or the emergence of secondary sexual characteristics before the age of 8

- **Hormones** – these are selective chemicals dispersed into the bloodstream, eventually arriving at bodily organs for health, maintenance, and growth
- **Gonadarche** – a biological event where the gonads begin producing more hormones, including testosterone (i.e., an androgen) and estradiol (i.e., an estrogen)
- **Menarche** – female version of gonadarche, marked by the onset of the menstrual cycle
- **Spermarche** – male version of gonadarche, marked by production of active sperm
- **Primary Sexual Characteristics** – physical changes directly involved in reproduction, such as menarche and spermarche
- **Secondary Sexual Characteristics** – physical changes not related to reproduction. Secondary characteristics may include breast development in females (i.e., thelarche), pubic hair growth, voice changes, or acne.
- **Disordered Eating** – troublesome eating behaviors (e.g., restrictive dieting, bingeing, or purging) which occur less frequently or are less severe than those required to meet the full criteria for the diagnosis of an eating disorder
- **Anorexia Nervosa** – a disorder marked by voluntary starvation. Diagnostically, this disorder involves a refusal to maintain body weight at or above a minimally normal weight for age and height (weight loss leading to maintenance of less than 85% of that expected); intense fear of gaining weight or becoming fat, despite explicit contradictory evidence; a disturbance in the way in which the body is perceived or experienced; and amenorrhea.
- **Bulimia Nervosa** – an eating disorder characterized by eating large amounts of food (i.e., bingeing) and consequently compensating for it in some way. The four main criteria for bulimia nervosa include recurrent episodes of binge eating, recurrent compensatory behavior aimed at losing weight, behaviors last twice a week for three months, and self-esteem is too closely linked to body image.

Critical Thinking Questions

1. Discuss the phenomena of puberty. In doing so, not only define it, but discuss the defining features and characteristics of puberty. Also discuss at least three correlates of pubertal onset.
2. In cases of precocious puberty, an individual experiences puberty much earlier than his or her peers. What may be some psychosocial consequences (or effects) of experiencing puberty early? Would there be potential sex differences with the types of consequences experienced with precocious puberty? Why or why not?
3. The majority of cases of eating disorders are in females. Why might this sex difference in the diagnoses of these disorders be apparent? Are there any scenarios whereby males may be predisposed to an eating disorder?

References

Amso, D., & Casey, B. J. (2009). Beyond what develops when: Neuroimaging may inform how cognition changes with development. In L. S. Liben (Ed.), *Current directions in developmental psychology* (pp. 85-94). New York: Pearson.

Diwadkar, V. A., Wadehra, S., Pruitt, P., Keshavan, M. S., Rajan, U., Zajac-Benitez, C., Eickhoff, S. B. (2012). Disordered corticolimbic interactions during affective processing in children and adolescents at risk for schizophrenia revealed by functional magnetic resonance imaging and dynamic causal modeling. *Archives of General Psychiatry, 69*(3), 231-242.

Feldman, R. S. (2008). *Adolescence.* Pearson: Upper Saddle River, NJ.

Giedd, J. N., Stockman, M., Weddle, C., Liverpool, M., Wallace, G. L., Lee, N. R., Lalonde, F., & Lenroot, R. K. (2010). Anatomic magnetic resonance imaging of the developing child and adolescence brain and effect of genetic variation. *Neuropsychology Review, 20,* 349-361.

Giedd, J. N., Stockman, M., Weddle, C., Liverpool, M., Wallace, G. L., Lee, N. R., Lalonde, F., & Lenroot, R. K. (2012). Anatomic magnetic resonance imaging of the developing child and adolescent brain. In V. F. Reyna, S. B. Chapman, M. R. Dougherty, & J. Confrey (Eds.), *The adolescent brain: Learning, reasoning, and decision making.* Washington, DC: American Psychological Association Press.

Greenberg, N. (1998). "The evolutionary physiology of creativity." Human Behavior and Evolution Society, Tenth Annual Meeting, University of California-Davis, July 12-13, 1998.

Lawler, M. & Nixon, E. (2011). Body dissatisfaction among adolescent boys and girls: the effects of body mass, peer appearance culture and internalization of appearance ideals. *Journal of Youth and Adolescence, 40,* 59-71.

Shaw, N. D., Butler, J. P., McKinney, S. M., Nelson, S. A., Ellenbogen, J. M., Hall, J. E. (2012). Insights into puberty: The relationship between sleep stages and pulsatile LH secretion. *Journal of Clinical Endocrinology & Metabolism, 97*(11), E2055-E2062.

Thompson, R. A. & Sherman, R. (2010). *Eating disorder in sport.* New York: Taylor and Francis.

Tither, J. M., & Ellis, B. J. (2008). Impact of fathers on daughters' age at menarche: A genetically and environmentally controlled sibling study. *Developmental Psychology, 5,* 1409-1142.

Wilson, J. (2012). Boys—like girls—hitting puberty earlier. *CNN.* Retrieved from http://www.cnn.com/2012/12/20/health/boys-early-puberty/index.html

CHAPTER 11

Cognitive Development in Adolescence

Concrete and Symbolic Thought

Adolescence may be viewed as an ideal, yet vulnerable stage for cognitive and intellectual development. In terms of being ideal, many theories of cognitive development suggest that adolescents become highly capable thinkers, able to solve problems and navigate situations in adult-like ways. Undeniably, one of the most striking cognitive developments in adolescence is the ability to engage in symbolic or **abstract thought.** Being able to think abstractly implies that individuals are free from considering only concrete and tangible objects; rather, they are able to handle more difficult or theoretical themes. On the other hand, as individuals move away from authority figure-centered familial and elementary school contexts to settings of enhanced autonomy and personal choice, there lie vulnerability for negative outcomes (e.g., dropping out of high school, addictions) (Chapman, Gamino, & Mudar, 2012). To illustrate, estimates suggest one adolescent drops out of high school every 26 seconds, leading to about one million drop-outs each year, the highest totals in American history (Herbert, 2009). Thus, while there is potential for higher order cognitive and intellectual development, not all adolescents realize it. Alberts (2009) argued that the increasing drop-out rate has direct connections to cognition; many students become terribly bored with school due to the need to consistently memorize terms and concepts, rather than engage their abstract and symbolic thought via more meaningful activities and discussions. The rate of drop-out notwithstanding, Piaget's theory may help clarify cognitive development.

Piaget

Recall Piaget proposed four general stages marked cognitive development. The stages that characterize childhood are laden with immature cognitive structures than impede logical and rational thought. Recall the "conservation problem," in which younger children may be adamant that the taller beaker has more liquid in it. One may ask the question: At what age do most individuals "get" the conservation task?

Many may argue that children would begin to understand there are equivalent amounts of liquid in each beaker at about the age of 7 or 8; and Piaget's theory would support this assertion. For example, older children are able to solve the "conservation problem" because they realize that even though it appears different, it must logically be the same as long as no water is spilled. Indeed, one could reverse the process (even hypothetically) and verify there are equivalent amounts of liquid in each beaker. If an individual is able to engage in such mental action, they are less prone to make this (and other) errors.

According to Piaget, an **operation** is an internalized mental action that is part of an organized structure, and becomes apparent during the concrete operational stage. Basically, whatever a child could not do before, they can during the concrete operational stage. **Concrete operations** are defined by the ability to reason and think in a more adult-like fashion, but only in relation to real, concrete objects. Thereafter, children (as they approach and enter adolescence) may engage in **formal operational** thought. The major development in this stage is abstract thinking. Those in a concrete operational stage may be restricted to "operate on reality," while individuals in a formal stage may mentally engage with "hypothetical" situations. Individuals in this stage can be rather scientific in their approach to problems; they can develop a theory and speculate on outcomes.

Some consequences of adolescents being able to think abstractly may be apparent. For example, they may have more advanced decision-making and conversational skills. They may be more aware of their social surroundings and dynamics. In addition, adolescents may no longer be restricted to the "concrete" messages from authority figures. Subsequently, they may question authority and test limits. Lastly, it may have implications for moral development.

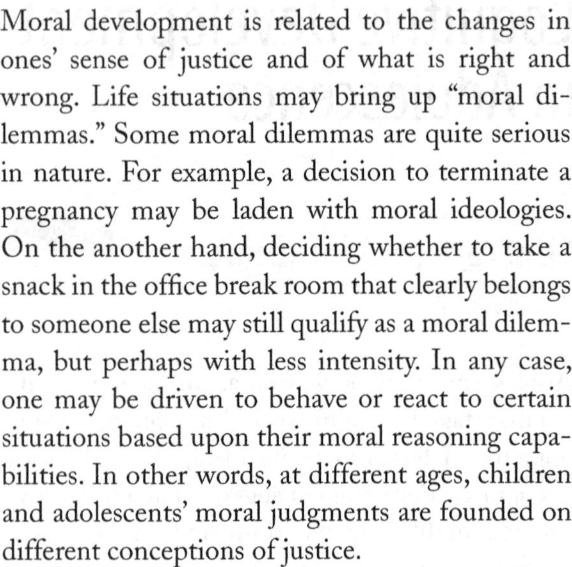

Moral Development

Moral development is related to the changes in ones' sense of justice and of what is right and wrong. Life situations may bring up "moral dilemmas." Some moral dilemmas are quite serious in nature. For example, a decision to terminate a pregnancy may be laden with moral ideologies. On the another hand, deciding whether to take a snack in the office break room that clearly belongs to someone else may still qualify as a moral dilemma, but perhaps with less intensity. In any case, one may be driven to behave or react to certain situations based upon their moral reasoning capabilities. In other words, at different ages, children and adolescents' moral judgments are founded on different conceptions of justice.

The three primary moral theorists are Jean Piaget, Lawrence Kohlberg, and Carol Gilligan. First, Piaget's general theory of cognitive development may be lent to moral development. That is, another consequence of a shift from pre-operational to operational thought may be in terms of moral reasoning. According to Piaget, individuals move from a **heteronymous** morality stage (approximately 4-7 years), which is marked by a rigid approach to rules; to an **autonomous** morality stage (about 10 years and older), which is marked by a fuller awareness of rules and their human construction. These particular stages seem to mirror notions of how children cognitively may become less restricted to their present (and concrete) surroundings to have a more abstract worldview.

Kohlberg's (1984) theory centers on issues of justice, and maintains some degree of similarity with

Piaget's theory of moral development. To arrive at his understanding of moral development, Kohlberg interviewed children and adolescents and used a series of moral dilemmas to evaluate moral reasoning. Perhaps his most famous example is the story of "Heinz." Consider this particular moral dilemma below, and ask yourself: Were Heinz's actions "right" or just?

> A woman was near death from a certain type of cancer. There was one drug—made from radium—the doctors thought might save her. The drug was expensive to make, but the druggist charged 10 times what the drug cost him to make. He paid $200 for the radium but charged $2,000. The sick woman's husband went to borrow money but could only come up with $1,000. The druggist would still not sell it; saying he invented the drug and wanted to make money. Heinz broke into the man's store to steal the drug. Should the husband have done that? (Kohlberg, 1984)

This dilemma is intentionally one that makes the reader consider a couple of stark perspectives. It should be noted there is not necessarily a right or wrong answer to this question. Many individuals might argue that the woman suffering from cancer has a right to receive medical care; and this right supersedes the right of the druggist to profit from the sale of this particular treatment. On the other hand, others may argue that stealing, regardless of context, is morally wrong. In any case, the thinking that one applies to such problems is referred to as **moral reasoning**, and was the basis for Kohlberg's theory.

Kohlberg (1984) offered three main stages through which individuals may progress in terms of moral development. In the **pre-conventional stage**, more typical of children, the primary focus may be on fear of punishment, eventually moving on to respect for authority. Imagine a child in a room with her parents. The child wants to play with an object in the room; however, playing with this object is forbidden, and this rule is typically enforced by her father. The child turns to the mother and states, "I want daddy to leave so I can play with this." In her mind, it is "right" if the immediate environment permits it, and punishment or reprimand may be avoided. In the **conventional stage**, moral judgments are based on an understanding of social order, law, justice, and duty. There are rules and laws in social contexts (e.g., homes, classrooms, athletic events, society) that must be adhered to. Generally speaking, following these rules will guide individuals to do what is legal, and very often morally "right." However, what is "legal" and what is morally right may diverge from time to time. In other words, laws and rules may not always neatly distinguish between what is right and wrong. Consider again the story of Heinz. Many may argue what he did was illegal, but morally right. Heinz may go to jail for his actions, but he may do so with a clean conscious. Such a scenario is reflective of the **post-conventional stage,** which evokes the consideration of universal ethical principles; one's moral judgments are based on notions of universal human rights.

Together, Piaget and Kohlberg offer theories of moral development that underscore an initial strict adherence to rules and those authority figures that may enforce rules, to more flexible, abstract conceptions of justice based upon the potential fallibility of manmade rules, and an understanding of universal ethical principles.

Carol Gilligan (1982) offered a slightly different theory on moral development, and one that highlights a gender difference in morality. In Gilligan's **morality of caring** perspective, she posits that males and females are fundamentally different in how they approach morality. According to her theory, males view morality adhering to general principles (e.g., justice). On the other hand, females develop morally on a more personal level (i.e., a responsibility to help others in the context of relationships). Together, Piaget, Kohlberg, and Gilligan theoretically conceive a certain level of cognitive maturity on the part of adolescents. There are some byproducts to such cognitive development, including egocentrism.

Egocentrism

Somewhat different than the egocentrism that may characterize young children, Elkind (1985) hypothesized about **adolescent egocentrism.** This egocentrism is thought to occur naturally, and as a byproduct of development. Adolescents tend to form clearer pictures of themselves (e.g., identity, self-esteem) by comparing themselves to and referencing others. Over time, adolescents begin to see the flaws and inferior qualities in others. Subsequently, this process may create anxiety about their own flaws, along with a sense—albeit irrational—that people are watching them with high degrees of intensity and duration. Moreover, they may begin to think their actions are at the center of everyone's thoughts. Teens have misconceptions called the personal fable and imaginary audience. An **imaginary audience** is akin to the idea that people are watching them to a degree that is not rational. As an adolescent walks down the hallway at school, although others may notice them, for the most part they are not being heavily watched. A **personal fable** is related to the idea that one is uniquely destined for magnificent outcomes. To understand a personal fable, one may consider what a classic fable (e.g., a Disney movie) entails. Typically, a protagonist (e.g., princess) has to deal with some adversity initially. However, the protagonist is relatively resilient to the difficulties that pass their way, and there is little doubt there will be a cheerful ending in terms of wealth and happiness. Moreover, there are numerous supporting characters that facilitate this rise. An adolescent elevating their own life story to that of a fable may be investing in an irrational thought pattern. It should be noted that adolescent egocentrism tends to subside through emerging adulthood.

Intelligence

Higher order cognition may be broadly linked with intellectual development, or intelligence. Many aspects of intelligence (e.g., history, definition, application, reliability, etc.) are contentious, and have stirred much debate over the decades. To further understand intelligence, it may be helpful to consider its history.

A cousin of Charles Darwin was influential in early conceptualizations of intelligence. Sir Francis Galton, who was also a renowned statistician at the time, attempted to demonstrate correlations between factors related to "success" (e.g., position, salary, and popularity) and performance on some simple laboratory tasks. Galton's main premise was that positive correlations would exist between success and task performance, indicating some underlying intellectual capability to handle real-world issues. Although Galton advanced the knowledge and use of correlational analyses as an analytic tool, he may have fallen short of confirming his hypotheses.

Decades later, Charles Spearman elaborated upon intelligence a bit. He proposed that skilled performance on tasks that involve thinking (broadly defined) would be highly correlated and predictive of enhanced performance on other tasks also requiring thinking. For instance, those that did well in mathematical areas would likely also do well in science; both require analysis and critical thinking. Akin to Galton's original premise, there may be an underlying intellectual capability that underlies many areas and tasks. Spearman called this **general intelligence**—abbreviated simply ***g***—and thought it was a core cognitive ability that could be applied in most situations (e.g., athletic, academic, and social). Although with the idea of ***g*** Spearman was theorizing about intelligence, he had no formal way to test and support his notions.

Binet and Simon were instrumental in formulating the first intelligence test, and the modern calculation of the **intelligence quotient (IQ)**. The main idea behind IQ is that when determining intelligence, an individual's age should be taken into account. Although this appears to make intuitive sense, it was a rather novel concept for Binet and Simon. Subsequently, **mental age** is compared to **chronological age**. Binet and Simon posited that an individual's chronological age should generally cohere with an expected performance level on various tasks. Accordingly, the actual IQ is calculated by dividing one's supposed "mental age" (as measured via testing) by their chronological age, and multiplying by 100. Thus, an individual of "average" intelligence would have an equivalent mental and chronological age—factoring down to 1.0 and then multiplied by 100 —yielding an IQ of 100. Consequently, IQ scores higher than 100 would purportedly indicate a higher mental age in relation to one's chronological age; IQ scores lower than 100 would presumably point to a lower mental age in relation to chronological age.

The Wechsler Intelligence Scale for Children (WISC) and the Wechsler Adult Intelligence Scale (WAIS) are common tests purported to assess intelligence. The WISC is typically used for individuals from ages 7 through 16, while the WAIS is used in anyone over 16 years of age. Thus, the intelligence of early and late adolescents may be assessed by different scales. The WISC and WAIS are used in a variety of contexts. Most frequently, they may be used to assess the presence of particular learning disabilities in childhood or adolescence. However, they may also be used in legal (i.e., assessing intelligence of defendants), neurological (e.g., tracking intelligence along with dementia), or organizational (e.g., recommending hiring based upon intelligence scores) contexts.

The WISC and WAIS involve the same general format, and all subtests and items relate to a verbal or performance scale. The **verbal scale** not only involves knowledge of language (e.g., vocabulary and mechanics), but also mathematical problems. The **performance scale** consists of items that require problem-solving skills for novel tasks (e.g., completing a puzzle, arranging blocks). The verbal scales may relate to a specific theoretical form of intelligence. More specifically, knowledge (i.e., vocabulary, facts and assertions about the world) individuals accumulate may be known as **crystallized intelligence**. On the other hand, the performance scale of the WISC or WAIS may assess **fluid intelligence**, which involves an individual's ability to reason and solve new problems. However, in one form or another, the WISC and WAIS are thought to assess general intelligence.

Sternberg theorized about successful intelligence, which in itself is broader than general intelligence. Concerning the latter, Sternberg strongly believed traditional intelligence tests were limited in nature, and may do more damage than good. **Successful intelligence** may be defined as "the ability to achieve success in life in terms of one's personal standards within one's own sociocultural context." Thus, intelligence may be understood according to the intellectual skills one employs to achieve personal success. This type of intelligence may vary between individuals and cultures. Moreover, Sternberg thought that successful intelligence was comprised of creative, analytical, and practical intelligence. Together, these are used to decide which problems are important to address, to solve those problems, and do so effectively.

Gardner went a step further than Sternberg, by hypothesizing about **multiple intelligences**. More specifically, intelligence may be demonstrated in numerous areas. Traditional tests may underscore verbal and mathematical abilities, but other forms of intelligence may exist. According to Gardner, there are eight general areas of intelligence:

- mathematical,
- verbal,
- interpersonal,
- intrapersonal,
- spatial,
- musical,
- kinesthetic, and
- naturalistic.

The first two forms (i.e., **mathematical** and **verbal**) are relatively self-explanatory and very academic in nature. The other six forms may also be understood as areas in which an individual may express intelligence. For instance, **interpersonal** intelligence is related to how one understands other individuals in a social context. On the other hand, **intrapersonal** intelligence is linked with self understanding. An individual with excellent self-awareness, emotional regulation, or both may be intelligent in this area. **Spatial** intelligence is related to one's ability to understand object placement in an environment. Another individual may express musical or kinesthetic intelligence. While **musical** intelligence is simply linked with musical capabilities, **kinesthetic** intelligence is related to the ability to use one's body. A skilled athlete may have enhanced levels of this form of intelligence. Lastly, **naturalistic** intelligence is associated with ability for dealing with natural phenomena (e.g., plants and animals). Together, there may be a variety of non-academic ways to understand and convey intelligence.

According to Gardner, one general intelligence score would not account for the unique skills, abilities, and talents that may be apparent in one or more of the aforementioned areas. Gardner once stated, "Ask not how intelligent you are, but how *are you* intelligent." According to this multiple intelligence theory, the WISC and WAIS—that only accounts for the mathematical and verbal forms—would fall far short of offering an accurate picture of intelligence. Along these lines, intelligence scores have often been scrutinized for their lack of general reliability.

To illustrate, a test that many adolescents take is the Standardized Achievement Test (SAT). While some may argue it is not technically a measure of intelligence, the modern SAT resembles the verbal portion of the WISC or WAIS, assessing linguistic and mathematical skills. Although SAT scores have been used as primary entrance criteria to many universities, the SAT has failed to be predictive of academic performance in college. In fact, it becomes less predictive over time. Universities have begun to abandon the SAT as a useful tool in determining students that may thrive at their respective institutions (Murdoch, 2007).

Notwithstanding potential differences in intellectual capacity between adolescents, many theoretical perspectives give adolescents credit for being able to think in very adult-like ways. While they do not necessarily apply their ability to think abstractly or reason morally, they may maintain the ability nonetheless. Together, adolescents may be more like adults than children in many cognitive domains.

Key Terms

- **Abstract Thought** – the process of being able to think abstractly implies that an individual is free from considering only concrete and tangible objects; rather, they are able to handle more difficult or theoretical themes
- **Operation** – a Piagetian term, this is an internalized mental action that is part of an organized structure, and becomes apparent during the concrete operational stage. Basically, whatever a child could not do before, they can during the concrete operational stage.
- **Concrete Operations** – the ability to reason and think in a more adult-like fashion, but only in relation to real, concrete objects
- **Formal Operations** – evident in the ability to think abstractly; individuals in a formal operational stage may mentally engage with "hypothetical" situations, being scientific in their approach to problems; they can develop a theory and speculate on outcomes
- **Moral Reasoning** – the thinking and logic one applies to moral dilemmas and problems involving notions of right and wrong
    - **Piaget: Heteronymous Morality** – encompassing approximately ages 4-7 years, this stage is marked by a rigid approach to rules in deciphering right and wrong
    - **Piaget: Autonomous Morality** – beginning at about 10 years of age, this stage is marked by a fuller awareness of rules and their human construction
    - **Kohlberg: Pre-conventional Stage** – more typical in children, the primary focus may be on fear of punishment, eventually moving on to respect for authority
    - **Kohlberg: Conventional Stage** – moral judgments are based on an understanding of social order, law, justice, and duty. There are rules and laws in social contexts (e.g., homes, classrooms, athletic events, society) that must be adhered to.
    - **Kohlberg: Post-conventional Stage** – moral reasoning evokes the consideration of universal ethical principles; one's moral judgments are based on notions of universal human rights

- **Gilligan: Morality of Caring** – a primary tenet of Gilligan's theory of morality, she posits that males and females are fundamentally different in how they approach morality; males view morality according to general principles (e.g., justice) whereas females develop morally on a more personal level (i.e., a responsibility to help others in the context of relationships).
- **Adolescent Egocentrism** – may be viewed as a byproduct of cognitive maturation, this egocentrism is thought to occur naturally. Adolescents tend to form clearer pictures of themselves (e.g., identity, self-esteem) by comparing themselves to and referencing others. Over time, adolescents begin to see the flaws and inferior qualities in others. Subsequently, this process may create anxiety about their own flaws, along with a sense—albeit irrational—that people are watching them with high degrees of intensity and duration.
    - **Imaginary Audience** – akin to the idea that people are watching them to a degree that is not rational
    - **Personal Fable** – related to the idea that one is uniquely destined for magnificent outcomes
- **General Intelligence (*g*)** – a supposed core cognitive intellectual ability that could be applied in most situations (e.g., athletic, academic, and social)
- **Intelligence Quotient (IQ)** – a ratio of one's mental age to their chronological age
    - **Mental Age** – someone's general and analytical capacity as evident in their ability to solve various problems
    - **Chronological Age** – someone's actual age in terms of years and months
- **Verbal Scale** – involves knowledge of language (e.g., vocabulary and mechanics), but also mathematical problems
- **Performance Scale** – consists of items that require problem-solving skills for novel tasks
- **Crystallized Intelligence** – the knowledge that individuals maintain about the world (i.e., vocabulary, facts, and assertions)
- **Fluid Intelligence** – related to an individual's ability to reason and solve new problems. However, in one form or another, the WISC and WAIS are thought to assess general intelligence.
- **Successful Intelligence** – the ability to achieve success in life in terms of one's personal standards within one's own sociocultural context
- **Multiple Intelligences** – a theoretical framework offered by Gardner; the basic idea that intelligence may be demonstrated in numerous areas; many of which would not necessarily be captured by traditional theories or scales of intelligence
    - **Mathematical** – related to the ability to solve problems involving numbers; a form of intelligence related to quantitative matters
    - **Verbal** – a form of intelligence linked with language and vocabulary
    - **Interpersonal** – a form of intelligence related to how one understands other individuals in a social context
    - **Intrapersonal** – intelligence linked with self understanding
    - **Spatial** – related to one's ability to understand object placement in an environment
    - **Musical** – simply linked with musical capabilities
    - **Kinesthetic** – related to the ability to use one's body. A skilled athlete may have enhanced levels of this form of intelligence.
    - **Naturalistic** – associated with ability for dealing with natural phenomena (e.g., plants and animals)

Critical Thinking Questions

1. general terms and using relevant terms from Piaget's theory, what are some of the cognitive capabilities that adolescents may maintain that distinguishes them from children? In your response, you may find it helpful to also discuss the Piagetian stages from earlier childhood units (i.e., sensorimotor, pre-operational).
2. Compare and contrast the ideas of three main moral theorists (i.e., Piaget, Kohlberg, Gilligan). How are these theories similar? How are they different? Regardless of the theory, what do they inform us of adolescent moral reasoning capabilities?
3. Discuss the theory of "multiple intelligences." What are the different types of intelligence, and how does this theory stand in stark contrast to the "general intelligence" theory (*g*)? What type(s) of intelligence do you feel you maintain? How do you know?

References

Alberts, B. (2009). The breakthroughs of 2009. *Science, 326,* 1589.

Chapman, S. B. Gamino, J. F., Mudar, R. A. (2012). Higher order strategic gist reasoning in adolescence. In V. F. Reyna, S. Chapman, J. R. Dougherty, & J. Confrey (Eds.), *The adolescent brain: Learning, reasoning and decision-making* (pp. 123-150). Washington, DC: American Psychological Association Press.

Elkin, D. (1985). Egocentrism redux. *Developmental Review, 5,* 218-226.

Gilligan, C. (1982). *In a different voice: Psychological theory and women's development.* Cambridge, MA: Harvard University Press.

Herbert, B. (2009, September 28). Peering at the future. *The New York Times.* Retrieved from http://nytimes.com

Kohlberg, L. (1984). *The psychology of moral development: Essays on moral development.* San Francisco: Harper & Row.

Murdoch, S. (2007). *IQ: A smart history of a failed idea.* Hoboken, NJ: Wiley.

CHAPTER 12

Socioemotional Development in Adolescence

One of the earliest conceptions of adolescence was that it was a time of "storm and stress"—a phrase made popular by G. Stanley Hall (1904). Originally, Hall believed this was a relatively universal phenomenon, prompted by biological forces, and all adolescents were predisposed to encounter difficult and tumultuous times. Such a view was not inconsistent with past views of the ages that typically encompass adolescence; even if the life stage was not formally termed "adolescence" yet (a term G. Stanley Hall himself popularized). Prior to Hall's (1904) work, philosophers and writers (e.g., Aristotle, Goethe, Rousseau) also characterized this life stage as being marked by social and emotional struggle (Arnett, 1999). Currently, most view adolescence as a time whereby some individuals do experience social difficulty or emotional crises; however, it is not necessarily a universal phenomenon to be expected of all adolescence. In a review in which more current scientific findings were applied to the storm and stress model, Arnett (1999) noted that adolescence does appear to be marked by higher levels of conflict with parents, mood disruptions, and risky behaviors. Importantly, there appears to be a high level of cultural and familial difference in the extent to which adolescent experience or exhibit such storm or stress. That is, social groups and contexts may inhibit or promote adjustment in adolescence.

Peer Groups

A **peer** is someone who is about the same age and level of maturity. To borrow some terms introduced in previous units, peers may be un-

derstood as members of a cohort, and peer groups may be conceptualized as a salient microsystem in adolescence. Generally speaking, the time individuals spend with peers increases dramatically throughout adolescence; meaning time spent with family members tends to diminish.

Thus, **peer groups** are composed of individuals of approximately the same age and status. Broader adolescent groups (i.e., crowds) may be **heterogeneous** in terms of race, ethnicity, and socioeconomic status (SES). However, narrower social circles will form (i.e., cliques) that may be more **homogeneous** in terms of sex (i.e., males *or* females). Homogeneity is also apparent in other ways, including in terms of age. Known as **age grading,** school systems are influential in organizing groups of students based on age.

An essential peer group to consider is a **crowd,** which are groups of individuals who share particular characteristic(s) but who may not interact with one another. Crowds are relatively large, and may carry some level of consistency. There is not a prescriptive list of crowds necessarily; they tend to form in the context of large adolescent settings (e.g., high school). Each researcher that studies crowds may have their own set of labels. For instance, Brown, Lohr, & Trujillo (1990) noted the differences in characteristics of "jock, druggie, nobody, normal, popular, and tough" crowds. Accordingly, one particular and consistent crowd may be the athletes, or "jocks." The members of this crowd share an interest in athletic participation and competition, and most high schools have a "jock" crowd. However, all members of this (or any) crowd do not necessarily all interact. The senior quarterback may not interact with a freshman volleyball player. Nonetheless, all members may claim membership in this crowd, and realize the benefits that may be associated with crowd membership.

Somewhat akin to how individuals display various levels of popularity, crowds have different statuses in the overall social milieu. Interestingly, though, benefit may be had from a position in most any crowd, as adolescents may naturally emphasize the positive aspects of their "in-group" and devalue aspects of their "out-groups" (Feldman, 2008). The lack of interaction between crowds and their constituent members may clarify why mis-perceptions abound between groups. In one study, researchers reported that adolescents overestimate the amount of drug- and alcohol-use and sexual behaviors that many of their peers are engaging in. At the same time, they underestimate the amount of time their peers spend on studying or exercise. Indeed, the "brainy" crowd studied on average about half of the the amount of time that their peers thought they did. The researchers conclude that adolescents conform not to what others do, but what they think others do. The lesson of this research is that adolescents are wrong—most peers aren't as risky as they may think (Helms, Choukas-Bradley, Widman, Giletta, Cohen, & Prinstein, 2014).

A narrower type of peer group is a **clique**, which are groups of between 2-12 people whose members have frequent social interactions. By definition, a group needs at least two members, so the lower limit of this definition is strict. However, it is possible a clique may exceed 12 persons. In any case, though, unlike a crowd, members of a clique do have high levels of interaction. Interestingly, a useful place to observe cliques may be school cafeterias. For an adolescent, they get to know fellow clique members (and possibly their families) well. These are the individuals they may hang out with on the weekends, and if genuine friendships endure beyond adolescence, many times the relationship originated in a clique.

Other key aspects of cliques are similarity in age, race, socioeconomic status, and gender, which may all be observed with cliques. Similar values also tend to be a unifying aspect. However, this homogeneity in cliques becomes less rigid in late adolescence. In a hallmark study (Dunphy, 1963), it was reported that early in adolescence, same-sex cliques are quite common. However, over time "high status" members of the cliques may form mixed-sex cliques, which fracture and weaken the original same sex clique. Thus, as dating and romantic activity increase into late adolescence, individual pairs may take precedence over cliques.

When being a member of a peer group such as a clique or crowd, there are some general benefits an adolescent may realize. For instance, peer support can benefit school achievement or compensate for lack of family support (Feldman, 2008). There are additional psychosocial forces that may be apparent in groups as well. Most notably conformity and peer pressure are evident in adolescent groups. **Conformity** is a general change in behavior or attitude brought about by a desire to follow the beliefs or standards of others. Such conformity may be akin to *peer pressure*, and adolescents may be more susceptible to it. However, it is important to note that being part of a group becomes *less* important as adolescents grow older, perhaps making them less susceptible to peer pressure. In addition to the informal groups covered thus far, more formal peer groups emerge.

Organized Activities

The percentage of adolescents involved in organized extracurricular activities is impressive. Based upon the National Survey of Families, it is reported that among youth ages 12-17, 57% participated on a sports team, 29% participated in lessons, and 60% participated in clubs or organizations after school or on weekends during the last year (Mahoney, Larson, Eccles, & Lord, 2005). Moreover, organized activities include, but are not limited to, civic (e.g., community service, volunteering), academic (e.g., math or chess clubs), and athletic (e.g., school or community sponsored athletics) programs or groups. These activities are not necessarily part of regular class curriculum, but rather include those that require after-school, or extracurricular, engagements, and may be sponsored by the school (e.g., interscholastic sport, debate club), or independent, community-based organizations (e.g., Babe Ruth Little League). Furthermore, these extracurricular activities are often categorized as being "organized" or "unorganized." The hallmarks of **organized activities** are structure, adult-supervision, and an emphasis upon skill-building (Eccles, 2005).

Studies have reported that participation in organized activities promote positive outcomes among adolescents (e.g., Eccles & Barber, 1999; Eccles, Barber, Stone, & Hunt, 2003; Feldman & Mat-

jakso, 2005; Fletcher, Nickerson, & Wright, 2003; Mahoney, Cairns, & Farmer, 2003; McHale, Crouter, & Tucker, 2001; Posner & Vandell, 1999; Zaff, Moore, Papillo, Williams, 2003). Various organized activities appear to offer distinct growth experiences, which subsequently promote specific kinds of adjustment. To illustrate, one study examined organized activity participation in 10th grade and subsequent outcomes two years later (Eccles et al., 1999). The researchers used five categories of activity involvement: pro-social (volunteer and community service); performance (band, drama clubs); athletics (inter-school athletics teams); school (student government); and academic (math, debate clubs) activities. Results revealed that participation in all activity categories was linked to higher levels of academic achievement and academic attainment (i.e., college attendance). Participation in pro-social and performing arts activities reduced the likelihood of engagement in risky behaviors such as drinking, skipping school, and drug use. Although athletic participation was associated with higher academic achievement, it actually predicted an increase in certain risky behaviors (i.e., alcohol use). Subsequent studies have expanded on such findings.

For instance, one relevant study inventoried high-school students about their learning experiences in various organized activities (Hansen, Larson, & Dworkin, 2003). Various activity-types were identified and compared: Faith-based and service activities, academic and leadership activities, performance and fine arts activities, community and vocational clubs, and athletics teams. Furthermore, learning experiences were conceptualized into personal (identity work, initiative, emotional regulation) and interpersonal (social skill building, peer network extension, social capital building) processes. Results revealed that the faith-based activities and community/vocational clubs offered more opportunities for identity reflection and emotional regulation. Furthermore, these activities offered more opportunities for leadership skill building and linkages to community. Academic/leadership organizations and performance/fine arts activities appeared to provide substantially fewer personal learning experiences than all other activities. Finally, athletics provided more opportunities for developing self-knowledge, physical skills, and emotional regulation. Together, organized activities appear to offer a range of benefits. Most pertinent to this particular unit, organized activity involvement may protect against poor social adjustment in adolescents.

Another study examined adolescent activity involvement and social adjustment (Barber, Eccles, & Stone, 2001). The longitudinal investigation tracked participants from the 10th grade through the 12th grade. Results revealed that loneliness decreased across time for all respondents, regardless of their degree of activity involvement. Moreover, athletes reported significantly less loneliness than adolescents in non-athletic activities. A similar investigation reported a consistent and positive relation between sport participation (i.e., total number of athletic teams that an adolescent participated in over one year) and social adjustment. Most notably, athletic participation appeared to promote social responsibility, reciprocity, and social skills (Rees & Howell, 1990). Similar findings have also been reported in other studies, in which athletics participation was linked with higher levels of perceived popularity (Melnick, Vanfossen, & Sabo, 1988).

Yet another related study investigated the impact that high school organized activity participation had upon social adjustment (e.g., loneliness) in emerging adulthood (Bohnert, Aikins, & Edidin, 2007). Findings revealed that more intense activity involvement was linked with better friendship quality in young adulthood for students that had experienced loneliness and social dissatisfaction in late adolescence, and that less intense activity involvement predicted loneliness and social dissatisfaction in students who had experienced poor quality friendships when compared to students who had experienced good quality friendships. In sum, participation in organized activities may be linked with gains in social adjustment areas.

Intimacy, Identity, and Friendships

Broadly speaking, **intimacy** is an affective sense of closeness and interconnectedness with another

person. It does *not* necessarily involve romantic or sexual intent or behavior, but it may in certain contexts. In fact, most intimate relationships are between friends or family members, and are nonsexual in nature. Intimate relationships emerge in adolescence as individuals may have a better understanding of themselves (i.e., identity) and others (i.e., perspective taking). This last idea raises an important theoretical consideration.

Erikson (1963) proposed that identity was a central psychosocial task in adolescence. This was a time for testing limits, breaking ties, and establishing a new identity; the major conflicts center on clarification of identity, life goals, and life meaning. Failure to do so may result in role confusion. Thereafter—into the emerging adulthood years—Erikson posited that developing intimate relationships was of primary importance. Accordingly, the fundamental developmental task is to form intimate relationships, including selflessness, sexuality, and devotion. Failure to do so may lead to feelings of alienation and isolation, creating fear and anxiety regarding future relationships. Putting these stages together, Erikson's model may suggest it is important to know yourself before being aptly suited to adopt and maintain close and intimate connections with others. This may make some degree of intuitive sense.

On the other hand, other theorists have suggested otherwise; the drive and need to formulate intimate relationships may precede understanding of one's own self. For instance, Sullivan (1953) had earlier offered a theory of interpersonal development, in which a need for intimacy and sexuality go before a need to "integrate into society." Admittedly, Sullivan did not necessarily specifically implicate "identity" into his theory, but the integration stage may include elements of forming sense of self and identity.

The most important consideration with these two theories may be the sequence of intimacy and identity work may be less important than the notion they are linked developmentally and both are salient in adolescence. Thus, there may be an interconnection between intimacy and identity formation. An adolescent may have a relatively well formed identity in one or more areas, and—based upon that knowledge—seek out relationships that seem to fit his or her own identity. On the other hand, adolescents may still be relatively undeveloped in terms of identity, and use peer relationships and groups to help form and crystallize their sense of self. These processes may be bidirectional and concurrent.

Dating

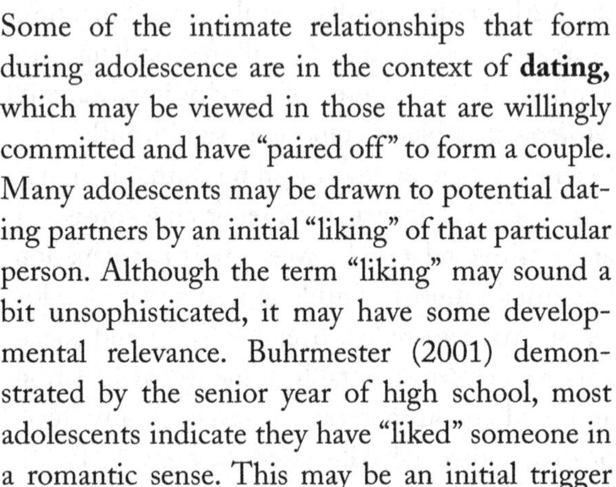

Some of the intimate relationships that form during adolescence are in the context of **dating,** which may be viewed in those that are willingly committed and have "paired off" to form a couple. Many adolescents may be drawn to potential dating partners by an initial "liking" of that particular person. Although the term "liking" may sound a bit unsophisticated, it may have some developmental relevance. Buhrmester (2001) demonstrated by the senior year of high school, most adolescents indicate they have "liked" someone in a romantic sense. This may be an initial trigger that perpetuates further relationship development. Along those lines, there are some theoretical stages of intimacy, including:

- infatuation,
- status,
- intimacy, and
- bonding.

As the name implies, adolescents in the first stage of intimacy may be marked by a level of **infatuation** with one another. They may be readily excited to be in a relationship and disclose personal information. While this may seem to the casual observer as a meaningful emotional stage of a relationship, it may actually lack some more genuine forms of emotion. In the second **status** stage, adolescents may date with an eye toward how others perceive the relationship. As adolescents age, dating may be viewed as normative and necessary to maintain or enhance a certain social status. Once again, this stage may lack some important emotional aspects. Upon entering an **intimacy** stage, adolescents may become more attuned to the emotional connection that exists between them and their partner. This type of emotional connectivity may be characteristic of mature relationships, and those that may more legitimately claim they "love" one another. The final theoretical stage of intimacy is **bonding**, which includes the consideration of long-term commitment. Many adolescent relationships may not maintain the bonding element that may otherwise permit a relationship to endure separation due to graduation from high school and the social changes that follow. Of course, not all adolescents progress through each stage; some short-lived relationships may not extend beyond an infatuation stage, when the partners become uninterested with each other. Some relationships may deteriorate during the status stage when the relationship is perceived by one or both partners as negatively impacting their reputation or social status.

In any case, dating is thought to have some potential psychosocial benefit. For instance, it may help build identity, as it offers another social context (in addition to families and peers) in which to understand oneself. In addition, dating may offer "practice" for future romantic relationships. Interestingly, dating in early adolescence may actually lack intimacy, marked more by a lack of self-disclosure, even when sexual activity is present.

Sexuality

During puberty in males, the testes accelerate the production of **androgens** (i.e., male sex hormone). Androgens are responsible for primary and sexual changes, but also **sex drive**. In adolescent males, androgen secretion is consistent. In females, there is increased production of **estrogens** and **progesterone**, and also some androgens. However, for females androgen secretion follows a less consistent, but cyclical pattern, corresponding to ovulation. This may seem to indicate females have a lower overall sex drive than males, but this is not necessarily the case. However, it does appear clear that adolescent males think about sexual activity far more than their female counterparts (e.g., Baumeister, Twenge, & Nuss, 2002; Mendelsohn, 2003). More specifically, about 50% of males report thinking about it daily, compared to 20% of females.

Sexual activity among adolescents is normative and rather pervasive, with up to 80% having engaged in intercourse before the age of 20 (Kantrowitz & Wingert, 1999). Almost two-thirds of women learn about intercourse by the age of 12, and their initial reactions may be shock or even disgust. Some societal trends have marked the contexts in which sexual activity may be apparent or acceptable.

For instance, Feldman (2008) outlines three such trends. First, the **gender double standard**—a perhaps outdated notion—that premarital sex by males was permissible, but not for females. Contemporarily, most may think premarital sex is acceptable for either gender (Hyde & DeLameter, 2003). In addition, **permissiveness with affection** implies that premarital sex is acceptable given an intimate, stable relationship between partners. Lastly, the idea of **friends with benefits** implies that sexual relationships that lack commitment (or even much intimacy or friendship) between partners. Together, there are social trends that may guide the occurrence of adolescent sexual activity.

There are a variety of risks that accompany sexual activity, including sexually transmitted disease and pregnancy. The latter possibility has been even made apparent thought television programs such as *Sixteen and Pregnant*, which highlights life as a pregnant teenager. Despite the high rates of intercourse in adolescence, there has been a rather consistent drop in teenage pregnancy over the past decade.

This trend may be due to several factors, including more formal sex education curriculum in school, increase condom availability and use, and also

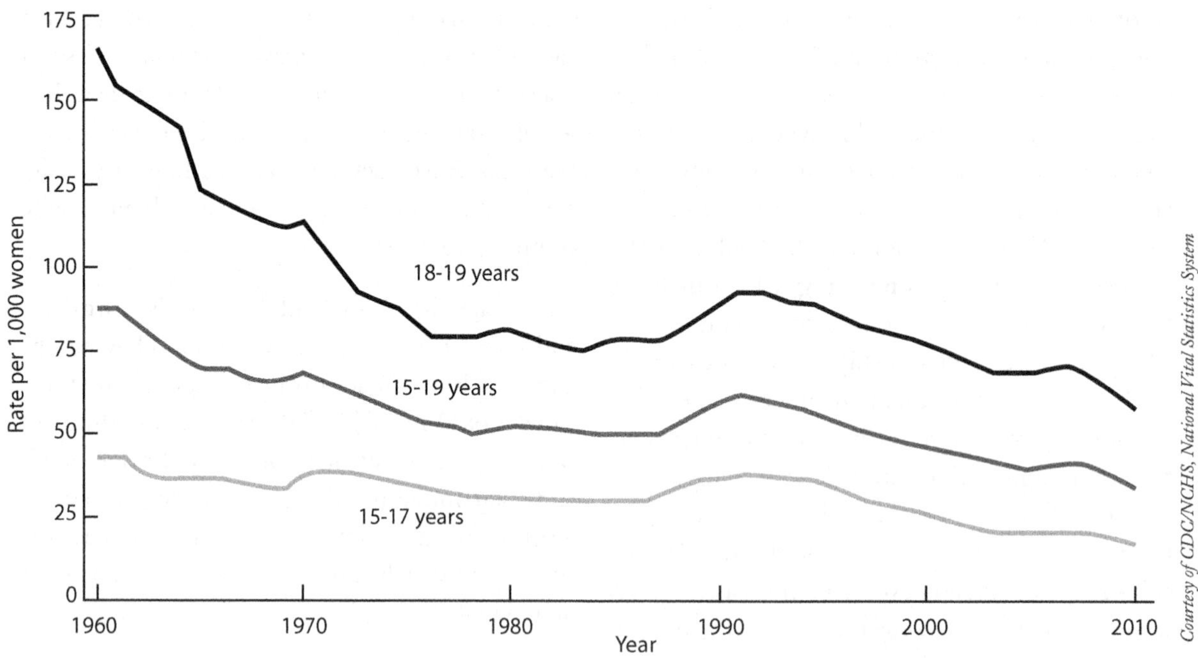

FIGURE 12.1 *Birth Rates for Teenagers Aged 15-19, by Age: United States, 1960-2010*

the legality of abortion (Martin et al., 2010). While the birth of a baby, at any age, has a variety of positive and fulfilling aspects for a mother, when a teenager becomes pregnant and gives birth, there are a variety of potential harmful consequences, including chronic stress, educational impact, and financial strain. Any or all of these may be further impacted by the presence or absence of the father, although as you can see in Figure 12.2, the overall proportion of unmarried mothers under the age of 20 has decreased over the years (Ventura, 2010). In Figure 12.3, it is apparent mothers under 20 years of age are much more likely to be unmarried as well.

Reconciling Cognitive and Socioemotional Development in Adolescence

In the preceding paragraphs, attention has been given to various aspects of adolescent development; many of which reflect ways in

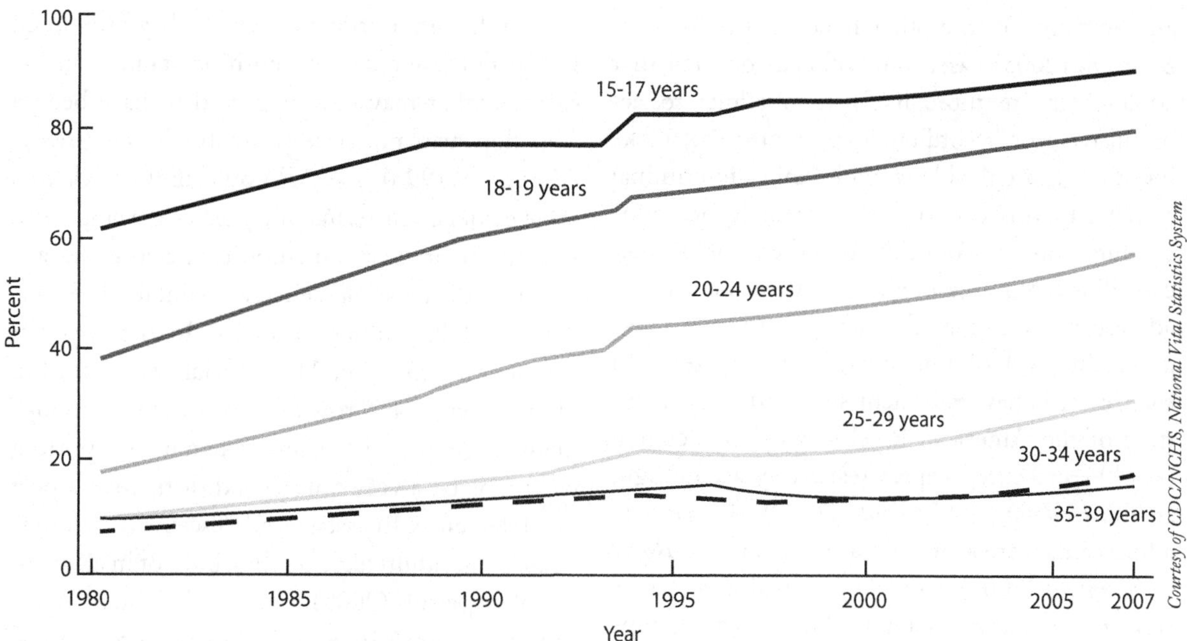

FIGURE 12.2 *Percentage of Births in each Age Group to Unmarried Women: United States, 1980–2007*

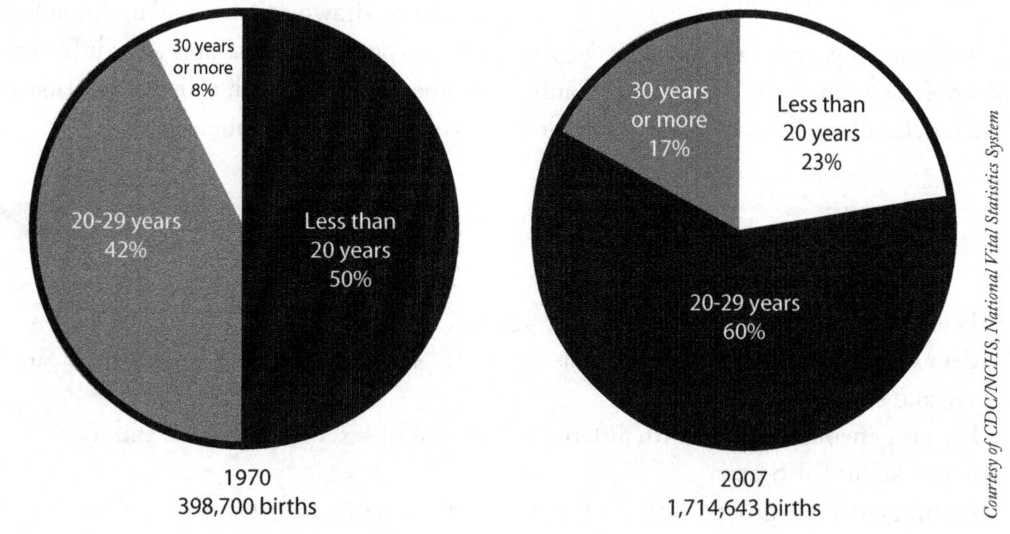

FIGURE 12.3 *Distribution of Nonmarital Births by Age: United States, 1970 and 2007*

which adolescence should be viewed as a distinct and unique life stage. That is, adolescents are not children, but they are also not adults in many ways. For instance, adolescents appear to be more mature cognitively than children, and may be adult-like in terms of cognitive capabilities and moral reasoning. However, in other instances (e.g., conformity, peer pressure) it appears as though adolescents may be more vulnerable than adults. A relevant question arises: How "mature" are adolescents? The answer to this question has been sought in high-profile cases presented before the Supreme Court.

More specifically, in the *Hodgson v. Minnesota* (1990) case, the court ruled that adolescents are capable of making mature decisions, and therefore do not need to notify parents before seeking an abortion. On the other hand, in the *Roper v. Simmons* (2005) case, court officials decided that adolescents are more likely than adults to act impulsively or according to peer pressure, making them less culpable when it comes to criminal activity. In this case, the death penalty for adolescents was not upheld. Together, the former case illustrated a case where relative maturity of adolescents was granted, whereas in the latter case a certain level of immaturity was apparent. In each case, behavioral scientists—and representatives of the American Psychological Association (APA)—presented expert testimony accordingly. In the *Hodgson v. Minnesota* (1990), they argued adolescents were as mature as adults; in the *Roper v. Simmons* (2005) case, they argued adolescents were *not* as mature as adults. This apparent "flip-flop" did not go unnoticed by court officials, and APA officials were called on to defend their seemingly contradictory viewpoints.

Thus, it became important to reconcile expert views of adolescent maturity. Steinberg, Cauffman, Woolard, Graham, Banich (2009) responded in an influential article in which they attempted to clarify these cases and position stands. On the surface, what may have appeared to have been a "flip-flop" was not necessarily. In the *Hodgson v. Minnesota* (1990) case, APA officials were asked to offer evidence in terms of *cognitive* development. Indeed, theoretical and empirical perspectives appear to indicate adolescents do maintain decision-making skills similar to adults. In the *Roper v. Simmons* (2005) case, APA officials were asked to offer evidence in terms of *socioemotional* development. Together, researchers were merely reporting what may be a very unique and distinctive aspect of adolescence. In essence, adolescents do demonstrate some adult-like qualities, but not in all areas. Steinberg et al. (2009) argue "...it is neither inconsistent nor disingenuous for scientists to argue that studies of psychological development indicate the boundary between adolescence and adulthood should be drawn at a particular chronological age for one policy purpose and at a different one for another" (p. 592). Such a distinctive aspect of adolescence should be embraced.

Key Terms

- **Peer** – someone who is about the same age and level of maturity
- **Peer Groups** – clusters of individuals composed of people of approximately the same age and status
- **Heterogeneous** – groups with differences in terms of sex, race, ethnicity, and socioeconomic status (SES), etc.
- **Homogeneous** – groups with similarity in terms of sex, race, ethnicity, and socioeconomic status (SES), etc.
- **Age Grading** – placement of individuals of the same age into groups; school systems are influential in organizing groups of students based on age
- **Classic Peer Groups:**
    - **Crowd** – a group of individuals who share particular characteristic(s) but who may not interact with one another. Crowds are relatively large, and may carry some level of consistency in terms of their nomenclature.
    - **Clique** – more intimate groups of between 2-12 people whose members have frequent social interactions
- **Conformity** – related to peer pressure, a general change in behavior or attitude brought about by a desire to follow the beliefs or standards of others

- **Organized Activities** – a relatively common social context for adolescents, these may scholastic (affiliated with a school) or non-scholastic (church-, community-based); the hallmarks of organized activities are structure, adult-supervision, and an emphasis upon skill building
- **Intimacy** – an affective sense of closeness and interconnectedness with another person; intimacy does *not* necessarily involve romantic or sexual intent or behavior
    - **Infatuation** – excited to be in a relationship and disclose personal information
    - **Status** – a relationship with an eye toward how others perceive the relationship
    - **Intimacy** – also a "stage" in this sense, apparent when partner(s) in a relationship become more attuned to the emotional connection that exists between them and their partner
    - **Bonding** – this stage includes the consideration of long-term commitment
- **Dating** – may be viewed in those that are willingly committed and have "paired off" to form a couple
- **Androgens** – during (and leading up to) puberty for males, the testes accelerate production of this sex hormone, which are responsible for primary and sexual changes, but also sex drive
- **Estrogens** – during (and before) puberty for females androgen secretion follows a less consistent, but cyclical pattern, corresponding to ovulation
- **Trends in Sexual Activity:**
    - **Gender Double Standard** – a traditional notion that premarital sex by males was permissible, but not for females
    - **Permissiveness with Affection** – implies premarital sex is acceptable given an intimate, stable relationship between partners
    - **Friends with Benefits** – the basis of sexual relationships that lack commitment (or even much intimacy or friendship) between partners

Critical Thinking Questions

1. What is a peer group? Moreover, what are two common types of groups? In discussing these peer groups, be sure to highlight the similarities and differences between the two, and also include personal examples from peer groups you may have had during adolescence. From which peer group(s)—if any—did more enduring friendships come from?
2. Discuss intimacy in adolescence. What are some of the defining characteristics of intimacy and stages that such relationships may progress through? Do you think romantic adolescent relationships have a significant level of intimacy? Why or why not?

References

Arnett, J. J. (1999). Adolescent storm and stress, reconsidered. *American Psychologist, 554,* 317-326.

Baumeister, R. F., Twenge, J. M., & Nuss, C. K. (2002). Effects of social exclusion on cognitive processes: Anticipated aloneness reduces intelligent thought. *Journal of Personality and Social Psychology, 83,* 817-827.

Bohnert, A. M., Aikins, J. W., & Edidin, J. (2007). The role of organized activities infacilitating social adaptation across the transition to college. *Journal of Adolescent Research, 22,* 189-208.

Brown, B. B., Lohr, M. J., & Trujillo, C. M. (1990). Multiple crowds and multiple lifestyles: Adolescents' perceptions of peer group characteristics. In R. E., Muuss (Ed.), *Adolescent behavior and society: A book of readings.* New York: Random House.

Buhrmester, D. (2001, April). *Romantic development: Does age at which romantic involvements start to matter.* Paper presented at the meeting of the Society for the Research in Child Development, Minneapolis, MN.

Dunphy, D. (1963). The social structure of urban adolescent peer groups. *Sociometry, 26,* 230-246.

Eccles, J. S. (2005). The present and future of research on activity settings as developmental contexts. In Mahoney, J. L., Larson, R. W., Eccles, J. S. (Eds.). *Organized Activities as Contexts of Development* (pp. 353-374). Mahwah, NJ: Lawrence Erlbaum.

Eccles, J. S. & Barber, B. L. (1999). Student council, volunteering, basketball, or marching band: What kind of extracurricular activity involvement matters? *Journal of Adolescent Research, 14,* 10-43.

Eccles, J. S., Barber., B. L., Stone, M., & Hunt, J. (2003). Extracurricular activities and adolescent development. *Journal of Social Issues, 59,* 865-889.

Erikson, E. (1963). *Childhood and society.* New York: Norton.

Feldman, R. S. (2008). *Adolescence.* Upper Saddle River, NJ: Prentice Hall.

Feldman, A. F. & Matjasko, J. L. (2005). The role of school-based extracurricular activities in adolescent development: A comprehensive review and future directions. *Review of Educational Research, 75,* 159-210.

Fletcher, A. C., Nickerson, P., & Wright, K. L. (2003). Structured leisure activities in middle childhood: Links to well-being. *Journal of Community Psychology, 31,* 641-659.

Hall, G. S. (1904). *Adolescence: Its psychology and its relation to physiology, anthropology, sociology, sex, crime, religion, and education* (Vols. I and II). Englewood Cliffs, NJ: Prentice-Hall.

Hansen, D. W., Larson, R. W., & Dworkin, J. B. (2003). What adolescents learn in organized youth activities: A survey of self-reported developmental experiences. *Journal of Research on Adolescence, 13,* 25-55.

Helms, S.W., Choukas-Bradley,S., Widman, L. Giletta, M., Cohen, G.L., & Prinstein, M.J. (2014). Adolescents misperceive and are influenced by high-status peer's health risk, deviant and adaptive behavior. *Developmental Psychology, 50.* doi: 10.1037/a0038178

Hyde, J. S. & DeLameter, J. D. (2003). *Understanding human sexuality* (8th ed.). New York: McGraw Hill.

Kantrowitz, B. & Wingert, P. (1999, October 18). The truth about tweens. *Newsweek, 134,* 62-79.

Mahoney, J. L, Cairns, B. D., & Farmer, T. W. (2003). Promoting interpersonal competence and educational success through extracurricular activity participation. *Journal of Educational Psychology, 95,* 409-418.

Mahoney, J. L., Lord, H., & Caryl, E. (2005). After-school program participation and the development of child obesity and peer acceptance. *Applied Developmental Science, 9,* 202-215.

Mahoney, J. L., Larson, R. W., Eccles, J. S., & Lord, H. (2005). Organized activities as developmental contexts for children and adolescents. In Mahoney, J. L., Larson, R. W., Eccles, J. S. (Eds.), *Organized Activities as Contexts of Development* (pp. 3-22). Mahwah, NJ: Lawrence Erlbaum.

Martin, J. A., Hamilton, B. E., Ventura, S. J., Osterman, M. J., Wilson, E. C., Mathews, T. J. (2010). Births: Final data for 2010. *National Vital Statistics Reports, 61*, 1-72.

McHale, S. M, Crouter, A. C, & Tucker, C. J. (2001). Free-time activities in middle childhood: Links with adjustment in early adolescence. *Child Development, 72,* 1764-1778.

Melnick, M. J., Vanfossen, B. E., & Sabo, D. F. (1988). Developmental effects of athletic participation among high school girls. *Sociology of Sport Journal, 5,* 22-36.

Mendelsohn, J. (2003, November 7-9). What we know about sex. *USA Weekend Edition,* 6-9.

Posner, J. K. & Vandell, D. L. (1999). After-school activities and the development of low-income urban children: A longitudinal study. *Developmental Psychology, 35,* 868-879.

Steinberg, L., Cauffman, E., Woolard, J., Graham, S., Banich, M. (2009). Are adolescents less mature than adults? *American Psychologist, 64*, 583-594.

Sullivan, H. S. (1953). *The interpersonal theory of psychology.* New York: Norton.

Ventura, S. J. (2010). Changing patterns of nonmarital childbearing in the United States. *NCHS Data Brief, 18,* 1-8.

Zaff, J. F, Moore, K. A., Papillo, A. R., Williams, S. (2003) Implications of extracurricular activity participation during adolescence on positive outcomes. *Journal of Adolescent Research, 18,* 599-630.

CHAPTER 13

Emerging Adulthood

Defining Adulthood

In this unit, the term "adulthood" will be applied for the first time. As is customary at the outset of a unit related to a distinct life stage, a definition is warranted. Recall adolescence may be viewed as beginning with puberty and ending with an age corresponding with the graduation from high school, typically at 17 or 18 years of age. The importance of receiving a high school diploma notwithstanding, many may argue that an individual does not qualify as an "adult" merely upon graduation from high school. Thus, as with adolescence, there is not necessarily a simple chronological marker to the beginning of adulthood. In this case, there may be other psychosocial factors that define adulthood, and surface over time. In fact, the life stage following adolescence may be referred to as *emerging* adulthood. In general, **emerging adulthood** begins after graduation from high school and extends through the late twenties and is primarily devoted to constructing an adult life. For instance, adulthood may be evident when an individual begins to:

- take responsibility for personal actions,
- decide on personal values and beliefs,

- maintain a more equal relationship with parents or other authority figures, and
- demonstrate relative levels of fiscal responsibility or independence (Belsky, 2010).

The above list is not intended to be an exhaustive list. Rather, it encompasses some general notions of adult characteristics. The first notion, that adulthood may be marked by taking responsibility for personal actions may be linked with cognitive maturity and self-awareness. In addition, deciding upon personal values and beliefs is reflective of a more crystallized identity, which may be more apparent in emerging adults than children and adolescents. When one has a solid identity and value system(s) they tend to be more assertive on certain points and less susceptible to group influence. Adulthood may be recognized also by some qualitative shifts in communication and dynamics between the emerging adult and other adults (e.g., parents, employers, professors, etc.). The social hierarchies and authority adults may exert toward children may be less evident as they interact with adults. Lastly, being financially responsible may be indicative of an adult.

When one disregards a simple chronological view of adulthood, and instead views it according to some social markers, it may be a bit more complex, but also more accurate. You can rarely take a "snapshot" of an individual in one particular dimension and accurately apply the "adult" label. For instance, consider a 28-year-old individual who lives at home with his parents. On the surface, one may be inclined to view this person lacking personal and financial responsibility. However, suppose this individual is otherwise quite adult-like, but happened to have lost his job due to reasons uncontrolled by him. Moving home was actually part of a sound financial move as he saves money during a job search. In the meantime he contributes to household duties and chips in financially when he can. On the other hand, imagine a 28-year-old who lives at home because he came to realize he was simply too comfortable being in a place where he could live rent-free, groceries were bought, laundry was done, etc. From these two divergent examples, one may appreciate adulthood should be viewed in context, and may not be achieved with the mere presence of one or two select variables. Moreover, during the emerging adulthood years, there may be numerous common milestones.

Social Clock

Some typical milestones may include the receipt of a bachelor's degree (for those that pursue a secondary education), the beginning of a career, the birth of children, and perhaps marriage. There is some degree of expected variability with these milestones, but when one adopts a group perspective, it may become apparent when the majority of individuals in a particular group (e.g., cohort, crowd, and clique) have achieved one of these milestones. For instance, an individual may be readily aware when many of their peers have graduated from college. Assuming this individual was also pursuing a college degree, they may identify as having graduated before, along with, or after most of their peers. This example illustrates the concept

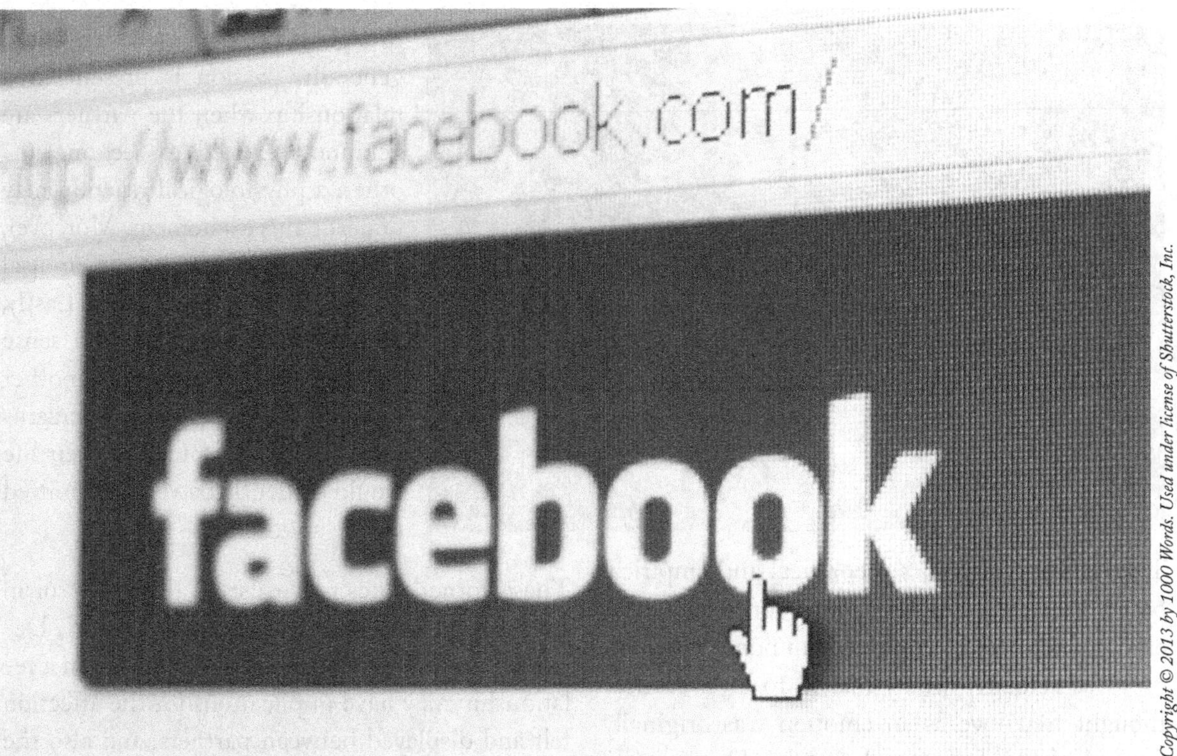

of a **social clock**, which is an understanding of societal appropriate age ranges at which some of the milestones are met. Given the social clock is socially derived; different groups of individuals are able to adopt and maintain different conceptions of a social clock. For instance, there may be gender or cultural differences in what one views as an appropriate age at which to get married or have children. Nevertheless, each individual may be knowledgeable about when most of their same-age peers have gotten married or had children.

Facebook and other social network sites seem to facilitate the social clock; when individuals get married they may make announcements and post wedding photos. In addition, many individuals announce pregnancies and births online. This would be used, in part, to formulate notions of what individuals are doing and when. Subsequently, there can be negative consequences to feeling off-time in relation to one's peers. One may imagine an individual who is feeling isolated because all of her immediate friends and distal associates of the same age have adopted and maintained a more long-term relationship, which she also desires, but has yet to achieve. As illustrated in this example, adopting and maintaining intimate relationships, including loving and romantic relationships, appears common in emerging adulthood.

Intimacy and Love

Intimacy and intimate relationships were covered in the adolescence unit, as these are purported to begin in adolescence, extending into the emerging adulthood years. Recall Erikson emphasized the role of intimacy in what are the emerging adulthood years. Erikson posited that intimate relationships should be formed during these years, at the risk of feelings of isolation. Moreover, Erikson's theory suggests an inability to form intimate relationships may be linked with fear and anxiety in future relationships. Intimate relationships may be particularly important in the emerging adulthood years, both theoretically and as a milestone in the social clock. Another affective sense that may figure prominently into relationships that form during the emerging adulthood years is love.

The notion of love has theoretical and empirical bases. Harlow's monkey study—originally covered in relationship to attachment bonds in infancy—was actually a study related to love. Harlow thought that love as an emotion was originally formed when infants were being fed. The trust, security, and emotional closeness that resulted from the caregiver-infant feeding behaviors prompted fundamental forms of love. Contemporarily, neuro-imaging studies have offered evidence that feelings of love reside in specific areas of the brain (Fisher, Aron, & Brown, 2005). Theoretically speaking, Sternberg's theory of love may help clarify what individuals do (or do not) feel when it comes to love. According to this theory, the three main cornerstones of love are:

- intimacy,
- passion, and
- commitment.

Briefly, **intimacy** may be defined in the traditional sense and as an affective sense of closeness and interconnectedness with another person. Thus, intimacy continues to indicate an emotional aspect of a relationship. Intimacy is also characteristic of friendship, and if this element is present in the context of a loving relationship, the partners appear to be solid companions. On the other hand, **passion** involves some type of physiological arousal and attraction. This does not necessarily have to imply sexual arousal and attraction, although it does many times. More generally, passion is present in a relationship when the partners are genuinely excited to see one another; a physiological reaction may underlie this excitement. Moreover, passion does include the arousal that leads to sexual activity. Lastly, **commitment** is related to a sense of long-term devotion to another individual. A couple that remains married for the course of their life would evidently be very committed to one another.

These cornerstones may exist on their own, or in conjunction with one or both of the others. Depending upon which elements are present in a relationship may have implications for the affection felt and displayed between partners, and also the longevity of the relationship. For instance, a relationship marked only by passion may be relatively short-lived as it was sparked merely by physical or sexual attraction. A relationship consisting only of a sense of commitment would largely be void of emotional and physical closeness, but may be long-lasting.

Perhaps more common notions of love become apparent when these elements are combined. For instance, passion and intimacy may merge to form what is commonly called **romantic love**. Perhaps most typical in the early stages of relationships, a couple may happily be together for months or years without having made firm plans for any type of commitment. **Companionate love** exists when intimacy and commitment are apparent. As the name implies, these partners are excellent "companions" or friends, who genuinely enjoy one another's company and maintain a stable, long-term relationship. What is missing in the relationship may be a passionate element, and perhaps void of sexual activity. Lastly, **fatuous love** is evident with passion and commitment, but without intimacy. Imagine a couple that are immediately attracted to (and passionate) about one another, making immediate long-term plans. This may be done before

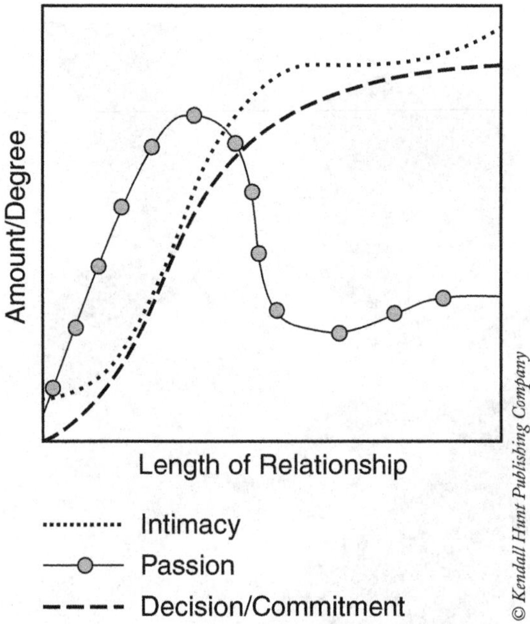

FIGURE 13.1 *Passion, Commitment, and Intimacy*

the couple has had time to emotionally connect. The term "fatuous" is synonymous with "inane" and may imply a critical element of love is missing (i.e., intimacy). When all three cornerstones (i.e., passion, intimacy, commitment) are combined, the most complete form of love is realized. Also called **consummate love**, it is thought to capture all elements of a classic love. Relationships that maintain consummate love tend to be mutually-beneficial, long-term, and sexually vibrant. As may be viewed in Figure 13.1, the strength of the three aspects of love—intimacy, passion, and commitment—tend to vary over the course of a relationship.

As some of the above examples illustrate, an absence of committed love may translate into relationships that are less enduring. Interestingly, neuroplasticity may play a role in love. More specifically, in loving relationships, a chemical called oxytocin is released. **Oxytocin** is a type of neuromodulator, which enhances or diminishes the overall effectiveness of existing neurological connections. The presence of oxytocin permits large scale neurological change—much more drastic than normal. Consider some of the circumstances in which oxytocin is released: during sexual orgasm for males and females, during labor and breastfeeding for females, and even when viewing one's own children and parenting (Doidge, 2007). Thus, oxytocin is involved in many events characteristic of intimate relationships, and may facilitate trust and attachment. Together, when two people "fall in love," they enter a period of enhanced plasticity—due to greater oxytocin release—and over time the couple may appear to customize their brains according to each other. It may not be so surprising that many couples (particularly those who are in love for many years) appear to have many similar attitudes, perspectives, and preferences.

Marriage and Cohabitation

According to one survey, marriage rates reached its lowest rate in 2010, at about 52% of couples seeking marriage. Overall, though, in recent years and decades the marriage rates have remained relatively stable. The attitudes toward and perceptions of marriage has changed greatly over time. Throughout history, marriage was largely based on practical concerns. Moreover, marriages were arranged without any notion of "love,"

which is a relatively novel idea when it comes to reasons why individuals seek marriage. Whereas marriage originally may have served as a function of male society, in the late twentieth century marriage was "deinstitutionalized." That is, some of the antiquated functions and views of marriage were fracturing. Some of the reasons behind this shift include the women's movement, lesbian and gay rights movements, as well as a rapid increase in the number of single parents, blended families, and cohabitation rates. Together, the definition of marriage and family is rapidly changing.

In a 2011 survey, about 39% of respondents thought marriage was becoming "obsolete." The response was coupled with a statistic that marriage hit an all-time low in September 2010 with only 52% of couples seeking marriage. Supporting these findings, at the time of the survey about 30% of children and adolescents under 18 lived with a single or unwed parent, and 6% lived with a cohabitating couple. The vast majority of respondents still said a "family" is a wedded couple with (or without) kids. However, 80% also agreed that unmarried couples were a family and 60% viewed same-sex couples as a family unit. Together, there appears to be an ever-expanding definition of marriage and family.

The notion that individuals marry another based upon feelings of intimacy and love is relatively new in the course of human history. In a book entitled, *Marriage, a History: From Obedience to Intimacy or How Love Conquered Marriage*, author Stephanie Coontz captures this—along with other historical issues related to marriage—very well. All in all, for centuries marriage has been a way of organizing social lives. Coontz (2005) was able to identify only one cultural group (i.e., the Na people of China) that has not integrated marriage into their sociocultural milieu. The Na is a group of about 30,000 people in the Southwestern province of Yunnan in China. For the Na, sibling relationships have more meaningfulness and emotional intimacy. That is, many Na siblings are "companions for life." However, these sibling relationships do not involve sexual contact. Rather, the Na people procreate via casual sexual encounters, but the father does not necessarily maintain an active role in the child's life. The brothers in a household maintain a paternal role with their sisters' children.

Throughout most other areas over the course of history, marriage was an integral part of society. For much of marriage history, in-laws had a "stake" in the marriage. The in-laws may have found an individual they deemed a suitable spouse (i.e., physically, emotionally, socially) for their child. The in-laws may have also stood to have financial benefit in the marriage of their children, through such customs as a dowry. Moreover, marriage was often based upon practical concerns (e.g., geographic, financial) rather than emotional needs or desires. Together, although married couples throughout history undoubtedly experienced an emotion of love, its development appears to have taken a different trajectory. Currently, couples may report love prior to an engagement or marriage, with relatively little input from in-laws. In fact, many may marry someone despite their in-laws objections. This is unparalleled independence when it comes to marriage. Coontz (2005) further argues that "never before had societies thought such high expectations about marriage was either realistic or desirable" (p. 23). Nonetheless, most societies in the world view marriage as a union ideally marked by some degree emotional and physical fulfillment.

The social shift in views toward marriage and family may be viewed politically. Patterson (2009) offered an excellent review of the psychological, legal, and political landscapes surrounding same-sex marriage and parenting. In 1990, no state offered any form of legal recognition for same-sex couples (Joslin & Minter, 2008). However, as of 2009, five states (Iowa, Connecticut, Maine, Massachusetts, and Vermont) offered marriage for same-sex couples (Patterson, 2009). In addition, although New York and Rhode Island did not offer a same-sex marriage option, they did recognize those that occurred in the aforementioned states. Thus, same-sex couples in New York and Rhode Island could be married in a nearby state (e.g., Maine, Massachusetts) and return to their home state being legally recognized as married. For a brief time, California recognized and offered same-sex marriage, but then rescinded the legality of it. Thus, although there were about 18,000 same-sex marriages in California, there are not new ones being conducted. Rather, California, along with New Jersey and New Hampshire offer same-sex civil-unions, which legally are equivalent to marriage. Semantically, however, it is still not called "marriage." Three states (Oregon, Washington, and the District of Columbia) offer domestic partnerships that carry some of the legal state-level rights of marriage. Lastly, Maryland and Hawaii offer even more limited forms of recognition of same-sex couples (Patterson, 2009).

Together, at the time of publication of the article, 15 states offer at least some type of legal recognition of same-sex marriage. However, federal level benefits (e.g., social security benefits) are not offered to same-sex partners in any state. Thus, even when a state formally recognizes a marriage in all

aspects, the federal government does not. Overall though, there appears to be a marked increase in the acceptance of same-sex couples in the 20-year period from 1990 to 2010. This is consistent with the survey results referred to above in which many report a broader—less antiquated—perspective on what constitutes marriage and family.

Concerning family, the same-sex marriage issue also has implications for children. That is, some child custody and adoption laws and judgments have been adjusted to parallel the state's marriage laws. For instance, in Massachusetts and California, a parent's sexual orientation is considered irrelevant in child custody cases. In other states, it may be considered relevant if the parent and/or lawyer have reason to believe it would negatively impact the child in some way (Patterson, 2009). In terms of adoption rights given to gay and lesbian parents, as of 2010 only Florida explicitly prohibited it. Some states (e.g., Arkansas, Mississippi, Utah) restrict adoptions to married couples. Thus, by extension they do not permit adoptions to same-sex couples as they do not support same-sex marriage. Overall, however, most states permit such adoptions. As briefly eluded to above, much of the legal and historical debates and cases of gay and lesbian parenting rights have centered on the impact (if any) it may have on the child(ren).

In particular, three general areas that faced scrutiny are gender development/sexual orientation, adjustment, and social relationships. That is, could one or more of these developmental areas be impacted in any way should a child be raised by gay or lesbian parents? Although it may sound outmoded to some reading this, some individuals may have argued that children raised by gay or lesbian parents may themselves develop gender atypical behavior or themselves identify as gay or lesbian later on. An inherent problem in such an argument is it implies gender atypical behavior and homosexuality is a problem. Patterson (2009) is very clear: "The APA and the American Psychiatric Association, among others, have long disavowed notions of homosexuality or non-normative gender behaviors as representing either disease or disorder" (p. 731). Ultimately, the majority of children raised by gay and lesbian parents identify as heterosexual (Bailey & Dawood, 1998). In relation to the other two developmental areas (adjustment and peer relations) the evidence does not support the idea that children raised by gay or lesbian parents are at greater risk for negative adjustment (e.g., anxiety, depressive symptoms, delinquency, substance use) or negative patterns or outcomes with peer relations (Patterson, 2009).

Another phenomena driving the changing definition of marriage may be a trend in **cohabitation**, which is evident when unmarried couples are living together. Cohabitation may be a risk factor for a variety of negative outcomes (Kamp Dush, Cohan, & Amato, 2003; Cohan & Kleinbaum, 2002; Stanley et al., 2004). This phenomenon has been termed the **cohabitation effect.** Rhodes, Stanley, and Markham (2009) reported those who cohabited *before* engagement reported lower marital satisfaction, dedication, and confidence as well as more negative communication and greater potential for divorce than those who cohabited only *after* engagement or not at all until marriage. It is important to note this same effect was not observed in those who cohabitated *after* engagement. Thus, there may be an important actual or symbolic commitment with engagement.

After marriage, honeymooners report the highest levels of marital satisfaction, perhaps because of the relatively high levels of intimacy, passion, and romance. Moreover, approximately 10% of couples retain a very high level of marital satisfaction, sometimes referred to as "bliss," throughout their marriage. However, for the other 90% marital satisfaction may decline, particularly in the first several years of marriage. The "downhill slope" of marital satisfaction levels out around year four of marriage, at which time a couple may pass the "danger zone." However, many do not, and seek separation or divorce during these years. There may be numerous reasons for why a U-shaped pattern is apparent for many couples in terms of marriage and marital satisfaction. One may be the emergence of young children. Although not all couples follow this social clock pattern, many couples may marry, and then have children a few years thereafter. There are many positive aspects of children, but they do negatively impact marital satisfaction. A primary reason this occurs is that new roles are being adopted. A couple that had happily assumed roles as husband and wife must now grapple with roles of father and mother, which can be stressful, confusing, and contentious. However, happiness can grow when children leave. Together however, some decreases in marital satisfaction should be considered normative. Figure 13.2 illustrates marital longevity may be linked with educational level; particularly for females, their marriages are more likely to remain intact as their education level rises.

Nevertheless, some couples may have particular difficulty returning to previous blissful stages of the relationship. These couples may be labeled "unhappy couples." Although each couple has unique aspects to their relationship, there may be some general qualities that are evident with unhappy couples. For instance, unhappy couples tend to:

- Have a low ratio of positive to negative emotions.
- Make personal attacks when arguing.
- Engage in demand-withdrawal conversations (Belsky, 2011; Lavnos & Bradbury, 2012).

Having a low ratio of positive to negative emotion would imply one person makes another feel negative (e.g., angry, frustrated, anxious, depressed) more than they are able to generate positive emotions. Simple learning principles may suggest eventually one or more partners would begin to avoid the other. The latter two items are broadly subsumed under "communication" difficulties. For instance, although arguing and disagreements in the course of relationships is typical, there are adaptive and constructive ways to go about them. Conversely, making personal attacks when arguing represent a maladaptive way of doing so. When this happens, couples no longer focus on the origin of the argument (i.e., a certain problem) but begin "hitting below the belt" with irrelevant personal attacks. Imagine a couple arguing over finances, and one partner begins attacking the other about his or her weight. In this scenario the original problem is no longer being tended to, and may get buried

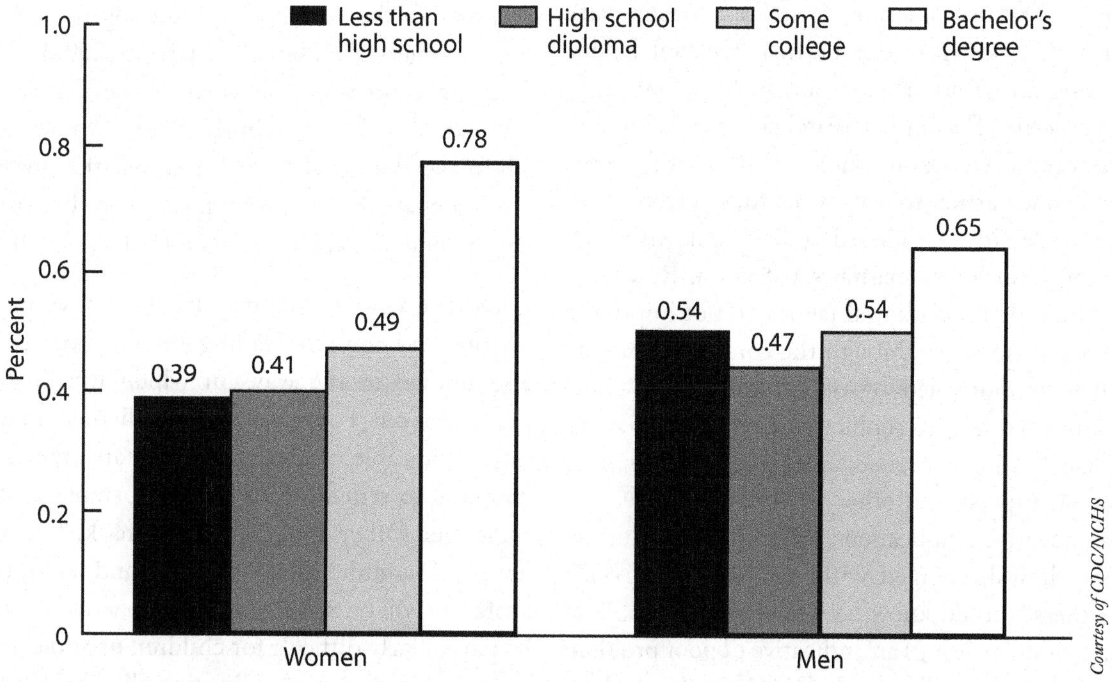

FIGURE 13.2 *Marriage Probability Relative to Education Level*

under layers of irrelevant, contentious material. Lastly, engaging in demand and withdrawal conversations is evident when one partner is seeking (i.e., demanding) emotionality or disclosure while the other does not provide it (i.e., withdrawal). In such a scenario, one partner may not be receiving an emotional component (e.g., intimacy) they desire. Recently, researchers have examined withdrawal tactics in couples. Withdrawal occurs when one partner retreats when they perceive they are "under attack." There is a direct link with such actions and lower marital satisfaction. Researchers state that withdrawal tactics do not imply the couple cannot get through the conflict. However, when accompanied by other problematic communicative issues, conflict can quickly be made worse. For instance, in couples where one or more person expects the other to "be a mind reader" has negative implications for conflict resolution. Withdrawal, coupled with an expectation one's partners "should know how to solve the problem" (i.e., mind-reading) are indicative of poor problem solving and conflict resolution (Nichols, Backer-Fulghum, Boska, & Sanford, 2014).

Divorce

As noted above, the rates in marriage have remained relatively stable. However, data suggest a consistent increase in divorce rates (Stevenson & Wolfers, 2007). Strictly speaking, **divorce** is a legal dissolution of marriage. The divorce rate has risen to rates whereby it may be considered relatively commonplace. To illustrate, for females there appears to be about a 33% chance of divorce within the first 10 years of marriage; this rate increases to 50% after 20 years of marriage (Bramblett & Mosher, 2001). Despite these trends, most engaged or newlywed couples maintain high levels of optimism about the long-term prospects of their own relationship (Helweg-Larsen, Harding, & Klein, 2011).

There are numerous reasons behind one or more partners in a marriage seeking a divorce. For instance, communication problems—two of which were covered in the last section—are often cited as a primary reason to seek a divorce. Moreover, an extramarital affair may intensify the communication difficulties beyond a reconcilable point. In one study, two out of three divorced couples were able to report the presence of an affair (on the part of at least one of the partners) surrounding the divorce event (Amato & Hohmann-Marriott, 2007). Thus, for many couples an affair may be the "last straw." Ultimately, and in the United States, women usually make the decision to leave, and this may be a result that women also appear more dissatisfied than men in unhappy marriages (Belsky, 2010).

Each divorcing couple may be distinctive in the reasons and motives leading to the divorce, but also unique in the ways in which the breakup plays itself out. For instance, some divorces may be rather amicable between partners, and they may continue to remain in healthy and stable contact thereafter. Other divorces may be marked by high levels of argument, contention, and emotional strife. As will be noted shortly, such a divorce may be particularly difficult for children or adolescents involved. In any case, a divorce will require a significant adjustment period on the part of each spouse, particularly if children are present. Some of the major issues for women in divorce include being a single mom, stepmom, or new mom. In addition, some issues for men in divorce include becoming part-time dads or disengaging as primary custody is typically granted to the mother. The divorce will also be an adjustment period for the children or adolescents involved.

Hartman, Magalhaes, and Mandich (2011) offered a useful literature review on the impact parental divorce has upon children and adolescents. In a review involving dozens of papers related to the impact of divorce, several general themes arose, five of which are outlined below:

- academic performance,
- deviant behavior,
- attitudes toward romantic and sexual relationships,
- psychosocial well-being, and
- parent-adolescent relationship.

Academic performance has long been an indicator of home-life. Sudden academic problems may often be a sign of emotional regulation difficulties that arise due to familial problems (e.g., divorce). The risk of academic problems is heightened when the divorce is particularly hostile and the child or adolescent seems to be "forgotten" about. The reviewers noted that parental involvement seemed to protect against academic problems leading up to and following a divorce. Thus, if one or more parents maintain a somewhat stable and consistent relationship with their child, it may protect against academic problems. (Hartman, Magalhaes, & Mandich, 2011). Second, deviant behavior—or behavior that is not viewed as societally acceptable—may be linked with divorce. Numerous other studies (e.g., Amato & Keith, 1991; Fergusson, Horwood, & Lynskey, 1992; Burt, Barnes, McGue, & Iacono, 2008; Hetherington, Bridges, & Isabella, 1998) have demonstrated a similar link between divorce and juvenile delinquency. Once again, this may be linked with emotion regulation; children and adolescents may seek out substances to cope with negative emotions. Once again, parental involvement appeared to reduce the likelihood of this outcome (Hartman, Magalhaes, & Mandich, 2011). Third, a child's attitude toward romantic and sexual relationships (and even marriage) may be impacted. To illustrate, a study of a large Norwegian sample reported—after years had passed—that children of divorce were more likely to delay marriage or not marry at all, divorce if they did marry, or marry other offspring of divorce (Storksen et al., 2009). Fourth, the well-being of the child or adolescent may be negatively impacted, including anxiety, depressive symptoms, and anger. Once again, positive relationships with adults (e.g., mentors, coaches, grandparents) appear to be protective in nature. Lastly, the relationship between the parent(s) and children may be impacted, including a heightened sense of being "caught in the middle" of two parents. Together, there are numerous potential negative effects of divorce for children, but it appears as though stable and healthy relationships with an adult (parent or not) may help guard against some of these negative outcomes.

Pregnancy and Parenting

In addition to marriage (and divorce), parenthood is a milestone commonly experienced in young adulthood, although not necessarily in that order. That is, while many couples delay having children until after they are married, many do not. Attitudes toward when marriage and parenthood are appropriate, and whether marriage should precede parenthood may depend upon religious or cultural values, or even one's interpretation of a social clock. In any case, many married couples consisting of young adults also have young children. Subsequently, couples that had previously understood each other as partners (e.g., husbands and wives) must now redefine their relationship to include the prospective roles of mother and father. This notion of redefining one's relationship refers to a transition to parenting.

Generally speaking, transition to parenting (i.e., the emergence of children in a household) has been

linked with decreases in marital satisfaction. There are multiple potential reasons for this. First, and as mentioned above, partner roles begin to compete with parental roles. Each of these respective roles require time, and an individual may now have to "share" their spouse in order to also be parents for the children. Moreover, one spouse's expectations for how the other should parent may not be met (Dew & Wilcox, 2011). Second, during a transition to parenthood, intimacy and romance (as defined in Sternberg's theory) tend to decline. Parenting issues may be contentious among couples, and children may generally take away from the time that couples once had to connect on intimate and romantic levels. Third, the financial responsibility or strain of raising children may also drive lower satisfaction (Guttman & Lazar, 2004).

Co-parenting and the Spillover Hypothesis

When it comes to parenting, one may reconsider the parenting styles (i.e., authoritarian, authoritative, permissive, neglectful) presented in an earlier unit. Parents may display one of these styles, and together, their collective parenting styles may resemble one of these four primary styles of parenting. Another important concept is that of **co-parenting,** which refers to the ways in which parents coordinate their parenting efforts (Gordis, Margolin, & John, 2001). There are many desirable aspects of co-parenting. When well coordinated, and assuming parenting behaviors complement one another well, there are documented positive effects on marital satisfaction and the adjustment of the children and adolescents in the family (Cui & Donnellan, 2009). However, co-parenting issues may also drive a negative trajectory for the family. For instance, co-parenting may also raise conflict over childrearing topics and how one or both parents do not support (or even sabotage) the other in his or her parenting efforts. In such a case, it appears as though parenting has been linked with decreases in marital satisfaction (Cui & Donnellan, 2009).

The **spillover hypothesis** may further clarify why parenting and marital satisfaction may be linked. According to this hypothesis, negativity in a parenting domain may be linked with negative impact in the marital domain, and vice versa (Engfer, 1988). Together, arguments and points of contention that exist in one area for a couple may "spill over" into another, causing further disagreements and contention. The potentially positive and negative experiences related to marriage and parenting are common for young adults.

Career Exploration

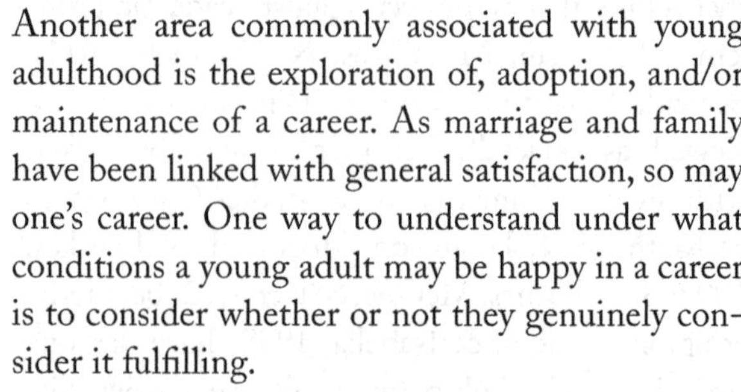

Another area commonly associated with young adulthood is the exploration of, adoption, and/or maintenance of a career. As marriage and family have been linked with general satisfaction, so may one's career. One way to understand under what conditions a young adult may be happy in a career is to consider whether or not they genuinely consider it fulfilling.

Generally speaking, motivation is related to the "why" question(s) of behavior. That is, why are humans driven to act in a certain way? Moreover, motivation theories attempt to clarify precisely why humans behave in certain ways. There is an element of intensity when it comes to motivation. There is the idea of **amotivation**—or a relative absence of motivation. On the other end of the spectrum is the highly motivated individual. The former is marked by a general lack of direction and interest in pursuing goals, while the latter is marked by a high degree of goal orientation and achievement. When considering motivation (as opposed to amotivation), the construct may be further broken down into two basic forms: instrinsic and extrinsic motivation (Cox, 2007; Vallerand & Lossier, 1999).

Briefly, **intrinsic motivation** is motivation that comes from internal sources. Intrinsically motivated individuals tend to engage in behaviors that they find genuinely stimulating and interesting. They do not engage in activities for short-term or long-term rewards other than the satisfaction that may be derived from the activity itself or mastering a new skill. There tends to be a high sense of volition and control with individuals that are engaged in certain tasks for intrinsic reasons. More specifically, this satisfaction may be related to a sense of newfound knowledge, accomplishment, or stimulation (Cox, 2007). Thus, an individual that is intrinsically motivated in his or her career may genuinely derive enjoyment from the primary tasks associated with their work. For instance, an individual may enter a scientific field due to a genuine enjoyment of making inquiries, collecting data, and answering questions. Another individual may be driven to help others, and pursue a career in nursing, and derive satisfaction on a daily basis at work.

On the other hand, **extrinsic motivation** is related to motivation that comes from external areas. Extrinsic motivation may be viewed with external reinforcements such as social praise and accolades, monetary rewards, or prizes (Deci & Ryan, 1991). A person that is extrinsically motivated to learn or perform a task is not driven by personal satisfaction but rather has an eye toward some form of external reward that typically comes from some social source, or social reinforcement (Terry, 2009). An individual entering a career for extrinsic reasons may do so for the salary associated with the position, or a certain level of prestige the position carries.

The two forms of motivation may exist on a continuum, and individuals may not categorically be either intrinsically or extrinsically motivated across all behaviors and situations. However, higher levels of happiness are reported by those that are intrinsically motivated at work.

Income and Happiness

Along with discussion of a career, it is natural to consider income as well. Indeed, even those that are intrinsically motivated must consider the salaries that certain positions command. In 1978, some researchers curious about happiness undertook a study. They assembled three groups: lottery winners, accident victims, and a control group. The lottery winners considered themselves no happier than the other groups. The lottery winners anticipated future happiness, but so did the other groups. The lottery winners took significantly less pleasure in daily activities than the other groups (Kohbert, 2010). Subsequent research has suggested that income does not necessarily predict happiness. More household income may—up to a certain point—alleviate financial stress, particularly for those struggling to make ends meet. In other words, for some individuals an increase in income may enhance happiness, but this linear trend does not continue. In fact, it tends to "level off" whereby past a certain point more income does not increase happiness (Kohbert, 2010). If income and happiness were consistently and linearly correlated, many of the world's wealthiest would be the happiest individuals, which is not necessarily the case.

Summary

The preceding paragraphs have included some issues and milestones typical in young adulthood (i.e., intimate relationships, marriage, happiness, careers, and income). Moreover, satisfaction and happiness have been interwoven into the picture, describing general relations that may exist between these experiences and the satisfaction individuals may report. It is evident that "people routinely mispredict how much pleasure or displeasure future events will bring" (Kohbert, 2010). This may be due, in part, to what is called the **hedonic treadmill.** People adapt to new and improved situations, including increased income, marriage and relationships, and careers, perhaps helping to explain why we cannot always continue to derive the same level of enjoyment from the same context.

Substance Use in Emerging Adulthood

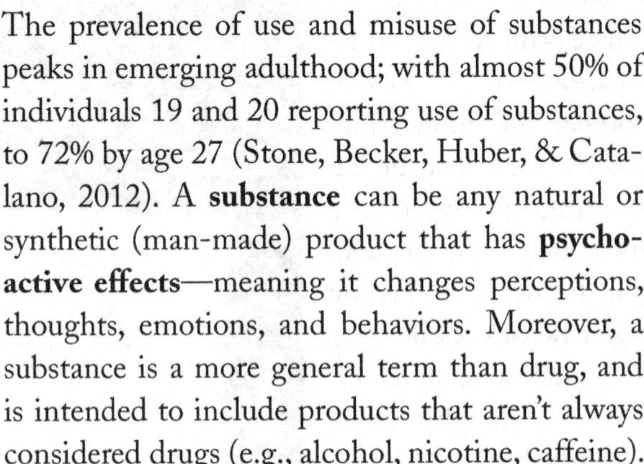

The prevalence of use and misuse of substances peaks in emerging adulthood; with almost 50% of individuals 19 and 20 reporting use of substances, to 72% by age 27 (Stone, Becker, Huber, & Catalano, 2012). A **substance** can be any natural or synthetic (man-made) product that has **psychoactive effects**—meaning it changes perceptions, thoughts, emotions, and behaviors. Moreover, a substance is a more general term than drug, and is intended to include products that aren't always considered drugs (e.g., alcohol, nicotine, caffeine).

Although substance users are not all necessarily abusing it, the high prevalence of substance use warrants attention. Alcohol, one popular substance, is used most frequently in young adulthood, including problematic forms such as daily use and drunkenness, and binge drinking (Johnson, O'Malley, Bachman, & Schullenberg, 2009). Substance use is linked with some forms of risk. For instance, substance use is associated with academic decline in college students. In a broader, and perhaps more serious sense, it has also been associated with injuries (sometimes fatal), and 75% of all deaths of those 20-24 years old is due to injury. Moreover, other causes of death in this age group (i.e., poisoning, vehicular and fire arm accidents) are also often substance involved (Stone et al., 2012). Emerging adulthood is viewed as a transition stage between adolescence and adulthood, and for some, substance related behaviors may become more pervasive, continuing through many adulthood years.

According to the fourth edition of the Diagnostic and Statistical Manual (DSM-IV), there are 11 main classes of substances one may consider. However, a simpler view offers four main classes of substances:

- depressants,
- stimulants,
- hallucinogens, and
- cannabis (i.e., marijuana).

The first class of substance, **depressants**, slows the central nervous system (CNS) and tends to dull the senses. They are used to induce muscle relaxation, drowsiness, and euphoric feelings as endorphin- and dopamine-like chemicals flood the nervous system. There are different ways in which depressants exert their influence, but they tend to either mimic the body's natural sedative chemicals or suppress the stimulation centers of the brain. There are **major depressants** such as alcohol, opioids (including morphine and heroine), and sedatives. Alcohol is the oldest psychoactive drug known, and is produced as a byproduct of fermented sugars or starches. There are also **minor depressants**, such as muscle relaxers, antihistamines, and other over-the-counter (OTC) depressants.

The second class of substance, **stimulants**, do the opposite, activating the CNS and the locus coeruleus (which releases the chemicals referred to below) by keeping certain energy chemicals (i.e., epinephrine, norepinephrine) in circulation. For example, **epinephrine** has considerable impact upon physical energy, while **norepinephrine** impacts feelings of self-confidence, motivation, and well-being. **Serotonin** and **dopamine**, which are also linked with energy and well-being are released as well, but to a lesser extent (Inaba & Cohen, 2004). Some more common stimulants include cocaine, amphetamines, nicotine, and caffeine. Stimulants promote a somewhat unnatural production and release of chemicals associated with energy. When an individual takes stimulants consistently, the body may run out of these energy stores, and the individual may experience a crash or withdrawal (Inaba & Cohen, 2004).

Hallucinogens, the third class of substance, cause sensory and perceptual disturbances and alterations. Substances such as acid (i.e., LSD), ecstasy, and peyote fit into this category. Most hallucinogens stimulate the sympathetic nervous system, causing increased heart rate and blood pressure, as well as dizziness, sweating, and dilated pupils. Hallucinogens interfere with normal neurotransmitter uptake; ultimately interfering with sensation and perception (Inaba & Cohen, 2004).

Lastly, **marijuana** (or cannabis) constitutes the fourth class of substance. Marijuana may be given its own class as it does not necessarily fit neatly into any of the other classes, and may have hallucinogenic, stimulant, or depressant effects. The most potent agent in marijuana is called **tetrahydrocannabinol (THC)** which—when ingested—has many psychoactive effects. Marijuana, like other substances, may disrupt normal neurotransmitter functioning. Interestingly, the areas of the brain most impacted by marijuana and THC are less centrally located near the brainstem, areas that are responsible for many essential automatic functions (e.g., heart rate, respiration). For this reason, it is much more difficult to overdose on marijuana when compared to many other depressants, stimulants, and hallucinogens (Inaba & Cohen, 2004).

Together, there are numerous substances—with varying psychological and physiological impact—that may be used and abused. It should also be noted not only are illicit drugs (e.g., cocaine, marijuana) used; prescribed and OTC drugs can also be abused (e.g., anesthetics, antihistamines, cardiovascular medications, muscle relaxants, or anti-inflammatory medications). With substance use, there are six general levels of use, including:

- abstinence,
- experimentation,
- social/recreational use,
- habituation,
- drug abuse, and
- addiction.

Patterns of substance use more typical of substance-related disorders (SRD) are associated with the last three levels (i.e., habituation, abuse, and addiction). The DSM-IV described four main types of SRD:

- substance intoxication,
- substance withdrawal,
- substance abuse, and
- substance dependence.

An Ecological Perspective on Substance Use

There are many factors (e.g., biological, social, emotional, economic, and legislative) to consider when clarifying who may (or may not) be at risk for an SRD. Given the numerous layers of influence on substance use and disorder, it may be appropriate to adopt an ecological perspective. In the following paragraphs, recall that substance use, which may develop into an SRD, develops over time. Therefore, when looking at an adult substance user, you may consider the childhood and adolescent factors that may have played a role.

First, consider the biological components of each individual residing in their respective ecological system. It appears as though SRDs may be heritable; it runs in families. Thus, although it has not been specifically identified, there may be specific gene(s) that otherwise disrupt hormonal and neurotransmitter production or reception, and subsequently prompt alcohol use (Stone, Becker, Huber, & Catalano, 2012). Another neurological indicator is an **event-related potential (ERP)**; specifically, an ERP generally indicates reaction time, and lower ERP scores have been linked with SRD onset (Courtney & Polich, 2009). There are also apparent sex differences, as males are more likely to experience an SRD; males are more likely to use marijuana; and males are more likely to drink heavily (Stone, Becker, Huber, & Catalano, 2012). These gender differences may be due to hormonal differences between the sexes. Thus, although it is not exactly clear the mechanisms responsible for biological predisposition to SRD onset, it does appear to have some biological bases. Moving outward in an ecological sense, the individual resided in multiple microsystems.

The family remains an integral microsystem for emerging and young adults. Above and beyond the genetic bases, adults that were once children and adolescents in households with an adult (e.g., parent) who abused a substance are more likely to do so themselves upon becoming an adult, perhaps due to modeling behavior. Such individuals are also more likely to drink heavily in young adulthood. In addition, some research has suggested that children and adolescents of divorce are more likely to engage in substance use (Stone et al., 2012). This familial influence may come not only from parents, but also older siblings as well. Another microsystem is peer groups, and—not surprisingly—individuals who associate with peers who use and/or abuse substances are more likely to do so themselves. This may be part of a socialization process, and it may also be related to group membership and peer pressure.

Recall mesosystems are related to how one microsystem may impact another. In terms of substance use, consider family management factors (e.g., guidelines, monitoring, and discipline). While family management may arise in the home, it may impact how the individual views and behaves with substances in other contexts. Generally, if there is consistent and apparent family management and

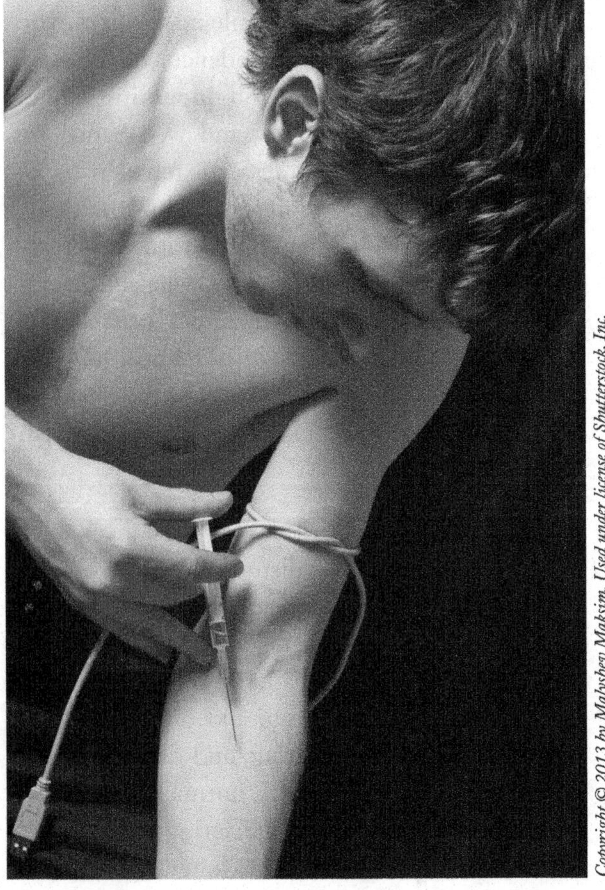

functioning, individuals are less likely to use or abuse substances in peer contexts, lessening the likelihood of adopting long-term problematic patterns of substance use.

The exosystem relates to contexts that the individual does not directly reside, but impacts them nonetheless. For instance, increasingly low and high levels of parental income may increase the likelihood of substance use. That is, a curvilinear pattern may exist between parental income and future substance use; whereby the lowest and highest incomes are at risk and moderate level of income less so (Stone et al., 2012). This may be a characteristic related to the parent's profession, and although the child does not necessarily accompany their parent(s) to work, it may impact them nonetheless.

There are numerous influences from the macrosystem level. First, social norms and customs related to substance use should be considered. For instance, on many college campuses, where access to substance use—particularly alcohol—may be a problem, heavy and consistent drinking may be viewed by many as typical of college life at that particular campus. There are also governmental regulatory elements that may impact in what ways an individual uses certain substances. For instance, states have minimum drinking ages, or may restrict the availability of certain quantities of alcohol or tobacco. In addition, certain substances (e.g., alcohol, tobacco, marijuana) may be more available in certain areas. This is not an exhaustive list, but rather some illustrations of how cultural or societal variables may impact substance use.

Lastly, from an ecological perspective, the chronosystem reflects the notion that all the aforementioned systems are subject to change over time. A once healthy functioning family may become dysfunctional due to death or divorce, thereby increasing the risk of substance use. A government may increase or decrease a legal drinking age or the penalties associated with driving under the influence. Administrators at a college campus may institute policies, procedures, and programs to modify the apparent drinking norms.

Key Terms

- **Emerging Adulthood** – a life stage that begins after graduation from high school and extends through the late twenties and is primarily devoted to constructing an adult life
- **Social Clock** – an understanding of societal appropriate age ranges at which some of the milestones are met (e.g., degree attainment, marriage, children, etc.)
- **Basic Forms of Love**:
    - **Intimacy** – an affective sense of closeness and interconnectedness with another person
    - **Passion** – physiological and/or neurological arousal and attraction. This does not necessarily have to imply sexual arousal and attraction, although it often does.
    - **Commitment** – a sense of long-term devotion to another individual
- **Composite Forms of Love:**
    - **Romantic Love** – comprised of the passionate and intimate elements
    - **Companionate Love** – exists when intimacy and commitment are apparent. As the name implies, these partners are excellent "companions" or friends.
    - **Fatuous Love** – evident with passion and commitment, but without intimacy
    - **Consummate Love** – thought to capture all elements of a classic love

- **Oxytocin** – a neuromodulator, which enhances or diminishes the overall effectiveness of existing neurological connections
- **Cohabitation** – evident when unmarried couples are living together
- **Cohabitation Effect** – the potential consequences (e.g., divorce, separation) associated with cohabitating before engagement
- **Divorce** – a legal dissolution of marriage
- **Co-parenting** – the ways in which parents coordinate their parenting efforts
- Spill-over **Hypothesis** – the hypothesis that negativity in a parenting domain may be linked with negative impact in the marital domain, and vice versa
- **Amotivation** – a relative absence of motivation
- **Intrinsic Motivation** – motivation that comes from internal sources (e.g., the satisfaction that may be derived from the activity itself or mastering a new skill)
- **Extrinsic Motivation** – motivation that comes from external areas (e.g., social praise and accolades, monetary rewards, or prizes)
- **Hedonic Treadmill** – the process of adapting to new and/or stimulating objects or situations; generally returning to a baseline level of life satisfaction
- **Substance** – any natural or synthetic (man-made) product that has psychoactive effects; a more general term than "drug," and is intended to include products that aren't always considered drugs (e.g., alcohol, nicotine, caffeine)
- **Psychoactive Effects** – capable of altering perceptions, thoughts, emotions, and behaviors
- **Depressants** – substances that serve to slow the central nervous system (CNS) and dull the senses
    - **Major Depressants** – alcohol, opioids (including morphine and heroine), and sedatives
    - **Minor Depressants** – muscle relaxers, antihistamines, and other over-the-counter (OTC) depressants
- **Stimulants** – substances that activate the CNS and the locus coeruleus by keeping certain energy chemicals (i.e., epinephrine, norepinephrine) in circulation
    - **Epinephrine (or Adrenaline)** – a hormone and a neurotransmitter that is capable of operating on most tissue in the body and has considerable impact upon physical energy levels
    - **Norepinephrine** – a chemical that may also function as a hormone and a neurotransmitter; impacts feelings of self-confidence, motivation, and well-being
    - **Serotonin** – a chemical linked with energy and a feeling of well-being
    - **Dopamine** – a neurotransmitter also linked with energy and well-being are also released
- **Hallucinogens** – any of a class of substance which cause sensory and perceptual disturbances and alterations; interferes with normal neurotransmitter uptake; ultimately interfering with sensation and perception
- **Marijuana (or Cannabis)** – given its own class as it does not necessarily fit neatly into any of the other classes, and may have hallucinogenic, stimulant, or depressant effects. Marijuana, like other substances, may disrupt normal neurotransmitter functioning.
    - **Tetrahydrocannabinol (THC)** – the most potent agent in marijuana; when ingested, THC has many psychoactive effects
- **Event-Related Potential (ERP)** – generally indicates reaction time; a neurological term

Critical Thinking Questions

1. Discuss some of the characteristics of happy and unhappy couples. In your response, be sure to cover any or all of the basic (e.g., passion, intimacy, commitment) and composite (e.g., romantic, fatuous, companionate) forms of love in terms of whether or not (un)happy couples may maintain such forms of love. Also, what characteristics may unhappy couples demonstrate that happy couples do not? You may also find it useful to discuss the "U-shaped" pattern of marital satisfaction.
2. What is the "cohabitation effect?" Given the prevalence of cohabitation, do you think the cohabitation effect still exists? Are there other positive aspects of cohabitation? If so, what are they?
3. Define and discuss the range of substances and their use. There are a variety of substances (e.g., depressants, stimulants, hallucinogens) that should be included in your response, as well as the levels of use (e.g., intoxication, withdrawal, abuse, dependence).

References

Amato, P. R. & Hohmann-Marriott, B. (2007). A comparison of high and low distress marriages that end in divorce. *Journal of Marriage and Family, 69*, 621-638.

Bailey, J. M., & Dawood, K. (1998). Behavior, genetics, sexual orientation, and the family. In C. J. Patterson & A. R. D'Augelli (eds.), *Lesbian, gay, and bisexual identities in families: Psychological perspectives* (pp. 3-18). New York: Oxford University Press.

Bramblett, M. D. & Mosher, W. D. (2001). First marriage dissolution, divorce, and remarriage: United States. Advance data from *Vital and Health Statistics* (no. 323). Hyattsville, MA: National Center for Health Statistics.

Belsky, J. (2010). *Experiencing the lifespan.* New York: Worth.

Coontz, S. (2005). *Marriage, a History: From Obedience to Intimacy or How Love Conquered Marriage.* New York: Penguin.

Courtney, K. E. & Polich, J. (2009). Binge drinking in young adults: Data, definitions, and determinants. *Psychological Bulletin, 135*, 142-156.

Cox, R. H. (2007). *Sport Psychology: Concepts and Applications* (7th ed.). New York: McGraw-Hill.

Cui, M. & Donnellan, M. B. (2009). Trajectories of conflict over raising adolescent children and marital satisfaction. *Journal of Marriage and Family, 71*, 478-494.

Deci, E. L. & Ryan, R. M. (1991). A motivational approach to self: Integration in personality. In R. A. Dienstbeier (Ed.), Nebraska Symposium on Motivation 1991: Vol 38. *Perspectives on motivation: Current theory and research on motivation* (pp. 237-288). Lincoln, NE: University of Nebraska Press.

Doidge, N. (2007). *The brain that changes itself.* New York: Penguin.

Dew, J. & Wilcox, W. B. (2001). If momma ain't happy: Explaining declines in marital satisfaction among new mothers. *Journal of Marriage and Family, 73*, 1-12.

Gordis, E. B., Margolin, G., & John, R. S. (2001). The relations among parents' hostility in dyadic marital and triadic family settings and children's behavior problems. *Journal of Consulting and Clinical Psychology, 69*, 727-734.

Guttman, J. & Lazar, A. (2004). Criteria for marital satisfaction: Does having a child make a difference? *Journal of Reproductive and Infant Psychology, 22*, 147-155.

Hartman, L. R., Magalhaes, L., & Mandich, A. (2011). What does parental divorce or marital separation mean for adolescents? A scoping review of the literature. *Journal of Divorce and Remarriage, 52,* 490-518.

Helweg-Larsen, M., Harding, H. G., & Klein, W. M. P. (2011). Will I divorce or have a happy marriage?: Gender differences in comparative optimism and estimation of personal chances among U.S. college students. *Basic and Applied Social Psychology, 33*, 157-166.

Inaba, D. S. & Cohen, W. E. (2004). *Uppers, downers, and all arounders.* Ashland, OR: CNS Publications.

Joslin, C. G. & Minter, S. P. (2008). *Lesbian, gay, bisexual, and transgender family law.* New York: Thompson West.

Kohbert, E. (2010, March 22). What can policymakers learn from happiness research? *New Yorker,* 72-74.

Lavnos, J. A. & Bradbury, T. N. (2012). Why do even satisfied newlyweds eventually go on to divorce? *Journal of Family Psychology, 26*, 1-10.

Nichols, N.B., Backer-Fulghum, L.M., Boska, C.R., & Sanford,K. (2014). Two types of disengagement during couples conflicts: Withdrawal and passive immobility. Psychological Assessment. Retrieved from: www.sciencedaily.come/releases/2015/1507131342.htm.

Patterson, C. J. (2009). Children of lesbian and gay parents: Psychology, law, and policy. *The American Psychologist, 64*, 727-736.

Stone, A. L., Becker, L. G., Huber, A. M., & Catalano, R. F. (2012). Review of risk and protective factors of substance use and problem use in emerging adulthood. *Addictive Behaviors, 37*(7), 747-775.

Terry, W. S. (2009). *Learning & memory: Basic principles, processes, and procedures.* (4th ed.) Boston: Pearson Higher Education.

Vallerand, R. J. & Losier, G. F. (1999). An integrative analysis of intrinsic and extrinsic motivation in sport. *Journal of Applied Sport Psychology, 11,* 142-169.

Vallerand, R. J., Rousseau, F. L., Grouzet, F. M. E., Dumais, A., Grenier, S., & Blanchard, C. M. (2008). Passion in sport: A look at determinants and affective experiences. *Journal of Sport and Exercise Psychology, 28*, 454-478.

CHAPTER 14

Middle Adulthood

There may be a prevailing notion that by the time someone has reached midlife—perhaps by the time they are 50 years old and well established as an adult—they are essentially who they are, and always will be, in terms of their personality, values, and preferences. To some degree this may be true. For instance, there may be core elements of personality that remain consistent; someone who was genuinely extraverted and outgoing in adolescence and emerging adulthood may continue to be sociable and engaging in midlife and even well into later life. However, recent research has revealed that in many cases humans are continually changing and adapting. In other words, in midlife (or really any life stage) it may be an illusion or misperception that we will no longer change in profound and meaningful ways (Quoidbach, Gilbert, & Wilson, 2013). Moreover, we tend to underestimate how much will change. In one study, researchers asked over 19,000 individuals (aged 18 to 68 years) how much that had changed (broadly in terms of personality, values, and preferences) over the past decade and how much they predict they would change in the next decade (in terms of the same factors). Interestingly, where people (regardless of age) can readily detect past change, they rarely report or expect future change. However, given even the older individuals consistently reported change, it appears to be occurring throughout the life span (Quoidbach, Gilbert, & Wilson, 2013). Humans tend to invest in the somewhat mistaken notion they will not change. As the authors of this study put it:

> Young adults pay to have the tattoos removed that teenagers paid to get, middle aged adults rush to divorce the people whom young adults rushed to marry, and older adults visit health spas to lose what middle-aged adults visited restaurants to gain. (Quoidbach, Gilbert, & Wilson, 2013, p. 96)

Together, it is important to note that changes continue through the life span, and certainly are apparent in **midlife**, a term which will be applied to those from the ages of 40 to 59 years. This development period may similarly be thought of as **middle adulthood**. In 2000, the U.S. Census reported almost 74 million individuals—comprising more than a quarter of the overall population—were in this particular age range. Moreover, it was the fastest growing segment of the population at the time of data collection. In the paragraphs that follow, attention will be given to some developmental issues that may be unique to midlife. When considering midlife, many may inevitably think of some type of "crisis." There are some reasons why this issue may prevail in many minds. First, there may be some anecdotal reports of parents or friends going through difficult life transitions during their forties or fifties that is conveniently labeled a "midlife crisis." Second, there may be some theoretical support for a crisis; Erikson (1997) suggested adults may consider generativity versus stagnation, and when this reaches salience during adulthood, individuals may struggle with how meaningful their life has been. Third, the connection between midlife and crises may exist due to a relative dearth (at least in previous decades) of research related to midlife issues. Brim (1992) argued midlife was the "last uncharted territory in human development" (p. 171). Since this statement, scientists have considerably more understanding of midlife issues, but the notion of a midlife crisis appears alive and well, at least in people's minds. Thus, discussion of the evidence related to such crises will be given in this unit, as will attention to other relevant issues, including:

- cognitive functioning,
- emotional development,
- social relationships,
- work, and
- health and physical changes (Lachman, 2004).

In terms of cognition, there is an assumption that middle-aged adults may not be as cognitively capable as young adults, but not as incapable as the elderly. Some aspects of cognition (e.g., working memory, processing speed) begin to decline in midlife, but gradually. The decline is not necessarily detectable, nor does it inevitably interfere with day-to-day tasks in midlife. Even when some form of cognitive decline is apparent, middle-aged adults often have the practical intelligence and knowledge to compensate for it. In terms of emotional development, middle-aged adults appear to have an emotional range and intensity more similar to younger adults than older adults (Mroczek, 2004). Moreover, middle-aged adults tend to have solid emotional regulation skills when compared to younger age groups, and they report far fewer depressive symptoms.

A major predictor of well-being in midlife is the quality of social relationships. Most notably, positive relationships with parents, spouses, and children appear to be the most satisfying area of life for many in midlife. While satisfaction may be derived from family, it must be done amidst changing roles. The empty nest transition (discussed later in more depth) is one relevant shift concerning children. Consider also how those in midlife must also confront changes in relationships with their parents, perhaps due to old age or physical health issues. According to one National Survey of Families and Households; upon *entering* midlife about

40% of individuals still have both parents. However, upon *leaving* midlife, more than 75% of individuals have lost both parents. Thus, a considerable portion of the population loses their parents during middle adulthood.

Besides family, work constitutes a major portion of life for middle adulthood. Many base a large part of their identity upon their professional work, and individuals tend to peak in terms of position and earning during these years. Of course, there are numerous ways in which work in midlife may be experienced. Some may remain in the same position, with the same employer throughout these years, while others move from job to job. This latter group—those seeking new employment during these years—may face what is known as "age discrimination" for the first time. While middle-aged workers are quite competent, and often valued senior members of an organization, they may also be preparing for retirement. At the very least, they may consider when (or if) they feel they may retire, and what their financial situation would be post-retirement.

For the most part, physical health in midlife is solid. According to one survey, about 7% in their early forties reported a disability. This figure doubles (about 15%) into the early fifties, and quadruples (about 30%) into the early sixties. Thus, there are increasing health problems during midlife, but it does not encompass the entire population. Many middle-aged adults are quite vibrant, staying active physically and perhaps even outperforming their younger counterparts on some physical tasks. If one observes activity at a local road race or gym, there are many active middle-aged adults.

The biological changes during midlife may be less marked than other life stages in which there are

more noticeable improvements and development (i.e., infancy, childhood, adolescence) or decline (i.e., later life). However, one of the major biological shifts in midlife is related to reproductive capabilities, particularly for females. More specifically, a typical age for women to experience **menopause**—the slowing and cessation of ovulation—is in her early fifties (Lachman, 2004). Although less salient, and less sudden in nature, some researchers have argued that males experience **andropause**, which signifies lower testosterone, and subsequently, lower sexual drive and muscle mass (Berger, 2011).

Together, midlife appears to be marked by some continuity, and also some change. The changes that do occur may be viewed as positive or negative, depending on a milieu of factors. In addition to the variables mentioned above, change (or lack thereof) may also be discussed in terms of personality.

Personality

Personality is typically well established by middle adulthood, and is a set of enduring personal characteristics and unique ways of responding to events in the world. Personality may be viewed in basic and special abilities, interests, social relationships, and many other psychosocial characteristics. In sum, your personality is "you" as viewed by others (Fernald, 2008). By definition, personality is relatively consistent. Theoretical and empirical accounts support the notion that the personality one demonstrates in middle adulthood is similar to the features of personality apparent in earlier life stages. One may envision a friend from high school going away to college, not to be seen or heard from in many years. However, at the 25th high school reunion, everyone maintains this person hasn't changed a bit. There may be certain underlying structures to personality that others come to evaluate in people they interact with.

First, you may reconsider the notion of temperament. Recall **temperament** may be viewed as behavioral and reactionary aspects of oneself that are thought to be innate, becoming apparent even in infancy. In an earlier unit, temperament was discussed in relation to easy, slow-to-warm-up, and difficult varieties. It is possible that one's temperament contributes to personality across the life span. Intuitively, research in this area requires a longitudinal design, collecting data on infants, and tracking them well into adulthood. In fact, some studies in this area have spanned 35 years or more (Hampson & Goldberg, 2006; Pulkkinen, Kokko, & Rantanen, 2012). Despite this apparent difficulty, some researchers have found support for this notion.

Caspi and Silva (1995) reported that temperamental qualities at age 3 predict some personality traits into young adulthood. For instance, young children with an "undercontrolled" temperamental quality appeared to be more impulsive, aggressive, and alienated in young adulthood; while "inhibited" children were less likely to act impulsively or aggressively (Caspi & Siliva, 1995). Although these researchers used different terminology related to temperament, the research did appear to support the idea that underlying qualities may predict future responses and behaviors. Since this study, others have also supported stability across the life span—well into middle adulthood—in core aspects of temperament and personality (Caspi, Roberts, & Shiner, 2005; Pulkkinen, Kokko, & Rantanen, 2012). This may be particularly apparent with traits such as extraversion, or how outgoing someone is. If they are outgoing in childhood, this may be something that lasts a lifetime (Hampson & Goldberg, 2006; Pulkkinen, Kokko, & Rantanen, 2012). Together, qualities apparent even in infancy may be apparent later on in life. As Caspi et al. (2005) put it, "childhood temperament should be conceptualized with an eye towards adult personality structure, and adult personality should be understood in light of its childhood antecedents" (p. 454). There are other competing perspectives on how and why personality may be consistent across time.

For instance, the **Five Factor model of personality** includes 5 underlying structures that may be apparent in all humans: openness, conscientiousness, extraversion, agreeableness, and neuroticism (OCEAN). Also referred to as the **Big Five**, there is not a mere presence or absence of these factors for each individual. Rather, each factor lies on a continuum for each individual. For instance, someone displaying high levels of **openness to experience** would be relatively inquisitive, spontaneous, and/or artistic. A person low on this dimension would exhibit rigid attitudes and be more close-minded. **Conscientiousness** is related to being orderly and respectful, as opposed to a general lack of this quality, demonstrated by impulsivity and disorganization. **Extraversion** is a dimension of personality many are already familiar with. Some individuals are extraverted and extremely outgoing, personable, and adjust well in most social contexts. On the other hand, some individuals are more introverted and prefer being alone and are perhaps less amiable. Being on a continuum, there is room for individuals to be somewhere in between these two extremes as well. Another factor, **agreeableness**, is evident in how good-natured an individual is. Some individuals are quite agreeable, while others are definitely not, being ill-tempered and contentious. Most individuals would probably fall somewhere in between these two extremes. The last factor is **neuroticism**, which relates to emotional stability. High levels of neuroticism would lean toward—but not necessarily predict—psychosocial disturbance. Someone that is particularly hostile, obsessive, or high-strung would have a higher level of neuroticism. A lower level of neuroticism is evident in those that maintain balance, emotional and social stability, and adjust well to life events and change. Figure 14.1 includes some additional terms which may describe an individual high or low on any one of these traits. Together, there is theoretical and empirical support regarding how individuals may stay the same over time and into midlife and beyond.

Interestingly, certain personality traits have been implicated as predictive of those who will eventually become **centenarians**—those that live to be 100 years old or more. While researchers may have traditionally looked for physiological differences (e.g., hypertension, cholesterol levels) as differentiating centenarians from non-centenarians, other researchers have looked at personality (Albert Einstein College of Medicine, 2012). Generally, it appeared that centenarians tend to reflect a positive attitude toward life, and they tend to be outgoing, optimistic, and easygoing. Moreover, centenarians considered laughter an imperative aspect of life and had relatively large social networks. In relation to some Big Five traits, the centenarians had lower scores on neuroticism scales and higher scores on conscientiousness than the average population. The authors of the study—which was part of the *Einstein's Longevity Genes Project*—asserted that it may be difficult to tell whether some of these variables (e.g., positive attitude, easygoing)

Openness to experience
Independent—Conforming
Imaginative—Practical
Preference for variety—Preference for routine

Conscientiousness
Careful—Careless
Disciplined—Impulsive
Organized—Disorganized

Extraversion
Talkative—Quiet
Fun-loving—Sober
Sociable—Retiring

Agreeableness
Sympathetic—Fault-finding
Kind—Cold
Appreciative—Unfriendly

Neuroticism (Emotional Stability)
Stable—Tense
Calm—Anxious
Secure—Insecure

FIGURE 14.1 *Five Factors of Personality*

were life-long attributes, or they developed later on. This notion brings up an important question: What might explain the ways in which people change over time?

Generativity and Socio-emotional Selectivity Theory

While some temperamental qualities and personality structures may be relatively enduring, individuals may approach, perceive, and otherwise understand life in different ways as they age. For instance, Erikson assigned the resolution of **generativity** versus a sense of stagnation to midlife. Erikson believed that individuals come to utilize their unique qualities to be creative and productive individuals, and hone a portion of identity more closely linked with giving to others. In fact, Erikson proposed that many of the qualities arising from earlier developmental stages (e.g., autonomy, skill, intimacy) are usefully employed in helping adults help others. Moreover, Erikson thought a "virtue" that arose for some was caring. Thus, for some that usefully begin to care for others, particularly the younger generations, there may be some profound changes to their respective attitudes. On the other hand, **stagnation** refers to being unwilling or unable to help others. Erikson thought this could be genuinely frustrating, and marked a pathological state of being marked by conflict (Erikson, 1997). Thus, individuals that were "stagnating" may also change in some ways due to emotional upheaval and distress.

Carstenson (1995) posited that starting in midlife; individuals may have shifting emotional priorities, which is at the core of a **socioemotional selectivity theory**. More specifically, younger individuals (i.e., adolescents, young adults) may often look to the future in terms of personal, familial, and professional goals. In doing so, they may often give up immediate desire to achieve a futuristic goal. However, older individuals may shift to a more present life perspective, which may prompt them to make the most of every moment and do what makes them feel good now. Moreover, this shift may be observed in how social priorities also change, as older individuals may devote concentration on their immediate and loving relationships. Theoretically, there are ways in which middle-aged adults may adopt and maintain life perspectives distinct from their younger counterparts. In addition, there may be some social shifts which are unique to middle-age, which carry some psychological and emotional sequelae.

Empty Nest

One such social shift is known as the **empty nest transition**—the period when children (presumably) permanently leave (or "launch" from) the parental home. This "launching" may be more immediate, when a teenager leaves more permanently after graduation from high school. The transition could be more extended also; offspring may move in and out depending on their circumstances. In either case, the empty nest transition is a relatively normative event—all parents can reliably expect it to occur—although there is some variation in how it may be experienced. For instance, it is widely presumed that mothers have a more difficult time with the empty nest transition. The prevailing notion was that mothers—when compared to

fathers—tend to have invested more time and energy into child-rearing, creating a stronger attachment bond. When the child(ren) leave, mothers are forced to surrender their day-to-day parenting role, which may incur emotional distress.

There are many ways the transition is thought to be manifest, with reports of depressive symptoms or emotional distress perhaps most common (Mitchell & Lovegreen, 2009). Other purported "effects" of the empty nest transition include alchoholism, identity crisis, and/or marital conflict (Hiedemann, Suhomlinova, & O'Rand, 1998). Previously, the empty nest transition even was labeled a "syndrome" akin to a psychiatric condition; medical journals included full-page advertisements for anti-depressant drugs that could alleviate the negative feelings associated with the empty nest transition. However, these negative feelings do not appear to be as inevitable as once thought.

Some studies have shed light upon the course and correlates of this social transition. For instance, studies indicated marital quality and life satisfaction may increase when children leave the home, as there is a time to reconnect with a spouse, or reinvest in personal interests and activities (Schmidt, Murphy, Haq, Rubinow, & Danaceau, 2004). For example, a couple may experience higher levels of intimacy and romance without children in the home, or a parent may pursue an education that was "put on hold" while children were young and in the house. Mitchell and Lovegreen (2009) reported that parents may bask in the sense they raised their children well, and thoroughly enjoy the newfound leisure time. Therefore, the empty nest transition is not necessarily a broad and consistently negative experience for the parents.

More contemporary notions of the empty nest transition underscore culture as well. For instance, successful nest-leaving in Westernized societies may be viewed as an indication of the parents having raised well-adjusted and responsible children, who are now ready to live on their own. However, in some non-Western cultures, nest-leaving (at least before marriage) may be viewed more negatively, and as an indication of some broken family ties and values (Goldscheider & Goldscheider, 1999). Together, individuals, families, and cultural groups may view and otherwise experience the empty nest transition in various ways. However, it appears clear that although this can be a difficult transition period for a family, there are also some reliable positive psychological consequences. This may debunk a myth of sorts related to the empty nest transition. Might there also be imaginary aspects of a more general "midlife crisis?"

Midlife Crises

Lachman (2004) offered a helpful review of issues relevant for midlife, and in doing so, helped answer the question: Is there such a thing as a "midlife crisis?" A **midlife crisis** is generally a period of time (during midlife) where there may exist greater likelihood for an individual to find themselves in the throes of emotional difficulties, identity crises, social transition, and the like. In the following paragraph, you may appreciate a solid answer to this question may be "not necessarily" or "it depends."

First and foremost, there appear to be some commonalities running through many individuals' midlife experience. For instance, many middle-aged adults focus on caring and concern for others in their day-to-day life. This is in familial contexts, where they may be caring for spouses, children, and/or grandchildren. Middle-aged adults may need to adjust how and when they care for family members as children leave the home or they become grandparents. The need to care for others may also arise in the work sector, where they may be managing, supervising, or otherwise attentive to younger individuals. This idea is consistent with Erikson's theory described above in that middle-aged adults are "often linked to the welfare of others" (Lachman, 2004, p. 306). While addressing the needs of others, middle-aged adults may also deal with the meaningfulness of their own work, and their mental and physical health. Concerning the latter, there are physical changes salient in middle age. For instance, females experience menopause, and a variety of other illness or disease may begin to surface (e.g., hypertension, high cholesterol, arthritis). While some illness and disease may be remedied with biological or behavioral treatments (e.g., prescription drugs, diet, exercise), they are nonetheless indications of an aging body. Lastly, midlife may be characterized by better emotional regulation and increased "wisdom." Together, there is a milieu of social, emotional, and physical changes prominent in midlife, which may (or may not) spark what many view as an inevitable crisis.

As noted above, there are other very positive explicit and implicit "symptoms" of midlife, including competence, knowledge, wisdom, and authority (Lachman, 2004). Thus, in some respects, midlife may be viewed as a time of peak functioning in many areas. Research has supported a more balanced notion of midlife, consisting of some difficult, but also some rewarding experiences. Based upon a review of the literature, Lachman points out "most people fall somewhere in the middle, doing fine with neither a peak nor a crisis" (p. 313). Thus, a crisis may be a misguided stereotype of midlife. The data seem to support this; approximately 25% of participants in relevant studies (see Lachman, 2004 for a full review) reported something akin to a midlife crisis. In addition, most of the crises reported occurred *before* 40 or *after* 50 years of age. In fact, some argue the transition to age 30 may be more difficult than the transition to age 40, giving rise to the idea of a "quarter-life crisis" (Robbins & Willner, 2001). Nevertheless, a core decade of midlife does not appear to be impacted by an inevitable crisis at all. Rather, what constitutes a crisis may be driven by events that are not reserved for midlife, such as job termination, divorce, financial difficulties, or even the realization one is getting older. Interestingly, those individuals that are high on neuroticism scales—as defined above—may be more prone to experience and report a midlife crisis (Lachman & Bertrand, 2001; Whitbourne & Connolly, 1999). Together, although individuals may experience states of crises, it is not reserved for—or even common—during midlife. Rather, it appears as though experiencing a classic midlife crisis may be the exception, rather than the rule.

Key Terms

- **Midlife** – a term applied to those individuals from the ages of 40 to 59 years
- **Middle Adulthood** – a term synonymous with midlife
- **Menopause** – occurring in females typically in midlife, it is the slowing and cessation of ovulation
- **Andropause** – a possible male equivalent to menopause; signified by lower testosterone, and subsequently, lower sexual drive and muscle mass
- **Personality** – a set of enduring personal characteristics and unique ways of responding to events in the world. Personality may be viewed in basic and special abilities, interests, social relationships, and many other psychosocial characteristics.
- **Five Factor Model of Personality (or Big Five)** – a model of personality which includes five underlying structures that may be apparent in all humans:
    - **Openness to Experience** – related to a tendency to be inquisitive, spontaneous, and/or artistic. A person low on this dimension would exhibit rigid attitudes and be more close-minded.
    - **Conscientiousness** – related to being orderly and respectful; as opposed to a general lack of this quality, demonstrated by impulsivity and disorganization
    - **Extraversion** – a dimension of personality evident in those that are outgoing, personable, and adjust well in most social contexts. On the other hand, some individuals are more introverted and prefer being alone and are perhaps less amiable.
    - **Agreeableness** – generally evident in how good-natured an individual is. Some individuals are quite agreeable, while others are definitely not, being ill-tempered and contentious.
    - **Neuroticism** – relates to emotional stability
- **Centenarians** – those that live to be 100 years old or more
- **Generativity versus Stagnation** – Erikson believed that individuals come to utilize their unique qualities to be creative and productive individuals, and hone a portion of identity more closely linked with giving to others. On the other hand, stagnation refers to be unwilling or unable to help others. Erikson thought this could be genuinely frustrating, and marked a pathological state of being marked by conflict.
- **Socioemotional Selectivity Theory** – a theory that younger individuals (i.e., adolescents, young adults) may often look to the future in terms of personal, familial, and professional goals; whereas older individuals may shift to a more present life perspective, which may prompt them to make the most of every moment and do what makes them feel good now.
- **Empty Nest Transition** – the period when children leave or "launch" from the parental home
- **Midlife Crisis** – an alleged period of time (during midlife) where there may exist greater likelihood for an individual to find themselves in the throes of emotional difficulties, identity crises, social transition, and the like

Critical Thinking Questions

1. What is personality? What is the Big Five factor model of personality? What ideas are there as to whether personality remains consistent (or changes) through and during middle-age years?
2. What is a midlife crisis? What might contribute to the hypothetical crisis? In your opinion, does it exist? Why or why not? In your response, be sure to include examples to support your points.

References

Albert Einstein College of Medicine (2012, May 24). *ScienceDaily*. Retrieved May 29, 2012, from http://www.sciencedaily.com /releases/2012/05/120524215339.html

Berger, K. S. (2011). *The developing person through the lifespan.* New York: Worth Publishers.

Bertrand, R. & Lachman, M. E. (2002). Personality development in adulthood and old age. In R. M. Lerner, M. A. Easterbrooks, & J. Mistry (Eds.), *Comprehensive Handbook of Psychology: Vol. 6.* Developmental Psychology, NY: Wiley.

Brim, O. G. (1992). *Ambition: How we manage success and failure in our lives.* New York: Basic Books.

Carstenson, L. L. (1995). Evidence for a life-span theory of socioemotional selectivity. *Current Directions in Psychological Science, 4,* 151-156.

Caspi, A., Roberts, B. W., & Shiner, R. L. (2005). Personality development: Stability and change. *Annual Review of Psychology, 56,* 453-486.

Caspi, A. & Sliva, P. A. (1995). Temperamental qualities at age three predict personality traits in young adulthood: Longitudinal evidence from a birth cohort. *Child Development, 66*, 486-498.

Erikson, E. (1997). *The life cycle completed.* New York: Norton.

Fernald, D. (2008). *Psychology: Six perspectives.* Thousand Oaks, CA: Sage Publishing.

Goldscheider, F. & Goldscheider, C. (1999). *The Changing Transition to Adulthood. Leaving and Returning Home.* Thousand Oaks: Sage Publications.

Hampson, S. E. & Goldberg, L. R. (2006). A first large cohort study of personality trait stability over the forty years from elementary school through midlife. *Journal of Personality and Social Psychology, 91,* 763-779.

Heidemann, B., Suhomlinova, O., & O'Rand, A. M. (1998). Economic independence, economic status, and empty nest in midlife marital disruption, *Journal of Marriage and the Family, 60,* 219-231.

Lachman, M. E. (2004). Development in midlife. *Annual Review of Psychology, 55,* 305-331.

Mitchell, B. A. & Lovegreen, L. D. (2009). The empty nest syndrome in midlife families: A multimethod exploration of parental gender differences and cultural dynamics. *Journal of Family Issues, 30,* 1651-1670.

Mroczek, D. K. & Almeida, D. M. (2004). The effects of daily stress, age, and personality on daily negative affect. *Journal of Personality, 72,* 354-378.

Mroczek, D. K. & Spiro, A. (2005). Change in life satisfaction over 20 years during adulthood: Findings from the VA Normative Aging Study. *Journal of Personality and Social Psychology, 88,* 189-202.

Pulkinnen, L., Kokko, K., & Rantanen, J. (2012). Paths from socioemotional behavior in middle childhood to personality in middle adulthood. *Developmental Psychology, 15,* 210-220.

Quoidbach, J., Gilbert, G. T., & Wilson, T. D. (2013). The end of history illusion. *Science, 339,* 96-98.

Robbins, A. & Willner, A. (2001). *The quarter-life crisis.* New York: Putnam Books.

Schmidt, P. J., Murphy, J. H., Haq, N., Rubinow, D. R., & Danaceau, M. A. (2004). Stressful life events, personal losses, and perimenopause-related depression. *Archives of Womens' Mental Health, 7,* 19-26.

U.S. Census Bureau (Nov. 2000). Resident population estimates of the United States by age and sex. Washington, DC: U.S. Census Bureau.

Whitbourne, S. K. & Connolly, L. A. (1999). The developing self in midlife. In S. L. Willis & J. D. Reid (Eds.), *Life in the middle* (pp. 25-46). San Diego, CA: Academic Press.

CHAPTER 15

Later Life

Later Life and Life Expectancy

After midlife, the stage of "later-life" begins. Being that midlife was inclusive up through the 59th year; **later life** may be applied to any individual older than 60 years and on through the end-of-life. The term "senior citizen" is applied frequently, but typically refers to someone 65 years or older, and traditionally viewed as a time to retire, collect Social Security or other retirement benefits, or even receive the "senior discount" at local restaurants. Regardless of age, some individuals may take offense to such terms! Thus, they should be used cautiously when describing someone in later life. Currently, one in nine individuals in North America is over 65; in Europe, the ratio is one in six. Put in another way, every hour, over 300 individuals turn 60; by the year 2030, 20% of the population will be 65 years of age or older; and the number of **centenarians**—individuals over the age of 100—doubles each decade (Pargman, 2012). This represents a major **demographic shift** in that it is a much larger ratio than in centuries past; at one time there were approximately 20 times more children than elderly in the world. This demographic shift is due to multiple reasons, including:

- decrease in fertility,
- increased longevity, and
- the aging of the Baby Boomer generation.

The first two factors (i.e., decrease in fertility and increased longevity) may be considered together. First, concerning a decrease in **fertility**, the average number of children a woman will have has steadily declined over several decades. At the same time, individuals can expect to live much longer. When considering the global population, there is a slower rate of infants being born *and* an enhanced life expectancy, thereby augmenting the portion of the population consisting of older individuals. In addition, the **Baby Boomer generation**—those born post World War II—have now

entered later life. This was a large and influential generation, and has always been a "booster shot" of sorts in many ways; their presence now being felt as they enter later life.

Life expectancy is an important factor originally introduced in chapter 1, and warrants reconsideration. **Recall life expectancy** is an average (or mean) based upon *if conditions in a particular region remain unchanged.* A low life expectancy does not imply all individuals living there will die younger when compared to other countries, but rather conditions are such that many do not live past a certain age. A related term that has relevance for this chapter, **late-life life expectancy**, refers to the number of years someone can expect to live past 65. As life expectancy generally increases globally, so does late-life life expectancy, and together individuals in later life capture an ever-increasing segment of the general population.

There are some other important and relevant terms that should be covered. First, later life may be further broken down into three main sub-stages. First, there is the **young-old** group, comprised of individuals in their 60s and up through 75 years of age. The young-old are still relatively healthy and financially stable; they may possibly be retired, but yet remain active. Second, the **old-old** group are those over 75 and also more likely to be characterized by disease or disability due to aging, and financial instability. And last, the **oldest-old** group are those over 85 years of age, who are generally dependent on others (e.g., family members, caretakers) for many day-to-day tasks. This is the last life stage applied to human development. It should be noted that while the above categories attempt to delineate between some important later-life stages, some do not prefer the usage of the term "old." Rather, terms such as *optimal* or *pathological aging* are applied (Berger, 2011). In any case, one of the primary ways in which the young-, old-, and oldest-old differ is in terms of physical health and capabilities.

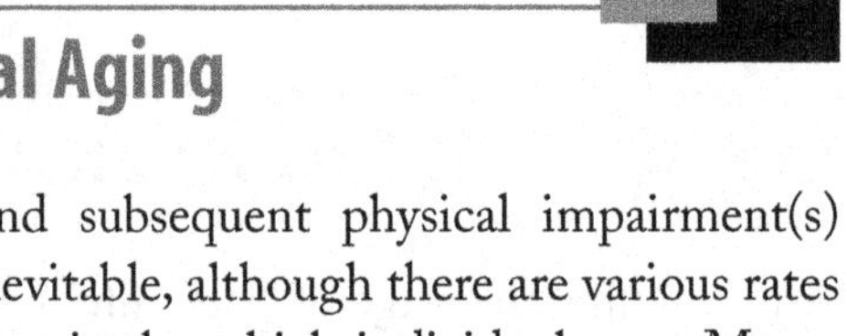

Physical Aging

Aging, and subsequent physical impairment(s) may be inevitable, although there are various rates and trajectories by which individuals age. Moreover, there are primary and secondary aging processes. **Primary aging** refers to the universal and irreversible physical changes that occur as we age. On the other hand, **secondary aging** is related to specific illnesses or conditions that may in part be linked with age, but also behaviors, habits, and other influences (Berger, 2011). For instance, cardiovascular capacity decreases in later life (i.e., primary aging) but this loss may be exacerbated by lack of exercise or smoking (i.e., secondary aging). Regardless of type of aging, disease prevalence does rise in later life. **Disease** may be understood as a condition that requires ongoing medical attention and/or interferes with day-to-day tasks for at least one year (Anderson & Horvath, 2004). Disease in aging individuals may be prompted by physical changes in numerous areas, including:

- cardiovascular system,
- immune system, and
- bone density.

First, in terms of the aging **cardiovascular system**, the heart will pump more slowly in later life than it did in earlier life stages. Moreover, the vascular system is less flexible, and together this may cause an increase in blood pressure, perhaps leading to hypertension. In addition, aging lungs take in less oxygen with each inhalation, meaning less oxygenated blood is traveling throughout the bloodstream. Second, the **immune system** becomes less effective in later life. Some of the cells that identify and destroy foreign substances (i.e., T-cells and B-cells) become less effective, allowing more pathogens to infect the individual (Berger, 2011). Third, bones become less dense, losing calcium and rigidity. In more extreme cases, **osteoporosis** may be apparent.

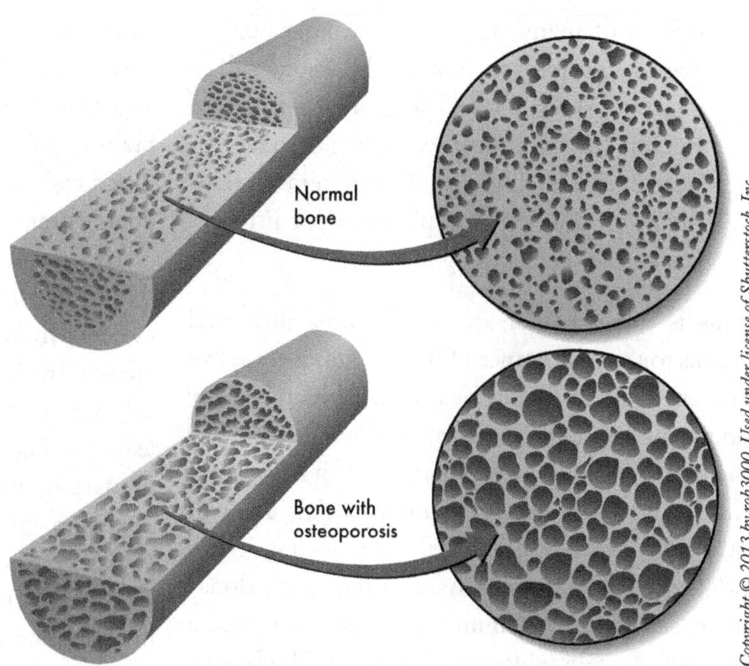

Due to decreased bone density, falling in later life may be particularly problematic. In fact, there are approximately 14,000 fall-related fatalities each year in the United States, a majority of whom are 75 years or older. Some individuals may be at greatest risk, including females, those that live alone, or have poor vision or balance (Pargman, 2012). When an individual with a more fragile skeletal system falls, they are more likely to fracture or break bones in more areas and with greater severity. Moreover, falling is more likely to cause infection or immobility in older individuals.

It should be noted the aforementioned areas (i.e., cardiovascular system, immune system, and bone density) is not an exhaustive list of the physical changes that occur in later life. Rather, they are but some of the areas in which aging may occur optimally or pathologically, and contribute to overall health and longevity. Other factors are linked with such longevity and quality of life. For instance, researchers have linked a sense of meaning and purpose to a longer lifespan. Researchers assessed "eudemonic well-being" - which is linked with sense of control, feelings that what you are doing is worthwhile, and a sense of purpose - and linked high well-being scores to about 2 more years of life (Steptoe, Deaton, & Stone, 2014). One may also consider neurological changes, and the impact they may have upon cognition and lifestyle.

Neurological Aging

Consider the following passage, taken from a book written by Norman Doidge, entitled *The Brain that Changes Itself*:

> Psychologically, middle age is often an appealing time because all else being equal, it can be a relatively placid period compared to what has come before. Our bodies aren't changing as they did in adolescence; we're more likely to have a solid sense of who we are and be skilled at a career. We still regard ourselves as active, but we have a tendency to deceive ourselves into thinking that we are learning as we were before. We rarely engage in tasks in which we must focus our attention as closely as we did when we were younger, trying to learn new vocabulary or master new skills. Such activities as reading the newspaper, practicing a pro-

> fession of many years, and speaking our own language are mostly the reply of mastered skills, not learning. By the time we hit our seventies, we may not have systematically engaged the systems in the brain that regulate plasticity for fifty years. (Doidge, 2007, p. 256)

This is somewhat of an unwelcoming idea, and speaks to the importance of being cognitively active and engaging in lifelong learning. Although many do remain mentally sharp well into later life, the aging processes do impact the brain, and it is apparent the human brain becomes somewhat less efficient over time. For instance, there is a reduction in the production of key neurotransmitters (e.g., dopamine, serotonin), a thinning of myelination, and a slowing of cerebral blood and neural fluids (Berger, 2011). Together, in later life neural impulses may proceed more deliberately and slowly through neural networks. This may be observed in reductions in speed of processing information; such as delays in remembering an event or responding to a question.

While there may be changes in speed of processing, there may also be changes in brain size. That is, the brain tends to get smaller as one ages. At a broad level, there is a reduction in the volume of gray matter in the brain—the areas responsible for information processing. Although gray matter reduction is inevitable, it appears clear that individuals that maintain neurological and cognition functioning have the *least* amount of shrinkage (Berger, 2011). Some of the processing areas that experience the most marked shrinkage include the hypothalamus and the prefrontal cortex. These brain areas have been linked with memory and thought coordination and response inhibition, respectively. If the area of one's brain responsible for response inhibition becomes smaller and less efficient, it may explain why some individuals may talk "too much" or with "off-target verbosity" (von Hippel, 2007).

For years a prevailing notion was that the brains of older individuals would be less neurologically active. However, this does not appear to be the case as the brain remains quite active in later life. Rather, older brains may *compensate* for inadequate brain regions by utilizing other, more fully functioning areas for thinking and problem solving. In a way, brain regions are "combining" in order to maintain functional capabilities. Similarly, researchers have demonstrated that many older brains demonstrate plasticity, but in different places. More specifically, when learning a new task, older individuals may experience more plasticity and change in white matter areas of the brain compared to the changes in cortical, gray areas which were more apparent in younger learners. Thus, older brains may be able to accommodate by increasing transmission efficiency from one brain region to another (Yotsumoto, Chang, Ni, Pierce, & Andersen, 2014). On the other hand, if in fact there is reduced inhibition in older brains, the brain will no longer be able to correctly pair the incoming information with the appropriate brain region. Sometimes referred to as a "wandering mind" perspective, information may flow more liberally through an older brain (Berger, 2011). These processes may, in part, impact memory.

Memory

Changes in memory capabilities are apparent across the life span (Terry, 2009). That is, the memory capabilities of an individual changes over time, from infancy and early childhood through later life. It is interesting that we seem to have a "double standard" when it comes to age and memory. If a younger individual forgets something, it most often is understood as simply that—they forgot. However, when an older individual forgets something, we may be more prone to think, "they are getting old, and their memory is poor." A classic study in age and memory was conducted in which three actors (a 20-year-old, a 50-year-old, and a 70-year-old) read an identical speech to an audience of different participants. During this speech, each actor made identical statements related to memory, such as "I forgot my keys." Study participants (i.e., audience members) were then asked to describe the speaker they just heard. Interestingly, only those who heard the 70-year-old give the speech described the speaker as "forgetful" even though the other actors had made the same speech. The term (or terms related to forgetfulness) was not used at all when the other speakers were being described (Rodin & Langer, 1980). These findings may suggest individuals maintain the idea that forgetfulness is a typical symptom of aging. However, the general idea that a negative correlation exists between age and memory ability may not be true.

Memory may be viewed in different ways. For instance, there are three proposed fundamental types of memory: procedural memory, semantic memory, and episodic memory (Tulving, 1985). Briefly, **procedural memory** is related to information that is automatically recalled without conscious effort. Many motor skills (e.g., walking, throwing) are ingrained in procedural memory systems. **Semantic memory** is akin to "declarative" knowledge and involves basic factual assertions about the world. Semantic memory may be viewed in the recollection of historical facts and real world objects. In a game of *Trivial Pursuit*, players are relying upon semantic knowledge. Lastly, **episodic memory** is comprised of information from the events of daily life, and is ongoing. You may have episodic memories related to what you ate last week, or the hike you went on yesterday—each general memory with respective details. Together, these three forms of memory may capture the overall uses and functions of memory (Zacks, Hasher, & Li, 2000). Subsequently, age differences may be discussed with all three type of memory.

In terms of procedural memory, older individuals tend to be very comparable to younger individuals. For example, an older individual can rather fluently engage in motor skills after many years. Thus, procedural memories are quite resilient to decay. In addition, semantic memories are relatively stable. Older individual can rather effortlessly recall important facts of the real world. In fact, many older individuals perform as well—if not better—than younger individuals on semantic memory tasks (Craik & Jennings, 1992; Zacks, Hasher, & Li, 2000). Episodic memories—those related to daily life events—appear to be the most fragile and subsequently the most susceptible to decline as one gets older. For example, for an older individual it may be more difficult to remember where they left their keys, or at what restaurant they ate last week. Together, older individuals do not *always* have a poorer memory than their younger counterparts.

This may be true in relation to episodic memory, and causes some individuals to forget items related to daily life, but it is not as consistently true in regard to other memory systems (i.e., procedural, semantic). Of course, there are a number of other factors related to individual differences in memory (e.g., gender, personality, and arousal) that may moderate the age-memory link, too (Terry, 2009).

It should be noted the aforementioned terms and concepts related to neurological aging and age differences in memory are prominent, but part of a normal course of aging nonetheless. In some more extreme cases, there is more prominent and irreparable neurological loss.

Dementia

The term **dementia** is a generic term which means "out of mind," and involves an irreversible, pathological loss of brain function due to organic damage or disease (Berger, 2011). The irreversible nature of dementia implies it is enduring, and should not be confused with **delirium**, which is a short-term loss of brain function. Most elderly individuals do not have dementia. In fact, only about 5% of individuals from the ages of 70 to 79 have some type of dementia. However, this rate jumps to 24% of individuals from age 80 to 89 (Plassman et al., 2007). This jump is consistent with a transition from a young-old to old-old life stage.

An early indicator of dementia may be **mild cognitive impairment**, which is lack of memory and loss of spoken fluency and is more pronounced than that which would be expected due to normal neurological aging. About one half of those with a mild cognitive impairment stay at that particular level of impairment (i.e., they don't get worse). In some cases, they even improve in terms of memory and verbal competence. However, mild cognitive impairment is also a well-recognized risk factor for other types of dementia, including Alzhemier's disease.

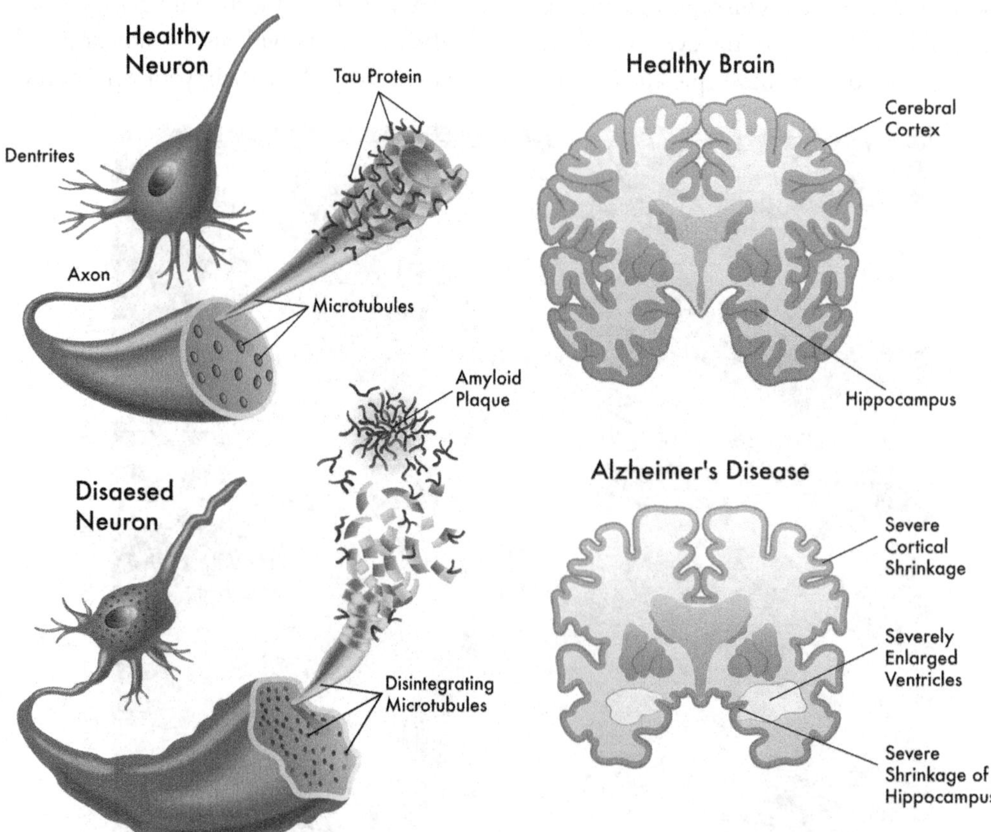

The most common form of dementia in the United States is **Alzheimer's disease**, which is marked by the proliferation of abnormalities in the cerebral cortex. These abnormalities inhibit the neural connection and communication. More specifically, the abnormalities are called plaques and tangles. **Plaques** are bundles of one type of protein, while **tangles** are twisted accumulations of another protein. While both of these proteins are naturally found in all human brains, in Alzheimer's patients they grow and reproduce in unhealthy amounts, disrupting normal brain functioning, including memory. The consequences of cortical functioning loss due to Alzhemier's can be significant; more advanced stages requiring full-time care of the individual. There are actually five recognized stages of Alzheimer's disease:

- Stage 1: Forgetfulness;
- Stage 2: Generalized confusion;
- Stage 3: Advanced memory loss;
- Stage 4: Full-time care; and
- Stage 5: Unresponsiveness.

In the first stage (forgetfulness) mild cognitive impairment may be evident, with some general inability to remember people, places, and more recent events. The next stage (generalized confusion) involved more marked memory loss—perhaps with short-term memory loss—as well as difficulty with concentration. In this stage, speech patterns may become nonsensical from time to time. In the third stage of advanced memory loss, the individual's inability to recall items may significantly interfere with day-to-day functioning, and may even pose safety risks. For instance, an individual in this stage may forget to dress properly for the weather, turn off an iron or stove, or even eat. The fourth stage (full-time care) requires that someone (e.g., spouse, family member, health care worker) care for the individual at all times. There is a general inability to communicate, or even recognize those that may care for them. Sadly, in the last stage (unresponsiveness), the individual may become completely unresponsive to people and stimuli in their environment.

Exercise in Later Life: Physical Benefits

Exercise has consistently emerged as a behavioral correlate of good health, and this remains true in later life. **Exercise** may be viewed as rigorous physical activity with the aim of improving one or more elements of personal fitness (Pargman, 2012). Exercise may have preventative qualities. Although the aforementioned effects of aging (i.e., loss of muscle mass and flexibility, vascular hardening and hypertension, loss of bone density) are ultimately inevitable, exercise may slow the impact of primary and secondary aging processes. In addition, exercise may be thought of as an intervention tool. After problems have arisen (e.g., hypertension, osteoporosis), some form(s) of exercise may be suggested by medical professionals. The U.S. Surgeon General, Dr. Regina Benjamin, has extolled the benefits of exercise, stating it is

a reliable type of "medicine" (Pargman, 2012). To that end, exercise may not only benefit individuals in intuitively physical ways, but it also stands to offer benefits in cognitive (e.g., memory) and psychosocial (e.g., well-being) areas.

Dr. David Pargman (2012) offered a very useful review of the benefits of exercise for older adults. In fact, the title of his book, *Boomercise: Exercising as You Age,* seems itself to speak clearly about the intent of the book and the target audience. It is useful to reconsider some of the aforementioned issues associated with aging, as they will reemerge as some of the same areas that are protected by exercise.

In terms of cardiovascular health, exercise induces short-term bouts of accelerated heart rate. Over time, this "strengthening" of the heart will permit it to eject larger quantities of blood with each pump, sending blood more efficiently to the desired destinations (i.e, organs). Consequently, this tends to lower one's resting heart rate. In addition, exercise increases the relative quantity of high-density lipoprotein (HDL) in the bloodstream. This HDL is a desirable substance that cleans out arteries and veins by washing away harmful plaque that accumulates over the years. Although genetics can also impact cardiovascular health, exercise is a behavioral variable that may consistently demonstrate benefits. Together, these results will tend to lower blood pressure, which otherwise tends to increase in later life. Moreover, these results of exercise ensure oxygenated blood is received in necessary amounts to all bodily organs, including the brain, fortifying health, functioning, and ability to stave off infection (Pargman, 2012).

The latter notion (i.e., better blood flow helps stave off infection) implies enhanced blood circulation directly impacts immune functioning. More specifically, the T-cells and B-cells travel more readily through the body to attack foreign and harmful agents. To illustrate, researchers have found that wounds on "fit" older individuals actually heal more quickly than wounds on those that are "unfit." However, it is important to note that moderate exercise enhances immune system functioning in older individuals; too much intense activity may actually have a negative impact on immune functioning (Pargman, 2012).

It was noted briefly in earlier paragraphs that falling in older individuals may be particularly problematic; bones that are less dense and immune systems that are less efficient may be an undesirable combination in this respect. Exercise may be a factor here, as those that do not engage in regular exercise are twice as likely to fall as those that do engage in physical activity. Once again, exercise may enhance the same areas (i.e., balance, bone density, immune functioning) that make falling so dangerous. Exercise activates and strengthens the neuromuscular pathways responsible for balance and coordination. In addition, exercise—particularly weight-bearing and resistance activities—can strengthen bones (Pargman, 2012). Together, Dr. Benjamin appeared to be on target when describing exercise as a form of medicine.

Exercise in Later Life: Cognitive and Psychosocial Benefits

As mentioned above, exercise facilitates the passage of blood (and oxygen) to bodily organs, including cerebral blood flow in the brain. Thus, exercise may also impact brain functioning, including a host of cognitive functions, including memory. Studies indicate older individuals who exercise regularly perform better on short-term memory tasks than those who do not exercise regularly (Pargman, 2012). Interestingly, in one study, researchers also implicated computer use into the equation. Geda et al. (2012) examined exercise and computer use in a sample of 926 individuals aged 70–93. Moderate exercise was viewed as brisk walking, hiking, aerobic activity, strength training, walking a golf course (i.e., no cart), swimming, tennis, yoga, martial arts, or other exercise machines. Results revealed of those who did not exercise or use a computer, 20% demonstrated

normal cognition, while almost 38% exhibited mild cognitive impairment. On the other hand, those who *did* exercise and use a computer frequently, 36% demonstrated normal cognition, while only 18% showed signs of mild cognitive impairment. With the substantial increase in computer use by older adults, the authors suggest it is important to continue to examine this link.

Rosenbaum and Sherrington (2011) looked at the connection between physical activity and well-being for older adults by performing a meta-analysis of the literature related to light or moderate physical activities on physical and psychological well-being in older adults. The researchers concluded that a minimum of two 45-minute light exercise sessions should be recommended to older adults in order to enhance mental health. The "mental health" the researchers refer to may in fact be "wellness."

Wellness may be understood as a general "perception of a satisfactory balance among the important life dimensions" (Pargman, 2012, p. 39). More specifically, some general life dimensions include:

- physical,
- mental,
- social,
- emotional, and
- spiritual.

Intuitively, physical activity certainly enhances **physical** dimensions for all the aforementioned circulatory and cardiovascular reasons. Many times, this is the dimension that is referred to as "health" or "fitness." Not only do individuals derive the physical benefits, but they may generate a sense of satisfaction from attending to something many family members, friends, and/or medical professionals may encourage. They may feel good it is an aspect of life they are not ignoring. Second, the **mental** dimension is associated with thinking and cognitive capabilities. Once again, exercise may positively impact this area for an aging person; as noted above, exercise can improve cognitive functioning. Third, the **social** component refers to interactions with people. It stands to reason that individuals engaged in regular exercise (i.e., outdoors, gyms, rec centers) also incur social interactions with friends, walking or work-out partners, fellow gym patrons and staff, or trainers as a result of their exercise behaviors. Thus, physical activity may also promote a social health. Fourth, the **emotional** dimension is related to how one identifies, regulates, and copes with emotions. Indeed, exercise may be used as a coping mechanism for negative emotions; it has distractory functions that may promote better emotional health. Lastly, **spirituality** is a part of wellness. Spirituality may be viewed in those that maintain or seek a relationship with a specific God, but it may also be evident in other areas as well. For instance, those that seek closeness to nature and earthly elements may also be fostering a sense of spirituality. Admittedly, it may be more difficult to envision how exercise may impact spirituality, but the preceding paragraph may make it relatively clear that exercise can impact many life dimensions for older individuals.

Together, if one senses these areas are in some type of balance, they may experience "wellness." A lack of wellness is apparent when there is some perceived imbalance among these life areas. For instance, one may exercise intensely alone (e.g., in the privacy of their home) but generally feel disconnected with others (e.g., family, friends) or their spiritual side. Thus, they may be physically fit, but not feel well overall. On the other hand, someone could be suffering from serious illness, but if they otherwise sense social, emotional, spiritual, and mental health, they may still be well overall.

In addition to the aforementioned physical, cognitive, and psychosocial benefits of exercise for individuals in later life, it may also increase one's life span. In one study, researchers pooled numerous large pre-existing epidemiological (i.e., related to the patterns, causes, and effects of health and disease) studies. In gathering all of these, they were able access biological health data for over 650,000 individuals! Of those 650,000, the researchers had data on over 82,000 deaths, giving them necessary data for life expectancy. Then, the researchers applied statistical analyses with predictive value to quantify the years of life that may be gained according to distinct levels of physical activity (Moore et al., 2012). The researchers defined the minimum amount for those in later life according to World Health Organization (WHO) standards, which is 150 minutes of moderate to vigorous physical activity per week. It was reported that individuals meeting this minimum requirement lived an average of 3.4-4.5 years longer than those who did not meet this minimum. Even engaging in moderate to vigorous physical activity for half the recommended amount of time (75 minutes) was associated with 1.8 years of longer life compared to those who did not exercise that much, if at all. Not surprisingly, these findings may imply that yet again some physical activity is better than none at all! Another interesting finding that emerged: being inactive and normal weight was associated with 3.1 *fewer* years of life expectancy compared to being active and obese. This latter finding suggests physical activity is important for life expectancy even when the exercise does not necessarily result in weight loss (Moore et al., 2012).

As much as physical activity may be a protective factor in later life, and one that may prolong late-life life expectancy; it cannot completely cease the course of aging. The impact of primary aging will be felt eventually for all individuals. With life expectancy increasing globally, so too does the number of individuals living with chronic disease, injuries, and mental health problems, such as depression. Currently, health problems more typical in aging populations (e.g., hypertension, bone, joint disease) have overtaken child malnutrition as the leading health concerns (People living longer, but sicker, 2012).

Key Terms

- **Later Life** – a term applied to any individual older than 60 years and on through end-of-life
- **Demographic Shift in Aging Populations** – referring to a much larger ratio currently of individuals 60 years or older than in centuries past
- **Fertility** – refers to the average number of children a woman will have in her lifetime
- **Baby Boomer Generation** – those born post World War II; this generation has now entered later life
- **Life Expectancy** – an average based upon the number of years a newborn can expect to live in a given country if conditions in that particular region remain unchanged
- **Late-Life Life Expectancy** – this term refers to the number of years someone can expect to live past 65
- **Young-Old** – comprised of individuals in their 60s and up through 75 years of age. The young-old are still relatively healthy and financially stable; they may possibly be retired, but yet remain active.
- **Old-Old** – those over 75 years of age and also more likely to be characterized by disease or disability due to further aging and heightened financial instability
- **Oldest-Old** – those over 85 years of age, who are generally dependent on others (e.g., family members, caretakers) for many day-to-day tasks; the last life stage applied to human development
- **Physical Aging:**
    - **Primary Aging** – the universal and irreversible physical changes that occur as we age
    - **Secondary Aging** – related to specific illnesses or conditions that may in part be linked with age, but also behaviors, habits, and other influences
- **Disease** – a condition that requires ongoing medical attention and/or interferes with day-to-day tasks for at least one year
- **Cardiovascular System** – the heart will pump more slowly in later life than it did in earlier life stages; vascular system is less flexible; and together this may cause an increase in blood pressure, perhaps leading to hypertension. In addition, aging lungs take in less oxygen with each inhalation, meaning less oxygenated blood is traveling throughout the bloodstream.
- **Immune System** – bodily system that combats disease, this system becomes less effective in later life. Some of the cells that identify and destroy foreign substances (i.e., T-cells and B-cells) become less effective, allowing more pathogens to infect the individual.
- **Osteoporosis** – bones become less dense, losing calcium and rigidity
- **Memory Types:**
    - **Procedural Memory** – related to information that is automatically recalled without conscious effort. Many motor skills (e.g., walking, throwing) are ingrained in procedural memory systems. It is the least fragile of the memory systems.
    - **Semantic Memory** – this type is akin to "declarative" knowledge and involves basic factual assertions about the world. It is moderately fragile.
    - **Episodic Memory** – comprised of information from the events of daily life, and is ongoing. It is the most fragile of the memory systems.

- **Dementia** – a generic term meaning "out of mind," and involves an irreversible, pathological loss of brain function due to organic damage or disease. The irreversible nature of dementia implies it is enduring.
- **Delirium** – a short-term loss of brain function
- **Mild Cognitive Impairment** – a lack of memory and loss of spoken fluency, and is more pronounced than that which would be expected due to normal neurological aging
- **Alzheimer's Disease** – the most common form of dementia in the United States which is marked by the proliferation of abnormalities in the cerebral cortex. These abnormalities inhibit the neural connection and communication.
    - **Plaques** – bundles of one type of protein
    - **Tangles** – twisted accumulations of protein
- **Exercise** – rigorous physical activity with the aim of improving one or more elements of personal fitness; maintains numerous benefits for all individuals, including those in later life
- **Wellness** – a general perception of a satisfactory balance among the important life dimensions
    - **Physical** – dimension of wellness linked with circulatory and cardiovascular areas; often referred to as "health" or "fitness"
    - **Mental** – associated with thinking and cognitive capabilities
    - **Social** – refers to interactions with people
    - **Emotional** – related to how one identifies, regulates, and copes with emotions
    - **Spirituality** – also a part of wellness, spirituality may be viewed in those that maintain or seek a relationship with a specific God, but it may also be evident in other areas as well

Critical Thinking Questions

1. What are some of the defining features of "later life?" How prevalent is this population? What factors are associated with the increase in the relative proportion of this population? What ages and stages constitute later life? What are some of the primary changes that impact individuals as they approach the end-of-life?
2. Discuss memory in later life. What are some of the perspectives on memory loss, as it occurs naturally, in later life? What is the difference between natural memory loss and dementia? Concerning the latter, what are some of the main characteristics of dementia? In your response, be sure to address key terms and concepts, and also integrate real or hypothetical examples.
3. What benefits does exercise maintain for individuals in later life? How would you prescribe an exercise routine for someone in later life who had not been active for many years prior? What unique challenges might you (as the consultant) or this individual (as the aging exerciser) face in adopting and maintaining an exercise regimen in later life?

References

Anderson, G. & Horvath, J. (2004). The growing burden of chronic disease in America. *Public Health Reports, 119,* 263-270.

Berger, K. S. (2011). *The developing person throughout the lifespan.* New York: Worth.

Craik, F. I. M. & Jennings, J. M. (1992). Human memory. In F. I. M Craik and T. A. Salthouse (Eds.), *The handbook of aging and cognition* (pp. 51-110). Hillsdale, NJ: Erlbaum.

Doidge, N. (2007). *The brain that changes itself.* New York: Penguin.

Geda, Y. E., Roberts. R. O., Knopman, D. S., Christianson, T. S., Pankratz, V. S., Ivnik, R. J., Boeve, B. F., Tangalos, E. G., Peterson, R. C., & Rocca, W. A. (2012). Physical exercise and mild cognitive impairment: A population-based study. *Archives of Neurology, 67,* 80-86.

Moore, S. C., Patel, A. V., Matthews, C. E., de Gonzalez, A. B., Park, Y., Katki, H. A., Linet, M. S., People living longer, but sicker (2012, December). *Associated Press.* Retrieved from http://www.usatoday.com/story/news/world/2012/12/13/people-global-diseases/1766831/

Pargman, D. (2012). *Boomercise: Exercising as you age.* Morgantown, WV: Fitness Information Technology.

Plassman, B. L., Langa, K. M., Fisher, G. G., Heeringa, S. G., Weir, D. R., Ofstedal, M. B., Burke, J. R. Hurd, M. D., Potter, G. G., Rodgers, W. L., Steffens, D. C., Willis, R. J., & Wallance, R. B. (2007). Prevalence of dementia in the United States: The Aging, Demographics, and Memory Study. *Neuroepidemiology, 29,* 125-132.

Rodin, J. & Langer, E. J. (1980). Aging labels: The decline of control and the fall of self-esteem. *Journal of Social Issues, 36,* 12-29.

Rosenbaum, S. & Sherrington, C. (2011). Is exercise effective in promoting mental well-being in older age? A systematic review. *British Journal Of Sports Medicine,* 45(*13*), 1079-1080.

Steptoe, A., Deaton, A., & Stone, A.A. (2014). Subjective well-being, health and ageing. The Lancet. doi: 10.1016/S0140-6736(13)61489-0

Terry, W. S. (2009). *Learning & memory: Basic principles, processes, and procedures.* (4th ed.) Boston: Pearson Higher Education.

Tulving, E. (1985). How many memory systems are there? *American Psychologist, 40,* 385-398.

von Hippel, W. (2007). Aging, executive functioning, and social control. *Current Directions in Psychological Science, 16,* 240-244.

Weiderpass, E., Visvanathan, K., Helzlsouer, K. J., Thun, M., Gapstur, S. M., Hartge, P., & Lee, I. (2012). Leisure time physical activity of moderate to vigorous intensity and mortality: A large pooled cohort analysis. *PLoS Medicine, 9,* 1-14.

Yotsumoto, Y., Chang, L., Ni, R., Pierce, &R., Andersen, G.J. (2014). White matter in the older brain is more plastic than in younger brain. *Nature Communications.* doi: 10.1038/ncomms6504

Zacks, R. T., Hasher, L., & Li, K. Z. H. (2000). Human memory. In F. I. M. Craik and T. A. Salthouse (Eds.), *The handbook of aging and cognition* (pp. 293-357). Hillsdale, NJ: Erlbaum.

CHAPTER 16

Death and Dying

Definition of Death

While this "death and dying" unit appears at the end of a life span development text and immediately following a unit related to later-life; death, of course, is not reserved for older individuals. Death may occur in any life stage for a variety of reasons (e.g., medical complications, illness, accident, or suicide). Accordingly, the following chapter is devoted to various aspects of death and dying.

Here are some descriptive statistics from a recent large scale study related to life expectancy and leading causes of death:

- Heart disease and stroke remain the leading cause of death across the world.
- Lung cancer has vaulted to the 5th leading cause of death globally, perhaps due to an increased ratio of individuals 65 and older.
- Globally, homicide is the 20th leading cause of death among men. In the United States, homicide is the 21st leading cause of death; in Latin America it is the 3rd leading cause of death.
- Suicide is the 21st leading cause of death worldwide, but ranks as high as 9th across portions of Asia, from India to China; an area has been termed the "suicide belt." Suicide ranks 14th in North America in terms of causes of death (Moore et al., 2012).

Before proceeding further, a formal definition may be warranted. **Death** is an irreversible cessation of bodily functioning, including heart beat, respiration, and brain activity. Many coroners or

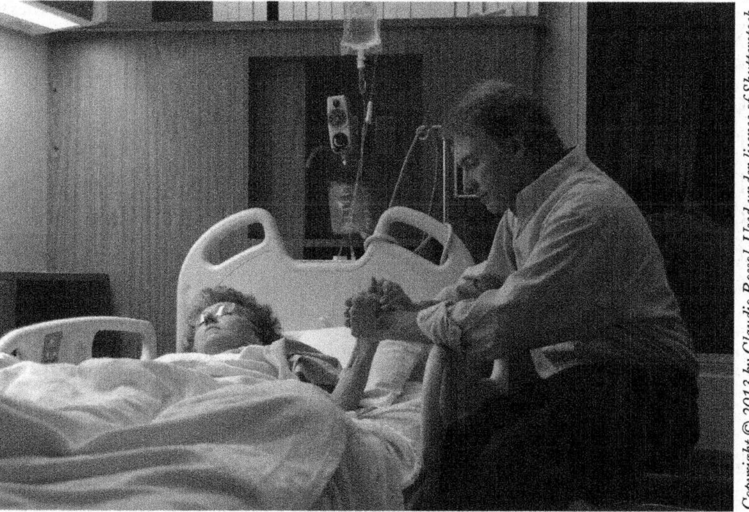

medical professionals may view lack of electrical brain activity as the truest marker of a biological death. Emanating from this definition of death arises four discernible realities of death:

- universality,
- irreversibility,
- non-functionality, and
- causality.

The first reality (i.e., universality) refers to the fact that death is a global and consistent truth. That is, death is inevitable for all living things. Second, death is irreversible and final. When an organism is legitimately "dead," the organism cannot become alive again. Third, death necessarily involves that all functioning in that organism has ceased. Fourth, ultimately biological factors cause death.

Death Perspectives

The scientific study of death is **thanatology.** This field captures not only the biological aspects of death, but also the social and cultural traditions surrounding death events. For instance, one historical change in death may be recognized in the typical age at which it occurs (i.e., life expectancy). That is, over time, there has been a "redistribution" of death from the young to the elderly, prompted in part by prenatal and pediatric health care (DeSpelder & Strickland, 2011). Moreover, there have been transformations in the ways in which death events are anticipated, viewed, and experienced. Much of the variation in how death is perceived may be clarified by culture in which the dying (or surviving) individual(s) reside. Consider the following passage:

> The distinctive stance towards death in a particular culture affects the behavior of its members as they go about their daily lives, influencing, for example, their willingness to engage in risky behaviors or their likelihood of taking out an insurance policy, as well as their attitudes towards such issues as organ donation, the death penalty, euthanasia, or the possibility of an afterlife. In a variety of ways, our culture helps us deny, manipulate, distort, or camouflage death so it is a less difficult threat with which to cope. (DeSpelder & Strickland, 2011, p. 27)

For example, in the United States, there are hundreds of recognized Native American nations, and each maintains unique views and practices related to death. In many nations, there is particular veneration for the dead, who are believed to become guardian spirits for their own people after death. There is much emphasis on past generations and ancestral influence. The guardian spirits maintain high rankings in social hierarchies, and to become a spirit is to "outrank" many others. Thus, death is viewed as a transition to another spirit world, and not something to be viewed with fear or negativity.

The view of a spirit world after death is not exclusive for some Native American nations. Some African communities, including the Nandi in Kenya, also believe that to be remembered after death is to be "alive in spirit form." Thus, according to the Nandi and other traditional African cultures, the "view of death is positive because it is comprehensively integrated into the totality of life" (DeSpelder & Strickland, 2011, p. 109). Thus, some cultural perspectives involve some degree of optimism toward death. This may be in stark contrast to other cultures, which maintain negative and anxiety-provoking views of death and/or an afterlife.

The earliest Christian views emphasized a "collective destiny." All individuals were mortal, would experience death, but eventually experience resurrection. In earlier centuries, this view was held rather strictly and literally, and may have mitigated the confusion or anxiety individuals had regarding death. Generally speaking, there were little or no debates regarding what happened after death, and it was a reassuring notion of sorts.

Thereafter, religious doctrines were put in place regarding the prospect of an afterlife; the quality

of which may be based on the relative presence or absence of "good deeds" being performed while living. As Westernized societies moved through ages of *Enlightenment*, along with the emergence of the sciences, a more ambivalent view of death was held. In other words, society no longer had a uniform view of death. Over time, and reaching into the 21st century, societal views of death transitioned from a "collective destiny" and understanding of death, into more personal awareness and ideas of death, and ultimately, into preoccupation with the deaths of loved ones (DeSpelder & Strickland, 2011). Death became a process and event that provoked much more confusion and anxiety.

Grief and Bereavement

The terms *grief*, *bereavement*, and *mourning* are often used interchangeably. However, they deserve distinction. At perhaps the broadest level, **grief** is a reaction to a loss, including death. The grieving process is multi-faceted, including social, emotional, and even physical components. There are understandably negative aspects of grief (e.g., sorrow), but there may be some positive aspects as well (e.g., acceptance). **Bereavement** is often associated with state of sadness, and is a specific state of being "deprived" of someone or something. An individual described as "bereft" is being depicted as being in a state of loss.

Kübler-Ross (1969) originally offered a model of grief that is not restricted exclusively to death and death events; rather, it may be applied more generally with loss. Individuals may sense loss and "grieve" for a variety of reasons, including job termination, divorce, or illness. The original notion was that when faced with some form of loss, individuals may pass through a certain set of stages, including:

- denial,
- anger,
- bargaining,
- depression, and
- acceptance.

In the context of death and dying, when an individual first hears news related to someone else having died, or even if they themselves receive a terrible diagnosis from a doctor, an initial reaction may be that of **denial**. Simply put, the individual may first not believe, or be incapable of believing, what they are being told; subsequently disowning the information. Upon hearing of grave news, a reaction such as "there must be some mistake" may be indicative of denial. Thereafter, some degree of **anger** may set in. Anger may be directed at physicians, family members, friends, oneself, or perhaps even a deity. Thought processes that prompt anger may be related to "why the illness was not diagnosed sooner" or "why are others that don't take care of themselves in perfect health?" Eventually, anger is thought to yield to **bargaining**, which is evident when an individual pleads for more time. This may be evident in a dying person when they plead with a deity to spare their life so they may live longer, perhaps to see grandchildren grow up, or to be sure their spouse will be taken care of. These emotional stages were thought to lead to a **depressed** state, which involves feelings of hopelessness and despair. Over time, however, some of the negative emotions (e.g., anger, depression) make way for a sense of **acceptance**. In such a state, the dying person may even look forward to the end. In others, they may accept that a loved one is actually gone.

In sum, this model may offer some useful notions regarding the emotions and issues confronting those individuals coping with loss. It is important to note individuals may not necessarily move sequentially and discretely through these stages. In fact, researchers have argued the uncritical adoption of the grief stage model may cause some to withdraw socially or emotionally from those that have died, or are in dying process, thereby negatively impacting a natural course of grief (Kastenbaum, 2004). In other words, it may be problematic should some bereft individuals (or counselors) view certain emotions and processes (e.g., depressive symptoms, anger) as a "stage" that should be passed through, rather than as an emotion or symptom that may be naturally processed, revisited, or both.

Interestingly, many years after the hallmark publication (Kübler-Ross, 1969) brought the idea that grief may be experienced in stages, Kübler-Ross affirmed the stage model was "never meant to help tuck messy emotions into neat packages" (O'Rourke, 2010, p. 68). Thus, grieving processes may be viewed as less of a "checklist" and more of an ongoing process accompanied by a range of biological, psychological, and social symptoms (O'Rourke, 2010). Thus, grief is an emotional process reactive to loss. Mourning, on the other hand, is the behavioral expression of loss.

Mourning

The process of mourning has specific sociocultural connotations. **Mourning** involves practices and traditions that individuals engage in surrounding a death event (e.g., funerals, processions, etc.) and may also involve matters of faith and religious practices. Some more traditional and contemporary mourning rituals include events such as **funerals**, which are ceremonies to remember or sanctify the deceased. Funerals may reflect the spiritual or religious affiliation of the deceased and/or the surviving family members. Funerals may be put on in churches, or at a non-denominational funeral home. Other familial preferences may guide whether or not there will be an open viewing of the body or not, or whether the body will be cremated. If the body is cremated, some surviving family members may choose to keep the ashes nearby, while others prefer to spread them in a location perhaps significant to the deceased. While these are some contemporary and typical ways to mourn, there are many others.

For instance, in two seemingly similar religious communities, the mourning process can be quite different. In Egypt and Bali, while both share a Muslim religious background, members of the former community view "waling and public lamenting" as appropriate, while the latter encourage a more private grief, along with demonstrating a cheerful outer appearance (DeSpelder & Strickland, 2011).

Earlier in the unit, it was brought out that many Native American nations view death as a transformative event, moving from an earthly existence to a spiritual one. Thus, their mourning practices may reflect how they care for the individual's body after death. For instance, the Ohlone (a nation in California) dress the corpse in decorative ways, including with feathers and flowers. Thereafter, the body is wrapped in blankets. The corpse is then burned in a funeral type ceremony, along with the deceased person's possessions, which is thought to facilitate a prompt passage to the spirit world. Through this ritual, it is important to get of rid of the deceased's earthly belongings—as well as refrain from uttering their name—as it may cause the dead spirit to remain in an earthly realm longer than necessary. In another example, the Cherokee nation maintains a multiple soul perspective of death, with the last of four bodily souls dying after one year. Thus, graves are tended to for one year after death, when formal mourning may end. Thereafter, the deceased has completed his or her journey to a spirit realm.

As noted, some African nations share the perspective that a spiritual existence begins after death. Therefore, some mourning practices involve preparing the deceased for this next stage. The deceased may be given messages to carry with them to transmit to others whom have previously died. In some cases, such as the LoDagaa of Ghana, mourning may last for several months, or even years. First, the body is prepared for burial, which may take several days. During this time, there are public ceremonies, and more private redistribution of familial roles and belongings. This first stage ends with body burial. Later on, there is an erection of an ancestral shrine on the grave, which is thought to signify transformation to an ancestral world. A final stage involves constructing a more final shrine, and a subsequent ceremony releases loved ones from obligatory mourning.

Some Mexican traditions also invoke the presence of spirits. This view receives particular attention on *Dia de los Muertos*, or the Day of the Dead. Food has an integral role to this day, and may reflect some core attitudes toward death.

Eating candy and bread in the shape of skeletons, including skull and bones, are thought to signify death may be viewed as a "companion" rather than an adversary. Moreover, the food and ceremonies aim to accustom individuals to the prospect of their own death. Candles light gravesites, to invite spirits back to celebrate (DeSpelder & Strickland, 2011). Together, there are numerous cultural variations in how individuals mourn the deceased. Therese Rando (1995) offered a model of mourning, outlining some supposed important aspects of it:

- recognize the loss,
- react to separation,
- recollect and re-experience the deceased,
- relinquish old attachments,
- readjust, and
- reinvest.

The first task is to **recognize the loss.** This involves understanding how or why the individual died, and accepting the finality. Recognizing loss would certainly be incongruent with Kübler-Ross' notion of "denial." **Reacting to separation** is related to the grief experience, and realizing all of the emotional and behavioral symptoms of grief. **Recollecting and re-experiencing** refers to an inability to remember the deceased in realistic ways. That is, when someone dies, it may be natural to be consumed with sadness and not want to recall memories of the deceased person, for fear it may elicit sadness. On the other hand, it may be natural to remember and elaborate only positive aspects of the deceased. Over time, however, a more realistic memory may set in. Thereafter, it may be vital to **relinquish** (or abandon) the roles and life that were evident with the deceased. In the absence of the deceased, social life may have a new context. Thus, the **readjustment** task involves exploring new roles and responsibilities in social contexts, while a **reinvestment** of emotional energy may be made toward other persons or activities. Together, these theoretical tasks move a person emotionally from initial grief toward healthy processing and readjustment. While these may be some underlying tasks, individuals move through them at different rates and methods. Moreover, mourning practices vary by culture, and may dictate how long it is appropriate for one to grieve the deceased.

Suicide

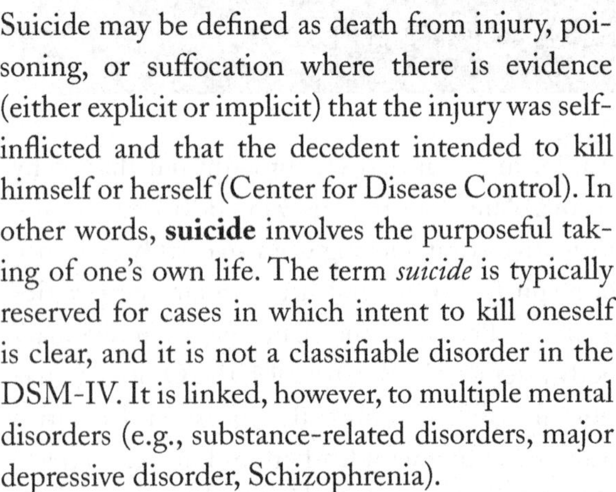

Suicide may be defined as death from injury, poisoning, or suffocation where there is evidence (either explicit or implicit) that the injury was self-inflicted and that the decedent intended to kill himself or herself (Center for Disease Control). In other words, **suicide** involves the purposeful taking of one's own life. The term *suicide* is typically reserved for cases in which intent to kill oneself is clear, and it is not a classifiable disorder in the DSM-IV. It is linked, however, to multiple mental disorders (e.g., substance-related disorders, major depressive disorder, Schizophrenia).

There are some observable descriptive statistics and demographic data related to suicide attempts and completions. Internationally, about 2 million individuals attempt suicide each year, and at least 5-10% of these attempts are successful. Together, yearly there are about 30,000 successful suicides in the U.S., and most prevalent among White and Native American individuals. In addition, suicide is one of the top 10 leading causes of death in the U.S., and rates of suicide increases substantially in early adolescence. In fact, it is the third leading cause of death among individuals ages 15-24. A survey of college students showed 9% said they had thought about committing suicide. There has been a 50% decline in suicide rates among older adults over the past few decades, but older adults, especially older men, are still at relatively higher risk for suicide.

There are also some apparent sex differences in relation to suicidal behaviors; women are more likely than men to attempt suicide, while males are more likely to successfully complete a suicide attempt. This difference may be due to the use of different methods (e.g., guns versus pills). In the U.S., women are three times more likely than men to *attempt* suicide.

There are several competing perspectives on suicide, ranging from biological to cognitive. For instance, biological perspectives on suicide may suggest particularly low serotonin levels (linked to depression). From a sociocultural point of view, some individuals may maintain a general lack of supportive groups (e.g., family, friends). In some group contexts (e.g., family, peer group) **social (suicide) contagion** may be apparent. More specifically, when one member of a group commits suicide, other members are at increased risk for suicide, perhaps because of modeling, increased acceptability, or the impact of the traumatic event on already vulnerable people. Lastly, from a cognitive standpoint, some individuals may be more prone to dichotomous thinking, where they more quickly and harshly negatively evaluate themselves. If they are not "good" at something, then they are "bad." Others may more consistently emphasize negative evaluations of self, and demonstrate an inability to recognize positive aspects of one's self or one's life. These perspectives rarely independently clarify why one may be suicidal—it may often be a complex combination of factors.

Individuals that do attempt suicide appear to have a clear intent to end their own life. However, there may be different underlying motives. Some, referred to as **death seekers**, may have felt alienated and disoriented from others and society, and otherwise are in the throes of deep emotional crises. In some contexts (e.g., the chronically ill, elderly) individuals may seek to end their own life to hasten what is an inevitable death. Individuals attempting or completing suicide for this reason are sometimes referred to as **death initiators.**

There are numerous warning signs for suicide, including changes in mood, affect, behaviors; major life changes (e.g., death, divorce); declarations about death or suicide; or perhaps other risky behaviors (e.g., cutting). Moreover, there are proposed stages to suicide, including:

- suicidal thoughts,
- suicidal plan,
- suicidal experimentation, and
- suicidal attempt.

In the first **suicidal thoughts** stage, an individual may contemplate the world, including family and friends, if they were to die. This stage is considered relatively normal, as most individuals contemplate their own death from time to time. In some cases, however, these thoughts become more intense and frequent, perhaps leading to a **plan**. In this development stage, more concrete plans and methods are considered and isolated. Thereafter, in an **experimentation** stage, individuals may actually begin to employ the plan(s) they have considered. While they may not necessarily go through with what may be considered a suicide attempt, they may engage in riskier behaviors. Lastly, a **suicide attempt** may take place. These attempts may be completed—in which case the person takes their own life—or incomplete—implying the individual did not take their own life. Individuals proceed through these stages with decreasing frequency. That is, while many individuals may have suicidal thoughts, fewer actually make plans; fewer than that experiment, and so on.

Euthanasia

Above, the term *death initiator* referred to someone who desires to hasten an inevitable death. This may be linked with the idea of **euthanasia,** which is when an individual assists another in killing themselves to end pain, many times physical pain. There is **passive euthanasia**, which hastens death by withdrawing life-saving interventions (e.g., feeding tube, oxygen tubes, etc). This type of euthanasia is legal, and individuals may spell out passive euthanasia in advanced directives (i.e., living wills, do-not-resuscitate orders, and do-not-hospitalize orders). On the other hand, **active euthanasia** is illegal across the globe except for Belgium, Luxemburg, and the Netherlands (Belsky, 2010). This process involves taking observable and deliberate action to help facilitate death for someone else, such as administering a lethal amount of a drug. In one disparate form of active euthanasia, at the appeal of a terminally ill patient, a physician may prescribe a drug that will accelerate death if taken in the right dosage. This is known as **physician-assisted suicide**, and it is legal in the state of Oregon as part of the 1997 *Death and Dignity Act*. Although cases related to euthanasia are relatively rare, the idea that some individuals—particularly those in pain due to a terminal illness—may desire to be as comfortable as possible in their remaining time is not. In fact, this was the basis for the "hospice movement."

Palliative Care: Hospice

Hospitals do not necessarily neatly treat the terminally ill or injured. A hallmark study demonstrated how terminally ill or injured patients were treated (Glaser & Straus, 1968). The researchers noted that patients were treated differentially based upon their supposed **dying trajectory**. More specifically, a patient's trajectory was a supposed "swift death," and was not expected to live very long due to medical circumstances (e.g., heart attack). Others were labeled as having a "lingering" death, in which case a slower decline was projected. Lastly, there were those patients categorized as "entry-reentry," describing those who are admitted and discharged regularly. A major finding from the study was that hospital staff may frequently err when it comes to giving a death trajectory to a patient, and when they do, there may be physical or emotional consequences. Consider when a patient was expected to experience death swiftly, and close family are called in to say goodbye. However, this patient stabilizes and actually "lingers" for a time. The emotional consequences for the patient and family in this scenario are evident. Consider also a patient who is supposed to linger for a while; they may be placed in a unit or area where they do not get the same intensity of care they necessarily needed, and their health could actually deteriorate further. Together, death does not necessarily occur in expected ways.

The **hospice movement** gained ground in the 1970s, and is based upon the notion that death is a natural process. While hospital staff is often in a position to prolong life and attempt to treat and "cure" disease, hospices emphasize comfort and care for the dying person. Thus, while many units within hospitals are "curative" in aim and scope, hospices are "palliative." While treatment at a hospital may focus on eliminating or slowing symptoms of disease; treatment at a hospice focuses on comfort, mitigating the physical and/or psychological distress a dying person may be experiencing. Admit-

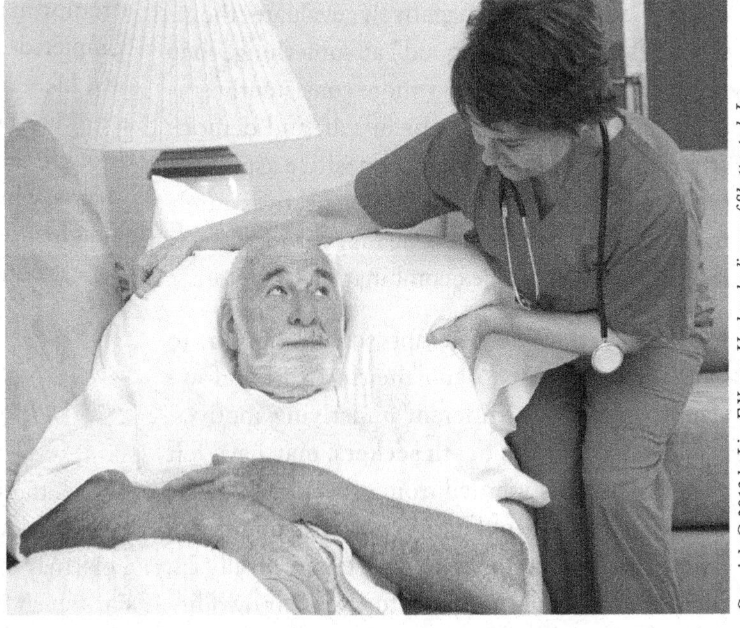

tedly, there are palliative care units in some hospitals, but hospices specialize in this end-of-life care (to see a hospice website and mission statement, see the URL: *www.bigbendhospice.org/).* Of course, hospice care is reserved for those who are terminally ill. A patient's personal physician and the medical director of the hospice verify the nature of the illness. This may represent an important phase of life for a dying patient, as they have perhaps come to terms with the progression of the disease and have turned toward being comfortable, rather than further seeking to extend their life.

Hospice staff not only includes nurses, but also medical directors, social workers, grief support counselors, chaplains, and sometimes even music therapists. In addition to a variety of services offered by these professionals, staff may engage and guide individuals in life reviews. These reviews are systematic and detailed recollections of events and memories used to create a framework of meaning and purpose into one's life, and in an attempt to achieve resolution. Hospices may even help a dying person and their family financially if costs for treatment are not covered. The traditional hospice is a "hospice house," with a select number of rooms for dying patients to receive care round the clock. This would be considered a form of in-patient care. However, hospices also offer out-patient care, whereby patients may choose to be at home (or elsewhere), with hospice staff coming to the person on a daily or semi-daily basis.

Widowhood

According to some researchers, **widowhood,** or the death of a spouse, ranks as high (or higher) than most other life events (Holmes & Rahe, 1967). It may involve a significant shift in identity. Even if the couple did not appear to get along well, being widowed in later life would imply a significant amount of time has been spent together, and the death of one spouse may cause physical, social, and psychological stress for the surviving partner. To illustrate, recall in a preceding paragraph that hospices often have volunteers. One of the important roles volunteers may maintain is to help the surviving spouse handle tasks that were perhaps traditionally handled by the other spouse (e.g., paying bills, managing housework or yard work, shopping, cooking, etc.).

It is more myth than fact that someone can "die of a broken heart." This notion makes for an excellent movie, as in *The Notebook*. From time to time, there may be anecdotal reports of a couple dying in such close proximity, this is what appears to have occurred. However, not since the 15th century has grief been a legitimate (or at least what a coroner can ascertain) a cause of death.

It is not necessarily the stress and grief itself that is problematic for the bereft widow(er). Rather, the important question is "how well can they cope with it?" There are numerous factors, including emotional regulation, prior mental health, social support, personality, and religious faith that facilitate coping. Although many may assume the grieving and mourning processes should be discrete, perhaps lasting for one year, this is not the case. Individuals tend to move at their own pace through some of

the difficult emotions linked with loss. There are several factors that may "complicate" grief, perhaps making it more long-lasting and the overall adjustment more difficult. For the widowed, these factors include, but are not necessarily limited to:

- Was the death sudden and unanticipated?
- Was the death a result of an excessively long illness?
- Does the surviving spouse view the death as having been preventable?
- Was the relationship between the dying person and surviving spouse marked by anger, ambivalence, or extreme dependence?
- Does the bereft widow(er) have previous or current mental health problems, which were intensified by the death?
- Does the bereft widow(er) perceive they have inadequate social support?

Intuitively, when the answers to any or all of the above questions are "yes," there may be heightened likelihood of a form of **complicated or enduring grief**. Such a process may not result in healthy social, emotional, and behavioral adjustment. Rather, it may be marked by extreme and long-lasting sadness, anger, anxiety, or despair. Rando (1995) argued that complicated grief aims to do one of two things; 1) repress or deny the loss, or 2) hold onto, or avoid relinquishing, the loss (DeSpelder & Strickland, 2011).

It is important to note that grief that is complicated is not "pathological" or "abnormal" in nature. Consider an individual who loses a spouse due to an unanticipated death. Due to the nature of the death, the surviving spouse may experience a complicated, yet expected, form of grief.

There is a prevailing notion that females grieve "better." This may be clarified by some of the points above. Women tend to be more embedded in other relationships (e.g., children, friends, siblings) in later life than men do. This trend may become apparent even in middle adulthood, when many women may report higher levels of emotional connection to others (e.g., daughters) than their husbands. Thus, they may have a better overall emotional support network during widowhood. Indeed, when husbands are preceded in death by their wives, they are much more likely to suffer physically, becoming disabled or even dying, when compared to the reverse scenario (i.e., husband preceding wife in death).

An Ecological Perspective on Grief

Given the attention to grief above, it may be apparent the course of one's grief may depend on a lot of different factors. Once again, an ecological perspective may be useful in determining who may experience a complicated grief and who may experience a "good grief." First, consider the individual and their own health. A history of mental instability or disorder may be aggravated by the loss of a spouse. Moreover, their physical health may play a role in terms of how well they grieve. For instance, if the individual was in good physical health, and not reliant upon his or her spouse for day-to-day mobility; this person may have been less dependent on the dying spouse, and subsequently less susceptible to experiencing a complicated grief. At the individual level, one's personality may also play a role. Some are naturally less "neurotic" (i.e., they're emotionally stable) and extraverted (i.e., they're likely to have a better social network). Speaking of social networks, this has direct relevance for a microsystem. As noted above, the presence of a solid social system including friends has important implications for grieving. Having others to turn to and/or empathize with grief may have a beneficial impact. Other microsystems may include extended family. If the surviving spouse has no children or siblings to support him or her, they may be more susceptible to complicated grief than one who has solid emotional ties with other surviving family members. Lastly, churches may be another important microsystem. The presence and influence of church leaders (e.g., reverends, pastors) and fellow congregation members may offer solace and comfort. Recall a mesosystem is when microsystems exert influence upon one another. In this case, a grieving widow may adopt the views and behaviors of her friends in grief, and maintain these among her family. Or, she may adhere strictly to what she believes is a customary grieving practice in her church, and act accordingly among friends and family. Even if church and religious organizations are not an identifiable microsystem for an individual, it still may impact one as an exosystem. For instance, those that do not attend church or claim a particular faith may still rely upon religious views and practices during the grieving process, in order to facilitate processing emotions and negotiating ambivalent views of death. Beyond the exosystem level, the macrosystem involves cultural and historical influences. Some important questions at the macro-level include: Is there ambivalence toward death, or does the culture view it in positive terms? What are mourning traditions, and do the bereft get "released" from a grieving period? Should the bereft demonstrate sadness overtly, or do so privately? The consideration of any or all of these may impact the natural course of grief.

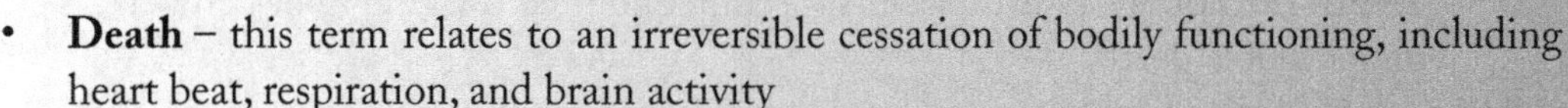

Key Terms

- **Death** – this term relates to an irreversible cessation of bodily functioning, including heart beat, respiration, and brain activity
- **Thanatology** – the scientific study of death; this field captures not only the biological aspects of death, but also the social and cultural traditions surrounding death events
- **Grief** – a reaction to a loss, including death; the grief process may be multi-faceted, including social, emotional, and even physical components
- **Stages of Grief (Kübler-Ross):**
  - **Denial** – a process by which the individual may first not believe, or be incapable of believing, what they are being told regarding a loss; subsequently disowning the information
  - **Anger** – this may be resultant of the frustration with loss, and may be directed at physicians, family members, friends, oneself, or perhaps even a deity
  - **Bargaining** – evident when an individual pleads for more time
  - **Depression** – a negative emotional state which involves feelings of hopelessness and despair
  - **Acceptance** – the bereft individual may acknowledge that a loved one is actually gone
- **Bereavement** – often associated with a state of sadness, and is a specific state of being "deprived" of someone or something
- **Mourning** – involves practices and traditions that individuals engage in surrounding a death event (e.g., funerals, processions, etc.) and may also involve matters of faith and religious practices
- **Stages of Mourning (Rando):**
  - **Recognize the Loss** – involves understanding how or why the individual died, and accepting the finality
  - **Reacting to Separation** – related to the grief experience, and realizing all of the emotional and behavioral symptoms of grief
  - **Recollecting and Re-experiencing** – refers to an inability to remember the deceased in realistic ways. Over time, however, a more realistic memory may set in.
  - **Relinquish** – the abandonment of the roles and life that were evident with the deceased
  - **Readjustment** – exploring new roles and responsibilities in social contexts

- Reinvestment – related to emotional energy that was initially given to grief and mourning, but which may be made toward other persons or activities
- **Funerals** – ceremonies to remember or sanctify the deceased; they may reflect the spiritual or religious affiliation of the deceased and/or the surviving family members
- **Suicide** – this term involves the purposeful taking of one's own life
- **Social (Suicide) Contagion** – when one member of a group commits suicide, other members are at increased risk for suicide, perhaps because of modeling, increased acceptability, or the impact of the traumatic event on already vulnerable people
- **Types of Suicide:**
    - **Death Seekers** – these individuals may have felt alienated and disoriented from others and society, and otherwise are in the throes of deep emotional crises. In some contexts (e.g., the chronically ill, elderly) individuals may seek to end their own life to hasten what is an inevitable death. Individuals attempting or completing suicide for this reason are sometimes referred to as
    - **Death Initiators** – individuals may seek to end their own life to hasten what is an inevitable death.
- **Stages of Suicide:**
    - **Suicidal Thoughts** – an individual may contemplate the world, including family and friends, if they were to die; considered relatively "normal," as most individuals contemplate their own death from time to time
    - **Suicidal Plan** – more concrete plans and methods are considered and isolated
    - **Experimentation** – individuals may actually begin to employ the plan(s) they have considered; they may engage in riskier behaviors
    - **Suicide Attempt** – attempts at taking one's own life may be completed or incomplete; the latter implying the individual did not take their own life
- **Euthanasia** – apparent when an individual assists another in killing themselves to end pain, many times physical pain
    - **Passive Euthanasia** – hastens death by withdrawing life-saving interventions (e.g., feeding tube, oxygen tubes, etc.). This type of euthanasia is legal, and individuals may spell out passive euthanasia in advanced directives (i.e., living wills, do-not-resuscitate orders, and do-not-hospitalize orders).
    - **Active Euthanasia** – involves taking observable and deliberate action to help facilitate death for someone else (e.g., administering lethal amount of a drug); illegal except for in Belgium, Luxemburg, and the Netherlands
    - **Physician-Assisted Suicide** – this term refers to an appeal of a terminally ill patient, for a physician to prescribe a drug that will accelerate death if taken in the right dosage; legal in the state of Oregon as part of the 1997 *Death and Dignity Act*
- **Dying Trajectory** – the rate at which an individual (e.g., a terminally ill patient) is expected to die. Terms such as "swift" and "lingering" have been applied to describe deaths that may occur quickly, or more slowly, respectively.
- **Hospice Movement** – this term refers to a surge in popularity of hospices in the 1970s, and is based upon the notion that death is a natural process; hospices emphasize comfort and care for the dying person
- **Widowhood** – this term refers to the death of a spouse
- **Complicated (or Enduring) Grief** – grief marked by extreme and long-lasting sadness, anger, anxiety, or despair

Critical Thinking Questions

1. What is a textbook definition of death? What are some differences in how death has traditionally been viewed? After having considered and discussed these disparate views, discuss how you personally view death. For instance, do you view death as a generally negative, anxiety-riddled event, or a cause for celebration or "homecoming" for the deceased? Or neither? Defend your responses with examples.
2. What are the stages of grief as offered by Kübler-Ross' theory? Be sure to describe them thoroughly, but also answer the question: Do you think these stages neatly capture the range of possible emotions and processes that a grieving individual will experience? Also, do the grieving necessarily need to pass sequentially through these stages, or can they move in and out, bypassing one stage completely? Why or why not?
3. What is euthanasia? What are the various forms of euthanasia? In your opinion, what form(s) of euthanasia should be legal, if any? Why or why not?

References

DeSpelder, L. A. & Strickland, A. L. (2011). *The last dance: Encountering death and dying.* New York: McGraw-Hill.

Glaser & Straus (1968). *Time for dying.* Chicago: Aldine.

Holmes, T. H. & Rahe, R. H. (1967). The Social Readjustment Rating Scale. *Journal of Psychosomatic Research, 11,* 213-218.

Kastenbaum, R. (2004). *On our way: The final passage through life and death.* Berkeley, CA: University of California Press.

Kübler-Ross, E. (1969). *On death and dying.* New York: MacMillan.

Moore, S. C., Patel, A. V., Matthews, C. E., de Gonzalez, A. B., Park, Y., Katki, H. A., Linet, M. S., Weiderpass, E., Visvanathan, K., Helzlsouer, K. J., Thun, M., Gapstur, S. M., Hartge, P., & Lee, I. (2012). Leisure time physical activity of moderate to vigorous intensity and mortality: A large pooled cohort analysis. *PLoS Medicine, 9,* 1-14.

O'Rourke, M. (2010, February 1). Good grief. *New Yorker,* 66-72.

Rando, T. A. (1995). Grief and mourning: Accommodating after the loss. In H. Wass & R. A. Neimeyer (Eds.) *Dying: Facing the facts* (pp. 211-241). Washington, DC: Taylor and Francis.

- **Abstract Thought** – the process of being able to think abstractly implies that an individual is free from considering only concrete and tangible objects; rather, they are able to handle more difficult or theoretical themes, 135
- **Acceptance** – the bereft individual may acknowledge that a loved one is actually gone, 206
- **Accommodation** – existing schema are modified to match up better with new events or experiences, 56
- **Active Video Games** – require the player to physically move to interact with video images. Game play and progression is predicated upon movement detected through a camera, infrared sensors, pressure-sensitive mats, lasers, or ergometers. 87
- **Adolescence** – a life stage beginning with puberty and ending with the ages corresponding with high school graduation, 123
- **Adolescent Egocentrism** – may be viewed as a byproduct of cognitive maturation, this egocentrism is thought to occur naturally. Adolescents tend to form clearer pictures of themselves (e.g., identity, self-esteem) by comparing themselves to and referencing others. Over time, adolescents begin to see the flaws and inferior qualities in others. Subsequently, this process may create anxiety about their own flaws, along with a sense—albeit irrational—that people are watching them with high degrees of intensity and duration. 138
- **Adoption Studies** – compares children with their biological and adoptive parents, 28
- **Age Grading** – placement of individuals of the same age into groups; school systems are influential in organizing groups of students based on age, 146
- **Agreeableness** – generally evident in how good-natured an individual is. Some individuals are quite agreeable, while others are definitely not, being ill-tempered and contentious. 183
- **All-or-None Principle** – electrical impulses travel through a neuron completely, or not at all. There is no partial activation of neurons. 22
- **Altruism** – the most genuine form of prosocial behavior; complete selfless behavior aimed at helping someone in need, 104
- **Alzheimer's Disease** – the most common form of dementia in the United States

which is marked by the proliferation of abnormalities in the cerebral cortex. These abnormalities inhibit the neural connection and communication. 195

- **Amniocentesis** – an analysis of the amniotic fluid. The amniotic fluid contains stem cells that may reveal the presence or absence of disorders. 41
- **Amniotic Fluid** – rich in stem cells, this fluid surrounds the developing organism(s) in the womb, 37
- **Amotivation** – a relative absence of motivation, 171
- **Androgens** – during (and leading up to) puberty for males, the testes accelerate production of this sex hormone, which are responsible for primary and sexual changes, but also sex drive , 151
- **Andropause** – a possible male equivalent to menopause; signified by lower testosterone, and subsequently, lower sexual drive and muscle mass, 182
- **Anger** – this may be resultant of the frustration with loss, and may be directed at physicians, family members, friends, oneself, or perhaps even a deity, 206
- **Animism & Anthropomorphism** – giving life and human characteristics to inanimate objects, 93
- **Anorexia Nervosa** – a disorder marked by voluntary starvation. Diagnostically, this disorder involves a refusal to maintain body weight at or above a minimally normal weight for age and height (weight loss leading to maintenance of less than 85% of that expected); intense fear of gaining weight or becoming fat, despite explicit contradictory evidence; a disturbance in the way in which the body is perceived or experienced; and amenorrhea. 129
- **A-not-B error** – this error may be demonstrated simply by taking an object and hiding it, first in location A (e.g., behind a pillow) and second in location B (e.g., under a blanket). If the object is initially hidden in location A, the infants may correctly find it there. However, when hidden at location B, even when the infant is able to see it being hidden, they continue to search at location A first. 57
- **APGAR Test** – given initially at 1 and 5 minutes after birth, the APGAR assesses relative levels of activity, pulse, grimace, appearance, and respiration in a newborn, 42
- **Artificialism** – the idea humans make everything, including natural phenomenon, 93
- **Assimilation** – existing schema work well to explain the world, including events, objects and experiences, 56
- **Attachment** – an emotional connection that is created between the infant and an immediate and nurturing adult, 66, 109
- **Attachment-in-the-Making Phase** – infants begin to show preference for particular caretaker(s). Not surprisingly, when preferences begin to emerge, so do protests when the infant is separated from their primary attachment figures. 67
- **Authoritarian** – discernible in high levels of demandingness in the form of structure, rules, and rule enforcement; as well as relatively low levels of responsiveness in these parents, 110
- **Authoritative** – more democratic in nature; an authoritative parenting style that combines high levels of demandingness and similarly high levels of responsiveness, 110
- **Autonomy versus Shame and Doubt** – during this time, Erikson thought it was particularly important for the infant to begin developing autonomy, or a sense of self-sufficiency. The most basic struggle is between a sense of self-reliance and sense of self-doubt. 29, 73
- **Axon** – this feature delivers messages away from the cell body. There is one axon responsible for dissemination of information through the neuron. 21
- **Babbling** – this type of infantile communication is distinct from cooing in that recognizable syllables are being uttered, but not in a sequence necessary for word formation, 53
- **Baby Boomer Generation** – those born post World War II; this generation has now entered later life, 189

- **Bargaining** – evident when an individual pleads for more time, 206
- **Basking** – apparent when a parent is deriving enhanced psychological enjoyment and fulfillment due to accomplishments and achievements of their children, 112
- **Bereavement** – often associated with a state of sadness, and is a specific state of being "deprived" of someone or something, 205
- **Biological Development** – related to one's physical self, health, and adaptive capabilities, and may be impacted by genetic and environmental influences, 8
- **Biological Theory** – underscores the role that physical systems have upon human development, including behavioral, emotional, and cognitive adaptations, 20
- **Birth Stage** – baby descends from the uterus—through the opening the cervix has vacated—and into the birth canal, 41
- **Blood Test** – a relatively common prenatal test; may demonstrate the relative presence or absence of various chemicals necessary for fetal growth. Moreover, blood tests are able to reveal whether some chromosomal abnormalities are present (e.g. Down syndrome). 40
- **Body Mass Index (BMI)** – a specific ratio of one's weight to height, 81
- **Brain Localization** – the notion specific regions of the brain are adapted for specific functions, 24
- **Bulimia Nervosa** – an eating disorder characterized by eating large amounts of food (i.e., bingeing) and consequently compensating for it in some way. The four main criteria for bulimia nervosa include recurrent episodes of binge eating, recurrent compensatory behavior aimed at losing weight, behaviors last twice a week for three months, and self-esteem is too closely linked to body image. 130
- **Bullying** – an aggressive act that is repeated, and involves a "disparity of power between victim and perpetrator", 106
- **Caloric Expenditure** – related to the calories that are used or burned, either through resting metabolic rates or physical activity, 84
- **Caloric Intake** – linked with food taken in and converted to calories for energy use, 84
- **Cardiovascular System** – the heart will pump more slowly in later life than it did in earlier life stages; vascular system is less flexible; and together this may cause an increase in blood pressure, perhaps leading to hypertension. In addition, aging lungs take in less oxygen with each inhalation, meaning less oxygenated blood is traveling throughout the bloodstream. 190
- **Causal Information** – lets one know—with reasonable accuracy—that one antecedent (phenomena A) tends to have a certain consequence (phenomena B), 8
- **Cell Body** – the main processing area for the neuron, 21
- **Centenarians** – those that live to be 100 years old or more, 183, 189
- **Centered** – children may get "stuck" on striking features (e.g., tallness) of immediate objects, 93
- **Cephalacaudal Principle** – the idea children tend to grow from the top down, 79
- **Cerebral Cortex** – this area of the brain consists of the entire upper portion of the brain, is responsible for most thinking, feeling, or activity. The "folded" appearance of the cortex is due to it being compressed, or "wrinkled" to fit into a relatively small space. 24, 50
- **Cerebrum** – a cortical brain region related to sensory and motor movement, 125
- **Cesarean Section (or c-section)** – a procedure in which the doctor enters the womb by making incisions in the abdominal wall to remove the newborn, 42
- **Childhood** – the life stage that begins when infancy ends and concludes with the onset of puberty, 77
- **Child maltreatment** – evident when a child's physical or emotional integrity is threatened, 111

- **Child Psychology** – the scientific study of behavior and mental processes of children, 1
- **Chorionic Villus Sampling (CVS)** – performed by inserting a catheter into the mother (abdominally or vaginally) and extracting a piece of the placenta. The piece of placenta then may be further examined to verify numerous chromosomal or genetic disorders. 41
- **Chromosomes** – threadlike strands of DNA located in the nuclei of cells that carry genetic material, 36
- **Chronological Development (or Chronological Age)** – the number of years and months since birth. Chronological age is just one—and rather crude—way of assessing development., 8, 139
- **Circular Reactions** – behaviors engaged in consistently to produce a particular result. These circular reactions facilitate schema formation. 55
- **Classical Conditioning** – behavior may be broken down into simple stimulus-response relations, consisting of (un)conditioned stimuli and (un)conditioned responses, 16
- **Clear-Cut Attachment** – an observable preference for one or more attachment figures, 67
- **Clique** – more intimate groups of between 2-12 people whose members have frequent social interactions, 146
- **Cognition** – this term broadly refers to mental activity (e.g., attention, concentration, decision-making, and memory), 54
- **Cohabitation Effect** – the potential consequences (e.g., divorce, separation) associated with cohabitating before engagement, 166
- **Cohabitation** – evident when unmarried couples are living together, 166
- **Cohort** – the group of individuals with whom you were born into the world concurrently, and pass through time with, 2
- **Commitment** – a sense of long-term devotion to another individual, 162
- **Companionate Love** – exists when intimacy and commitment are apparent. As the name implies, these partners are excellent "companions" or friends. 162
- **Complicated (or Enduring) Grief** – grief marked by extreme and long-lasting sadness, anger, anxiety, or despair, 212
- **Concrete Operational Stage** – characterized by the ability to "mentally act" upon the concrete and tangible object and situations, 94
- **Concrete Operations** – the ability to reason and think in a more adult-like fashion, but only in relation to real, concrete objects, 136
- **Conditioned Response (CR)** – the learned reaction to the CS, 17
- **Conditioned Stimulus (CS)** – the CS becomes paired with the UCS and the learner—in a passive sense—associates the old (UCS) and new stimuli (CS), 17
- **Conformity** – related to peer pressure, a general change in behavior or attitude brought about by a desire to follow the beliefs or standards of others, 146
- **Conscientiousness** – related to being orderly and respectful; as opposed to a general lack of this quality, demonstrated by impulsivity and disorganization, 183
- **Consummate Love** – thought to capture all elements of a classic love, 163
- **Context** – the circumstances surrounding a particular experience or event, 1
- **Contractions** – muscular fluctuations at the base of the uterus, that occur with increasing frequency as the birth event approaches, 41
- **Control (Placebo) Group** – this "otherwise" group lets the researcher(s) know what would have happened had there been no intervention, 10
- **Cooing** – after crying, cooing is the first observable stage of communication (language); infant cooing broadly captures the noises they may make, 53
- **Co-parenting** – the ways in which parents coordinate their parenting efforts, 170
- **Corporal punishment** – methods of bodily or physical punishment, 110

- **Correlational Design (Associational Design)** – this design is aimed at capturing the direction and strength of the relation between two variables. Although quite useful, this design also does not imply causation. 10
- **Creeping Obesity** – weight gain that occurs (and ultimately results in obesity) slowly over time, perhaps undetectable over the course of many years, 85
- **Critical Period** – a chronological window of time that is ideal for acquiring a new behavior or establishing a connection, 65
- **Crowd** – a group of individuals who share particular characteristic(s) but who may not interact with one another. Crowds are relatively large, and may carry some level of consistency in terms of their nomenclature. 146
- **Crowning** – the emergence of the head from the birth canal, 41
- **Crystallized Intelligence** – the knowledge that individuals maintain about the world (i.e., vocabulary, facts, and assertions), 140
- **Cyberbullying** – an indirect form of bullying viewed as aggression through personal computers (e.g., email, instant messaging, social network sites) and cellular phones (e.g., text messaging), 107
- **Cycle of Self-Esteem** – a phenomena observable when children with high self-esteem in a certain area appear more likely to approach novel tasks and situations or new people, as they are more confident in their abilities to successfully navigate the task or situation. On the other hand, children with low self-esteem may be less likely to put forth effort toward tasks where they predict failure. 102
- **Dating** – may be viewed in those that are willingly committed and have "paired off" to form a couple, 150
- **Daycare Center** – a daycare center is an institution whose administration and staff maintain a primary focus upon caring for infants and children, 71
- **Death Initiators** – individuals may seek to end their own life to hasten what is an inevitable death. 209
- **Death Seekers** – these individuals may have felt alienated and disoriented from others and society, and otherwise are in the throes of deep emotional crises. In some contexts (e.g., the chronically ill, elderly) individuals may seek to end their own life to hasten what is an inevitable death. Individuals attempting or completing suicide for this reason are sometimes referred to as, 209
- **Death** – this term relates to an irreversible cessation of bodily functioning, including heart beat, respiration, and brain activity, 203
- **Delirium** – a short-term loss of brain function, 194
- **Demandingness** – a variable related to parenting style; this is related to the relative presence within a household of clear rules, boundaries, and expectations for their children, and—when rules are broken or expectations are not met—the consequences, 109
- **Dementia** – a generic term meaning "out of mind," and involves an irreversible, pathological loss of brain function due to organic damage or disease. The irreversible nature of dementia implies it is enduring. 194
- **Demographic Shift in Aging Populations** – referring to a much larger ratio currently of individuals 60 years or older than in centuries past, 189
- **Dendrites** – these features resemble the branches of a tree, and are largely responsible for receiving information and guiding it toward the cell body. There are numerous dendrites in any one neuron. 21
- **Denial** – a process by which the individual may first not believe, or be incapable of believing, what they are being told regarding a loss; subsequently disowning the information, 206

- **Depressants** – substances that serve to slow the central nervous system (CNS) and dull the senses, 173
- **Depression** – a negative emotional state which involves feelings of hopelessness and despair, 206
- **Developmental Psychology** – the study of the changes and adaptations (over time) to human behavior and thought processes, 7
- **Differential Sibling Exposure Design** – these studies employ a design that compares siblings and captures genetic similarity that exists between siblings, 28
- **Diffusion Tensor Imaging (DTI)** – offers scientists information related to interior changes in white matter in the brain. Water reacts differentially when placed in white matter containing strong, consistent nerve fibers (i.e., more connected) when compared to white matter with weaker and inconsistent nerve fibers (i.e., less connected). 125
- **Dilation** – responsible for the widening and opening of the cervix, 41
- **Disease** – a condition that requires ongoing medical attention and/or interferes with day-to-day tasks for at least one year, 190
- **Dishabituation** – an increase in the strength of a response after a change in stimuli, 56
- **Disordered Eating** – troublesome eating behaviors (e.g., restrictive dieting, bingeing, or purging) which occur less frequently or are less severe than those required to meet the full criteria for the diagnosis of an eating disorder, 129
- **Divorce** – a legal dissolution of marriage, 168
- **Dopamine** – a neurotransmitter also linked with energy and well-being are also released, 173
- **Dying Trajectory** – the rate at which an individual (e.g., a terminally ill patient) is expected to die. Terms such as "swift" and "lingering" have been applied to describe deaths that may occur quickly, or more slowly, respectively. 210
- **Ecological Theory** – a developmental theory that posits development depends upon the interaction of multiple sources (or systems) of influence, 25
- **Egocentrism** – the inability to see another's point of view, 93
- **Embryonic Stage** – the prenatal organism has not yet developed human-like features. However, the brain and spinal cord begin to emerge. 37
- **Emerging Adulthood** – a life stage that begins after graduation from high school and extends through the late twenties and is primarily devoted to constructing an adult life, 159
- **Emotional Regulation** – the ability to manage, modify or regulate ones' emotional state, 103
- **Emotional** – related to how one identifies, regulates, and copes with emotions, 197
- **Empathy** – the ability to feel what another person is feeling, or being able to "put yourself in another person's shoes", 104
- **Empty Nest Transition** – the period when children leave or "launch" from the parental home, 184
- **Endocrine System** – consists of the endocrine glands and functions to regulate body activities, 23, 126
- **Energy Balance Equation** – a ratio comparing caloric intake to caloric expenditure. The presumption is when intake exceeds expenditure, weight gain occurs; when expenditure exceeds intake, weight loss occurs, 84
- **Energy Dense Food** – foods typically high in fat and have a large amount of calories in a relatively "small package", 85
- **Epigenetics** – the study of environmental factors that may produce permanent changes in gene activity, 38
- **Epinephrine (or Adrenaline)** – a hormone and a neurotransmitter that is capable of operating on most tissue in the body and has considerable impact upon physical energy levels, 173

- **Episodic Memory** – comprised of information from the events of daily life, and is ongoing. It is the most fragile of the memory systems. 193
- **Erikson's Theory** – suggests humans develop according to eight psychosocial tasks that must be negotiated across the life span, 185
- **Estrogens** – during (and before) puberty for females androgen secretion follows a less consistent, but cyclical pattern, corresponding to ovulation, 151
- **Ethology** – the study of behavior in animals (including humans) in natural settings, 65
- **Euthanasia** – apparent when an individual assists another in killing themselves to end pain, many times physical pain, 209
- **Event-Related Potential (ERP)** – generally indicates reaction time; a neurological term, 174
- **EvolutionaryTheory** – a biological theory that posits humans develop over the course of their own lifetime, but may also be part of a larger ancestral chain, where adaptations—ultimately aimed at survival—are genetically transmitted, 24
- **Excitatory and Inhibitory Responses** – when a neurotransmitter enters a dendrite, it serves to excite or inhibit that particular neuron. While an excitatory response would facilitate continued passage of a neural signal, an inhibitory response would suggest a certain pathway will not activate. 22
- **Exercise** – rigorous physical activity with the aim of improving one or more elements of personal fitness; maintains numerous benefits for all individuals, including those in later life, 195
- **Experimental Design** – considered the most useful design in capturing causal relations between variables, it incorporates random assignments and maintains the presence of a control group, 10
- **Experimentation** – individuals may actually begin to employ the plan(s) they have considered; they may engage in riskier behaviors. 209
- **Extraversion** – a dimension of personality evident in those that are outgoing, personable, and adjust well in most social contexts. On the other hand, some individuals are more introverted and prefer being alone and are perhaps less amiable. 183
- **Extrinsic Motivation** – motivation that comes from external areas (e.g., social praise and accolades, monetary rewards, or prizes), 171
- **Family Daycare** – an individual who cares for a relatively small group of children in their home, 71
- **Fatuous Love** – evident with passion and commitment, but without intimacy, 162
- **Fertility** – refers to the average number of children a woman will have in her lifetime, 189
- **Fertilization** – when the sperm of a male and egg of a female combine to form one cell, 35
- **Fetal Development (or Stage)** – the second and third trimester are marked by further body development and refinement; human features are apparent, 37
- **Fine (or Precise) Motor** – those movements that require the activation and use of smaller muscular units, 80
- **Five Factor Model of Personality (or Big Five)** – a model of personality which includes five underlying structures that may be apparent in all humans. 182
- **Fluid Intelligence** – related to an individual's ability to reason and solve new problems. However, in one form or another, the WISC and WAIS are thought to assess general intelligence. 140
- **Forebrain** – located at the front of the brain and responsible for most higher-order thinking (cognition) and feeling (emotion), 23
- **Formal Operations** – evident in the ability to think abstractly; individuals in a formal operational stage may mentally engage

with "hypothetical" situations, being scientific in their approach to problems; they can develop a theory and speculate on outcomes, 136

- **Friends with Benefits** – the basis of sexual relationships that lack commitment (or even much intimacy or friendship) between partners, 151
- **Frustration-Aggression Hypothesis** – the idea that most aggressive acts are prompted by feelings of dissatisfaction, annoyance, and frustration, 105
- ***functional* MRI, (*f*MRI)** – brain activity is assessed through blood oxygenation levels. Thus, *f*MRI not only offers insight into the brain structure, but also the relative levels of activity within the brain. 125
- **Funerals** – ceremonies to remember or sanctify the deceased; they may reflect the spiritual or religious affiliation of the deceased and/or the surviving family members, 206
- **Gender** – a psychosocial construct related to "acting or feeling" male or female, 114
- **Gender Double Standard** – a traditional notion that premarital sex by males was permissible, but not for females, 151
- **Gender Identity** – the fundamental sense of being male or female, begins to form early in childhood, 115
- **Gender Schema Theory** – children may recognize early they belong to one of the two sexes. Thereafter, they develop schema, which are organized knowledge structures consisting of the information related to the behavior, attitudes, and social variables linked with gender. 114
- **General Intelligence (*g*)** – a supposed core cognitive intellectual ability that could be applied in most situations (e.g., athletic, academic, and social), 139
- **Generativity versus Stagnation** – Erikson believed that individuals come to utilize their unique qualities to be creative and productive individuals, and hone a portion of identity more closely linked with giving to others. On the other hand, stagnation refers to be unwilling or unable to help others. Erikson thought this could be genuinely frustrating, and marked a pathological state of being marked by conflict. 29, 184
- **Genetic Determinism** – a rather strict and narrow evolutionary perspective that refers to the notion that individuals are completely biologically pre-programmed for a certain developmental sequence irrespective of environmental conditions, 25
- **Gerontology** – the scientific study of behavior and mental processes in aging populations, 1
- **Gestational Phase** – the stage of prenatal development, which in humans is approximately 40 weeks long, 35
- **Gonadarche** – a biological event where the gonads begin producing more hormones, including testosterone (i.e., an androgen) and estradiol (i.e., an estrogen), 126
- **Grasping Reflex** – infants tend to wrap their fingers around objects placed in their palm, 52
- **Gray Matter** – brain matter associated with information processing areas, and consists mostly of cell bodies and some extracellular space, 124
- **Grief** – a reaction to a loss, including death; the grief process may be multi-faceted, including social, emotional, and even physical components, 205
- **Gross (or Mass) Motor** – movements that require the activation and use of large muscular systems, 80
- **Growth Spurt** – more typical in pre-adolescent (late childhood), this term refers to a lengthening of the limbs and overall body growth, reducing the ratio of head size to body size and giving an individual a more adult-like appearance, 79
- **Guided participation** – perhaps an extension of Vygotsky's zone of proximal development; it is the process and system of involvement of individuals with others, as they communicate and engage in shared activities, 108

- **Habituation** – the gradual decrease in the strength of a response after repeated exposure to a particular stimulus, 56
- **Hallucinogens** – any of a class of substance which cause sensory and perceptual disturbances and alterations; interferes with normal neurotransmitter uptake; ultimately interfering with sensation and perception, 173
- **Hedonic Treadmill** – the process of adapting to new and/or stimulating objects or situations; generally returning to a baseline level of life satisfaction, 172
- **Heterogeneous** – groups with differences in terms of sex, race, ethnicity, and socioeconomic status (SES), etc., 146
- **Hindbrain** – located toward the rear and typically responsible for automatic processes including breathing, blood circulation, and digestion, 23
- **Holographic Speech** – syllables are deliberately and consistently used to form words and communicate specific desires, 53
- **Homogeneous** – groups with similarity in terms of sex, race, ethnicity, and socioeconomic status (SES), etc., 146
- **Hormones** – these are selective chemicals dispersed into the bloodstream, eventually arriving at bodily organs for health, maintenance, and growth, 126
- **Hospice Movement** – this term refers to a surge in popularity of hospices in the 1970s, and is based upon the notion that death is a natural process; hospices emphasize comfort and care for the dying person, 210
- **Hypothalamus** – maintains control over the pituitary gland, and subsequently the endocrine system, 23, 126
- **Identity achievement** – this is evident in the presence of exploration and commitment, 114
- **Identity** – a term akin to a self-concept; it involves a "self-portrait", 112
- **Identity Constancy** – scary mask turns a person into a monster, 93
- **Identity diffusion** – according to Marcia's identity status model, this status is marked by uncertainty, with neither reflection nor commitment to form of identity, 114
- **Identity foreclosure** – in this stage, an individual begins to commit to aspects of their identity, without having explored it deeply (if at all), 114
- **Identity moratorium** – this stage is marked by exploration, but a lack of commitment, 114
- **Immune System** – bodily system that combats disease, this system becomes less effective in later life. Some of the cells that identify and destroy foreign substances (i.e., T-cells and B-cells) become less effective, allowing more pathogens to infect the individual. 191
- **Implantation** – the process of the zygote descending into the uterus and attaching to the uterine wall, 36
- **Imprinting** – the idea that newborns tend to follow and prefer a certain stimulus, 65
- **Industry versus Inferiority** – the child needs to expand his or her understanding of the world, and learn basic skills required for school success. The basic task of industry relates to setting and attaining personal goals, and failure to do so results in a sense of inadequacy. 101
- **Infantile Amnesia** – refers to a general inability to remember specific events prior to about three years of age, perhaps due to neurological immaturity or a lack of linguistic sophistication, 58
- **Infant Mortality** – infant death that occurs within the first year of life, 44
- **Initiative versus Guilt** – the basic task is to achieve competence and initiative. If children are given freedom to select personally meaningful activities, they tend to develop a positive view of self and follow through with projects. If they are not allowed to make their own selection, they tend to develop guilt over not taking initiative. 29, 101

- **Insecure Avoidant Attachment** – infant shows little or no interest in exploring the new environment or interacting with the stranger in any way. In addition, they appear to avoid contact with the caretaker when they return. Together, they appear to "avoid" contact and exploration, and lack the emotional and behavioral reaction to separation and reunion that are present in other attachment styles. 69
- **Insecure Resistant Attachment** – infants show a general reluctance to explore the new environment, even when in the presence of only their caretaker. When the stranger does enter the room, the infant is wary and avoids interaction, and is extremely upset (greater in intensity and duration) when they notice the caretaker has left. Often, they continued to be upset even upon reunion with the caretaker and surprisingly do not seek contact with them. 69
- **Instrumental Aggression** – harmful actions (physical or non-physical) that occur as a result of a pursuit of a goal, 105
- **Intelligence Quotient (IQ)** – a ratio of one's mental age to their chronological age, 139
- **Intimacy** – an affective sense of closeness and interconnectedness with another person; intimacy does *not* necessarily involve romantic or sexual intent or behavior, 149, 162
- **Intrinsic Motivation** – motivation that comes from internal sources (e.g., the satisfaction that may be derived from the activity itself or mastering a new skill), 171
- **Late-Life Life Expectancy** – this term refers to the number of years someone can expect to live past, 65, 190
- **Later Life** – a term applied to any individual older than 60 years and on through end-of-life, 189
- **Law of Effect** – the notion that when an individual engages in a certain behavior and it yields a positive or rewarding outcome, he or she is more likely to engage in that behavior again, 18
- **Law of Forward Conduction** – the standard sequence by which information is received by the dendrites, passed along to the cell body (including the nucleus), and then sent along through the axon. Neurological signals do not travel in the opposite direction. 21
- **Learning** – a relatively permanent change(s) in behavior that occurs due to experience. This term is akin to conditioning. 16
- **Life Expectancy** – an average based upon the number of years a newborn can expect to live in a given country if conditions in that particular region remain unchanged, 45
- **Life Expectancy** – an average (or mean) based upon whether conditions in a particular region remain unchanged, 2
- **Life Expectancy** – the average number of years one can expect to live, given various conditions (i.e., physical, social, economic) remain the same, 190
- **Lifespan Developmental Psychology** – the term refers to the scientific study of human growth and adaptation across the life span. This field was sprung from two "bookends" in child psychology and gerontology. 1
- **Lock-and-Key Principle** – the idea that distinct neurotransmitters are only able to fit into certain receptor sites on dendrites, 22
- **Logical Thought** – perhaps akin to operational thought, the ability to think rationally and readily solve problems, 93
- **Longitudinal Design** – allows researchers to observe and collect data over time (i.e., weeks, month, years, decades, etc.) to verify physical, social, and/or psychological changes, 11
- **Long-Term Memory** – these types of memory may be stored for many years or decades, consistently available for retrieval, 58
- **Low Birth Weight** – this may occur due to slow prenatal growth with an on-time birth, or premature delivery. A standard cut-off to

determine which infants are of low-birth and which are normal weight is 5.5 pounds. 43

- **Magnetic Resonance Imaging (MRI)** – MRI employs magnetic forces, radio waves, and intricate software to recognize signals from brain tissue, providing very accurate pictures of the human brain, 124
- **Major Depressants** – alcohol, opioids (including morphine and heroine), and sedatives, 173
- **Marijuana (or Cannabis)** – given its own class as it does not necessarily fit neatly into any of the other classes, and may have hallucinogenic, stimulant, or depressant effects. Marijuana, like other substances, may disrupt normal neurotransmitter functioning. 173
- **Memory** – the storage of images and ideas for later retrieval, 58
- **Menarche** – female version of gonadarche, marked by the onset of the menstrual cycle, 127
- **Menopause** – occurring in females typically in midlife, it is the slowing and cessation of ovulation, 182
- **Mental** – associated with thinking and cognitive capabilities, 197
- **Midbrain** –located above the hindbrain, responsible for processing some auditory and visual information, 23
- **Middle Adulthood** – a term synonymous with midlife, 180
- **Midlife** – a term applied to those individuals from the ages of 40 to 59 years, 180
- **Midlife Crisis** – an alleged period of time (during midlife) where there may exist greater likelihood for an individual to find themselves in the throes of emotional difficulties, identity crises, social transition, and the like, 185
- **Mild Cognitive Impairment** – a lack of memory and loss of spoken fluency, and is more pronounced than that which would be expected due to normal neurological aging, 194
- **Minor Depressants** – muscle relaxers, antihistamines, and other over-the-counter (OTC) depressants, 173
- **Moral Reasoning** – the thinking and logic one applies to moral dilemmas and problems involving notions of right and wrong, 137
- **Motor Skill (or Coordination) Disorder** – among other criteria, the primary feature for diagnose of this disorder is an apparent and significant delay in motor skill attainment, often observable in a failure to meet motor milestones, 81
- **Mourning** – involves practices and traditions that individuals engage in surrounding a death event (e.g., funerals, processions, etc.) and may also involve matters of faith and religious practices, 206
- **Multiple Intelligences** – a theoretical framework offered by Gardner; the basic idea that intelligence may be demonstrated in numerous areas; many of which would not necessarily be captured by traditional theories or scales of intelligence, 140
- **Myelination** – a process that strengthens the protective covering (i.e., myelin sheath) surrounding the axon of the neuron. Along with synaptogenesis, myelination facilitates neurological maturation. 50
- **Natural Childbirth** – birth may occur in the home or a birthing center, and may generally lack many of the traditional factors of a hospital birth, including the staff, room, and even anesthetics, 41
- **Nature and Nurture** – these two terms relate to biological and genetic (nature) or social and environmental (nurture) factors and their relative influence of any aspect of human behavior or development, 16
- **Neural Stem Cells** – stem cells capable of generating neural tissues, 37
- **Neural Stem Cells** – the stem cells that were reserved for the formation of the nervous systems (e.g. central and nervous systems), 20
- **Neural Tube** – the preliminary formation of the brain and spinal cord, 37

- **Neurological Pathways** – meaningful connections between neurons that permit the transmission of neural messages from the nervous systems to the brain and vice versa, 21
- **Neuron** – the most basic cellular unit in the nervous system, 20
- **Neuroticism** – relates to emotional stability, 183
- **Neurotransmitters** – these chemicals are stored in small sacs at the end of the axon, and within the synapse. The nerve impulses trigger the release of the chemicals into the synapse, where they are potentially absorbed by the dendrites of adjacent neurons. 22
- **Non-Shared Environmental Influences** – factors that are exclusive to respective environments, 28
- **Norepinephrine** – a chemical that may also function as a hormone and a neurotransmitter; impacts feelings of self-confidence, motivation, and well-being, 173
- **Normal weight** – indicated by BMI scores from the 5th to the 85th percentiles, 82
- **Nucleus** – located in the cell body, all information must pass through the nucleus, 21
- **Obesity** – a term reserved for those who rank above the 95th percentile of BMI scores for any gender and age; indicating a relatively large amount of weight for their height in comparison to others in their age group, 82
- **Object Permanence** – a basic understanding that objects continue to exist even when unseen, unheard, or unfelt, 56
- **Oldest-Old** – those over 85 years of age, who are generally dependent on others (e.g., family members, caretakers) for many day-to-day tasks; the last life stage applied to human development, 190
- **Old-Old** – those over 75 years of age and also more likely to be characterized by disease or disability due to further aging and heightened financial instability, 190
- **Openness to Experience** – related to a tendency to be inquisitive, spontaneous, and/or artistic. A person low on this dimension would exhibit rigid attitudes and be more close-minded. 183
- **Operant Conditioning** – this theory, developed by B. F. Skinner, elaborated upon the law of effect; that the consequences of a behavior alter the probability (enhance or lessen) of the behavior's reoccurrence, 18
- **Operation** – a Piagetian term, this is an internalized mental action that is part of an organized structure, and becomes apparent during the concrete operational stage. Basically, whatever a child could not do before, they can during the concrete operational stage. 92
- **Operation** – central to Piaget's theory, this term refers to an internalized mental action that is part of an organized structure, 136
- **Organized Activities** – a relatively common social context for adolescents, these may scholastic (affiliated with a school) or non-scholastic (church-, community-based); the hallmarks of organized activities are structure, adult-supervision, and an emphasis upon skill building, 147
- **Osteoporosis** – bones become less dense, losing calcium and rigidity, 191
- **Overweight** – indicated by BMI scores that lie between the 85th and 95th percentile, 82
- **Oxytocin** – a neuromodulator, which enhances or diminishes the overall effectiveness of existing neurological connections, 163
- **Passion** – physiological and/or neurological arousal and attraction. This does not necessarily have to imply sexual arousal and attraction, although it often does. 162
- **Peer Groups** – clusters of individuals composed of people of approximately the same age and status, 146
- **Peer** – someone who is about the same age and level of maturity, 108
- **Percentile Score (or Rank)** – indicates the percentage of scores that fall at or below an infant's personal measurement(s). In infancy, these are often given in terms of length, weight, and head circumference. 51

- **Performance Scale** – consists of items that require problem-solving skills for novel tasks, 140
- **Permissive** – does not clearly create and enforce rules, but does display relatively high levels of emotional warmth; sometimes referred to as "indulgent" parenting, 110
- **Permissiveness with Affection** – implies premarital sex is acceptable given an intimate, stable relationship between partners, 151
- **Personality** – a set of enduring personal characteristics and unique ways of responding to events in the world. Personality may be viewed in basic and special abilities, interests, social relationships, and many other psychosocial characteristics. 182
- **Physical** – dimension of wellness linked with circulatory and cardiovascular areas; often referred to as "health" or "fitness", 102 , 197
- **Pituitary Gland** – capable of releasing hormones into the bloodstream, eventually arriving at bodily organs for health and maintenance. In this way, the hypothalamus controls internal bodily processes (e.g., hunger, fatigue, sexual drive, body temperature, etc.). 23, 126
- **Placental Expulsion** – removal of the placenta and other materials that were necessary for prenatal development, but unnecessary post-birth, 41
- **Placenta** – the "lifeline" between the fetus and the mother; this feature must form shortly after implantation for essential nutrients to reach the developing embryo and subsequent fetus, 36
- **Plaques** – bundles of one type of protein, 195
- **Plasticity Principle** – the idea the human brain is constantly reorganizing itself in response to outward experiences. Neurological connections unused may fade away and disconnect, while new experiences may generate and lubricate new pathways. 24
- **Popularity** – related to peer-likeability and salience. That is, in determining popularity, two important questions must be answered: Are peers aware of a student *and* are they liked? 106
- **Practitioner** – professionals who aim to intervene and modify human developmental trajectories, 7
- **Pre-Attachment Phase** – from birth to about 3 months, infants are relatively indiscriminant when it comes to adults. At this time, they are not necessarily showing preference. 67
- **Precocious Puberty** – evident when an individual experiences primary sexual change (e.g., menarche) before the age of 9, or the emergence of secondary sexual characteristics before the age of 8, 128
- **Prenatal Diagnostic Tests** – any of a variety of tests that offer insight into the embryonic and fetal health and progression, 40
- **Preoperational Stage** – following sensorimotor, this stage may be evident from approximately ages 2 through 7, and one that exists *before* proper operational thought exists, 92
- **Primary Aging** – the universal and irreversible physical changes that occur as we age, 190
- **Primary Sexual Characteristics** – physical changes directly involved in reproduction, such as menarche and spermarche, 127
- **Procedural Memory** – related to information that is automatically recalled without conscious effort. Many motor skills (e.g., walking, throwing) are ingrained in procedural memory systems. It is the least fragile of the memory systems. 192
- **Pro-social behavior** – caring about others and acting upon that by helping where necessary. The most genuine form of pro-social behavior is altruism. 104
- **Protective Factors** – variables that protect against the undesirable outcomes or increase the likelihood of a positive outcome, 4

- **Proximodistal Principle** – the idea children tend to grow from the inside out, 79
- **Psychoactive Effects** – capable of altering perceptions, thoughts, emotions, and behaviors, 172
- **Psychological Development** – subsumes numerous mental activities that may change over time (e.g., memory, self-esteem, cognitive processing, etc.), 8
- **Puberty** – marking the beginning of adolescence, puberty is the "awakening of a complex neuro-endocrine machinery in which the primary mechanism is still unclear", 126
- **Quasi-Experimental Design** – Generally the same as an experimental design, but lacking random assignment, which may be impractical in a given setting. Causal information may be inferred from this design. 11
- **Racial Identity** – a sense of group or collective identity based on one's perception that he or she shares a common heritage with a particular racial group; often based upon skin color and may prompt individuals to categorize themselves into groups based upon that feature. 116
- **Racial Socialization** – the process by which individuals develop a racial identity, 116
- **Random Assignment** – a process thought to equalize groups; helps ensure the groups have the same "complexion" in regard to a wide array of pre-existing differences. In doing so, random assignment helps to ensure that the primary way the groups differ is the intervention. 10
- **Reacting to Separation** – related to the grief experience, and realizing all of the emotional and behavioral symptoms of grief, 208
- **Readjustment** – exploring new roles and responsibilities in social contexts, 208
- **Recognize the Loss** – involves understanding how or why the individual died, and accepting the finality, 208
- **Recollecting and Re-experiencing** – refers to an inability to remember the deceased in realistic ways. Over time, however, a more realistic memory may set in. 208
- **Reinvestment** – related to emotional energy that was initially given to grief and mourning, but which may be made toward other persons or activities, 208
- **Relational Aggression** – a non-physical form of aggression comprised of acts designed to hurt a person's social relationships, 105
- **Relinquish** – the abandonment of the roles and life that were evident with the deceased, 208
- **Responsiveness** – an element of parenting style linked with emotional warmth and a high degree of involvement, 109
- **Reversibility** – what was done may be undone, 93
- **Risk Factors** – variables that increase the likelihood of an undesirable developmental outcome, 4
- **Romantic Love** – comprised of the passionate and intimate elements, 162
- **Rooting Reflex** – another instinctual movement in which infants turn toward touches on their cheeks, 52
- **Schema** – these "organized rules" are mental structures that make sense of experience. The "experience" in this case is motor movement. The "structures" are akin to thinking patterns related to the experience. 55
- **Scientist** – professionals who examine what changes occur, why they may happen, and when, 7
- **Secondary Aging** – related to specific illnesses or conditions that may in part be linked with age, but also behaviors, habits, and other influences, 190
- **Secondary Sexual Characteristics** – physical changes not related to reproduction. Secondary characteristics may include breast development in females (i.e., thelarche), pubic hair growth, voice changes, or acne. 127
- **Secure Attachment** – demonstrated by infants who explore strange environments freely while their caretaker is there, and also

noticeably (but controllably) upset when they realized they had been separated. Upon reunion, the securely attached infants greet and seek contact with their caretaker. 68

- **Self-Esteem** – an affective sense of generally feeling good or bad about one's level of competence; it is derived from evaluating oneself in relation to others. 102
- **Semantic Memory** – this type is akin to "declarative" knowledge and involves basic factual assertions about the world. It is moderately fragile. 192
- **Sensorimotor Stage** – this is a Piagetian term referring to the first stage of cognitive development, encompassing infancy. During this time, infants are literally stumbling into experiences; the infant moves around and interacts with people and objects. In doing so, cognitive activity occurs concurrently with the physical activity. 54
- **Separation Anxiety** – an infant who has established an attachment will more regularly fuss and protest when they sense they are being separated, 67
- **Seriation** – related to ordering or grouping objects, 93
- **Serotonin** – a chemical linked with energy and a feeling of well-being, 173
- **Sex** – the biological assignment of being male or female, 114
- **Sexual identity** – this term encompasses all the attitudes, knowledge, and behaviors related to one's sexual self, 112
- **Shared Environmental Influences** – those factors shared by respective environments, 28
- **Single-Subject Design (Case Study)** – a close examination of select individual(s); case studies tend to be very thick in descriptions and qualitative data. This design provides little or no causal information. 9
- **Social Clock** – an understanding of societal appropriate age ranges at which some of the milestones are met (e.g., degree attainment, marriage, children, etc.), 161
- **Social Development** – the ways in which one interacts with others, 8
- **Socialization** – a subtle sociocultural process whereby children may be made aware of useful ways to think and act in society, but also gives them an opportunity to "act like adults" during imaginative play sessions, 108
- **Social Learning Theory** – this theory gives humans a bit more credit as being thinking, dynamic organisms than the classical and operant models permit. A central tenet of this theory is "modeling," that suggests an important part of human learning occurs through observing others. 19
- **Social** – refers to interactions with people, 197
- **Social (Suicide) Contagion** – when one member of a group commits suicide, other members are at increased risk for suicide, perhaps because of modeling, increased acceptability, or the impact of the traumatic event on already vulnerable people, 209
- **Socioemotional Selectivity Theory** – a theory that younger individuals (i.e., adolescents, young adults) may often look to the future in terms of personal, familial, and professional goals; whereas older individuals may shift to a more present life perspective, which may prompt them to make the most of every moment and do what makes them feel good now. 184
- **Sociometric Procedures** – a procedure to assess popularity is relatively straightforward. In a classroom, all students could be issued a peer nomination form which they name the one (or more) peers they like the most, and also the peer(s) they dislike the most. 106
- **Spermarche** – male version of gonadarche, marked by production of active sperm, 127
- **Spill-over Hypothesis** – the hypothesis that negativity in a parenting domain may be linked with negative impact in the marital domain, and vice versa, 170
- **Spirituality** – also a part of wellness, spirituality may be viewed in those that maintain or seek a relationship with a specific God, but it may also be evident in other areas as well, 197

- **Stem Cells** – undifferentiated cells capable of increasing in number and forming various structures, 37
- **Stimulants** – substances that activate the CNS and the locus coeruleus by keeping certain energy chemicals (i.e., epinephrine, norepinephrine) in circulation, 173
- **Strange Situation Paradigm** – a research method that manipulates and captures the reactions and behaviors that occur when an infant is separated from (and reunited with) their attachment figure; used to assess attachment style, 68
- **Stunting** – the cessation of physical growth, often due to having either too little caloric intake in infancy and childhood or too little nutritional variety during that time, 79
- **Substance** – any natural or synthetic (man-made) product that has psychoactive effects; a more general term than "drug," and is intended to include products that aren't always considered drugs (e.g., alcohol, nicotine, caffeine), 172
- **Successful Intelligence** – the ability to achieve success in life in terms of one's personal standards within one's own sociocultural context, 140
- **Sucking Reflex** – an automatic and instinctual movement in which infants suck rather frequently and indiscriminately on objects that touch their lips, 52
- **Suicidal Plan** – more concrete plans and methods are considered and isolated, 209
- **Suicidal Thoughts** – an individual may contemplate the world, including family and friends, if they were to die; considered relatively "normal," as most individuals contemplate their own death from time to time, 209
- **Suicide Attempt** – attempts at taking one's own life may be completed or incomplete; the latter implying the individual did not take their own life, 209
- **Suicide** – this term involves the purposeful taking of one's own life, 208
- **Symbolic play** – involves pretending and requires imagination. Importantly, a child may engage in symbolic play by themselves or with others (e.g., peers, siblings, parents). 107
- **Symbols** – becoming more evident in the preoperational state, language, make believe play, and drawing are all examples of symbols and symbol use, 93
- **Sympathy** – to feel sorry for another who is experiencing difficulty at home or school, 104
- **Synapses** – the microscopic spaces between neurons that serve to connect neurons to one another, 22
- **Synaptogenesis** – the capacity to generate entirely new neurons in certain regions, 24, 50
- **Tangles** – twisted accumulations of protein, 195
- **Taste Aversions** – may occur when an individual associates the taste of a certain food with some symptoms of sickness; people may become disgusted by said foods, 17
- **Telegraphic Speech** – this particular stage is marked by words being connected to one another to form more complete ideas or desires, 54
- **Telomeres** – sequences at the tail ends of the chromosome that protect it from deterioration and fusion with other neighboring cells, akin to the casings that protect the end of shoelaces, 36
- **Temperament** – may be viewed as behavioral and reactionary aspects of oneself that are thought to be innate, 63, 109, 182
- **Teratogens** – any substances that may cross the placenta and harm the embryo or fetus during gestation, 39
- **Tetrahydrocannabinol (THC)** – the most potent agent in marijuana; when ingested, THC has many psychoactive effects, 173
- **Thalamus** – located in the forebrain, the thalamus initially receives the neural messages sent to the brain, and subsequently transmits them to appropriate areas of the brain for processing. Thus, many forms of human activity will stimulate neural activity in the thalamus as it is a sort of "entry gate" to many other brain regions. 23, 126

- **Thanatology** – the scientific study of death; this field captures not only the biological aspects of death, but also the social and cultural traditions surrounding death events, 204
- **Theory** – somewhat like a complex "educated guess," theories relevant for developmental psychology are created to aid researchers and practitioners in clarifying and predicting behavioral phenomena, 15
- **The Scientific Method** – a process related to answering questions; involving steps related to observing and forming hypotheses akin to human phenomena, then orchestrating steps to test those hypotheses, 8
- **Trimesters** – segments of the larger gestational stage. There are three trimesters approximately three months long each. 36
- **Trust versus Mistrust** – the first of the stages in Erikson's eight psychosocial task model, this stage is related to whether or not significant others offer basic physical and emotional needs, in which case the infant develops a sense of trust. However, if needs are not met with enough quality or consistency, an attitude of mistrust develops, especially toward interpersonal relationships. 29, 72
- **Twin/Adoption Studies** – compares identical twins who have been raised apart, or otherwise maintain some type of difference in their development or environment, 28
- **Twin studies** – a family of studies that compare identical and fraternal twins on certain abilities, 27
- **Ultrasound** – offers nurses and parents an actual image of the fetus. Ultrasound images allow doctors and nurses to track prenatal growth, and observe structural development. 40
- **Unconditioned Response (UCR)** – an unlearned reaction; instinctual reaction, 17
- **Unconditioned Stimuli (UCS)** – a naturally occurring stimuli in the environment to which someone has an UCR, 17
- **Underweight** – indicated by a BMI score at the 5th percentile or less; suggesting very light weight for their height when compared to their peers, 82
- **Uninvolved** – this parenting style is marked by low levels of demandingness and responsiveness; sometimes referred to as "neglectful", 110
- **Variables** – anything that is likely (or at least, able) to change; a broad set of biological, behavioral, psychological, social, and emotional phenomena that may fluctuate between individuals, or between points in time for the same individual, 9
- **Verbal Scale** – involves knowledge of language (e.g., vocabulary and mechanics), but also mathematical problems, 140
- **Very Low Birth Weight** – a term reserved for infants weighing less than 3.25 pounds at birth, 43
- **Vocabulary Spurt** – typically occurring toward the latter portion of infancy, this refers to a rapid increase in the words infants appear to repeat and apparently grasp, 54
- **Wellness** – a general perception of a satisfactory balance among the important life dimensions, 197
- **White Matter** – brain matter that derives its color and name from the presence of myelin, the fatty insulating material that covers axons; white matter in the brain has connective properties and capabilities, 125
- **Widowhood** – this term refers to the death of a spouse, 211
- **Working Memory** – this type of memory is more short-term in nature, and necessary for day-to-day tasks. This type of memory does not typically remain beyond the time period that it is required. 58
- **Young-Old** – comprised of individuals in their 60s and up through 75 years of age. The young-old are still relatively healthy and financially stable; they may possibly be retired, but yet remain active. 190
- **Zone of Proximal Development (ZPD)** – perhaps Vygotsky's most famous notion, this term refers to the distance between what a child can do alone versus what he or she can do with some assistance from an expert or mentor, 97
- **Zygote** – combined sex cells, 36

CPSIA information can be obtained
at www.ICGtesting.com
Printed in the USA
LVOW03s1934090216
474423LV00016B/93/P

9 781465 279477